JUNGIAN PSYCHIATRY

Heinrich Karl Fierz

Jungian Psychiatry

DAIMON
VERLAG

The material comprising the chapters of this book and the Foreword by C.T. Frey-Wehrlin were translated into English by Stephen Waller. The original German-language sources of the various chapters are the two books, *Klinik und Analytische Psychologie* (Rascher Verlag, Zurich and Stuttgart, 1963) and *Die Psychologie C.G. Jungs und die Psychiatrie* (Daimon Verlag, Zurich, 1982), both by Heinrich Karl Fierz (1912–1974). This English language edition was edited by Liza Burr, John Peck and Robert Hinshaw, ably assisted by Anne and Robert Imhoff, who also set the type.

With special thanks to Mrs. Cara Denman of London, the Klinik am Zürichberg and the Linda Fierz Fonds of Zurich, whose financial support made possible this English language publication of the writings of Heinrich Fierz.

Cover design by Hanspeter Kälin.
Cover illustration: "winged goddess"
by a 57-year-old patient (see Chapter XX).

ISBN 3-85630-521-1

CONTENTS

CONTENTS

Illustrations

FOREWORD

The fact that Jung spent the first ten years of his career working in clinical psychiatry had a decisive influence on his lifelong endeavors. Not only do we find his later discoveries foreshadowed in certain passages of the early writings which were the fruit of intensive daily contact with psychotic patients (Jung, 1907, 1914). There are also good grounds for arguing that concepts such as the collective unconscious and the archetypes, as well as the notion of their priority over the personal unconscious, could only have come out of clinical experience, bearing in mind that the fantasy of a psychotic compared to that of a neurotic or of anyone else, for that matter, is like a fresco compared to a copperplate engraving.

It is all the more surprising in view of this that so few of Jung's pupils should have followed his example. If the period of internship every doctor wishing to become a specialist has to go through is disregarded, then the number of Jungian analysts who have worked in clinical psychiatry for any length of time and published their findings can be counted on the fingers of one hand. One of them, and probably the one with the longest experience, is Heinrich Karl Fierz.

*

Fierz was born in 1912 in Basle. His father, a Professor of Chemistry at the Technical University in Zurich, wrote among other things, a "History of Chemistry" (H.E. Fierz-David, 1945), in which unusual attention is given to alchemy. His mother was one of Jung's earliest pupils (cf. Linda Fierz-David, 1947). Fierz studied medicine in Basle, Zurich, Berlin and Paris and was certified in 1938. He received his psychiatric training at the Burghölzli Mental Hospital in Zurich under H. W. Maier and Manfred Bleuler. His analytical and psychological training came from C.G. Jung. It is interesting to note that this pupil of Jung wrote his doctoral dissertation in 1941 on the subject of electroshock therapy.

Though he was to specialize in psychiatry and psychotherapy, Fierz also had an excellent medical training with Professor Löffler in Zurich, which served him well in the first four years of his clinical career; they were spent, not in psychiatry, but in the medical sanatorium at Mammern. As the writings that resulted from that experience show, even in medical practice, he never lost sight of the whole person (e.g., "The Attitude of the Doctor in Psychotherapy," p. 193 of this volume).

In 1949, Ludwig Binswanger, the founder of "Daseinsanalyse," appointed him director of the clinical department of Sanatorium Bellevue in Kreuzlingen. There, alongside his busy schedule of clinical duties, Fierz extended his activities to various other fields. The following deserve particular mention:

– a series of training analyses which he gave in addition to his outpatient therapy and which were especially valuable in training the young doctors. This was important for the Jungian school as a whole because, for a variety of reasons, the recruitment of a new generation of doctors was proving difficult at that time, which meant that the school was in danger of losing touch with its roots in clinical medicine.

– his teaching at the Zurich Jung Institute, founded in 1948, which he took up at around that time and maintained until shortly before his death.

– the enduring results he achieved as an active member of the International Society for Medical Psychotherapy, serving for many years as secretary on its council. There he maintained regular contact with colleagues and through his many lectures introduced the Jungian point of view to professional circles around the world.

The resonance of this work drew a growing number of fellow doctors and therapists to Kreuzlingen where they wished to complete their professional training under the supervision of H. K. Fierz. It was there that I also came to know him and over a three-year collaboration received the benefit of his considerable experience and skill as a teacher. It was there, too, that the core of the staff came together, with which we were to open "our" Zürichberg Clinic in 1964.

This brings me to the next and, in my view, most important stage in H.K. Fierz's career, which is his work as Medical Director of the Zürichberg Clinic in Zurich.

The basis of all therapy and the factor that has priority for Fierz is the attitude of the therapist. I would like to describe what that means in words that he himself approved and which can therefore be considered accurate: "A readiness to share the patient's experience, a willingness to learn despite growing experience, an awareness of what is unchanging in human nature and a mind that is open to the discoveries of modern science – only a combination of all four of these qualities can help the patient and foster understanding in this difficult field."

This is a good place to mention something that is fundamental to H.K. Fierz's nature, namely, the wealth of opposites it embraces, or rather the ability to endure the tension of opposites without sliding off into comfortable one-sidedness. For Fierz, one of the cornerstones of the treatment of psychotic conditions was analytical psychotherapy in the Jungian style. In practical terms that meant that every patient received an average of three hours of individual psychotherapy per week. It also meant that, in group therapy, milieu therapy and "body work," the spontaneity of the unconscious was always respected. But then that cornerstone was complemented, qualified and dialectically challenged by the second approach which Fierz, no doubt ironically, referred to as "normal psychiatry." This meant that the discoveries of modern psychiatry, primarily in the field of pharmacology, were applied to the full, but also that no irresponsible risks – of the sort often wrongly termed "psychotherapeutic" risks – were taken. Fierz's expectations regarding the environment of the clinic could also be described in terms of opposites: it should be friendly, but not false! His way of dealing with colleagues, as the expression of his leadership role, was not harmlessly predictable either. He was always available, his advice was practical and his criticism was constructive, though it could be aimed as much at the individual as at the facts and his interventions could be painful at times. He was a man of his generation in that his style was distinctly authoritarian, but – and here we see the opposite – at the same time he showed great tolerance and ability to delegate. In public he always took complete responsibility for those working under him.

A further outstanding quality was his correctness. His word was absolutely reliable, a fact recognized by all of the authorities who had dealings with the clinic. Whenever he managed to find a way out of a seemingly impossible situation, it was never by trickery. Instead one was left with the impression of having overlooked a perfectly obvious solution. This dependability, pre-dictability almost, was counter-balanced, however, by his capacity for unexpected, lightning-quick reactions in which his superior function, intuition, came to the fore.

I do not wish to reveal what is to come in the essays that follow, but I would like all the same to draw attention to two passages from the chapter, "Psychotherapy and the Shadow," which are particularly characteristic of Fierz's way of thinking. They are the remark about the abandonment of professional principles as a sign of the transference situation and the statement that, in cases of psychosis or near psychosis, dreams should be "understood directly from the images they contained, rather than interpreted."

*

Looking back now on more than twenty years as a pupil, colleague and friend, I can say that being together with this richly endowed, exceptional and many-sided, even contradictory person was always enriching, often enjoyable and sometimes difficult.

In an account of Jungian psychology published in German many years ago, Fierz described individuation in the following words, which surely can also be understood in an autobiographical sense:

"If someone really faces up to the problems he meets in the encounter with his own unconsciousness, he sets out along the path of progressive development which Jung called individuation. The encounter with the unconscious leads first of all to the differentiation of the ego from other psychic contents. I have to recognize how little 'ego' and how much of various other factors goes into making me what I am. The basis of that differentiation is the confrontation with one's own affectivity. This confrontation is a challenge. Again and again, one is struck by how shocked patients are to discover that something else apart from their ego is at work within them. Yet, assuming the person does not try to avoid the problem, he will constantly be coming up against questions which introduce him to the world of the unconscious. The archetypal situations he encounters will demand a new sort of typical response from him, and that often faces him with very subtle conflicts of duty which demand a sharper conscience. He will have to adapt his persona accordingly, not in the sense of becoming 'deeper,' but rather of becoming more of an individual and thus, in the eyes of the majority – which loves collective uniformity – almost an impossibility, though he is accepted in the end, still with some suspicion, but not in an unfriendly way. Being an individual, he will find, can easily cause offense."

(H.K. Fierz, 1976, p.76)

*

The publication of these collected essays would not have been possible without the generosity of Mrs. Cara Denman of London, who recognized the particular importance of these works for the English-speaking world and financed their translation. To her, therefore, we owe a special debt of gratitude. Thanks are also due to the Zürichberg Clinic which honored a promise I made in my earlier capacity as managing director of that institution, with a financial contribution of its own. Frau Dr. Antoinette Fierz-Monnier has supported the project from the outset and made available the copyright on her late husband's work.

Caspar Toni Frey-Wehrlin
Zurich, Summer 1989

References:

FIERZ, H.K. (1976): *Die Jungsche analytische (komplexe) Psychologie.* Kindler Verlag, Munich.
FIERZ-DAVID, H. E. (1945): *Die Entwicklungsgeschichte der Chemie.* Eine Studie. Birkhäuser Verlag, Basle.
FIERZ-DAVID, L. (1947): *Der Liebestraum der Poliphilo,* Rhein Verlag, Zurich.
JUNG, C.G. (1907): *Über die Psychologie der Dementia praecox* / "The Psychology of Dementia Praecox," in The Collected Works of C.G. Jung, Princeton University Press, in CW3.
JUNG, C.G. (1914): *Der Inhalt der Psychose* / "The Content of the Psychoses," in CW3.

PREFACE

I first met Heiner Fierz at the Burghölzli Clinic in 1938. At that time he was what in America is called a psychiatric resident. I was working with C.G. Jung and with Toni Wolff, and was a part-time extern, as it was called then, at Bleuler's clinic. Both Heiner and I had worked with Jung for considerable periods of time, which created an immediate connectedness between us. We were also brought together by our psychiatric duties, particularly in regard to a new treatment for schizophrenia that had just been devised, namely, insulin shock. It was discovered by accident because somebody gave a patient suffering from diabetes an overdose of insulin. The patient happened to be schizophrenic, and when he came out of his convulsions, he was as clear as a bell. This treatment spread all over the place with amazing speed and was being used very often at Burghölzli, so that Heiner and I had to attend some of these shock therapy sessions together. I shall never forget the patients going into what the doctors call opisthotomy. Every muscle in the body goes into spasm, the back is arched and all the back muscles are in spasm, and you could hear the vertebrae grinding on each other; it was not uncommon to have lumbar fractures in the lower back from the treatment. Because of our connection through Jung and through our experiences at the clinic, Heiner and I were able to talk about things like animuses and animas and introverts and extroverts and shadows and all those good things. And so that started our friendship.

Then the war intervened, and when I returned to Switzerland, Heiner was working together with Ludwig Binswanger, so-called young Binswanger, at Sanatorium Bellevue in Kreuzlingen. Their collaboration was a very nice blending of existentialism and Jungianism, and I think Heiner and Binswanger got along pretty well. That clinic became a place where some of the early trainees at the Jung Institute (which was founded in 1948) made their first acquaintance with psychosis under the tutelage of Heiner by accompanying him on rounds, attending conferences, etc.

I did not get back to Switzerland again until years later, at which time the then-Jungian Klinik am Zürichberg was under way with Heiner as clinical director, assisted very ably by his successor, Toni Frey. I attended some of the weekly conferences there run by Heiner, and they were always a joy, because Heiner not only had an ever-ready supply of wit, but he was also very wide-ranging and didn't let silly little barriers interfere with his freedom of thought. The result was that he was very creative, and was by then becoming in the Jungian world what in English we call a gadfly. This isn't meant to be a term of disparagement; a gadfly is a person who activates and challenges others, which Heiner did several times a minute. It was incredible. So that was a very important experience, sitting there watching Heiner run those meetings.

Not too long after that, Heiner came over to the United States for a memorable two-week visit in San Francisco. He and his wife Antoinette stayed with us, and I set him up for a lecture – I was on the staff of the University of California Medical School – in Langley Porter Clinic, which is the medical school's equivalent of the Burghölzli. He gave a very well-received lecture, again sparkling with wit, and then he gave a public talk which also went over very well. Many of our trainees wanted to go and have an hour with him, presumably so that they could boast, "Oh yes, I've just had an hour with Dr. Heinrich Fierz; perhaps you've heard of him."

In the meantime, Heiner had not been idle with the pen. He was writing articles and turning out a lot of material which is now at long last being translated into English. This means that those of us who didn't hear him delivering some of his papers can now enjoy them.

Heiner's personal qualities strongly reflected his Swiss nationality. While he was staying with us over the weekend at our house north of the Golden Gate, I took him for a walk on Mount Tamalpais, which is a state park and therefore a wilderness. It was evident that this walk in the wilderness delighted him, and that, like all good Swiss, he felt renewed and grounded by it. In a country where being trilingual is not unusual, Heiner was one of the leading exponents of trilingualism. Every three years at our international congress, he used to delight his audience with a speech given in three languages that had the entire room rocking with laughter, and sometimes shouts of indignation when he said something particularly blasphemous. But everybody always looked forward to these occasions as a special treat.

And so with Heiner's death, we lost one of our pioneer analysts and one of our most gifted friends.

Dr. Joseph B. Wheelwright

I

PRINCIPLES FOR THE PRACTICAL APPLICATION OF ANALYTICAL PSYCHOLOGY

Analytical psychology is the name C. G. Jung himself gave to the school of thought founded on his own work to distinguish it from Freudian psychoanalysis. What it describes is not a theory, but an attempt to give an account of the phenomena we encounter when we observe the psyche.

The practical application of analytical psychology is to be demonstrated with reference to psychotherapy. In order to have a clearer idea of what exactly psychotherapy is, I will start with a brief survey of the subject.* Any such survey is by nature schematic, but that should not lead anyone mistakenly to suppose that analytical psychology itself is schematic in its approach. We will return to this question when we come to consider the commencement of therapy.

The *method* of psychotherapy is medical. Psychotherapy aims to establish a diagnosis. To this end it draws up a case history. In psychotherapy, however, every case history is also the life story of a human individual. Working from information on the origin of the suffering and from observation of the patient's symptoms,

---

* I am using here, in part, a survey report produced in 1935–36 by the Commission on Psychotherapy of the Swiss Society for Psychiatry. The members of the Commission were C. G. Jung, Bally, de Saussure, Ewald Jung, Forel, Morgenthaler, and C. A. Meier (*sauf erreur et omission!*). The report was put up for discussion by the Swiss Society for Practical Psychotherapy at an international congress on psychotherapy held in the context of the bicentenary of the Zurich Scientific Society in 1946. Its use here is all the more appropriate in that the influence of C. G. Jung's personality on its drafting was considerable.

the aim of psychotherapy is to identify the specific form of mental illness involved.

Diagnostic examination shows that there are illnesses which cannot be accounted for, either at all or satisfactorily, in terms of physiological processes alone, and which have to be understood either wholly or in part from a psychological point of view. Psychotherapeutic diagnosis focuses, therefore, not on the organic factor of physical illness, but on the psychic make-up of the afflicted personality. We call this form of psychotherapeutic diagnosis *exploration*. Exploration takes into consideration all forms of self-expression of which humans are capable: language, spontaneous thoughts, fantasy, dreams, symptoms and symptomatic behavior, affectivity, and general behavior and attitude.

Deeper exploration reveals that mental aetiology extends beyond the limits of consciousness of the personality. The areas of the psyche that lie beyond consciousness are hidden from the personality and yet form part of the personality. Since Freud, this hidden part of the personality has been known as *the unconscious*.

The *task of psychotherapy*, insofar as it is not exclusively concerned with consciousness, is to elucidate the unconscious circumstances that made the illness possible in the first place and sustain it in the present. Its primary concern is the analysis and interpretation of all forms of self-expression from the patient – in other words, understanding the patient.

In-depth investigation leads, among other things, to the discovery of *fixations* at certain stages of psychic development on important situations and figures from childhood. These fixations seem, on the one hand, to be the cause of the illness (though it remains doubtful whether they are in fact the real cause); on the other hand, they also set the tasks that will prove decisive in later life.

Let me give an example. The father of Paracelsus, the great medieval scholar and physician, was an illegitimate scion of the noble family of von Hohenheim from Alsace. Ildefons Betschart,[1] writing of the father and of Theophrastus, the son, says:

"Paracelsus' father, illegitimate scion of noble blood, plucked out of a great family line, himself without tradition, cannot have adapted to life in a strange and constricting milieu (the Einsiedeln valley) without psychological wounding. It is no coincidence that a sudden and violent antipathy towards the ruling classes, and in particular towards the hereditary and intellectual aristocracy, should break through again and again in the writings of his son, placing him in defiant opposition to the upper ranks of society. And is it so hard to understand when, in the heat of battle, repressed feelings of personal worth erupt with explosive force from within his rich temperament?" The fixation on his father was, in one respect the cause of Paracelsus' chaotic nonconformism and cost him his place in society. But it was also the source of the revolutionary creativity that freed medicine and science from the shackles of medieval dogmatism, opening the way for a new concept of nature, and that secured for Paracelsus a place in the history of thought. This goes to show how a fixation can be both a curse and a blessing.

The psychotherapeutic process rests on the *relationship between therapist and patient*. It is a dialogue between two people, which forms the basis for a dialogue with society and an attempt to adapt to the environment.

The relationship between therapist and patient may take the special form of *transference*. Then the therapist is cast in the role of one of the important figures from childhood involved in the fixation. Investigation of the transference reveals its biographical background by reducing it to its origin. In detail, however, the content of the transference also reveals ideas that point to the future. For example, if a female patient regards her male analyst more or less as Jesus Christ, you may find that there is a strong paternal bond. But you may also find that you open up the whole problem of Christianity and of religion itself, so that the transference is not merely reduced but also positively integrated.

In psychotherapy, *treatment* is determined by the circumstances of the case in hand. One of the options to be considered is: *practical advice*. This is to be given with great caution and a proper sense of responsibility. It may be fair to say that advice is often no more than medical routine, and is not all that dangerous since it is generally ignored. But if you know the patient well, you also know how he usually reacts. You know, for example, that the patient will follow your advice if you adopt an authoritarian approach. In that case you bear a heavy responsibility. If your advice is more cautious, though still plain enough, you may know in advance that the patient will do the opposite of what you suggest. Or perhaps you have sufficient experience to know that the patient is simply incapable of doing something or other unless you expressly forbid it. So even in rational therapy – which is what practical advice is – you cannot hide behind the excuse that your advice was to do this or that, and that the patient is to blame if he did something else. On the contrary, you have to take the patient's irrational reactions into account as soon as you become aware of them, and to accept responsibility not only for the rational content but also for the probable irrational consequences of your advice. If you do not, you are acting dishonestly. If, for example, an analysand raises the question of whether to try a different analyst, there are cases where you know full well that as long as you tell the patient he can go to a different analyst any time he likes (after all freedom in one's choice of doctor is safeguarded by law), then he will never make up his mind to do it. In such cases you cannot simply avoid the issue, unless you are convinced that any change of analyst is to be discouraged on therapeutic grounds and wish to influence the patient accordingly. Otherwise the problem has to be dealt with analytically and examined for psychological factors (for example, changing from a male to a female analyst). And so, whoever thinks of giving advice should remember the words of Theodor Storm:

One man asks himself: what will be the consequences?
The other merely: is it the correct thing to do?
That is the difference
Between the free man and the slave.

Other options in psychotherapy include *suggestive intervention, conscious suggestion,* and *hypnosis;* then there is simple *confession* as well as *abreaction* of one or more traumatic moments. That these require a responsible attitude on the part of the analyst goes without saying. Confession and catharsis in particular can only play a significant role if the patient is confident that he is dealing with an attentive and critical therapist who understands but who also judges.

If it proves necessary to investigate the infantile situation at the source of the problem – the fixations – and if transference, general behavior and attitude have to be analyzed, the *analysis of dreams,* possibly also of other unconscious material such as fantasies, is usually indispensable. That is because the questions thrown up by analysis exceed as a rule the limits of consciousness of the personality. A transference, the identification of the therapist with a figure from the patient's childhood, for example, hardly ever results from conscious motivation. Even if the patient says to the therapist, "I am appointing you to be my father because I never had one of my own," further questioning soon reveals that the patient did have a father after all and, what is more, that that father represents for him a central problem.

If despite successful adaptation to everyday life, despite analysis of transference and attitude, there is still no improvement in the patient's condition, therapy has to continue, allowing the patient's *inner development,* his attitudes towards the therapist or towards third parties, to express themselves naturally. The prerequisites for this development are constant attention to unconscious material and a nonreductive, integrative approach to the contents of the transference. In other words, one is not primarily trying to get rid of a fixation, on the mother for example, but rather to unravel the meaning of the fate in which the figure of the mother has entangled the patient. Generally, this raises the question of opposites. Things that at first sight seem wholly negative often have a positive side that holds the key to the future; thus, *diabolus* becomes Lucifer, the bearer of light. To recall the dual significance of the father in the case of Paracelsus, the important thing is not that Theophrastus was molded by his father into a socially unacceptable nonconformist, but that his father's background gave him the urge and the strength to strike out in new directions.

Finally, it has to be emphasized that the analysis of the fixation and of the transference, as well as the prospective psychotherapy, should not get stuck at an intellectual level. In the transference situation the analyst always has an *educative task* to fulfil by insisting that the patient put the insights he has achieved into practice in his daily life with a proper sense of responsibility and seriousness.

Following this survey, which if not specifically concerned with analytical psychology is nevertheless strongly influenced by Jung, we turn now to the *commencement of treatment* in analytical psychotherapy and immediately find ourselves confronted by one of those complex psychological phenomena where everything seems at first impenetrably interwoven. Of course, we have some idea of the task and goal of psychotherapy as outlined above. But there can be no question of our simply interrogating the patient or otherwise asserting our authority. When beginning treatment, what matters is not what we ourselves consider important but what is important for the patient; it is not a question of what the therapist expects from the patient, but of what the patient expects from the therapist. You have to be ready to wait and see, and you also have to be ready to react spontaneously and naturally when occasion demands. Such readiness is best achieved in a relaxed and uninhibited atmosphere. At first sight this might seem to speak in favor of using the analyst's couch; lying on the couch the patient would calm and relax. Use of the couch is not to be recommended, however, since it requires the patient to adopt an unaccustomed position, one that contrasts, furthermore, with that of the therapist, who is seated. If on top of that the patient is unable to see the therapist, any symmetry there may have been in the relationship is destroyed and the tension is greater. The desk, forming a barrier between therapist and patient, does not help to create a relaxed atmosphere either. The best thing, therefore, is for the patient to sit facing the therapist in a comfortable chair, as if for a friendly discussion. Needless to say, this arrangement is not sacrosanct. If it seems appropriate in the circumstances, psychotherapy may begin during a walk in the open air, while sitting on a garden bench, or in some other way. In any case, externals are not so important when what you are talking about is a person's soul. Whatever the arrangement, the important thing is that the patient feel he is dealing with the therapist as a fellow human being. He should be able to see the therapist's face and know that the therapist can see him, too. It is absolutely essential that human reactions such as surprise, disbelief, embarrassment, delight, and so on, are freely exchanged between the two people engaged in psychotherapy.

The therapist has to be *attentive*. He will listen to what the other has to say, and listen carefully, since to start with he does not know what the patient is concerned about. *Not knowing*, in this context, includes uncertainty as to whether what is troubling the patient calls for psychotherapy at all. Sometimes, for example, one comes across cases of diabetes mellitus or carcinoma and I have occasionally found myself in the position of having to diagnose a somatic disorder when the patient had previously been referred to psychotherapy by the medical consultant. Criminal offences and other legal issues may also be involved. Physical illness is the most likely diagnosis when serious, supposedly psychogenic symptoms are found alongside undisturbed consciousness and normal affectivity, that is to say, when the symptoms indicate psychosis whereas open-minded observation of the patient suggests that psychosis is most unlikely (cf. p. 238).

The less both partners in the analytical relationship are hampered by preconceived notions, the sooner what Jung called *constellation* is likely to occur. The course that therapy will take in any one case is unpredictable. All the same, the therapist will be expecting one or other of the issues I touched on in the introductory survey to be brought up; though, as remarked, additional issues should not be overlooked. The outward situation is typically one of expectation. The therapist waits expectantly to see what happens, and generally the patient is equally tense despite all efforts to create a "relaxed atmosphere." Constellation is an automatic response that occurs entirely involuntarily and that no one can control.[2] The therapist will observe closely the development that takes place under the influence of the constellation. It would be quite wrong to launch into interpretations and therapeutic commentaries right away after only a few minutes. That could only prevent what is really important from becoming visible. The constellation between therapist and patient cannot be reduced to a routine. It is new every time, unique and unrepeatable. Not only is every patient a unique individual; the assumption also must be that the same patient would not be constellated in the same way by a different therapist. The constellation is, therefore, not just a function of the patient but also depends on the personality structure of the therapist.

What is constellated and what determines the situation are psychic contents that somehow belong together and that in their totality have some bearing on the patient's problem. These clusters of related psychic contents we call *complexes*.[3] It is not to be taken for granted that the complex constellated in the therapeutic encounter is the complex that defines the patient's problem. This is explained by the fact that the psychic contents we take to be the cause of the patient's problem are not in all respects integrated into the psychic whole – which is why they are a problem. Hence the tension that exists between the psychic whole and the problem contained in the complex, a tension that generates energy. Jung says accordingly that the complex at the root of the patient's problem has an energizing effect. The aim of therapy consists, therefore, in integrating the problem contained in the complex into the psychic whole, a process referred to as the assimilation of the complex.

The suspense felt by both therapist and patient at the start of therapy is a situation in which, on account of its own specific energy, the complex is activated; this is what is meant by constellation. The contents constellated as a complex can be contents of consciousness, guilty recollection of some wrong deed, for example. In that case you are dealing with a conscious complex which circumscribes the memory of a vividly emotional, but unassimilated, psychic situation. By far the more common case is one in which the complex is not conscious, whether because the emotional situation has been repressed or because the complex has never entered consciousness in the first place. Accordingly, the complex often remains invisible in the therapeutic situation and there is simply an agreement to continue therapy. If the complex does manifest, it should be discussed objectively, with due attention paid to any aspect that is relevant. If an objective discussion of the problem proves impossible, be it because the problem itself is not yet clearly visible or because the patient's behavior makes any such discussion seem inadvisable, the therapist may reasonably ask himself what could be causing the difficulty. To help answer this question, it is useful to have a clearly thought out concept of the task of psychotherapy, such as I have attempted to provide in this introductory survey. One is then in a position to ask oneself: Is it a situation that calls for practical advice or is it a matter of completing the exploration? Are suggestive measures appropriate? Are we dealing with a problem of attitude? etc.

If either at the beginning or at a later stage in therapy, the way forward seems blocked, *dream analysis* becomes appropriate. For as we might say, if consciousness cannot help, then you have to ask the unconscious. The need to address this question to the unconscious is so overriding that there are instances when treatment more or less comes to a halt and has to be continued on a wait-and-see basis until dreams start occurring.

Generally speaking, though, one proceeds with dream analysis only when rational therapy can go no further. However, should the patient spontaneously report a dream right at the outset, one should as a rule give it one's attention. The only time that you should not do so is if the patient's consciousness seems weak and insecure, in mild twilight states for example, or when one finds manifest symptoms of a schizophrenic nature, such as delusions. In cases of that sort, the first thing is rather to try to distract attention from dreams and the unconscious and to bolster rational consciousness. Often one has to change the subject with some remark such as "That is unhealthy." The sense in which the therapist must nevertheless take the dream content into consideration has yet to be discussed.

In any case, it is important in the early stage of therapy to determine whether the patient's problem lies on the side of *consciousness* or of the *unconscious*. Cases where what is needed is a *strengthening of consciousness* should not be made worse by insisting on dream analysis at all costs. It is in this context that the psychiatrists' often repeated warning against the analysis of psychoses and prepsychoses is to be understood. The warning is justified insofar as it could be wrong to analyze the dreams of patients in such states. Yet it is not wholly right, in the sense that one's primary purpose should not be to analyze dreams at all but rather the psychic condition of the troubled person; and the result of that analysis will give an indication of where best to start, which may turn out to be with consciousness.

Dreams do always have to be taken into account and analyzed, however, in the analysis of fixation and transference. That is because, as I have already mentioned, it is a safe assumption that fixation and transference are to an extent determined by the unconscious part of the psyche, so that any manifestations of the unconscious in consciousness (which is what dreams are) have to be included in the investigation.

As a rule, before proceeding with dream analysis, it is a good idea to give the patient an outline of one's own position on the issue. Usually I also tell patients who already know something about analysis, in a few words, how I myself stand with regard to dream analysis. This gives me an opportunity briefly to describe my own position. I start with something along these lines: If you do not have any useful ideas during the day, while you are awake, it may be that you will at night, while you are asleep. Ideas that occur to you while you are asleep are called dreams. So dreams are ideas that you have in your sleep. However, the thinking you do in your sleep takes place at a lower level of consciousness.

That is why dreams do not speak the language of logic and concepts but express themselves in images, in the way that children or primitives think. Dreams present us with images, as do fairy tales and myths. As a result, in the light of ordinary waking consciousness, their meaning is often ambiguous and hard to grasp. On the other hand, when waking consciousness is for once switched off, and habitual but unnoticed preconceptions disappear, it is possible that something vital will occur to you. Obscure and metaphorical as dreams may therefore often appear, it is important to understand them.

What I actually say depends on the case I am dealing with at any one time. There will be ample opportunity as analysis proceeds to return to such basic considerations. The actual analytical work on a dream begins with the patient's associations, the choice of associations naturally being decided by the patient himself. One does, however, have to see that the patient keeps to the subject. Extended free association is only to be permitted if it becomes apparent that what is in play is of major concern to the patient. It can happen that a particular dream figure prompts a chain of associations that develops rapidly and ends on a theme that may have nothing to do with the dream but nonetheless touches on the patient's core problem. The discussion of the dream has in that case simply acted as a catalyst to open up a new area of concern; there has been no analysis of the dream properly speaking. Normally, though, the patient should always be brought back to the original dream figure and asked for associations to that particular figure only. Through this procedure the dreamer constantly substitutes other, similar but more familiar and comprehensible figures for the incomprehensible dream figure. For example, if a priest appears in a dream, the associations might include: the father, the brother, God, and the therapist. One might also ask: Is the priest Catholic or Protestant or even pagan? Is he old or young, short or tall? If he is Catholic, is he an ordinary priest or a Benedictine or a Jesuit? Is he friendly or threatening? Is he important in the dream or not? One always has to remember, though, that the figure that appears in the dream is the only true representation of the facts. *If the dream figure were fully understood, there would be no need for associations.* As long as the figure is not fully understood, the patient is asked to substitute through association other figures that he knows and understands. In this way the incomprehensible dream figure is, as it were, "circumscribed." It is circumscribed with other images that are not quite as appropriate but that the dreamer can understand, thus aiding the eventual comprehension of the dream. Jung called this process whereby the associations circle around the dream material *amplification.* It is a process of gradual approximation, comparable to the method of approximation (iteration) used to solve problems in mathematics. Amplification relies on the personal associations of the dreamer; without them it can go on forever, and the particular significance of the dream for the patient gets lost. On the other hand, it is possible by using the amplification method to bring out the universal and typical features of the dream figure, those that Jung called the *archetypal* features. This enables us to situate the individual case in a general context (cf. pp. 42, 81, 109).

On the whole, the *therapist's contribution* to dream analysis is likely to be cautious and sparing. When dealing with inexperienced analysands it is sometimes helpful to suggest an example of how and where to start the process of association. Analysis is always, among other things, a lesson that the therapist gives to the analysand, and the analysand has to learn how to enter into conversation with his own dreams. However, because the personality structure of every individual is subtly different, any association that the therapist suggests constitutes a significant intervention, which can only be justified if one is aware from the outset that the whole dream analysis rests on the constellation given in the analytical relationship. If one has made that sufficiently clear to oneself, one need not worry unduly about contributing associations of one's own, since one knows that even the patient's associations are strongly influenced by the personality of the therapist, whether one says anything or not. And also, it is sometimes better to make this influence explicit rather than to have it continue unspoken and so often be all the more powerful. The therapist's main contribution to the discussion with the patient remains, however, his spontaneous, natural reactions. If one of the patient's associations strikes one as incomprehensible or strange, one should say so. After all, if one does not understand the patient's associations, one will not understand the patient either. It is important in such instances that one's response be both immediate and unambiguous. Even if I do not understand the patient, he at least must be able to understand me or we will not get very far.

One should also bring it to the patient's attention if part of the dream has been left out in the process of association, and if one can, insist with due firmness on a complete interpretation. For example, if a particular dream figure is overlooked, one immediately comes up against the question of *resistance* (why has this figure been "withheld"?) and one has the opportunity to expose a fixation on a figure or situation from the patient's own life. Often it is also useful to point out how the dream is divided into an exposition, a development, a peripeteia, and a lysis. Viewing the dream as a shorter or longer *drama*[4] highlights the way dreams imitate experience and makes it easier for the analysand to work on the dream through associations, without destroying its personal character.

When it is a question of elucidating the *relationship of the dream to consciousness,* the therapist is permitted a more active role. This relationship is bound to be at least touched on in any dream analysis. In practice one asks oneself: What could be the purpose of the patient's having this particular dream? Needless to say, dreams, being natural phenomena, do not in themselves have a purpose in the sense of a conscious intention. My old science teacher taught me long ago that "nature has no purposes; only man has purposes." Nor is the purpose – the goal-orientedness – of dreams an intention but rather a purposeful automatism, comparable, say, to the purposeful reactions of cells in biology.

The investigation of the relationship of the dream to consciousness leads us to consider the *meaning of the dream*. According to Jung, for example, it is possible to distinguish four types of meaning in dreams, of which the first three[5] belong together, while a fourth group[6] occupies a special place. Clearly, one cannot be dogmatic about any such grouping.

First, a dream may represent an unconscious reaction to a conscious situation. In such cases the dream contents clearly relate to an impression received during the day and complement that impression. Dreams of this type cannot occur without the direct stimulus of a specific impression from the day before.

Second, there may be some spontaneous activity on the part of the unconscious, such that it cannot be said with any certainty that the conscious situation itself caused the dream. Consequently, there is a conflict between the conscious situation and the unconscious urges. (The dreamer thinks, I want to do such-and-such; but the dream says, You do not want to do that.)

Third, the dream may be aimed at bringing about a fundamental change in conscious attitude. Significant and memorable dreams of this type result in a complete revolution in attitude. Take the famous chemist, Augustus Kekulé, for example. He was researching the chemical structure of benzol when he dreamed of the serpent biting its own tail: the *uroboros*. Kekulé's whole understanding of chemistry was suddenly altered; he recognized the ring structure of benzol, thus laying the foundations for the advance of organic chemistry in the nineteenth century.[7]

These three groups of dreams show a clear relationship to consciousness, while a progression can be seen in the way the emphasis shifts away from consciousness towards the unconscious. However that may be, the dreams in all three groups stand in opposition to consciousness, in effect counterbalancing consciousness, hence Jung's use of the term *compensatory* to characterize such dreams.[8] The question remains in each case whether the images that appear in these dreams relate to the psyche of the dreamer (*interpretation on the subjective level*[9]) or to real-life people and situations (*interpretation on the objective level*[10]). Above all, one must ask oneself whether both interpretations are not equally possible and useful. Always remember that a dream has many aspects: Janus-faced, it gazes both inward *and* outward, but also both backward into the past and forward into the future. Gazing into the future is especially characteristic of a fourth group of dreams. Those dreams represent an unconscious process that bears no discernible relationship to the conscious situation. Dreams of this type are strange and, being of such a singular nature, often hard to interpret. Frequently the dreamer himself is astounded by the dream, even positively overwhelmed by it. Jung notes that such dreams are known among certain primitives as "big dreams."[11] Often they point far into the future; they present an image of destiny that sometimes can only be understood decades later. They may also occur before the onset of mental illness, when a psychic content suddenly breaks through, leaving a deep impression on the dreamer even though he may not understand it.*

Precisely in regard to this fourth group, though for some patients in regard to the simplest dreams too, associations are often few and frequently indeed completely lacking. It may also be, as suggested previously, that a discussion of the dream with the patient is not appropriate. Nevertheless, dreams like these have to be considered. If associations are lacking, it is rarely advisable to attempt an interpretation from guesswork. The absence of associations is to be respected too, as it can sometimes indicate justified resistance: The dream content cannot be assimilated by consciousness because, as things stand, it would be far too dangerous for consciousness to take it in. In such cases (as also in those where any discussion of dreams is avoided for therapeutic reasons), the therapist should, however, at least acknowledge the affective content of the dream experience. For example, a young man dreams that he is being attacked by a giant, many-legged serpent, but produces no associations what-

---

* Alongside the literature cited, this discussion of the meaning of dreams also takes into account a seminar given by C. G. Jung in 1938/39 at the Swiss Federal Polytechnic University, in which I participated as a junior doctor at the Zurich University Psychiatric Clinic.

soever. The therapist should try to visualize the dreamer's situation as he is being pursued by the monster; that way he will be able to appreciate how he himself would feel in the same situation. Then he will say in the appropriate tone of voice, "That is a nasty situation." In other cases where there are no associations to work with, one can pick up on the dream image itself with a contribution of one's own. If, for example, in the dream the dreamer is *standing by* another person, then one might ask, "Do you think perhaps you should *stand by* that person?" Or if in the dream there is a beautiful view in the background, one's commentary might be, "The outlook is promising."

Dreams to which associations are lacking should always be recorded, since they could prove important at a later stage in therapy and may also be better understood then. If the dreamer does not write them down, then the therapist should do so himself. This is especially important because dreams recorded without the patient's associations sometimes begin to make sense once they are looked at in sequence. A single, isolated dream is usually only worth interpreting as an academic exercise, whereas some very remarkable results can be obtained by studying a series of dreams. It is often possible to discern formal developments within the series, a numerical or geometrical-pictorial development, for example. It was through the observation of such developments that Jung was led to assume the existence of *unconscious processes,* that is to say, of ongoing developments in the unconscious part of the psyche which are responsible for the formal development that can be observed in the sequence of dream images. His most detailed observations on this phenomenon are contained in *Transformations and Symbols of the Libido*[12] and also in the individual dream material published in *Psychology and Alchemy*.[13]

The investigation of a dream series is carried out by tracing individual motifs through the series. The aim is to see to what extent these motifs develop or change, and how the position of a particular motif within the dream alters. The procedure is the same as that followed in other sciences: We start with single items of data and try through interpolation to find a general law of development. The single items of data are understood as stages in a process; accordingly, the dream material can only tell us something about a psychic process if more than one dream is studied.

The study of the development of motifs within a series of dreams and other unconscious material led Jung to think about such questions as change and numerical proportion (trinity, quaternity), and above all the question of centering as a factor in the development of the personality (Self). In practical psychotherapy, these questions certainly have to be considered; but – at least at the beginning of therapy – they should not be discussed with the patient, or only with great caution. Concepts such as individuation, self, and so on, which serve to describe the process taking place in the psyche, should not be used in talking to patients; this will only encourage them to intellectualize.

The idea that the dreamer should record all his dreams in the course of analysis is well known and goes without saying. The associations (context) should likewise be noted down. In practical therapy, however, this demand cannot always be met. With many patients one must be thankful if one receives an oral account of dreams, and one cannot always persuade a person to write down his dreams without the risk of losing contact. Psychic phenomena are often fleeting, after all, and the most important things are not always to be had in black and white.

Finally, a word about the *handling of the transference* in analytical psychotherapy. In principle, transference fantasies are dealt with like dreams, using the method of amplification. Since in a series of transference fantasies or dreams the carrier of the transference is readily identifiable, whereas the way the motif is elaborated in detail hardly ever stays the same, transference analysis also lends itself to the study of single motifs as they develop. It is often in the course of transference analysis that an unconscious process first makes itself felt. If treatment has been going on for some time, the therapist need have no hesitation in raising the question of an identification with the father, mother, brother, or sister, since these are obvious possibilities. For behind every transference lies the problem of incest, what Jung[14] termed the *endogamous tendency,* the tendency that symbolizes unification with one's own being.[15] The fact that dreams should be discussed during transference analysis has already been mentioned. At the same time it is questionable, precisely with transference, whether rules can be laid down and kept at all. A transference cannot usually be "handled." It is an event that affects both patient and analyst. It is not an event that can be controlled; often one has to be thankful if one emerges from the tangle more or less unscathed. What the therapist needs above all, therefore, is a clearly thought-out *attitude* to the transference phenomenon. He has to recognize that the incest situation that generally obtains in the transference enables the patient to make contact with the parent of the opposite sex, basically in other words, with his own inner opposite. The therapist must appreciate that this means contact with the unconscious, contact that must be made if wholeness of the personality is to be ensured. He must also know that a transference occurs when contact with the unconscious cannot be achieved by direct means, so that a mediator is necessary. If the therapist thus clearly appreciates the vital importance of the transference for the patient, he will devote himself to the difficulties of the transference phenomenon in the same way that a mother devotes herself to her child or a teacher to his pupil. It is always a relief not to have to cope with all the difficulties and pressures of a transference, but the transference cannot simply be evaded. It will always be the central pillar of any thorough psychotherapy. That is why in analytical psychotherapy freedom and lack of constraint in the therapeutic alliance is essential; even for the therapist simply to take notes can often be too distracting.

The transference usually affects the therapist too, since every transference calls forth – openly or secretly – a countertransference. Contents that would normally remain hidden are activated in the therapist's unconscious. The effect of the transference on the psyche of the therapist is like that of an infection. It is vital, therefore, that the therapist have experience in dealing with his own unconscious. The completion of a training analysis and constant attention to the manifestations of one's own unconscious are essential requirements for serious psychotherapy. I would like to quote Jung on this matter of the difficulties involved in the transference phenomenon:[16]

The greatest difficulty here is that contents are often activated in the doctor which might normally remain latent. He might perhaps be so normal as not to need any such unconscious standpoints to compensate his conscious situation. At least this is often how it looks, though whether it is so in a deeper sense is an open question. Presumably he had good reasons for choosing the profession of psychiatrist and for being particularly interested in the treatment of the psychoneuroses; ... And the psychotherapist in particular should clearly understand that psychic infections, however superfluous they seem to him, are in fact the predestined concomitants of his work, and thus fully in accord with the instinctive disposition of his own life. This realization also gives him the right attitude to his patient. The patient then means something to him personally, and this provides the most favorable basis for treatment.

In the *clinical application of psychotherapy,* the question now facing us is how much time we have. For out-patient analytical treatment it was Sigmund Freud who introduced what has since become general practice: The intangible psychic phenomenon is dealt with in hourly measures, the one-hour consultation, and with a simple financial measure, the consultant's fee. Strict measures of time and money may seem utterly inadequate in relation to the needs of the psyche, yet they provide a meaningful link with practical reality. Very often, however, the clinician, and the clinical psychiatrist in particular, finds it impossible to organize his work on the basis of hour-long consultations. Consequently, he is confronted with a *time problem.*

The practical side of the clinician's time problem becomes apparent if one considers how much time he ought to have for each patient and how little he actually does have at his disposal. Closer inspection of the facts, however, shows that this is more than just a practical question, that there is a theoretical time problem too. The theoretical discussion of time is, in the first place, the concern of physics. Modern science and in particular Albert Einstein's theory of relativity have shed new light on our understanding of the world. As W. Braunbeck put it: "With Einstein's formulae and their interpretation ... a decisive step was taken: a step away from the evidence of the senses. Einsteinian space-time cannot be visualized because it runs counter to primitive feeling on various points."[17]

The physicist's reference to "primitive feeling" is very interesting. This "primitive feeling" of time – or, perhaps better, "primordial feeling" – is a fundamental form of psychic experience. The experience of time always has two sides to it: time is experienced as something continuous, as a steady flow, and it is experienced as an isolated measure of duration. Classical physics still conceived of time as an objective, external fact. Isaac Newton, in his *Philosophiae naturalis principia mathematica* of 1687, made a distinction between "absolute ... time that flows on without check" and "relative time" (he called it "normal time") "an external measure of duration accessible to the senses."[18] Absolute time, time as a continuous flow, can be seen as a typical conception of the life process. As a typical conception it is a psychic phenomenon. The human tendency to objectify this subjective, psychic conception as "time" or even to personify it (the "tooth of time," for example) reveals the archetypal character of absolute time, in accordance with C. G. Jung's definition.[19] Relative, measurable time arises from man's need for orientation, and is based typically on the perception of the movement of the earth and stars. The crowning achievement of this desire for orientation is the clock. Man's need for orientation is likewise a psychic phenomenon.

Accordingly, if since Einstein we see time more than ever as a psychic phenomenon, then we must immediately ask ourselves, as always when we use the word "psychic," *Who,* which psyche, has *which* time? The clinical psychiatrist is particularly well placed to make his own observations in this respect. He does not see his patients in hour-long consultations (in "relative time"), but shares their life in the clinic on a time continuum over days, weeks, often years. He needs a schedule, of course, a structure (a "relative time"), but if he shares the experiences and developments of his patients, he will also experience "absolute time." All psychology is highly theoretical and eminently practical at the same time. Everyone in the clinic – the doctor, the patient, the nursing staff – has his own time problem. Let us consider the patient and the doctor. The purpose here is not to offer advice or instruction, but simply to examine the facts of the situation.

First the patient. It is well known that the speed at which time passes in manic-depressive states is different from average experience. To the melancholic, minutes seem to creep by, hours seem an eternity. For the manic, months fly past like hours. The subjective experience of time is not necessarily uniform, though. Ludwig Binswanger[20] reports a case in which the neurotically irregular life-style of the patient was accompanied by a dissociation in the sense of time. The patient felt that she was living at two different speeds simultaneously, and evidently found it impossible to synchronize her experience. Cases like that are rare, however; L. Binswanger refers to the one he reports as an "unusual find."

A more common and obvious phenomenon is the displacement and alteration of the passage of time in acute schizophrenic psychosis. In acute psychosis the patient often loses all sense of relative, measured time. The patient can rave or hallucinate in a state of semiconsciousness regardless of the time of day; hours, days, weeks cease to have any meaning. A patient of mine who had lapsed into an acute schizophrenic phase once said to me in a brief, more or less lucid moment, "I have fallen out of time into eternity." The perception of absolute time with its unbroken flow may well correspond to what we commonly imagine to be eternity. The patient lives in and for the inner world, which has no sun or stars and is subject to its own timeless laws. G. Benedetti,[21] in his work on the treatment of schizophrenics, also contributes material on the schizophrenic's immersion in the inner world (for example, when he writes of one patient that "his hallucinosis was for him the only place where he could exist"). If in addition to this, the inner world is experienced as something encountered not only internally but also deludedly – in hallucination – as an "outside," then the result is a distorted view of the world. Eternity holds sway, or at least a completely different time scale from that of the real outside world, which follows the movements of the sun and the stars.

The significance of experiences such as these has to be acknowledged. J. N. Rosen,[22] G. Benedetti, and others have shown how important it is that inner experience be taken seriously. If the patient can be helped through the acute, timeless phase, a new aspect of the time problem begins to emerge. The patient has to find his place in society. So long as he remains immersed in the flow of absolute time, he is largely asocial. He lives exclusively for himself in an autistic manner. To help him adapt and join in activities with other people, he needs a routine: days, hours, and minutes have to be heeded once more. The patient cannot simply start to do something at any hour or minute of the day, since he is likely to disturb somebody else. At this stage, therefore – we will return to this question in a later chapter (p. 162) – it is of the utmost importance to establish a strict daily routine. It is only when relative time, the hourly measure, comes into force that the patient can do anything or join in any activity that will free him from his autism by building up contacts with others.

I realize that I am not saying anything new here. It is perhaps useful, though, to point out that an explicit diagnosis of the patient's time situation can often be a help. One patient may have a good reason for dreaming time away. Another, however, may need rousing from his absorption to be set in a routine of work. Conversely, it is possible for a person to do violence to himself with a schedule out of an obstinate sense of duty, while all the time – from a psychological point of view – he has every right and indeed a duty to devote himself to his inner life. Again, what was true yesterday may not be true today. Immersion in the timelessness of the inner world can be a very positive thing, but the experience of absolute detachment is also frightening and seductive, and there are many who, for want of being called back to order, have found eternity in suicide. Naturally, a diagnosis of the time situation can only be established through an examination of the individual case and, as indicated, panic and suicidal impulses are always important factors; thus we have to consider whether liberation from daily routine or rather a return to the discipline of ordered activity is more urgent.

We can see, in the patient's case, how relative time with its hours and minutes regulates the passage of time and so makes social relationships possible: working together, for example. While social relationships in shared time are often for the patient a goal, for the doctor this "ordered existence in relative time" is the starting point. The doctor has to see many different patients and many members of the nursing staff, so nothing could be more natural than that he should set himself a timetable with regular visits, individual consultations, staff meetings, and free periods. Any timetable of this sort is bound to be disrupted on occasion by unforeseen circumstances. Whenever a patient steps outside the timetable, he upsets the doctor's plans. Acute outbreaks demand immediate attention, sudden attacks of panic require help and intervention, and often new patients arrive at inconvenient moments. Consequently, the doctor is inwardly torn: He is supposed to keep to a fixed timetable and – at the same time! – to be available for anything that arises. Rather like L. Binswanger's patient, he must try to synchronize two competing demands on his time. This dilemma is becoming all the more urgent now that we understand better how important it is that the psychotherapeutic psychiatrist be on hand to support the patient when inner experience erupts with no regard for time or place. One solution, of course, would be to increase the number of doctors. But when inner experience erupts regardless of the time of day, there is no measure of time and often, therefore, no limit to the demands on the doctor. Soon we would reach a situation in which, to do justice to the therapeutic task, there would have to be a doctor for every patient. Such an increase in the number of doctors is obviously an impossibility.

Accordingly, the doctor cannot escape the problem, indeed the conflict, of "synchronization." Like any other conflict, it can only be overcome through personal effort. The doctor has to make a conscious decision to be available both in relative, measured time and in absolute, continuous time. His presence, his "being there" in a literal sense, has to encompass both aspects. As far as relative time is concerned, it is likely he will set himself a relatively flexible and not too rigid schedule of visits, consultations, and meetings. Within this framework he can legitimately refuse some of the demands patients make on his time, especially if he sees that a patient merely hopes to monopolize the doctor and have him all to himself. Besides his scheduled attendances, though, the doctor ought to be there in the clinic, as it were, continuously. That is to say, in spirit he is always there. His presence is felt in the clinic night and day. The nursing staff will be a second pair of hands for him, so that the patient can say, as a patient of mine did on one occasion, "The doctor can always see me, whether he is here or not." And if the right spirit is instilled into the clinic, every moment contributes, every passing nod or brief handshake, every little sign that *doctor and patient belong together*. No planning or great show of activity is needed. In the time continuum of life Pestalozzi's maxim holds true: "You must wait patiently and unselfishly and in time you will see results."[23] Follow his advice and you will always be there at the right time.

The "synchronization" of the daily schedule and of the need to be constantly present in the clinic, the doctor's "being there" for each and everyone: These are things that every doctor will manage differently according to temperament and character. Every success will be a creative achievement. Basically, though, "synchronization" is not something complicated; it is simple. Anyone who lives and works unreservedly in the present, anyone who has a feeling for the individual personality of each of his patients and colleagues, anyone who consequently understands the clinic as a living whole, will have little difficulty in finding his own individual solution.

II

THE FATHER ARCHETYPE
AS A CURSE AND AS A BLESSING

The figure of the father is a momentous experience for the child. For the adult, too, the relationship to the father is fundamental, and the image of the father often bears superhuman traits. In the Christian world God is addressed as "our Father."

In view of the superhuman traits of the father and of man's fundamental relationship to what is called father, we can say that the father is one of the primordial and typical experiences of humanity. That is what C. G. Jung called an archetype.

The archetypal aspect of a person's situation is not always immediately apparent. Often one has to search for it. One may find it in a person's fantasies or in his dreams, as Freud clearly demonstrated.

The archetypal image, as found in dreams, is a symbol. It has both reassuring and threatening features, and frequently appears when strong emotions are aroused or at times of crisis. But the symbol is not itself the force that produces the emotion or the crisis. That force is hidden; it can be neither seen nor clearly grasped; it lies beyond the scope of our imagination. An irrational force can produce a symbolic, or archetypal, image such as that of the father. Through the archetypal image, therefore, a force comes to bear on the individual.

In practical psychotherapy, the first task is to look for what is typical about a particular case. If a case is judged on the basis of arbitrary opinion, there is a risk of damage to the psyche, the structures of which are often delicate and complicated. We must therefore look not only for what is typical but also for the archetypal features of the case, for those features, in other words, that portray the primordial and typical experience of humanity. If we can find the archetype, we have hold of something that permits us t generalize without overlooking the individual. We have something that concerns both the patient and humanity at large, including the doctor.

Let me give an example. A twenty-five-year-old woman from a simple background has the good fortune to marry a wealthy husband. She has never been very disciplined, but is able to win the man with her charm. The difficulties start soon after the wedding. The woman becomes restless and feels ill and unhappy, despite the fact that the husband is able to offer her all the comforts of middle-class affluence. Within a few years two little daughters are born; the husband, fully tied up in his job, is often away on business. One day the husband begins to suspect that his wife has a lover, and soon he has proof. The woman has been having an affair with an extremely primitive individual with a bad reputation. None of this is all that abnormal, nor all that astonishing. The husband discovers, however, that his wife's affair is not the only thing. She drinks, too – mainly aperitifs and cocktails, and in large quantities. She also takes sleeping pills in considerable quantities. Naturally, the husband could have seen the way things were going long before. He chose instead not to notice anything, preferring a peaceful family life.

Sheer laziness made him shut his eyes. This laziness is itself perhaps a passion; La Rochefoucauld says of it, "Of all vices laziness is the one we ourselves are least aware of; it is also the most dangerous because it operates imperceptibly and the damage it causes is deeply concealed."

Finally, however, the husband can shut his eyes no longer. In trying to discuss the situation with his wife, he realizes that she has completely lost her mental balance. A furious quarrel is the only result of his attempt. Further heated discussions follow, but they merely serve to show what a chaotic state the household is already in. The husband has to admit to himself that his wife will continue to drink and take sleeping pills despite his reproaches.

Frequently he finds her in a stupor. And so the husband comes to the conclusion that the problem is no longer one of social behavior or morals; rather it is a medical problem. So he calls in a psychiatrist. The doctor feels that ambulatory treatment is out of the question and recommends a stay in a clinic. There it is impossible for the patient to drink or take sleeping pills. But still the woman is not cured. Her abnormal irritability persists even after several months in the clinic. The patient's thoughts and speech also remain noticeably incoherent and dissociated. Therefore, a change of clinic is considered necessary. In the second clinic every discussion ends in a hysterical scene, so that eventually the patient has to be interned in the closed unit of the clinic.

There the doctor alone is in charge. Circumstances lead the doctor to assume the role of a *substitute father*. Thus we can see from this case how the role of father can be directly transferred to the doctor. Where there is chaos, where there is a lack of discipline, where the confusion becomes a danger, the paternal order comes into force. The image of the father that we see here is that of the father who imposes order and the *avenging father*. The father who punishes imposes his will by force. Obviously, the doctor is not himself the avenging father. He too has to obey the paternal principle, since chaos cannot be tolerated in a clinic. The paternal spirit of order should govern the clinic, though the clinic itself, as an institution that receives and protects people, is a maternal symbol. Certainly to the patient, the doctor may seem to have the features of the terrible, avenging father. But that is a projection of a symbol onto the person of the doctor and not a banal, external reality.

Through her excited and distracted behavior the patient has conjured up the symbol of the father. The case visibly borders on psychosis. In an openly schizophrenic case the connection between pathological emotionality and the father archetype is even clearer. Daniel Paul Schreber, one-time president of the high court of Saxony, provides in his *Memoirs of a Psychiatric Patient* a remarkable document of psychosis. He had almost daily to perform what he called the "bellowing miracle." The purpose of this miracle (Schreber had to bellow out loud) was to remind God (the father), who was poorly informed about people on earth, of the sick man's existence.[1] We have here the early childhood experience: By screaming, the baby calls for its parents. And if the child screams too long or too loud, then not only might the mother come to feed it, the father might also come to punish it.

It emerges from what has been said that the behavior of our patient is still infantile. When circumstances compel the doctor to adopt the role of a provisional, substitute father, the image of the father comes into play and restores order. The father role of the doctor in such cases is provisional, and so too is the order deriving from the transference. But order is the first requirement if psychotherapy is to proceed, since chaos makes any treatment impossible.

At the same time, through the projection of the image of the father onto the doctor, contact is established with the patient. This makes it possible to discuss the situation with her and to look for a solution. The situation is not straightforward. The patient is virtually a prisoner, and her husband is thinking of divorce. And since she is guilty of adultery, she stands to lose everything: the children, the money, and her social position. It is difficult to see a way out. Whatever happens, the woman's attitude to life needs to be completely reshaped. All of this is just theory, though, and there is nothing to be gained from a rational discussion of these issues with the patient. If discussion is not getting us any further, then the moment has come, as Jung put it, to ask the unconscious. At such moments the unconscious often begins to speak of its own accord. During the first period of treatment, the patient consistently maintained that she did not have any dreams; but now, having encountered the image of the father – that is, having had to obey – she reports a dream. Here we see an important characteristic of the archetype: The archetype exerts an organizing influence on consciousness and the unconscious. In response to this influence, the situation begins to change, things start moving, and the unconscious is activated. The woman starts to take note of her dreams and is also prepared to tell them to the doctor.

Consciousness never has any genuinely new perspective on a problem. But during sleep, when the light of consciousness is extinguished, a new idea may take shape. The new idea is expressed in an archaic language, in a dream. Dreams do not speak logically, but in images. To understand dreams you have to understand the language of primitives and children.

The patient's dream occurred immediately before she was clinically interned. Interestingly, she had already had the same dream once before, around the time that her husband first called in the psychiatrist. The dream went as follows:

"I have just arrived after a journey. In the station I am standing at the foot of a flight of steps. The steps lead to a platform where my husband is standing. He wants to give me a ladies' glove."

From a psychotherapeutic point of view, it is important that a dream like this not be interpreted on the basis of a preconceived theory. The main thing is that the patient should accept the interpretation. The doctor's knowledge, the patient's associations, and even those of the doctor can all be drawn into consideration; and on no account should the affective contact with the patient be allowed to break off. If contact is ever lost, one has to try to reestablish order, in our case for example, by invoking the authority of the father whose image lies behind the doctor's role. If that has no effect, the patient can end up playing an often quite endearing game with the doctor whereby any therapeutic benefit is lost. Of course authority, the father archetype, is not the only thing that helps maintain contact. Often contact is sustained by an instinctive reaction on the part of either the doctor or the patient. But if simply keeping up the affective contact is a problem, it is often useful to look carefully at the archetypal elements of the therapeutic situation. In situations of this kind the doctor can be not only father but also, for example, mother, brother / sister, friend or enemy, savior, devil, and much more besides; and any such transference always defines the patient's role, too. The actual interpretation of the dream should in any case produce a result that is understandable and that makes sense to both partners in the discussion, patient and doctor.

The dream we are talking about is the first the patient recounts during this period of treatment and it has already occurred once before, right at the start of clinical treatment. It is also striking that the dream recurs precisely when treatment begins, as it were, for a second time, when the patient is interned. A dream that is characterized in this way by the moment at which it occurs is known as an *initial dream*. Often the dream gives us an overall view of the patient's problem and simultaneously outlines a program of treatment.

The dream begins with the patient's arrival at the station. The journey is an image of development and change. Arriving at the station (the "terminus," where she gets out) means the process of change is completed.

In connection with this motif, I would like to cite the ancient Egyptian myth of Isis and Ra, as it will be important later in our discussion. It is a typical transformation myth and, as synopsized by E. A. Wallis Budge,[2] runs as follows:

The goddess Isis wishes to become Queen of the World as Ra is King of the World. She cherishes this wish in her heart (Isis is not the wife of Ra, but rather his mother). Ra is old. His majesty is great, but he trembles; his steps are unsteady, and the aging god's saliva drips to the ground. Out of the saliva and earth Isis forms a snake. She forms a dangerous snake and throws it at the feet of the old god. With the help of the snake, she hopes to force him to tell her his name. When she knows his name, she will have power over him. The snake bites. Ra feels the wound; he knows that he is going to die. And he says that he has been wounded by something that he does not know. He, the creator of the world, has never before seen the creature that wounded him. He grows weak. Isis demands that he tell her his name. He says that he is Ra, but Isis is still not satisfied. She wants to know what the name means, what Ra really is. And Ra replies: "I am the creator of the world. Heaven and Earth are my work. When I open my eyes, it is day; when I close them, it is night." In explaining his own nature, he dies. But no, he does not die; he is transformed. Out of Ra, at the moment of his death, the eye of Horus is born, as the new sun. And Isis, his mother, triumphs. She says, "Horus lives and the poison dies."

Seen in the light of the myth of Isis and Ra, the beginning of our dream enacts the moment when Horus, the new perspective, is born, the moment when Horus opens his eyes. The transformation is complete.

Next the dreamer climbs a flight of steps, ascending to a higher level. Under the auspices of Horus, the new god, life begins to unfold. The patient has to find a higher level (platform) in life; it is obvious that the previous level was fairly low. On the higher level she can join her husband. This part of the dream seems promising since, from a practical point of view, the patient's chief problem is how to win her husband back. The means of achieving that, which he himself gives her, is the ladies' glove.

The result of the discussion of the "glove" is as follows: The woman had constantly demanded trust. Now that she has failed (now that the clay serpent has undermined the old position), she cannot expect any trust; her husband has no reason to show her any. On the contrary, he has good reason to mistrust her. She always demanded things, never giving anything in return. At present she has first of all to reassure her husband. She should handle him with care, "with kid gloves," and be tactful with him. In itself this wisdom is neither surprising nor new: Every wife ought to know that there are times when she should be tactful in the way she deals with her husband. If she does not know that, she is a child, not a woman. Here, however, the patient has to recognize that she cannot find the tact she needs – the glove – within herself; it is mediated by the husband. She has to be attentive to her husband. She has to recognize that the husband is an ordinary human being with his own reactions and his own ideas of family life, which she cannot simply ignore. She should not disappoint him too greatly, and she should obey him. She has always made demands, but the husband has justifiable demands of his own.

The relationship between man and wife cannot be founded one-sidedly on the demands of the wife, not even if those demands seem justified. She has to see that the husband also expects something from her.

It is a general fact that the relationship between two people, be it between neighbors or in a marriage, consists of two things: We expect something from the other person, but the other person also expects something from us. So my relationship with another person does not belong to me alone; it is the common property of myself and the other person. To find the right relationship I have to acknowledge the personality of the other person. In the relationship between I and Thou, therefore, the *persona*, the appropriate manner,[3] plays an important role. Our patient, for example, was too naive, too childlike. She exposed the husband to her every reaction, thinking it was her right, indeed her duty to do so. She believed that a reaction that was not childlike and naive was not sincere either. In that way she overruled her husband's feelings.

In antiquity, the persona was the mask worn by actors. Our patient thought that the persona of the wife would bring falsehood into her marriage. In that she was thoroughly mistaken. Even in the happiest of marriages, if the husband came home for lunch at midday to find his wife stark naked in the dining room, he would be extremely surprised. The wife ought, on the contrary, to be dressed as befits a woman in her position. The same applies on a psychological level. If the woman shows herself as psychologically naked, irritable, and egocentric, if the husband is greeted not with a smile but with hysterical tears, and if instead of a quiet lunch break all he can expect is quarreling and shouting, then he starts considering divorce. If our patient wants to save the situation and keep her position, she cannot simply demand that her husband be gentle with her on the grounds that she is easily upset, for example. Sensitivity can never be an excuse. No, the husband has to be handled "with kid gloves"; she must be tactful with him, because he is rightly indignant. So she must pay attention to her husband, take his reactions seriously, and also take his views seriously. She must, in the language of her dream, go to her husband to find her glove. In sum she has to recognize that there are certain rules in life, and that the wife of a factory director, if she wants to avoid divorce, cannot behave like a small child.

What we have seen so far, however, does not help us understand the patient's disorders. A program for the future has been given, but that still does not explain the previous negative development. A further dream helps us see more clearly. This dream occurred before the dream discussed above, but was not reported by the patient until much later, in fact not until the day she was released from the clinic. It will be seen that the point at which it was reported was significant.

The dream is simple and immediately understandable. It went like this: "I am in a church. There I marry my father." Clearly it represents a (reversed) Oedipus complex. The dream, which occurred a considerable time before the start of treatment, showed that the patient still had an infantile attachment to the father. She herself said that at the time of the dream her father had been dead for some months. She had loved him (and always rejected her mother). As a child and as a young girl, she had always been able to go to the father with any problem. Her father always knew the answer, and she revered him. Later, however, he was for a long time ill with a heart condition. Evidently the illness caused a change in his character. He became stubborn, irascible, and unapproachable. Our patient felt this change deeply and missed her father's good advice.

Simply in view of the plain reality, the patient's dream bears all the hallmarks of the *impossible*. She cannot possibly marry her father: It is not legally permitted, and anyway her father is dead. These realistic considerations will help us understand the dream better. While the patient was still a child, the father taught her the laws of life; he knew everything. But there comes a time when a person is too old to be seeking advice from the father. And the father too is an old man, too old to give advice. In the present case, it seems that the natural father was, long before his death, incapable of representing the paternal principle. He was old, sick, and unapproachable. The paternal world was no longer to be found in him; even before he died, he had already withdrawn from reality. Consequently, our patient lost the paternal principle. The result for her of losing that spiritual perspective was that impulse gained the upper hand. Pierre Janet describes this phenomenon as an *abaissement du niveau psychologique*.[4] Impulse takes over and, as a result, the balance of the patient's mind becomes disturbed. The patient finally loses all inhibitions.

We may recall here the myth of Isis and Ra: The father is the old sun god, Ra. Isis, matter, has killed Ra. That is to say, time, the changeable nature of our bodies, makes the daughter grow up and the father grow old. Thus the moment arrives when the daughter can no longer project the father symbol onto the natural father. Yet in spite of age, in spite of death, the image of the natural father remains a part of the patient's fantasy life and appears in dreams – that is the aging Ra, the *dying* Ra. As long as she looks back to the natural father, the image of the father is in reality lost. That is the *night*.

The patient has to find a new order if she is to find her way in the world, respect the reactions of others, and grasp the persona problem. That would be the new perspective, the *new sun god*, Horus. It is important in this connection that the dream occurred at the end of treatment. The impossibility of the event enacted in the dream indicates that it is not the natural father we are dealing with here, but an unnatural or even supernatural father. It is a father the patient can, amazingly, marry. And she can marry him even though he is supposedly dead. Only a small child really wants to marry her father ("when I'm big, I'm going to marry Daddy"). Accordingly, as long as she looks back, the patient is infantile. The impossibility of the marriage can also have a positive sense, though. In real life the marriage is undoubtedly impossible. The task is rather to seek a union with this supernatural father in the inner life. The patient should look forwards, not backwards. Then it would be possible to see in this second dream, as in the first, a program for the future. The second program does not concern the relationship to the external world, but rather to the inner world. The patient has to find a personal relationship to the paternal principle of order. She has to become united with that principle (in metaphorical terms, "married") and to accept it of her own free will as a necessity of life – of her own free will, as if she were to go to the altar with the man of her choice. She must find within herself the ability to organize her life and accept the reality of another person. In other words, she must find within herself the paternal principle that creates order out of the chaos of matter.

The ability to accept the order of the world reflects a very general principle; and yet every individual has his own solution. The way a person organizes himself depends on his personal constitution, not least on the typology inherited from his ancestors. It is understandable, therefore, that the supernatural father within is most often represented in dreams by the natural father. Our example shows, however, that if you examine the facts, the dream figure turns out to be no "ordinary natural father."

Generally speaking, there is a lot of sense in the paternal principle's being represented by the natural father. The similarity between the natural father and the supernatural paternal principle makes the transition from childhood to adulthood less of a rupture. Even when you have found the paternal principle within yourself, your whole personality structure is not turned upside down if the "new father" is not unlike the father of your childhood. Thus the paternal principle acquires a certain stability, which can also strengthen the family. The natural father does not have to be rejected. The adult who carries the paternal principle within himself can look back on his natural father and say, "Yes, that is father, my father, the father I love." In this way a person can detach himself from his father without destroying family ties.

Once our patient has found the paternal principle within herself, she has, of course, not only to tackle the persona problem, that is to say, the relationship to the external world; she also has to work on the relationship to the inner world. In this relationship, what we called the "inner father" is also a prefiguration of the animus archetype. The animus is the more masculine side of a

woman, which provides contact with emotionality. We are em-
barking on a different subject here, but the animus problem must
be mentioned since the future course of events in the case of our
patient cannot be judged before we have seen how the animus
question is resolved.

We can see now why the patient did not recount the dream of
her father until the end of treatment. If the dream had been
understood simply in terms of external reality, a very negative
impression would have been created. Once the second dream (of
the glove) had been discussed, however, it was possible to see the
positive side of the first dream. The fact that the first dream was
withheld for so long can thus be attributed to a self-regulatory
mechanism in the patient. It is very dangerous to become aware
of an archetypal problem without seeing both the positive and the
negative aspects. The doctor, too, often needs to trust his instincts
in such cases. When a problem assumes archetypal proportions,
the patient should not be made to see it if only negative aspects
are visible. And in practical psychotherapy one should respect the
patient's self-regulatory tendencies and not, for example, probe
for dreams that the patient does not recount voluntarily. It is not
uncommon for mistakes to be made in this regard. When that
happens, it is not for nothing that analysis is said to be dangerous
for a person's mental equilibrium. Naturally, that equilibrium
does not have to be protected under all circumstances; now and
then one comes across people whose illusory balance of mind
urgently needs upsetting and who need to wake up quickly because they have slept far too long already!

In the course of our investigation of this case, we have encountered two typical aspects of the father: the *good father* who
knows everything, represented by the father of the patient, and
the *avenging father*, represented by the organization of the clinic
and projected onto the person of the doctor. We find the same two
aspects of the father in the Bible: the good father (God the father)
of the New Testament and the irascible, avenging father (Jehovah)
of the Old Testament.

Even the young child experiences the father both as a good

father and as a terrible, threatening father. Everyone is familiar with the first aspect, the beloved father. One has only to think of the words of Victor Hugo, "My father, the hero with the gentle smile." And Marcel Jouhandeau gives us a good example of how a child can experience the terrible father in his book *My Father and Mother*:[5]

> A butcher's shop in Chaminadour, the barking dogs, the smell of blood, the apprentices, the customs and festivals of the trade; in the shop, the massive figure of the master butcher with the enormous hands (his "paws"), the sensual or enraged nostrils, the eyes, often laughing, often suddenly grim. Then the butcher as a man: calculations and resentments, childish passions, adulteries, a sudden temper that all but made a criminal of him. From his corner, the child looks on him with an almost religious awe: son of a butcher is what he is and always will be, son of a murderer and sacrificer.

Here the superhuman, archetypal aspect of the father is prominent: The father is both murderer *and* sacrificer. And his profession, which likewise bears many resemblances to that of the sacrificer, will decide the child's future. It is interesting to see how the author experiences the mother who belongs to this brutal and awe-inspiring father; he refers to her as "my little mother." The *brutal father* can destroy a life, and the danger becomes all the more real when both mother and son are in the Oedipal situation: "my little mother." In Jouhandeau's case the negative development is avoided, as we shall see, but the danger is there all the same. Jung reports a corresponding case in "The Significance of the Father in the Destiny of the Individual."[6] There the father, a onetime soldier in the Swiss Guard, was a harsh tyrant who demanded military discipline in the home and who even beat the mother. The mother died early, broken by sorrow. The son, Jung's patient, was impotent and also slightly homosexual. He subsequently married the divorced wife of his older brother. Since the older brother strongly resembled the father, the impression was that, in so doing, the patient hoped to take his father's place and marry his mother. The marriage was a disaster. And then when the patient for the first time met a woman he really liked, he did not have the strength to react positively. Instead, he became nervous, depressed, and even suicidal. His vital energy had already been sapped by the father, and when life offered him an opportunity he escaped into neurosis.

The opposite case, however, that of the *loving* father, is not without its dangers either. Such a father can also poison a life. There is an example of this too in Jung's work.[7] A woman came to the doctor complaining of palpitations, disturbing dreams, and depression. She said that her father was happily married to her mother and that her mother revered her father. The father was a good-looking, dignified, and intelligent man; he died of a stroke while the patient was still a child. At the age of twenty-four the patient became acquainted with a widower, a tall, dignified man just like her father. She married him. After four years of marriage the husband died of a stroke. Much later, at the age of forty-six, the patient began to feel a need for love. This time she took the first man that came along, a sixty-year-old farmer, who had already been divorced twice on the grounds of brutality and unacceptable behavior; she was, however, perfectly aware of the man's past history. Five difficult years followed, at the end of which she was divorced. The neurosis started shortly after that.

These two case histories correspond to one another. In both, the father is too strong, whether in his brutality or in his goodness. The son of the brutal father is unable to find his own way in life. He loses his instinct, becomes impotent, and repeats in his own life, though at a lower level, the life of his father (he too beats his wife). When he does eventually find a woman he could love, he falls ill. The daughter of the good father, though, is also unable to find her way. The first marriage is simply a repetition of her parents' marriage. Then when the need for love re-emerges before the menopause, she marries a brutal and dubious father substitute. In general, therefore, *too strong a father* can falsify a life; usually the life of the parents is repeated at a debased level. The worst damage is to the instincts, so that if ever a tiny instinct should happen to make itself felt, the strength to express it is lacking and all that comes of it is a neurosis.

To sum up what we have seen so far, the natural father teaches the child the laws of life. This is in line with the traditional roles: The mother is full of loving care while the father governs justly with goodness and authority. And the father knows; he is wise, too. It can happen, of course, that the father plays much more the role of the mother in a family. This tends to happen when the father himself was powerfully influenced by his mother and still has an Oedipal attachment to her. Conversely, the mother may have many of the attributes of a father if she herself stands in the shadow of her own father. The real father figure in such cases, the one that governs the child, is the grandfather on the mother's side.

One way or another the child will have to learn that the laws of life must be accepted, and sooner or later it will have to discover them for itself. The completion of this task is made that much more difficult if the natural father exerts too strong an influence, since to find the laws of life you have to take part in life. Anyone who is afraid of the father will also be afraid of life. He will think to himself, if father was terrible then the paternal laws of life must be even worse. And anyone who reveres the father too much will think, the advice of my dear father is much easier than this law of life that can only be cruel and dangerous. It is fear that stands in the way of life, fear of life and death, fear born of *laziness*. If consciousness rejects life, vital energy withdraws and finds expression on an earlier, outlived level. Whatever instinct remains leads the individual into a seemingly new situation that in fact merely repeats the old one on a lower level. And real life is lost. Jung says of this development:[8] "Flight from life does not exempt us from the law of age and death. The neurotic who tries to wriggle out of the necessity of living wins nothing and only burdens himself with a constant foretaste of aging and dying..." So the libido, finding the way forward blocked, regresses and seeks an outlet in neurosis.

That is the development we saw in the two cases outlined above. Needless to say, neither the brutal nor the good father was easy to cope with. But no father, however imposing, can excuse anyone from having to face up to life. If the father is brutal, he will have to be overcome. And if he is the embodiment of goodness, revered by the mother, then he will have to be exposed for what he is: probably an ordinary man, full of the enjoyment of life, who died early as a result of alcohol abuse or even venereal disease. Only the person who refuses to let himself be intimidated or fascinated by the natural father will find the paternal law of life.

Let us return now to Jouhandeau. Jouhandeau took the image of his wild father into his heart. And behind the brutal features he discovered another face, the face of the father-Titan which was that of his father as a young man and was to re-emerge when he was dying. For Jouhandeau this was the face of the man he could love, and he calls him "my little father." Once again he gives his father an archetypal name: Titan. Thus Jouhandeau's image of the father includes the murderer, the sacrificer, and the Titan. Certainly the law of the father can be cruel. Before order can be established, the instincts have to be curbed, and laziness and fear have to be sacrificed. But to maintain order, one has to be able to fight and conquer like a Titan. In that respect the father is a guardian. But if the old order of life should ever become suffocating, then the father has to be overcome so that he may be reborn. Thus Isis killed Ra in order that Horus (the Titan) might be born. Then the child has to conquer the mother and kill the father.

At this point I would like to go back to the myth of Isis. Order, the paternal principle, brings instinct and desire under control; but an order that becomes repressive has to be overthrown. It is important, therefore, in a clinical case when the father is experienced as an oppressor, to ascertain whether that father (who can also, for example, be the law in a narrower sense) is the aging, exhausted Ra or the new god Horus. If he is the old Ra, one can say to the patient, you must rebel and liberate yourself. But if he is Horus, one will say, you must accept and obey.

If the existing order is not superseded, if it still has life in it, then matter, everyday reality, will not be able to poison it. On the contrary, the order will shape reality. In the Egyptian myth, Isis outwits Ra with the snake. She also plays a dangerous game with Horus, the young god. Plutarch describes in *On Isis and Osiris* how the maternal principle can appear in two guises: as Isis, mother of Horus, and as the dragon Typhon, symbol of the dangerous, terrible mother. Isis secretly releases the dragon that Horus has tamed. She does it to avenge Ra, whom Horus has supplanted. Horus, however, furious at this treachery, confronts his mother, snatching away her crown and with it her power. Thus Horus, the new god, the Titan, emerges victorious over the dragon-mother. This illustrates the archetypal struggle of the sun hero against the dragon, symbol of the terrible mother.

Where can we see this myth in practical experience? A child goes to school to learn grammar, mathematics, and discipline too, of course. The organization of the school is the young Ra, the Ra who rules over matter and attends to the education of the raw material we call a child. But the child outgrows the narrow confines of the school, completing a development which corresponds in the myth to the killing of Ra by Isis. It should not be overlooked, however, that the school with its rules is not merely a father to the child. As an institution, it is also a mother; it affords him the security of knowing what has to be done and what has to be learned. When the point is reached where the school's rules are no longer adequate to the young person's needs, he should leave the school. He then must find a new perspective for coping with life and at the same time a new framework for his life. In our schools, which build on the experience of generations, this transition is generally accomplished quite naturally. The final examination signals the change. But where the training is, for example, a clerical apprenticeship, there may come a moment when the young person has to declare: "No, I cannot accept this subordinate position any longer. If I can get no further in my career here, I will leave my job and find my own way." That is then Horus snatching the crown away from Isis.

It is often far from easy to decide whether the paternal principle needs renewal or whether it should be obeyed. In such cases the unconscious can provide guidance, for instance in dreams.

Two examples will illustrate how, despite obvious outward similarities in two people's situations, their personal, inner circumstances can be very different.

The examples concern two twenty-year-old young men. One of them was studying at the university to become a teacher. One day, however, he began to doubt whether that was a good idea. It emerged in discussion that his opportunities were limited; it would not be easy for him to change direction in his studies or even to look for something completely different. The father was not very well off and would have been glad if the young man were soon in a position to support himself. Yet one hardly dared counsel against a change of profession on those grounds alone. The patient was as a result of his uncertainty extremely inhibited and also unable to work. Then he had a dream: "I see some cogwheels. Together they form a chain of cogwheels." This is an image of compulsion, in which every movement triggers a second movement and every turn of one wheel is caused by the turning of the next. It depicts a paternal law that is powerful and harsh. Anyone who refuses to accept that law will get caught in the machine. It is true that the father of this young man was a peaceable and good-natured man, but the fact that he had no money seemed – looking at the dream – to be inescapable. Any thought of changing careers had to be sacrificed; the young man had to work. As soon as he had grasped that he did not have to work because he enjoyed it, but because he was obliged to by the inexorable laws of life, he found new energy and was able to work properly again. Whoever has to obey the paternal laws must know what those laws are and consciously accept them.

The second patient was a commercial trainee. He was nervous and depressed. His parents were concerned and took him to a doctor, who suggested psychotherapeutic treatment. In the course of this treatment the patient drew a picture showing three cogwheels; the middle cogwheel was broken. The three cogwheels belonged to a machine which was supposed to drive a dynamo that supplied current to a lamp. Here the situation is different from the previous case. The cogwheels no longer function; one wheel is broken. This means that the law which supposedly compelled the young man to continue his commercial training was already ineffective. That fact had to be recognized if the patient's depression was to be understood. He found himself in the dark. The light that was supposed to clarify the situation was not working. A law always provides us with a perspective that helps us understand, in other words, that throws light on the situation. The therapist considered the meaning of this image and advised the parents to find a different profession for their son, one that was more congenial to him. The success of this advice was very convincing. I did not treat this case myself, so I cannot say whether the patient's father had much money or not.[9] But it is obvious that in the patient's unconscious the old law (the aging Ra) had already died, so that a complete change in external circumstances was called for. After all, a young man can find his own way in life even though his father is poor. Horus, the young god, conquers Isis, or matter. One way or another the patient seemed to have been poisoned by arguments foreign to his nature. He had to find his own way; and when Horus has thus been born, he can become a father in his own right. The case of the brutal father cited by Jung comes to mind in this connection. There the patient lacked the courage to break the father's law; he became impotent and was never himself a father.

Until now we have been discussing the problems of the father who has to be obeyed and of the father whose power has to be overcome. There is another, extremely important aspect of the father archetype in which even the very young child is interested. Jung gives an example in "Psychology and Education."[10] A four-year-old girl started screaming one night. The mother went to her. The child asked, "What is Daddy doing, what does he say?" And the mother replied, "He's asleep; he doesn't say anything." The little girl said mockingly, "No doubt he will be ill again tomorrow." Now, shortly before that, when the father had been ill, the child had suspected that he had "a plant in his stomach." She probably thought that the father had "something in his stomach" again; he might be going to have a baby, like the mother. But the child mocked at the idea. Of course the mother could have babies, but where from? The child faced a very subtle question: If the father cannot have children, what does he do? Does he do anything at all?

Thus we encounter the symbol of the *father as creator*. Does not Ra say of himself, "I am he that created Heaven and Earth"? The first chapter of the Bible also shows us God as the creator of the world and of man. The image of the *creator-father* seems at first sight banal. At the same time, it is by no means easy to appreciate why he is the father and how he accomplishes it. The child's question can be answered in biological terms, though it is notoriously difficult to say how the parents should answer it, and there are no rules. The answer is not simple at a psychological level either. Whatever you say of such an archetypal problem, you always risk oversimplifying and so distorting the picture. But as long as you are aware of the risk, you can attempt an answer.

We have already discovered that the father has something to do with a perspective; one could also say, a way of seeing. We will try to apply this idea to the beginning of the book of Genesis by examining the tremendous myth that shows us God the father as the creator of the world. The treatment is not intended to be exhaustive, of course; all we aim to do here is look more closely at the question of the father as creator.

Our starting point is consciousness. We need consciousness in order to perceive objects. We cannot perceive anything if we do not have a perspective (a point from which to view things). At the same time, the qualities of the perceived object enable us to say something about the consciousness that perceives it.

Let us take the first verse of Genesis: "In the beginning God created heaven and earth. The Earth was without form and void, with darkness over the face of the abyss." What sort of a being must it be that perceives such a world, the world before the first day of creation? It must be a blind worm that cannot yet perceive the qualities of the world. To it the earth is still empty ("void"); it can merely assume that something else apart from the earth exists – heaven – which is hidden from it in darkness.

Then God said: "Let there be light!" And he separated light from darkness. So evening and morning came. The being that perceives this *first day* is still largely unconscious. All the same, it is no longer blind. But its consciousness can only distinguish night and day and the transition between them, evening and morning.

On the *second day* God created the vault that separates the waters above from those below. The being that perceives this day is therefore capable of distinguishing above from below.

Then God created dry land; he separated the land from the water. He also created the gathering of the waters, the sea. And God caused the earth to produce seed-bearing plants and fruit-bearing trees. A being that can consciously perceive this knows the landscape and can orient itself in the geography of the rivers and the woods. It knows trees that bear fruit. It still orients itself in time solely according to day and night. That is the being of the *third day*.

On the *fourth day* God created lights in the vault of heaven to serve as signs for festivals, seasons, and years. Accordingly, the being that perceives this day is aware of time in the passing of days and the yearly cycle. God also created a greater light to govern the day and a lesser light to govern the night. The being that perceives this therefore knows that it is the sun that causes the day. But it still cannot distinguish itself from the other beings that populate the earth.

On the *fifth day* God created the living creatures in the sea and the birds that fly above the earth. The creature that perceives this day realizes that there are apart from itself creatures of the water and of the air, but it cannot yet distinguish itself from the land creatures.

The distinction between the various land animals, on the *sixth day*, brings not only the distinction between man and the animals, for God creates man and woman at the same time. Now the being can perceive itself not only as human, but also as man or woman.

Human consciousness comes into being, not yet as individual consciousness, but distinguished according to sex.

If we consider God's creation of the world in relation to the nature of the being that perceives it, the creation is an image of a developing consciousness. This development can be seen as that of the human race as a whole, which doubtless ran parallel to the phylogenetic development described by Darwin. But it can also refer to ontogenetic development. The blind creature is the child before birth (before the first day). The newborn child, who to start with is merely aware of night and day, is the being of the second day of Genesis. The child who knows that its dog is a dog, that today is an autumn day, and that it, a boy (as it can clearly see), differs from its little sister, is the being of the sixth day of Genesis. After that, there is a pause in the development: On the *seventh day* God rested from all the work he had done. A certain time will elapse before the child encounters sin and moral conflict the poison that the snake treacherously insinuates into his heart.

Who is he then, this creator-father, who made the earth? It is not God who resembles man, but man who resembles God. However, the biblical myth expresses it with singular caution. It says: "God created man in his own image; in the image of God he created him." The "image of God" is mentioned twice and so highlighted. This is an excellent definition of the archetype. Man can only see God in an image. The actual source of the image cannot be grasped. And it is that source which generated the image. When God created a human being that was conscious of itself, he also created the idea called God, the image of God. The same relationship of source to image applies to the whole of the archetypal world. We cannot visualize the archetype, only the archetypal image; but the image is produced by the archetype.

From this point of view (which, as we said, is in no way comprehensive), we are like God and God is like us. That is why it seems to us that the creator-father is human. We know, however, that that is just an image. The force of the creator-father demands *development*. In a psychological context this development is an unfolding of consciousness. Every day that the creator-father is at work, the consciousness of the being that perceives the world expands. To begin with, it knew only heaven and earth, then day and night, until finally it knew that it was a human being, indeed a man or a woman, and it could recognize the animals, birds, and fishes, the whole of nature and time. The creator-father desires the development of consciousness, and it is consciousness that creates the world.

It is indeed consciousness. Modern physics, as created by Einstein and Planck, demonstrates the fact. In modern physics distances within the universe are uncertain, and the state of things seems paradoxical to our understanding. In the universe, which is full of so-called fixed stars, space and time are by no means fixed quantities. If, on the other hand, one looks, say, at a house, an apparently solid building, one knows that one is in fact looking at a collection of infinitesimal particles whose position in space cannot be determined with any certainty. Macrocosm and microcosm are in a paradoxical state. But man has seeing eyes. He sees day and night, mountains and lakes, birds and fishes; he sees animals and he sees himself. Thus out of a paradoxical chaos a world is created. Admittedly, it is a world that is not a reality, but an image. The image is real enough, though, and it is a world in which one can love and hate, suffer and rejoice; it is a world in which one can live. It is consciousness that creates the world. And every time consciousness takes a step forward – impelled by the creator-father – the world changes. Our world is not that of our ancestors, and it will not be that of our children, because the creator God lives and continues to work.

The eye of consciousness gives form to chaos. From the father's perspective the maternal principle, matter, is that chaos. But that is not the case. The maternal principle is not chaos; matter is what is given form by the paternal principle. Chaos, however, is what one could call the state that arises through the *loss of the father,* for want of an organizing perspective. This became very clear in our first case, where the patient wanted (in her dream) to marry her dead father. There it was necessary to revive the paternal principle to make an ordered life possible once more. That is because the paternal principle organizes matter ("the mother") by imposing a perspective.

The perspective allows us to see a particular aspect of the world; other aspects remain invisible. Every perspective has the effect of making certain things visible while excluding others. Consequently, the paternal principle with its perspective is not only an organizer but also an oppressor. As a principle, it is both good and bad, and it often rules with force and violence. Thus, for example, the scientific perspective of the nineteenth century made possible an astonishing advance in science and technology. But the reality of the soul, which lay beyond the scope of that perspective, was lost.

What is important is that there always comes a creative moment when a change of perspective is due. In a stable situation the paternal principle allows a certain development to take place, for instance, that of the nineteenth century. But in a stable situation only limited aspects of matter can be apprehended. The development that began with a given aspect of matter becomes with time more and more distant from the true nature of matter. This creates a tension, which is the father's most powerful creative force. Towards the end of the nineteenth century, for example, matter and the soul of man, too, were weary of the mechanistic view of things; there was a longing for a new perspective, and a spirit of rebellion emerged. The mechanistic perspective had to be overcome, as it had exhausted its potential and no longer satisfied the needs of the age. Everywhere there was a reaction against the mechanistic spirit. That is the moment when the saliva of Ra falls to the earth, saliva that is the image of creative sperm. And that is the moment when Isis forms out of the saliva and earth the snake that is to kill Ra. So the tension between an increasingly one-sided development and the necessities of matter constitutes the real strength of the creator-father: He kills himself in fertilizing the earth. And the earth answers by transforming him into Horus, the new perspective. The new creator-father will sacrifice the old ideas, those of the mechanistic age, for example. Thus the old father is sacrificed by the new father; the father is both sacrificer and sacrifice.

To give an image of the creative energy that can be released by such a sacrifice, I would like to quote Jung.[11] In speaking of the bull of Mithras, a symbol of transformation, he says: "In the light of the Persian legend, and on the evidence of the monuments themselves, this sacrifice should be conceived as the moment of supreme fruitfulness. This is most beautifully portrayed in the Mithras relief at Heddernheim. On one side of a large ... stone slab there is a stereotyped representation of the overthrow and sacrifice of the bull, while on the other side stand Sol with a bunch of grapes in his hand, Mithras with the cornucopia, and the dadophors bearing fruits, in accordance with the legend that from the dead bull comes all fruitfulness..."

A further interesting detail is that on the monuments depicting the sacrifice, a dog always appears alongside the dead bull. The dog is a symbol of instinct and specifically of instinct controlled by man (the dog is a domestic animal). This shows how, at the moment of creative transformation, man needs an instinct to help him find the new perspective. C. A. Meier[12] draws attention to the fact that to the Indo-Germans the dog was man's guide in the beyond. The "beyond," however, is always the new, that which lies beyond the comprehension of the old perspective. The dog is well suited to the task, thanks to its keen sense of smell and its ability to see into the future. The dog has also to do with birth and death. The dog's most important gift, its ability to detect things, is, as C. A. Meier says, a quality that also characterizes a good doctor. The god of medicine, Asclepios, also has a dog for a companion. It can be assumed, therefore, that when the old world collapses the new path has to be found by instinct.

The fertility symbolism found in the Mithras cult does not, however, reach the level of Christian symbolism. In the Mithras cult it is the animal, base instinct that is sacrificed, as naturally seemed appropriate in a sensual age. In Christian symbolism, by contrast, through the sacrifice of the Man-God, the commitment of the whole personality is demanded for the sake of higher goals.

In general terms, the relationship of the paternal principle to the maternal principle corresponds to that of husband and wife.

To the child, the natural parents seem to represent both principles. Later, symbolic aspects come to the fore. The tension that develops between the one-sided, linear paternal development and maternal matter always issues in a new union of the two principles. Thus the new perspective is born out of the encounter of the father with the mother. We have cited examples for this process: the patient who had to find the paternal principle within herself, and the young man who had to find his own way independently of his parents. To these we can add the transition from the mechanistic perspective of the nineteenth century to the perspective of the twentieth century, the full significance of which is still by no means entirely clear. In every case the transformation is the result of a new union of the paternal and maternal principles, as exemplified in the myth of Isis and Ra. Ra, the king, is old; his saliva drips to the earth. Isis, the evil one, forms a snake out of the saliva and earth, and the snake poisons Ra. Thereupon Horus, god of the new sun, is born and Isis triumphs.

The union of father and mother is an archetypal symbol that encompasses the union of opposites. As a symbol, it is the *coniunctio oppositorum*, the *hieros gamos*, the heavenly marriage. It is the myth of rebirth through fathering. We find the same myth of the divine union represented in the *Iliad*:[13]

> So speaking, the son of Kronos caught his wife in his arms. There underneath them the divine earth broke into young, fresh grass, and into dewy clover, crocus and hyacinth so thick and soft it held the hard ground deep away from them. There they lay down together and drew about them a wonderful golden cloud, and from it the glimmering dew descended.

Who would want to burden the human individual who is our father with the weight of such symbolism? It is true that the parents are often to blame for their children's difficulties. But one should beware of accusing the natural father when in a clinical case one finds symbols such as God, the sun, the sacrificer, the thunderbolt, the avenging force, or the arrow (image of direction and development). A person does not fall ill because his father is a god, whether a loving god or an enraged one. The natural father is no god. A person is ill if he believes that his father (or his mother) is a supernatural being. A person has to learn that the forces transmitted to him by his parents are not identical with the natural parents. And he has to recognize that those forces are nevertheless a reality to be acknowledged and feared. He must accept those forces and not burden an ordinary mortal with an archetypal symbol.

The influence of the father on the child is undeniable. What is important, however, is not the sum of his virtues or weaknesses. What is important is that he is the one who first transmits to the child the great and mighty law of the paternal principle. Of such laws Jung wrote, "[They are] not laws devised by the wit of man, but the laws and forces of nature, amongst which man walks as on the edge of a razor."[14]

III

THE MOTHER ARCHETYPE
AS THE SUBJECT OF THEORETICAL DISCUSSION

Analytical psychology is not the only scientific method that seeks to understand human existence and the human mind. It exists alongside other methods; this leads to discussions that can help to throw some light on its theoretical premises.

In 1953, at the request of Gustav Bally, I set forth my own position with regard to Medard Boss's account of the concept of the archetype. Boss published his views in *Dreams and their Interpretation*; the relevant chapter is entitled "The Negation and Incorporation of the Artificial and Abstract Concept of the Archetype in the Underlying Concrete Whole of a Human Phenomenon."[1]

The clinical material that formed the basis for Boss's argument derived from a three-year-long psychoanalysis of an engineer in his forties who had had to undergo psychotherapy owing to severe depressive moods and complete sexual impotence. The treatment was accompanied by a series of 823 dreams.

In the course of treatment it became strikingly apparent to what extent the patient had in truth been a prisoner of his own life-destroying, mechanistic attitude of mind. Boss's way of seeing things, which, as we shall see, is quite unmechanistic, was therefore admirably suited to the handling of this case. Generally, in reading Boss's account, one is impressed by the remarkable therapeutic achievement. If, as Boss says, the treatment brought about a "phylogenetic development" in the patient, an evolution from the vegetable to the animal to the human, that is not least due to his careful and patient approach.

In what follows, I will look at individual points in Boss's statement of his views. In order to be able to discuss the concept f the archetype with reference to his account of the case, I would ike to pick up at the point in the material where Boss himself saw n opportunity to discuss the concept, namely at the point towards the end of treatment where a variety of mother figures appear. As far as possible, my method will be first to discuss the material from the perspective of Jungian psychology and then to compare that standpoint with the one adopted by Boss.

I have to assume that I will not be able to discuss the concept of the archetype properly in relation to a single case, and will only return to it when I have examined what our one patient experienced. Properly speaking, a type, and therefore also an archetype, cannot be studied in an individual case since a type presupposes a multiplicity of typical examples.

The findings in our patient's case are as follows: He dreams of motherly figures, varying from plain, unfamiliar mothers pushing prams to scenes in which his grandmother gives him his milk bottle and then powders his bottom. He dreams a naturalistic dream of incest with his mother; he dreams of mother-angels looking after a baby Jesus. He meets in his dreams a gigantic good fairy with flowing blond hair and huge breasts spouting cascades of milk. In the analytical sessions he would have a sudden desire to be carried in the analyst's arms; he was convinced the analyst had the beginnings of female breasts. Finally – after the experience of the mother figures, if I understood correctly – he met a dream lover "in loving togetherness."

While this development was taking place, those around the patient (analyst, wife, colleagues) saw something else happening. Previously so sober and coolly calculating, deprived of human contact, severely schizoid, the man seemed to become quite childish. He even wanted his wife to put him to bed. He became very talkative towards his secretary and cried in her presence. In his dealings with his boss he was greedy for compliments. His subordinates found him ridiculous because he assumed a foolish lisp. People were beginning to have serious doubts about his sanity. The analyst too observed peculiar behavior in the patient, accompanied simultaneously by interesting and striking dreams.

In this brief recapitulation, there is a difference between my own presentation of the facts and the way Boss presents them. Boss gives what the patient experiences and what those around the patient see combined in one. I have separated the two things, first saying what the patient experienced and then saying what the others saw. I will come back to this point in greater detail later, but for now I will just point out that in Jungian psychology the question of who experiences what is always foremost.

First, the patient experiences the mother in the most varied forms. In most cases, as far as I could see, it was a kindly mother, whom he strived towards. We know, since Freud, that the mother is not always a positive figure, that she can also appear in a terrible, engulfing form. The mother that our patient dreams of is by no means always the natural mother, but something more, in which even the male analyst is included. In his dealings with the people around him, the patient also encounters his own childlike nature, which eventually enables him to escape his schizoid isolation through appeal to others.

Needless to say, the mother that the patient experiences and the childhood he encounters are both aspects of an original whole. Jung describes this whole as the archaic identity of object and subject,[2] or also, following the French researcher Lévy-Bruhl, as *participation*. The archaic identity of object and subject is disrupted, however, if a personal consciousness comes into being in the subject, for example, in the patient. Nor can I hide the fact that Jung was very concerned, on therapeutic grounds, to foster even the most rudimentary personal consciousness. The reason he felt personal consciousness to be so important was that it alone can bring a sense of responsibility. And he believed that personal responsibility is what is needed at the present time. But Jung did not overlook the fact that the emergence of a personal consciousness destroys the unity of things; where there is a subject, there must also be an object, and so the world falls unpleasantly apart. Nevertheless, his view is that the destruction of the unity of things is a necessary part of the development of a personal consciousness, a first stage, which he calls the "ego-stage." The creation of distinctions within what was originally an undifferentiated whole is also, as L. Binswanger says, the essence of cultural development ("the work of culture").[3] According to Jung, the problem arising from the object-subject split is depicted in the following images: 1. The biblical Fall with the lost Paradise; 2. The dismembered Osiris of Egyptian myth, who must be made whole again if salvation is to be achieved; 3. The Freudian castration complex, which offers a particularly stark image of separation and the consequent impotence, and which can be observed at the moment in therapy where the difficulties of subjective consciousness start.

The starting point in our patient's case is the fact that he senses a disorder. He is somehow not at one with himself, otherwise he would hardly have sought psychotherapeutic treatment. In the course of treatment he finds, both in daily life and in his dreams, the experience of the mother who attracts him and who allows him to be childlike or to live out the childlike experience that was perhaps already within him. As a result, a living relationship forms, a relationship to the maternal object and a relationship to others perceived in maternal terms. It is impossible to say whether it is he that seeks the mother until he finds her, or whether he is imperceptibly drawn to the mother, or whether the mother is summoned by his childlike nature. But we do know that what he sees and experiences is called mother and that it is more than his natural mother. It is also possible to see how the split between object and subject is progressively overcome through the growing relationship between mother and child. This particular stage of treatment is, from a Jungian perspective, very convincing since it is during this stage that the incest with the mother takes place. In contrast to Freud, who tends rather to fear incest, Jung holds the view that, in the final resort, the patient has to go through with the incest, on an inner level, of course. The mother whom the patient experiences leads him, as previously mentioned, out of his schizoid isolation and into a new, ordered, and meaningful life.

Running parallel to this development, those around the patient also notice a change in his state of mind. At first, it is decidedly off-putting and makes them wonder whether he is still in his right mind. When we say that this change occurred in connection with the appearance of the mother, we are looking at the case primarily from the point of view of the dreamer; we center the events around what happens in his consciousness, be it in dreams, be it in thoughts and aspirations. This perspective is justified because it is in a true sense human to give importance to personal experience. Humans and animals alike are driven by instinct. But the idea that what we perceive of these drives and what we think of them makes all the difference is specifically human. I think it all the more fair to make this point, since both Boss and I not only describe events during treatment, but also consider it relevant to say what we think of it all.

I will summarize – very briefly, of course – the investigation (such as it is) of the facts on the basis of Jungian psychology. The patient was schizoid and lacked human relationships. In the course of treatment he experienced something of a kind, maternal nature and at the same time he experienced his own childlike nature. During this experience he was so strange to others that they questioned his sanity. In a way that was connected with this experience, he discovered a relationship to his fellow men.

Boss himself points out that the "maternal" experience of the patient would in Jungian psychology be called the mother archetype. As I said in my introductory remarks, it is impossible to study the typical aspects of a thing by looking at just one case. Boss correctly characterizes the archetype as a concept. A concept is by derivation a composite (something complex held in a single grasp!). Concepts are based on similarities among things. If I come across the same phenomenon repeatedly on several occasions, if a case such as that summarized above is observed regularly, then it may be possible to establish a concept. The fact, however, that a concept is applied to the material of experience should not mislead anyone into thinking that the concept corresponds to an underlying (e.g., archetypal) substance.[4]

Jung discovered from his own observations and experience that in difficult situations people perceive images that have a general significance. The appearance of these images is accompanied by movements of consciousness similar to psychosis, and is followed by a reordering of consciousness that resolves the original difficulty. The general nature of the images prompted Jung to call them typical images. The fact that they are to be observed not only in the present but also far back in the past led him to speak of them as arche-typical images. From the point of view of the individual involved, the impression is that the disturbance of consciousness and its subsequent reordering is brought about by an energy mediated by the image.

The features attributed to the archetype match our own case very well. The patient is in difficulties, namely in a state of schizoid isolation. He encounters an image familiar to man since time immemorial: that of the mother. He appears almost psychotic. A reordering takes place when the patient's capacity for relationships is reawakened.

When, taking the patient's point of view, we attribute to the image a disorienting and reordering energy of its own, it may seem a daring hypothesis. But sometimes one sees cases where it really seems as if the patient had been directly overwhelmed by the archetype. This is particularly striking in cases that end badly, where there is initial disorientation, but the reordering lysis is missing. Such cases do, unfortunately, occur; they are the genuinely pathological cases, whereas a phase of disorientation followed by reorientation cannot be regarded as pathological in the sense of a psychosis, even though the patient may seem to those around him at the time to be quite insane. But when a worthy Swiss skiing instructor who once had the job of giving skiing lessons to a king, afterwards neglects his job and social obligations because he now only ever refers to himself as the "Royal Skiing Instructor," and when he begins to degenerate more and more as he waits for the next royal customer, then you get the strong impression that the poor man has been destroyed by the king archetype and its energy. I was once told about this very case.

For the sake of completeness, let me add that when a person experiences an archetypal image, it is usually possible to see something else too, namely what the person involved and the image together represent; it is perceived by other people, on occasion also by the person involved if he recognizes himself in his own situation. It is the *archetypal situation* – itself yet another image if it is seen as a whole. In our case, in relation to content, the archetypal situation would be defined by the mother-child archetype which appears in European ecclesiastical art in the form of the Virgin with child. In relation to form, it is a question of the unification of what is separate and yet belongs together, and of what Jung calls the coniunctio archetype; Boss calls it loving togetherness.

It is simple to classify the archetypal experiences, to group together the images that appear at times of need, that seem often to disturb, but then often also to save us, within the concept of the archetype. And it would be simple if you could leave it at that. But there are difficulties. One is that the apparent variety and yet inner similarity of the images, their blend of personal and universal features, make it seem unlikely that the images themselves derive primarily from the individual material of the person concerned. It would seem that behind the images there is something else at work, creating related and yet ever new, shimmering images, in the same way that, in our patient's case, the image of the mother is expressed again and again in new forms. Whatever lies behind the images, however, is not accessible to direct experience; and since all the theoretical knowledge we can have is bound to the conditions of experience, it also lies beyond theoretical discussion. Yet whatever it is that produces the images is a reality. This reality would thus be philosophically identical with the noumenon, and the noumenon is then theoretically (and literally) something "merely thought of," that is to say, imaginary, although from a psychological point of view it is precisely what is most significant, namely the psychic substance. The philosophical noumenon corresponds closely to Kant's "thing in itself": It is unknowable for us owing to the fact that knowledge is conditioned by the laws of the senses (space and time), but can be intuited as a limit. Accordingly, Jung says of the psychic substance that we cannot have any knowledge of it, at least not with our present means.[5] In itself, that would be no more than a conceptual difficulty and, as far as philosophy is concerned, we could leave it at that. In the context of psychology, however, the difficulty goes beyond the merely conceptual when Jung surmises that the psychic substance that lies behind the archetypal images is not just a concept, that there are grounds for supposing that it does correspond to something in reality. It is not impossible that, where a person has the experience of an archetypal image, aspects of that image are also to be found in his surroundings, sometimes maybe even in totally fortuitous objects. This problem, which has not yet been satisfactorily studied, is the motive for Jung's interest in the horoscope and the Chinese *I Ching* (where it is assumed that three coins, thrown six times, will fall in a way that reflects the archetypal constellation of the person who throws them), in parapsychology, and so on. Jung tried, with his idea of "synchronicity,"[5] to sketch out a scientific approach to this question. He hoped that a satisfactory answer would come from the atomic physics of the future; it might provide the Archimedean point "outside." But that point is lacking so long as only psyche can observe psyche,[6] which is why, until that time, the psychic substance has to remain a noumenon (something merely thought of).

When we say that an archetype is a concept, we must not overlook the fact that a concept can only work if a particular perspective is adopted. In themselves, natural phenomena appear chaotic; it is only when we consider them from a specific point of view that they gain coherence. Every point of view, of course, contains within itself the germ of a judgment. In science, however, we strive beyond the perception of form towards experience. And we only have experience if our earlier perceptions are used in judging later perceptions.[7] To do that, we have to order them through concepts that isolate and grasp what is identical in the diversity of phenomena. That is nothing unusual or theoretically extravagant. We do as much every day with our language when we describe things with words that are themselves little abstractions and that are used uniformly by all those that know the language. Anyone who does not want to use the abstractions of language will have to do as the Balnibarbians in Swift's *Gulliver's Travels* did. Because to them words did not designate things, they carried the things they wanted to talk about around with them and showed them to each other. That way you would not need to learn any foreign languages either!

We have to ask ourselves, therefore, from what perspective it is that Jung orders phenomena in order to arrive at the concept of the archetype. As I have already mentioned, his is a point of view that ascribes great value to the individual personality and its consciousness or unconsciousness, which is logical insofar as we imagine ourselves to be talking about these things as conscious individuals. But then, precisely with the archetype, it emerges that humankind does not splinter into innumerable individual personalities, but that it is bound together by common psychic foundations, the collective. I would like here to dispute G. Bally's criticism that Jung's psychology reduces the problem of human relationships to that of the projection of individual psychic contents.[8] On the contrary, Jung's psychology describes people as beings whose contents are to a lesser extent defined by individual psychology, to a major extent, however, by a collective psyche.

In accordance with the starting point of his psychology, namely the interest in the psyche of the individual, Jung calls the process of personal growth, in which the individual's capacity for relationships develops and in which plant, animal, and human follow one another as partners, as exemplified by Boss's patient, the path of individuation. The development of human relationships leads beyond the ego stage towards individuation through relationships. The lone individual is no longer characterized by his subjective ego, but by the variety of his relationships both in his inner life and in his social life with other people. Of course, the ego retains an important place as the center of personal consciousness and the bearer of responsibility.

Jung's perspective not only shows the human individual as the focus of his psychology, it also gives the observed material – as Boss correctly noticed – a systematic, scientific order. And the experiences gathered through that perspective and from the material are represented by means of concepts, among which is that of the archetype. Throughout his account of the case, Boss opposes Jung's point of view. However, I do not consider his proposal that we should replace the "old, scientific instruments of thought" with a new way of thinking a happy one, and I will attempt to approach the argument from a different angle.

Boss is correct in highlighting the inner relationship between scientific psychology and modern physics. But his suggestion that we should put aside such scientific methods of analysis is one-sided and certainly goes too far. When he concludes – logically, from his own point of view – that in the end physics leads to the intellectual dilemma of an unpredictable acausality and that it reduces the things of the world to skeletal mathematical forms that cannot be visualized, then he comes up hard against reality. Firstly, the fact that the psychiatrist cannot imagine the formulas of physics does not prove at all that they do not mean anything or that they are inappropriate. Secondly, what may seem an intellectual dilemma to us because we lack the necessary background knowledge to understand it, is not simply the invention of a few oddball physicists, but the scientific basis for the tremendous progress made by atomic physics over the past decade. The atomic bomb is not just a theory of the physicists, and we can only hope that the reality of modern atomic physics proves as fruitful in peace as it is destructive in war.

My advice would rather be, let's not throw the baby out with the bathwater. Which is why I would like to investigate the opposition that exists between the viewpoint of Jung and that of Boss in more general terms, taking my cue from the concluding remarks of Boss's essay. He calls for "a style of inquiry that lets itself be guided by phenomena themselves and that lingers over them." He finds the traditional concepts – and, going by his previous remarks, the views of Jung in particular – to be crystallized, rigidly dogmatic, abstract unrealities. Accordingly, we have to investigate what contrasting standpoints are offered in Boss's essay. For that purpose we need a *tertium comparationis* that can combine the two otherwise completely different points of view. I have tried to take my bearings from the point in history where the scientific age was first born and where, accordingly, the ways of thinking that contrast with scientific thought were still visible. Therefore, I went back into the seventeenth century and turned to Pascal. In the first section of his *Pensées,* Pascal discusses *esprit,* which here corresponds roughly to a "way of thinking." In fact, he distinguishes between two forms of *esprit*; he discusses the "*Différence entre l'esprit de géométrie et l'esprit de finesse.*"[9]

Pascal says of the *esprit de finesse*: "*Dans l'esprit de finesse, les principes sont dans l'usage commun et devant les yeux de tout le monde. On n'a que faire de tourner la tête, ni de se faire violence ... il faut avoir bonne vue.*" * Further, he says: "*Il faut tout d'un coup voir la chose d'un seul regard, et non pas par progrès de raisonnement.*" ** This *esprit de finesse* corresponds roughly to what Boss envisages, namely the intuitive grasp of phenomena: One just has to look carefully so as to grasp comprehensively the total phenomenon and seeing things (*la chose*) at a single glance. That is why, in his report of the case, he records the experiences of the patient and the perceptions of others mixed together in a single perspective, in whatever order they seem to belong, whereas I – as I have stressed – in applying the Jungian point of view to the material, gave the experiences of the patient and the perceptions or experiences of the others separately.

So how does this *esprit de finesse* see the *esprit de géométrie*? Pascal says in this regard: "*Et les esprits fins ... accoutumés à juger d'une seule vue, sont si étonnés – quand on leur présente (l'esprit de géométrie) – des propositions où ils ne comprennent rien et où pour entrer, il faut passer par des définitions et des principes si stériles, qu'ils ne sont point accoutumés à voir ainsi*

---

* "In the subtle mind the basic principles are those in common usage and in full view of everybody. One has but to look, no effort is required. It is only a question of good sight."
** "We must see the matter at once, at one glance, and not by a process of reasoning."

en détail, qu' ils s' en rebutent et s' en dégoutent." * Boss voices this same reaction of the subtle mind against the geometrical mind when he describes a concept such as Jung's archetype as "a hypostatized abstraction from intentional objects that have been theoretically isolated, but that originally belonged to the full oneness of immediate experience," when he feels such things to be dogmatically hardened, abstract, unreal.

For his part, Pascal sees possibilities in the geometrical spirit. He says, *"On a peine à tourner la tête de ce côté-là, manque d' habitude: mais pour peu qu' on l' y tourne on voit les principes au plein; et il faudrait tout à fait l' esprit faux pour mal raisonner sur des principes si gros qu' il est presque impossible qu' ils échappent."* **

The *esprit géométrique,* therefore, directs its attention to principles. Thus, in the shattering experiences of individuals Jung saw what was general and typical. If, in an hour of need, the sufferer is able to see the general, human side of his predicament, the archetypal side precisely, then he is released from a dangerous isolation, without diminishing the integrity of personal destiny. Hence the effectiveness of the diagnosis of archetypes in psychotherapy. Diagnosis of the archetypal situation allows the therapist to understand the individual case by setting it in a general context, and that understanding promotes a relationship between therapist and patient. In difficult situations careful observation and empathy are not always enough by any means; it is often necessary to appreciate the facts on a higher level. It is particularly necessary where a person feels driven, whether from within or from outside, threatened, and overpowered. That person can be rescued if the typical form of reacting and acting – instinct – helps out.[10]

---

* "Subtle minds, on the contrary, being thus accustomed to judge at a single glance, are so astonished when they are presented with propositions of which they understand nothing, and the way to which is through definitions and axioms so sterile, and which they are not accustomed to see thus in detail, that they are repelled and disheartened."

** "From want of habit, it is difficult to turn the mind in that direction; but if one turns it thither ever so little, one sees the basic principles fully; and it would require a completely inaccurate mind to reason falsely from principles so clear that it is almost impossible for them to escape notice."

Insofar as man has consciousness at his command, the typical, instinctive way of acting includes the typical way of looking at things, what Jung called the archetype.[11] So when a person suffers without instinct or grasp of his bearings, the archetypal image, the way man typically imagines the world, comes to his assistance: It makes orientation and instinctive action possible. On the other hand, instinctive action calls for the corresponding typical view of things, the archetypal image. Jung accordingly describes the archetype as the self-portrait of instinct. In practical therapy, the diagnosis of the archetype is to be carried out when a consciousness of instinct is needed, an inner view of the life process. The forms of this way of seeing things, the archetypes, are not personal, but arise from a general human disposition which Freud called a "precipitate of the earlier experience of the species."[12]

But Pascal also says that a geometrical mind that is only geometrical is in danger of no longer seeing what is in front of its eyes and making itself ridiculous, even intolerable. On the other hand, it seems equally unsatisfactory to him when a subtle mind is merely subtle: *"Et les fins qui ne sont que fins ne peuvent avoir la patience de déscendre jusque dans les premiers principes des choses speculatives et d'imagination, qu'ils n'ont jamais vues dans le monde, et tout à fait hors d'usage."* *

In claiming that Boss's view corresponds more to that of the *esprit de finesse* and that of Jung – at least on a conceptual level, which is where Boss criticizes it – to that of the *esprit de géométrie,* I must also insist, following Pascal, that it is to one's advantage not to be one-sided and not to neglect either of them. Jung, for his part, pointed out in an extensive study, namely in *Psychological Types,*[13] that when two people see a thing entirely differently, so differently that the gap seems unbridgeable, then a typological contrast is usually involved. Since the views of both Boss and Jung are scientific views, we have to examine which of

---

* "And subtle-minded men who are only subtle cannot have the patience to reach the first principle of things speculative and conceptual, which they have never seen in the world, and which are altogether out of the common."

the two rational functions identified by Jung (thinking and feeling) determines each standpoint. Again, we can take our starting point from Pascal. Following his description of the *esprit de géométrie* and the *esprit de finesse*, he says:[14] *"Ceux qui sont accoutumés à juger par le sentiment ne comprennent rien aux choses de raisonnement, car ils veulent d' abord pénétrer d' une vue et ne sont point accoutumés à chercher les principes. Et les autres, au contraire, qui sont accoutumés à raisonner par principes, ne comprennent rien aux choses de sentiment, y cherchant des principes, et ne pouvant voir d' une vue."* *

It would appear from this that the *esprit de géométrie* probably has something to do with what Jung calls the thinking type, the *esprit de finesse* with what he terms the feeling type. However – and here Boss will agree with me – a scientific view can never be considered in isolation; it is always also a human product bound up with the person who holds that view. Consequently, we shall have to examine both Jung's and Boss's views to see what psychological attitudes they express. Of course, we cannot derive a psychological diagnosis from their views on the problem of the archetype that would characterize Jung and Boss as people. After all, both scientists also wrote other things. Nevertheless, it seems likely that Jung's concept of the archetype is the result of an effort of thought, of the application of the *esprit de géométrie*, whereas Boss's reaction represents the voice of feeling and is the result of the application of the *esprit de finesse*. Let us just briefly consider a crucial point in Boss's essay. The lysis in the patient's psychic development is seen in the fact "that the patient, in loving togetherness (with his dream lover), enacts the highest fullness of being attainable to man." Logically, that may be less than transparent: "enacts a fullness of being"; but it carries a strong emotional charge and a clear judgment – as is consistent with the

---

* "Those who are accustomed to judge by feeling do not understand the process of reasoning; for they like to understand at a glance and are not used to examining principles. Others, on the contrary, who are accustomed to reasoning from principles, simply do not understand matters of feeling; they study principles and are unable to see at a glance."

function of feeling – in this case, a positive one. Jung would perhaps see in the encounter with the dream lover the archetype of the *coniunctio,* the *hieros gamos,*[15] and raise the situation up to the conceptual level, placing it in a historical context simply through the use of foreign words, in other words tackle it intellectually.

Linguistic considerations would generally provide some interesting perspectives on our subject. I refer the reader to an article by H. Biaesch.[16] Language, and the concepts it contains, are initially tools for understanding oneself and others. Then man gives each sound an emotional and objective meaning and uses language as a vehicle capable of sustaining a tradition so as to develop his relationship with the world, both for mastery and for protection against overwhelming force. Thus, says Biaesch, we choose our concepts under the pressure of the existential dilemma of power and impotence. The Latin model of our mode of thought probably exerted the greatest influence on the development of the Western, and in particular the exact, sciences. Jung is obviously indebted to this tradition; it is no coincidence that he should have chosen for certain of his concepts words from the classical languages (animus/anima, archetype, individuation). That is why one still senses in Jung's concepts something of the original vitality of language that can protect and also help us when the primordial chaos of natural phenomena threatens us, and when irrational psychic forces become overpowering. Precisely the concept of the archetype, for example, has a peculiar, almost artistically chosen ring to it that somehow captures the overpowering force and so opposes reason to the irrational. Boss speaks quite differently. His language – as we have already seen – avoids conceptual clarity. In that sense, it is not Latin. Rather, it strives for something closer to what we find in Chinese. The Chinese language avoids words that could be called logical or conceptual. It displays concrete imagery and a great potential for forming associations, all characteristics that we try, as a rule, to avoid in our scientific statements.[17] In that way, Boss seeks to formulate human concerns. The strength of the *esprit de finesse* lies precisely not in conceptual synthesis, but in the clear grasp of detail. Again I quote Pascal: *"Or, l'omission d'un principe (de l'esprit de finesse) mène à l'erreur; ainsi il faut avoir la vue bien nette pour voir tous les principes, et ensuite l'esprit juste pour ne pas raisonner faussement sur des principes connus."* * [18] Above all in practical psychotherapy that attitude is particularly valuable since, of all the many individual traits that in their totality make up the character of the individual, none is neglected.

And so, I agree with Boss when he undertakes, after all the successes of the *esprit de géométrie* – often dangerous successes, such as the atom bomb! – to help the *esprit de finesse* to its rights. He champions a standpoint that is a very necessary corrective to the scientific way of thinking. But I do not agree with him when he rejects scientific thinking. There is nothing modern about looking for a new point of view because the old one no longer satisfies us. That is a demand of the times that has always been met; and so, since time immemorial, geometrical and subtle, realistic and nominalistic ages have followed one another in rhythmic succession. It is modern, however, to recognize that the world can be viewed from various standpoints and that that is so because people are different in ways that are a never-ending source of amazement. And it is modern to recognize that seemingly incompatible points of view also complement one another: *"Soyez esprit et fin et géomètre."* Then the spirit will be right; the wrong solution is described by Pascal: *"Mais les esprits faux ne sont jamais ni fins ni géomètres."* For that reason too, I do not believe that Boss is right when he despairs of ever seeing the various schools of thought and their conceptual frameworks brought into a harmonious relationship. He is right in that it will not be possible to amalgamate them. An indistinct mixture of different systems is not a good thing. But, as in relationships between individuals, the so-called schools, in their relationships to each other, can take into consideration the possibility of a

---

* "Now, the omission of even one principle leads to error; so one must have very keen sight to see all the principles, and, in the next place, an accurate mind to avoid drawing false conclusions from known principles."

second, even of several standpoints. Then, it may well turn out that in accepting the variety of schools, the variety of people is also acknowledged, and that it is precisely the diversity of theories in psychology and psychotherapy that comes to be seen as a guarantee that the scientific and therapeutic goal is achieved in the best possible way. That goal is understanding the nature of human beings.

However, Boss's point of view also raises an interesting question concerning his disagreement with Jung. As far as the conflict of views is concerned, as I have attempted to characterize it with the help of Pascal's *Pensées,* may I cite Wittgenstein with reference to the points of view of Boss and of Jung (as Boss sees it)? On the subject of the dualistic perception of an object, he says: "Today we know that it cannot be left to the observer to decide which of two possible aspects he chooses to see, but that both are equally necessary ways of seeing, both equally necessary if we are to say anything of validity. A thing seen dualistically is a living whole."[19] Boss, however, does not merely set himself up in opposition to Jung; rather he strives for an account of things that is not dualistic in itself, whose dualism is only apparent insofar as it opposes the traditional dualistic way of seeing things. Curiously, here too – exactly as in the style of writing – we come across something reminiscent of certain Chinese forms. I would almost venture to say: Boss is aiming for a presentation that embraces everything that exists; he strives after a meaning that lies between words, between gestures, between body and soul, signifying and encompassing both in one. I say I venture this description because the words I have chosen to describe Boss's presentation could also be used to paraphrase the Chinese word *tao:* a representation of the One that appears to us as a duality or antinomy.[20] He does not get rid of the conflict of human knowledge – the leopard cannot change his spots. But in stating his opposition to Jung's concept of the archetype, he shows where the conflict lies today. Nowadays, the question is no longer this or that psychotherapeutic school, nor even this or that religion, nation, class, attitude. Rather it is school therapists or a unifying perspective above the schools, and then also a particular religion or a religiosity above confessional differences, patriotism or a supranational attitude, etc. Today, the question is not the one or the other, but unity and dividedness. Yet here too both are valid; the difficulty has only been displaced, reformulated. A lot could be done to help reformulate this human problem if representatives of both points of view would talk to one another.

IV

THE IMPORTANCE OF THE FAMILY
FOR THE PSYCHIC HEALTH OF THE INDIVIDUAL

Psychology ought to contribute not only to the advance of science and therapy, but also to the prevention of psychological problems, in other words, to psycho-hygiene. The nature of psycho-hygiene requires that we express ourselves clearly and demonstrate the importance of psychological factors in daily life.

Since 1900 psychological science has been significantly stimulated by the development of psychoanalysis. Sigmund Freud, Carl Gustav Jung, Alfred Adler, and later many of their pupils have created modern psychotherapy; they also demonstrated the reality of psychic and spiritual life.

Considering that the founders of the psychological movement, which has dominated psychology since 1900, were doctors, it is understandable that pathological disorders of mental life should have been their particular interest. It was natural that they should have sought to develop the treatment of these disorders, namely psychotherapy, and to establish its theoretical foundations. The means of psychotherapy are themselves of a psychological nature; the important factors are personal contact, understanding, the making conscious of unconscious tendencies, along with conversation and the mutual reactions of patient and therapist. And a loving, educative attitude will always play a role. Among the special psychotherapeutic aids, several deserve specific mention.

The study of dreams: Things that a person either does not want to see or cannot recognize for what they are during the day, enter consciousness during sleep in the form of a dream fantasy. If the fairy-tale language of the dream can be deciphered, there are often some surprising insights to be gained.

The transference: When patient and therapist become close on a human level, there is often – without it being intended – a repeat of the particular situation in the patient's past life that he has still not come to terms with. Imperceptibly, the therapist is made to take the place of the person who, at that earlier moment, through the influence he had on the patient, confronted him with problems that have remained unresolved ever since. That is what we call the transference.

Group psychotherapy: When a therapist treats patients not individually, but in a group, then the difficulties of human relationships often emerge particularly clearly. This provides an opportunity to tackle those difficulties and to foster the capacity for human relationships.

The study of dreams reveals not only that dreams speak the language of children and fairy tales, but also that, through that world in which he does not think but rather dreams his own fairy tales, the dreamer is tied to his childhood; it is a world that holds both the threat of destruction and the promise of salvation. The transference shows that the person whose influence has not yet been overcome, the person, in other words, whose role the therapist takes over, is in the overwhelming majority of cases the mother or father of the patient. And in group psychotherapy it emerges that the problems the patient has in his relationships as an adult were already present in his youth and are often characteristic of the family situation in which he grew up.

In general the results of psychotherapy indicate that most mental disorders are rooted in early and earliest childhood. So the psychotherapy of an individual gives us an insight into the *structure of the family*. The picture that the therapist sees is mostly horrifying. The patient has been damaged by a brutal or dissolute father, for example. Or his vitality has been undermined by an overprotective mother who furthermore considered her one-sided, narrow views to be general truths. Or the patient is crushed by stronger, insensitive siblings.

For half a century psychotherapists have been striving to make these facts visible and to find ways of curing the damaged individuals. All too seldom, however, have the appropriate preventive, psycho-hygienic measures that follow from that psychological knowledge been taken. If it is true that a disturbed family atmosphere can ruin a person's life and make him ill, then we bear a heavy responsibility. If it is true and we know it, then whoever fails adequately to foster the family or even allows it to fall apart, is guilty of a crime. He is guilty of negligence and of causing grievous harm to his relatives. Our responsibility in these matters is a moral, ethical one. The criminal law and the judges rarely have anything to say on the subject. It is worth mentioning, though, that Article 125 of the Swiss Penal Code says: Anyone who, through his own negligence, damages another person's health will, on request, be punished with a prison sentence or a fine. If the damage is serious, the perpetrator will be officially pursued. And in Article 134 it says that anyone who neglects a child under the age of sixteen, of whom he is the guardian, so badly that the child's health or mental development suffers or is seriously threatened as a result, will be punished with a prison sentence of not less than one month. I am not trying to say that parents who neglect their family and so damage the mental development of their children should be thrown into prison. I simply want to show that I am not exaggerating when I call neglecting the family a crime.

Increasingly, it will be the task of psychotherapy to talk not merely about how to treat and cure psychic injury ("trauma" as Freud called it), but also about how to avoid it. Knowing how to avoid mental disturbance is not only the doctor's business, however. The doctor's main job is curing; he can point out certain dangers. The preventive task, however, psycho-hygiene, calls for the collaboration of other faculties besides the medical. There is scope here for psychologists, for educators, and of course also for priests. But beyond that, society in general also has an interest in the matter. These problems have to be acknowledged publicly. Nor can the politician keep aloof. Every responsible citizen should participate. General hygiene is not something the doctor can look after on his own. The problems of the supply of drinking water, of hygienic living conditions, and of a healthy diet, for example, are not just problems for the doctor to worry about either. They are problems that concern the general public. What use are pure water, clean and dry houses, or a sensible, vitamin-rich diet if people are being damaged mentally because we are blind and apathetic, because we refuse to see the threat to the psyche?

The tasks to be assessed if we want to appreciate the importance of the family for the mental health of the individual are various, so various that we hardly know where to start. Let us consider the parents first.

The *father* should point the way. A man knows what he wants. There are some men who are always surprised and indignant whenever the woman does not know what she wants. Those men have not yet noticed that there is a difference between men and women. Where the father fails to point the way and give a lead, the children too will have no direction in life. Paternal guidance is often achieved less through direct influence than through example. Clear attitudes towards the family, work, and politics leave their stamp on the child. The child learns respect for order and authority. It acquires an understanding of what is acceptable and what is not. A serious disturbance can be caused in a child if it sees its father as anything other than respectful towards his superiors or fair towards his subordinates. The father should mediate a proper understanding of the social hierarchy. It is well known that a brutal father who gives no guidance and instead breaks the child is dangerous. It is less well known that the seductive father, who draws the child to him intellectually without regard for the child's personality and without revealing his own paternal personality, is equally dangerous. Everything becomes indistinct; the child loses its sense of direction and will never find its way in life.

Finally, an extremely unsatisfactory type of father for the children is the one that is never there, the father who is always busy. It is true to say, however, that even the most demanding job need not be an obstacle, and that a man can always manage to put in an appearance despite his lack of time if he has once recognized the importance of his task as a father.

It is not only the natural father who will have to answer for the child. The teacher, the priest, the superior, everyone who is supposed to bring up and educate young children has to assume responsibility for the paternal principle of direction and order.

The first duty of the *mother* is to look after the child. All the stages of childhood and youth demand motherly care. However, psychotherapy can show (René Spitz[1]) that the first weeks, months, and years are particularly crucial for a person's development and that the absence of the mother during that period has the most serious consequences. As she bends over the tiny child, the mother helps it recognize the form and nature of a human being. In cases where the mother was absent in early childhood, the child is often totally incapable of coming to terms with its mental and emotional life; not infrequently, the result is mental illness. But the mother's warmth is needed in later years too, particularly in times of illness and, generally, in the field of personal hygiene. In that way the child develops an awareness of its body. Spiritually, the mother's job is to represent, at least on a more emotional level, the principles we know as "right" and "wrong." Schiller's Stauffacherin, Pestalozzi's Gertrud and Gottfried Keller's Frau Regula Amrein are beautiful examples of this. Here too, as with the father, good example is worth more than words. How did Frau Regula Amrein bring up her youngest child?[2] "How she actually set about it and put her plan into effect," Keller writes, "is difficult to say. Because in fact she did as little educating as possible and her contribution consisted almost entirely in the fact that the child, cast in the same mould as her, grew up in her presence and followed her example." And Keller goes on to make the following useful observation: "It is usually only the frightful air of importance and arrogance with which most good housewives go about the business of buying and preparing food that arouses in the children the greed ... that later, when they are grown up, becomes a tendency towards a life of luxury and extravagance. It is curious that among all the Germanic peoples the best housewife is thought to be the one who makes the most noise with her pots and pans."

The teacher can also be a mother figure for the child, along with other women. But there is no substitute for the natural mother any more than there is for the natural father. Particularly during the first years of life, which is when a person's character is formed, there is a special rapport when, as Gottfried Keller says, the mother figure and the child are "cast in the same mould."

Nonetheless, a woman's going out to work is no obstacle to her fulfilling her role as a mother. The contact between mother and child is not measured by the clock, but according to its inner value; the mother is not a hired help, and the decisive factors are above all her attentiveness and the strength and warmth of her heart.

The greatest problem for the working mother is not so much the lack of time as a certain sense of exhaustion. This permits the level of attentiveness to fall and often leads to irritability; here, self-control out of a sense of duty is the best solution. Frequently too, it is necessary for the father, contrary to tradition, to take over some of the duties of looking after the children. The trend nowadays is for the strict separation of the mother's and the father's duties to become more flexible.

So, since father and mother convey the basic principles less through direct teaching than through personality, they have a duty to look after their personality. What is especially dangerous for children in this respect is what has to be called the dissociated personality. The dissociated personality is not at one with itself; it lives on two levels that have nothing to do with one another. There are secret, criminal relationships that imperceptibly poison the family atmosphere, far more dangerous than open conflicts. There is dishonesty in the running of the business; nobody knows about it, and yet it spreads the spirit of bad faith. Here, it is generally the father who is the culprit. Mostly, he is also the guilty one when there is a lot of talk about duty and honesty while at the same time considerable amounts of alcohol are consumed.

The mother, on the other hand, is guilty in cases where she believes herself to be sacrificing herself to caring for the family, whereas in fact she is simply using washing day, floor cleaning, and the rules of the household to make the family feel her tyrannical power.

Another thing that is extremely damaging is the dissociated *parental couple*, the couple that is not united, that is in fact split. Such parents find it impossible to talk to one another. Man and woman are opposites, in fact one of the really basic pairs of opposites. It should be an opportunity for the child to learn how meaningful the encounter between such different partners in conversation and in daily life can be. Here, the child receives guidance on how to surmount the conflicts of life. That is why, as we all know, children from broken homes are at risk. Yet it is even more worrying when a marriage is kept going despite the fact that both partners hate each other – ostensibly for the sake of the children, but mostly for reasons of prestige. Open conflict is always preferable to the poison of concealed hatred. The parents' duty in such cases is not to keep up appearances by continuing to live together, but to engage in genuine and frank discussion. Both form *and* content are expected. One feels like shouting at them: Talk to each other! Or even: Learn to quarrel with a bit of decency!

The meaningful dealings of the parents with one another are the source of the family atmosphere, of the emotional and intellectual climate in the family. This climate is not determined by how much the parents know or by how well educated they are, however valuable knowledge and education may of course be. The climate that makes the family valuable is determined by the relationship of the parents to one another and, in particular, by the degree of honesty and truthfulness that is between them. This climate must give the children the strength to stand up to the dangers and temptations of life.

The world our children find themselves in is considerably more dynamic and complicated than that of our parents. Even the small child, scarcely out of the cradle, is offered sweets on all sides; the choice of toys for all age groups is too vast to appreciate. Picture books with stories of robbers, available on every street corner, have replaced the grandmother who used to tell stories to her grandchildren. Outside the home, cinema and sporting events are a constant attraction; at home, you only have to turn a switch and you have music and television at your disposal. Needless to say, whether young people still assimilate it all properly is a different matter. Everything is made so easy, it all demands so little concentration, that often the result is a tendency towards superficiality and distraction. Cinema, television, and illustrated magazines, along with spectator sports, are not necessarily beneficial to the development of a mature personality. Impressions are absorbed entirely passively through the eyes, and all the images come from outside. What is taken in is often extremely impersonal and conventional. Individual creative fantasy is excluded and crippled, and the development of an alert intelligence, confident in its own judgments, is held back, even in basically gifted individuals.

In this context, an ordered family life is a vital support. Father and mother should not only share the interests of the children, above all they should also allow the children to share in their interests. The relationship of the parents to the children has constantly to draw on the relationship of the parents to one another. Precisely sport and leisure can be meaningful if they are experienced in the context of a well-governed family.

How far the parents want to influence the children in such questions has to be left to their tact and feeling in each particular case. Two points, however, should be mentioned:

Sex education demands special tact. It is a commonplace, nowadays, that children are factually enlightened before their parents even think of raising the subject. Often, it is all the more important that, in erotic-sexual matters, the parents maintain the traditional discretion which preserves sexuality from profanation and protects its emotional value. On the other hand, it is absolutely vital that the parents warn their growing children against the danger of sexual criminals. The children must realize that they may be risking their lives by accepting an invitation from a strange man to enter a house or even a car.

And later, when the children are almost adults, even when they have passed their majority, the parents should do everything they can to discourage the mania for cars or motorbikes. On the whole, it is probably a good thing that relationships between parents and children are more flexible and more gentle nowadays than in the hard, old, patriarchal times. But modern traffic knows no mercy. It is usually very young drivers who are to blame for serious road accidents, and here the parents have a very great responsibility to bear, one that demands decisive measures. News reports such as the following convey an all too familiar message:

Neue Zürcher Zeitung, 5.11.1962, Kloten: The driver of a sports car that left the road while speeding in the Homburg forest near Kloten on Saturday night and collided with a tree, killing two young passengers, was a twenty-three-year-old youth who did not know how to control his thoughtless delight in speed.

It is not just modern life that requires the counterbalance of family life. The attitude of contemporary youth demands it too. Youth today is curiously different from that of earlier times. It is subject to a displacement which reaches deep into the somatic sphere and which is known scientifically as acceleration. Young people today are taller, but lighter in weight. They are sexually mature at an earlier age, but later in reaching personal maturity. Acceleration has the result that young people are arrogant and insecure at the same time, and display a strange combination of childishness and adulthood. Today's youth is neither more stupid nor less gifted than that of earlier times. In many respects it may even be more clear-sighted and critical, often more skeptical. However, it is often conspicuously lacking in independence. This creates difficult problems for teachers and, at times, one has the impression that our whole school system is beginning to totter. A family that has at its center a parental couple, a father and mother who are prepared to talk with each other and with the children, is what these uncertain and yet precocious young people urgently need.

Talking to one another should not be confined to the natural parents. We saw how other people from the children's environment can, in the right circumstances, become father or mother figures. We mentioned, in the first place, teachers. They belong to the group of people that, together with the natural parents, are the child's fathers and mothers. The idea that the fathers and mothers should work together, in other words that the parents should enter into discussion with the teachers, is the proper basis for the relationship of parental home and school. There should be no thoughtless abuse of teachers in the home. And the school, the teachers, should take the questions and complaints of the parents seriously and not simply dismiss them as unjustified. They should talk to each other. The time taken up with talking is not wasted.

Above and beyond that, the parental home has a positive function to fulfil with regard to the school. The parents should appreciate that it is the family's task to prepare the child for school. Heinrich Pestalozzi specifically emphasizes this point in his essay "How Gertrud Teaches Her Children." He writes, "The child has to have acquired a high level of visual and linguistic skills before it is sensible to teach it to read or even to spell." He says, furthermore, "The child's range of visual experience has to be expanded all the time." Needless to say, the school cannot do this on its own. Talking and seeing are things the child learns at home. And broadening its experience is a task for school and family working hand in hand. Pestalozzi recommended for small children the use of picture books, which has become accepted. Later, the parents should tell the children stories from real life, explain things they see and events that take place around them, perhaps occasionally visit the sights with them: a zoological garden, for example, a historical museum or a medieval castle, all things that are likely to stimulate a child's fantasy and expand its horizons. In this way, the family can contribute to the children's education, for the parents should not imagine that the education of the young can be left entirely to the schools and teachers.

Another important responsibility of the family is the safe-guarding of the religious outlook. So long as the children are still small and incapable of judgment, the parents are gods to them. The father is the "strongest," the mother "the dearest," and what either of them does or says may be felt positively or negatively, but is always absolutely valid. Things cannot stay that way, though. Sooner or later the child will see the darker side of the parents, and if they do not then stop being gods, the young person effectively finds himself in a world that is ruled by evil or corrupt divinities. The results can be read about in the case histories compiled by psychotherapists. Therefore, the family has to provide a vessel to contain the divine and to protect the parents from false deification. That vessel is the religious outlook. Of course, it is the church that administers religion. But, as an institution, it cannot sow the seeds of the religious outlook, or at least only with considerable extra effort. The mother's bedtime prayers with the children and, on the father's part, sufficient respect not to take the name of God in vain are worth a great deal. A person's views on religion will always be his own responsibility. But it is the responsibility of the parents to ensure that he is in a position to answer the religious question, and that this question raises itself for him in the first place.

So long as the children do not persist in regarding the parents as gods, there is no harm in their seeing that their parents are not perfect. That way, they can also see their parents as people. You do not have to be a model parent to cultivate family life. That would be asking too much. What is dangerous for the children is the dissociated personality that, against its own better judgment, lives on two levels. What is dangerous, then, is above all hypocrisy.

One particular form of hypocrisy that can creep in almost unnoticed is parental egoism. A thing is declared to be in the best interests of the child when, in fact, it serves only the parents' interests. The child is forced or encouraged to take a job that the parents think is good or advantageous. The children are expected to be successful at school and in society for the sake of family prestige. And then there is general astonishment when suddenly, apparently for no good reason, suicide puts an end to a young life. Manslaughter, a psychologist might call it in many cases! Another dubious thing is when a daughter, out of gratitude, devotes herself to caring for her parents and misses out on life, ending up as a mummified old spinster. Let no one imagine that old spinsters do not exist nowadays. True, forty or fifty-year-old daughters still living at home with their parents have become rare. But the sort of daughter who has a job, for example as a secretary, but whose private life is centered around the parents and their needs, so that she is cheated of her own life, is still common. The parents' egoistic art of seduction is often naive and unsophisticated, but it can also be as beautiful and seemingly noble as it is deadly. A classic description of such a case is found in Thomas Mann's novel *Buddenbrooks*. Mann shows how the daughter of the Buddenbrook household, Toni Buddenbrook, is twice maneuvered into an unsuitable marriage out of pure pecuniary greed, until finally she has to cry out: "There are moments when you cannot take comfort in anything, God help me, when you lose faith in justice, in goodness … in everything. Life breaks so many things inside us, it wrecks so many beliefs."

The most dangerous thing of all, more dangerous than egoism, is the hypocrisy of false excellence. Again and again, it seems that parents who, to all appearances, are the embodiment of goodness and who maintain an ordered family life, have children who are, as they say, a failure. If you examine the circumstances more closely, you find that the parents have forbidden themselves, in a way that is both unhelpful and artificial, to live out their conflicts so as to be more like the ideal of excellence. You might think that the strain would show in the parents sooner or later. Often, however, something else happens, something almost sinister. The explosive material of the conflict, the emotional tension, is transferred onto one of the children. That child then acts out in its own life and behavior the dark side that the parents wanted to make invisible; it becomes the so-called black sheep of the family. For that reason, honesty and forthrightness within the family demand that the parents accept their own darkness, their own human imperfection. Anyone who tries to disprove the existence of his own darkness and strives for excellence above all else may find that the same thing happens to him as happened to the proverbial vicars whose children – as the saying goes – "hardly ever or never turn out well."

The family does not consist only of parents, though. There are brothers and sisters too. The parents do not just have to think of one child; mostly, they have to deal with a number of children. It is important that they see to fairness between the brothers and sisters. The children must learn to treat each other with respect, even with politeness. They must also learn to develop a mutual sense of responsibility. Thus the relationships between the brothers and sisters provide a basic training in social responsibility. Comradeship and kindness, but also competition and conflict, need social forms of expression. We say that all men are brothers. But that is only true if brothers are really brothers.

Children often expect their parents to exercise justice. And that is what they receive. But it must never be a schematized sort of justice. Usually the children are of different ages. They are also different in sex and character. Each should be treated accordingly, so that the children can see that there are differences between people, and that the needs and merits of each are different. We have to recognize that "All men are brothers" does not mean "All men are equal."

In dealing with the children, parents often face the far from simple question of how far they should evade the generation conflict. It is a nice idea to empathize with the thoughts and aspirations of the child. It is also often easier, easier than giving guidelines, enduring opposition, and imposing one's will. But let it not be forgotten that, without an older generation with its own principles, the younger generation will have a difficult development (cf. also p. 257).

The parents' active role can also bring them up against the problem of punishment. It is very important that the brothers and sisters of the child to be punished are involved in the punishment.

If a child is punished, then the other children should understand why. Even within the family, on a small scale, the principle of law should apply: that every punishment should have not only an expiatory, but also a preventive purpose. The guilty one is punished and the innocent are warned.

We have to have punishment, because even a child has to learn that injustice has real consequences. Punishment given in blind rage is wrong. For punishing is not easy; it is an art that should demonstrate a law. Soft parents often forget that life is hard and that many of life's laws are of iron. Therefore, one safeguards the child's future by knowing how to punish appropriately. The art of punishing demands tact and often imagination too. One should only forbid something, or keep a child at home when it is due to go out, if the child can be engaged in an educational activity at home. Sending a child to bed or locking it in its room only makes sense if the parent then comes to the child and talks with it. And as for corporal punishment, well certainly a cuff on the ear at the right moment can work wonders, but it calls for the very greatest restraint. Corporal punishment requires a form of ceremony that is more important than the physical act itself. I used to know a teacher who punished ink blots in exercise books with a stroke of the ruler on the palm of the hand. The whole class had to be silent; he would not tolerate a sound. The culprit had to come to the front of the class, his hand was held out flat, and the ruler had brass edges. The effect of the punishment was excellent despite the fact that the blow itself was very light and merely symbolic. The punishment did no harm to the dignity of the school, the pupil, or the teacher; but then, he was an expert.

In the relationship of the children to each other, the social hierarchy should be respected. The older, the stronger, or even the cleverer ones should have more duties and more responsibility. Then any privileges will seem deserved. Here too the family should prepare the children for the larger family of state and society.

The family also includes *grandparents*. The figures of the grandparents can prepare the children for the problem of old age, for that period of life that is still so far off and yet is hard to come to terms with later if you are not already prepared. On the other hand, grandmother's or grandfather's stories provide contact with a distant past. Thus the grandparents point both to the future and to the past and show that man is not the product of an instant but a historical being, that each individual has a life history which is itself embedded in the history of mankind.

Changes in living conditions have meant that it is becoming increasingly rare for the grandparents to share the same household with the family. Often they are taken care of in a home. Anyone that knows the importance of the grandparents in the family will expect the children to visit the grandparents, not simply out of piety, but also so that they can learn something.

The father and mother have brothers and sisters too: the uncles and aunts. The importance of *uncles* and *aunts* in the family is often greatly underestimated. The importance of uncles and aunts has to do with what Gottfried Keller said about "the child, cast in the same mould as its mother." Parents and children are from the same mould; they have a similar genetic make-up and are on the same wavelength. But at the same time, they are also individuals in whom the genetic material is reproduced one-sidedly. Therefore, it can be extremely valuable for a child to see and experience what other possible realizations of that same genetic material there are. Often the child is drawn to something particular in its uncles and aunts; often it finds in them what it needs, the right model. For reasons of psychological hygiene, therefore, it is good to cultivate the wider family circle that includes brothers and sisters, as well as more distant relatives, of the parents. Whoever recognizes this can say that a so-called family reunion, when insofar as possible all the members of the extended family come together, is not an outdated, but a modern institution.

Finally, the family circle also includes the *friends* of the family. It is a gain both for the children and for the marriage partners if the father does not just meet his friends in the pub or the mother hers at women's gatherings or in the street. For if relatives are cast in the same mould, friends are from a different mould altogether. The presence of friends and visitors in the house shows the family situation in a new light, from a different point of view. And the same applies if the children are allowed to bring friends home and are invited to their friends' houses. There should be open doors everywhere, since the families can only get to know each other through reciprocal contacts. Then the family becomes the core of a vital society.

A family, all of whose members are tied to each other as in a living organism and in which all the members live in mutual, human responsibility, is not an artificial cultural product. Family life is deeply rooted in nature. The *family instinct* belongs to the natural drives. Anyone who wants to can see this if he looks at a family of swans: The father swims majestically at the head, and behind him comes the mother, calm and protective, with the grey signets. If danger approaches, the father spreads his wings, ready to defend his family, and hisses threateningly. The mother gathers the young ones around her and leads them to safety. Such collaboration is nature, not civilization. The family thrives on an instinct, the loss of which would be the ruin of society. So, upholding the family is a human duty. And as is natural for humans, the family instinct should be filled with meaning and culture. An increase in the number of neglected families in a society leads to an accumulation of ill-developed, stunted, or neglected people. What a society or state built by such people would look like need hardly be described in detail. I can illustrate what I mean by ill development and neglect with the following short newspaper report:

Neue Zürcher Zeitung, 12.11.1962: The instant expulsion a few months ago in Bern of four pupils from the municipal secondary school shortly before their final exams caused a considerable sensation. Over a period of a year, the four pupils had carried out a number of clever burglaries. While the real ringleader, who was also the youngest, had already been sentenced by the juvenile court, the other three were to appear before the Bernese criminal court. The three accused – a vicar's son, an engineer's son, and the son of a government official – said that they had acted rather out of a thirst for adventure than out of greed for money. Boredom at school, isolation, and conflicts with their parents had led them to form a *pact of destiny*, not, however, initially with the aim of committing crimes. Only later did they decide to break into a kiosk. When, contrary to expectations, that first escapade went off without a hitch, further break-ins, sometimes involving just two of them, sometimes involving all four, followed at regular intervals. A variety of tools, torches, and face masks was stolen. In one sports shop 480 francs in cash and a mountain climber's outfit were taken, in a restaurant an amplifier, and in a warehouse 31 bottles of whisky, to transport which one of the youths brought along his father's car disguised with cardboard number plates.

What is remarkable about this story is not only that the young people concerned were the children of respectable families, whose fathers were a vicar, an engineer, and a government official. What is also remarkable is the way they spoke of sharing a common destiny. This unhealthy pact then turned into a criminal gang. When we contrast these dangerous gangs with the true community of the family, this does not in any way imply that we approve of family arrogance and false family pride. The family, which is a genuine community of destiny, is a sphere of modesty and warmth.

Nurturing the family demands that we be alert and watchful at all times. It is essential to nip any trouble in the bud and not to complain afterwards, when – as all too often – it is too late. Theodor Fontane gave moving poetic expression to this idea in his novel *Effi Briest*. Lacking support from her parents, Effi Briest loses her way in life. An unhappy marriage and a love affair break her, and she goes to her grave still a young woman. And in the evening, her father and mother are sitting in front of the house, filled with sorrow. The mother says: "Not a day goes by since she died without my having to ask myself the question, could it be that it's *our* fault? Should we perhaps have taken her in hand? Are *we* to blame?" But the father replies evasively: "Let's not talk about it, Luise … it's too big a question."

It may be that, afterwards, looking back full of guilt when it is all over, it is too big a question. But like a garden, the family needs tending every day of the year. Then it is never too big a question. If we neglect it, the garden will become overgrown with weeds. But if we do our duty, we can hope for a rich harvest.

V

RAPPORT IN CLINICAL PSYCHIATRIC THERAPY

The introduction of psychoanalysis into psychiatric clinics at the beginning of this century by Eugen Bleuler in Zurich and his then senior registrar, C. G. Jung, did not lead to the adoption of psychoanalysis as the normal method of treatment for the more serious forms of mental illness. Nevertheless, as M. Bleuler[1] points out, "with psychoanalytic training a much closer relationship between doctor and patient could be established than previously, which was all to the benefit of the treatment."

The following is an attempt to clarify the possibilities and show the place of analytical psychotherapy within the framework of clinical psychiatric treatment, focusing on the phenomenon of rapport. In basing my argument largely on the work of C. G. Jung, I do not mean to deny the validity of other psychological schools of thought. We shall come back to how psychotherapy can be practiced in very different ways in a later chapter (p. 199). All the same, it is important that the therapist have a clearly defined point of view since, without it, no meaningful therapeutic encounter between doctor and patient can take place. For both doctor and patient, the psychotherapeutic situation is one in which the "Thou" can be experienced. The first thing either party feels is spontaneous sympathy or antipathy. Wherever we feel sympathy of any sort, we also have the feeling that we have found rapport. In the introduction to *The Psychology of the Transference,*[2] Jung described this process as a chemical – or alchemical – allegory of the impending union of two different elements, in other words, of the beginning of the synthesis of opposites. The above-mentioned work, which centers around a discussion of the alchemical imagery of the *Rosarium Philosophorum* (Frankfurt, 1550), was aimed primarily at doctors and practicing psychotherapists; it provides the main scientific basis for this investigation.

In modern chemistry we call the tendency of certain substances to combine with others "affinity." Medieval alchemy referred to that same force as *nuptiae, coniugium, amicitia, attractio,* and *adulatio.* One hundred and fifty years ago the German expression for affinity was "elective affinities." Goethe's novel *Elective Affinities* is a careful attempt to show the importance of chemical or physical metaphor in social life.

Since 1937 Szondi has accumulated extensive practical evidence to support the description of the curious phenomenon of elective affinities in his theory of the analysis of destiny.[3] When he puts spontaneous sympathy and antipathy down to the latent genes, he is fully aware that that is a rationalization. "Anything that is not rooted in the irrational," he says, "is not a discovery, and moreover – in my opinion – it is not science."

In situations where the only reaction is antipathy, however, psychotherapy is utterly impossible, since the synthesis of opposites that is supposed to take place in the psychotherapeutic encounter – as an overt or concealed "union of the elements" – cannot then get underway. But where the presence of sympathy, even if it is only the beginnings of sympathy, makes it possible to proceed, the symbolic, alchemical images described by Jung, or Szondi's image of the genes, show us just how large a part the irrational plays in the phenomenon of rapport. The very spontaneity of rapport leads one to suppose that the unconscious of the patient and that of the doctor often have more to say in the matter than consciousness, reason or judgment.

However, analytical psychotherapy cannot rely solely on spontaneous rapport. The doctor should realize that rapport has to be consciously acknowledged and constantly renewed, fostered, and preserved. Only in that way can a genuine, human relationship come out of the original, primitive, spontaneous rapport. In psychotherapy, as L. Binswanger says,[4] "the sick individual is not merely an object of study, but a partner in a human relationship, in a process of communication." It also has to be assumed that, wherever rapport makes true communication possible, the unconscious and thus also transference and countertransference will have a part to play. In practice, of course, we are glad to be spared the difficulties of transference analysis in any particular case.

On the emotional side, it is vital for the development of rapport that the problems the patient has to cope with be explicitly acknowledged. It is not enough to know that the patient is suffering; you must say it loud and clear. And where words are not enough, you should not hesitate to hold the patient's hand so that he can feel through the physical contact that somebody else is there and is supporting him. Patience and dedication are essential if the patient himself is to learn to be patient and dedicated in his suffering. That suffering is like the *opus* described by alchemists in images, whereby out of the initial confusion, the chaos of the *nigredo,* new life is to emerge. "Often the *opus* demands all the patient's energy, and a capacity for suffering that ought not leave the doctor unaffected" (Jung). The patient's *opus* is in effect the doctor's too.

The image of the *nigredo* means that the conflict-laden cause and the final goal of the suffering lie invisible – unconscious – in the "blackness." Faced with this situation, it is very important that the doctor does not undermine the rapport by insisting on knowing everything. The initially unknowable individual component can only be respected if the doctor works on the basis of *not knowing.* Then, the patient feels that the doctor is in solidarity with him, sharing his not knowing and his darkness.

Understanding, love, and patience, however, do not imply blind trust in the patient. That would be far too simple, naive even. We are all too familiar with the negative side of the *adulatio,* the endless flattery of the therapist that keeps the analyst in lucrative employment and gives the patient the assurance that, despite years of "analysis," his carefully guarded secret will never come out. The patient cannot demand to be trusted; where necessary, the therapist should show suspicion, since rapport without natural reactions to what we encounter in the "Thou" is sterile. Only when the therapist reacts can the process get underway. At this point, I would like to introduce a practical example.

Case 1. A fifty-year-old woman sought voluntary admission to the sanatorium, suffering from severe depression with all the characteristic signs, such as lack of energy, mourning, insomnia, and a tendency to gastrointestinal disorders. From time to time she experienced intense panic attacks. The woman had lost her husband the previous year, but – and here the patient herself agreed – the depression clearly went far beyond a purely reactive condition. To start with, although the patient trusted me, I had difficulty in establishing any closer rapport. So I just had to wait the way, for example, a doctor sometimes has to wait when a birth does not seem to want to proceed. (I use this metaphor deliberately. In cases like this it is not initially a question simply of carrying out a psychoanalysis; first, the doctor needs a suitable personal, analytical, and psychological attitude, and the importance of the right attitude is borne in upon us most clearly by an image. This means that an *active projection* on the part of the doctor becomes an integral part of the act of empathy. I will come back to the importance of images as a guide to orientation at the end of this chapter.) In time, despite the fact that the depressive symptoms were becoming rapidly more severe, I achieved better rapport with the patient. This led to the first situation that called for a psychotherapeutic reaction. While the patient became ever more insistent with her assurances of how much she trusted me, my trust in her diminished rapidly and I had the growing impression that she could become suicidal. I asked her, therefore, to agree to the appointment of a private twenty-four-hour nurse; after considerable initial resistance, she acquiesced. With this vote of no confidence, which circumstances had forced upon me, an emotional barrier seemed to have been broken. Whereas, up until then, she had only expressed complaints of a general nature, now the patient began to tell me what was going on inside her. She said she was plagued by a peculiar series of images that both fascinated and frightened her, a succession of images that was like a river. – I cannot go into these images in detail here; I can only emphasize that it was the doctor's vote of no confidence that prompted the patient to talk. As a result, the autonomous images produced by the unconscious became visible too, which is to say, they were drawn into the conversation; in that way, through contact with the doctor, contact was also established with the unconscious. From then on the treatment also changed insofar as the doctor's analytical stance was no longer determined by an act of empathy relying on images, nor by his conscious intention, but by the patient's unconscious. The autonomous images generated the material that could provide the compensatory orientation to the doctor's conscious attitude of "not knowing." The task of understanding the images provided access to the patient's problems without destroying the individual component. In fact, the images were of a very general kind (tower, child, cross), clearly collective and archetypal in nature. One of the images showed graphically how the patient had got things out of proportion in her own mind. The patient was troubled by the image of a crucified St. Christopher. This image signifies presumption. Christ, the God-Man, the highest spiritual value, he is the Crucified. Our feeble ego can only try to bear that problem and, like St. Christopher, we often find that hard enough by itself. Psychologically, putting St. Christopher in the place of Christ shows the identification of the ego with the Self. This identification is always a symptom of dangerous psychotic or near-psychotic disorders. Furthermore, the tendency to mortify the natural man (the crucifixion of St. Christopher) corresponds in clinical terms to a suicidal tendency.

Collective images of that sort, precisely because they are collective, are understandable to others, in this case to the doctor, since they show the individual and the universal combined. Consequently, analysis of such images produces both individual data and the general evaluation and meaning of the individual circumstances. Here I will just add that the particular question arising from this individual case concerned the significance and evaluation of an apparently morally dubious action on the part of the deceased husband of the patient; she had learned of that action shortly before his death. I must also briefly consider the fact that the succession of images was like a river. The flow of images enables doctor and patient to receive knowledge about the meaning and solution of the conflict from an independent, superordinate source: from the primordial images, the archetypes of the collective unconscious. That knowledge then furthers psychic development, the growth of consciousness. It could reasonably be said, therefore, that rapport makes it possible for the therapist to react and that his *reaction* sets the psychic process in motion.

But rapport is not achieved simply through compassion and sincere reactions. The doctor must also relate to the patient's character, his ideas, his imagination, his feelings and emotions, his views and his ways of expressing himself. The fact that it is possible for the therapist to do so is in itself something irrational and a result of spontaneous affinity, or sympathy. It is especially important that what those around the patient – and often enough the patient too – regard as "illusions" and therefore trivial, are not dismissed out of hand. The intensity with which the patient clings to his illusions shows how important they are to him personally. The illusions are representations of the unconscious reality of the patient, though in the form of projections. But new contents of the unconscious that have the potential to give consciousness a new direction often manifest themselves in projections. Let me give a practical example of this:

Case 2. A twenty-five-year-old man is in love with a young woman. He hopes to marry her, but she proves aloof and unfaithful. He gets into an agitated, slightly bewildered, and somewhat depressive mood, is often hopeful, then discouraged again, but in general so disturbed emotionally and mentally that he considers himself ill and decides to undergo psychotherapy. In the course of treatment a curious state of affairs comes to light: As soon as the patient sees the girl, even if only briefly, his symptoms become more severe; he even becomes so depressive and agitated that, to those around him, he seems thoroughly disturbed. When he has calmed down again, he is able to discuss his disorder with friends or with the doctor. Naturally, the suspicion is that the girl does not suit him and is only harming him. But the minute he begins to realize this, the same symptoms of inner disorientation reappear with renewed force. The disorder develops to such a degree – it is the old story of the unhappy love breaking the lover's heart and robbing him of his sanity – that hospitalization is necessary. The clinical condition is clearly that described by P. Janet[5] as *abaissement du niveau mental,* with a loss of inner tension and orientation. The unattainable, intolerable, and yet unrenounceable girl causes in the patient a state similar to that observed in primitives and described by J.G. Frazer[6] as "loss of soul."

In the clinic the symptoms were displayed in almost paradigmatic form. Told that he had no hope of ever winning the object of his affection – and the woman was by anybody's standards, even the patient's, completely unsuitable for him – the patient fell into a state of agitation resembling psychosis, talked wildly to himself and was deathly pale with distorted features. But if he was given hope, he soon became calm and in every respect normal and inconspicuous. He nevertheless had to remain in hospital because as soon as he was set free, he would hurry to his sweetheart, only to suffer a prompt relapse into the state of *abaissement*; a single experiment along those lines was sufficient proof. The hopeful enthusiasm, directed outwards, corresponded simply to an inflation (a false, illusionary, puffed-up state) that led to maladjusted behavior towards the external world, which in turn severed contact with the external world. Hence the disappointment in the face of the reality of the woman he loved, a disappointment that was experienced subjectively as a catastrophe. The threat to psychological development implicit in such disappointments has been investigated by R.L. Denkins[7] with interesting results. When it is a matter of finding a solution in a case of this kind, you do not have to look for dream material. The image of the sweetheart whom it is vital to attain, but whose physical presence is deadly, is material enough. The patient should not be deprived of the hope of eventually winning his sweetheart, however illusory it may seem. You have to carry on looking until a satisfactory position is reached, one that guarantees the possibility of future development. The corresponding, often tedious discussion with the patient should not be avoided. What you are aiming for is not simply an analysis of the unconscious material (the *imago* of the loved one), but above all a didactic reorientation of consciousness in the direction of self-knowledge and discipline. In the event, the outcome was as follows: Evidently, in the eyes of the patient the girl has all the features of the "distant, unattainable lover," the king's daughter, in honor of whom and to win whose favor in the Middle Ages the young knight, his lady's vassal, had to tread the path of battle, without ever being able to see or directly to woo her. It appears that the young man is not mature enough to survive the encounter with his sweetheart and that all outward contact with her is forbidden. In her honor he has to travel the path of inner growth. This formulation made sense to the patient, and he was then able to adopt a new inner orientation, so that discharge from hospital became possible. But above all, this way of speaking preserved the rapport with the psychotherapist, whereas whenever the patient was simply dissuaded from the planned marriage and told it was a nonsense, the rapport immediately broke down, resulting, among other things, in an attempt to escape from the clinic. If a patient has to keep the image of the sweetheart and the hope of ever being united with her within him, without being allowed to see her, then it is fair to assume that he is typologically an introvert. Our formulation of the further inner development threw our patient back on himself, with the result that he brought up the question of his typology of his own accord. It emerged that he had previously read a book by Kretschmer and had recognized himself as leptosome and therefore, as he thought, inferior. Since Jung's introvert and Kretschmer's leptosome describe – albeit from different angles – something similar, if not identical, it proved possible to open the patient's mind to an understanding of his own inner disposition. He was not an inferior introvert or leptosome; on the contrary he had to recognize the value and sense of his introverted nature and not try to live against it. Recognition of this fact had a positively liberating effect; he spontaneously exclaimed, "That's it!" A psychological conclusion that does not have a similarly convincing effect on the patient is mere theory and insubstantial. It remains to consider the psychic event that took place in the patient. His initial, purely impulsive interest in the woman revealed a naive, unconscious attitude. There was a corresponding identity of subject, the passionate ego, and object, the sweetheart. Lévy-Bruhl[8] described this subject-object identity as a frequent phenomenon among primitive peoples and called it *participation mystique*. In the case of our patient, however, this identity gave rise to a disorder and so became the object of criticism. It was obvious that something was not right. A vital psychic factor – you could almost say, a part of the soul – seemed to be in the possession of the sweetheart. The loss of that factor through the giving up of the sweetheart involved a loss of soul with corresponding *abaissement du niveau mental*. And yet the attempt to win back the missing part of the soul by seeking an external relationship with the object of his love, by identifying the missing psychic factor with the objective person of the sweetheart, caused the same disorder. What was needed, therefore, was the dissolving of the *participation,* of the identity of the subjective, psychic factor with the object. Accordingly, one could say that the part of the soul that was projected onto the sweetheart as an *imago* had to be detached from the object. But when we talk of a projection, we have to be clear in our minds that, in the kind of case we are concerned with here, it is not a psychic content that is projected by consciousness and that has subsequently to be reversed. It is a *passive projection*, produced spontaneously by the unconscious. The new content is first encountered by consciousness in projection and the re-collection of the projection into consciousness is not a reversal, but the acquisition of a new psychic factor as part of the development of personality. The formulation "his lady's vassal" indicates what factor we are talking about. The sweetheart whose physical presence is poison is transformed into a figure of inspiration, an image of woman in honor of which the challenge of life is pursued. It is clearly a projection of the anima. Nevertheless, the successful formulation of the problem does not mean that the projection has been withdrawn and so put out of operation. All that has happened, initially, is that a position has been reached from which it is "as if" the projection were no longer in operation: The patient must not see his sweetheart, but must conduct his life in her honor. However, this attitude guarantees an inner development in which – under therapeutic guidance – the projected content can be seen more and more for what it is: an inner emotional factor ("anima" has something to do with "animosity," for example). And then the recognition of the truth does not involve a disappointment but the dissipation of illusion and the discovery of inner, emotional reality. Through the re-collection of the projection, the anima works to the advantage of the individual and aids adjustment to inner necessity. As an archetype, it is universally valid and comprehensible: It is the princess, the fairy, the mistress of the soul. As a psychological factor, it is the partly unconscious female side of a man. Accordingly, in medieval alchemical literature, the anima was represented less as a wife than as a sister (*soror mystica*); the literal representation, then, of a man's relationship to his anima is the marriage of brother and sister. But, as Layard[9] has shown, even among primitive peoples, there is extreme resistance to any literal, external solution to this question. And he believes that if the solution is not possible in the external world ("in the flesh"), then it has to be achieved in the spirit. In the case under consideration, the solution was obviously impossible on a naive, projective level. The "soul relationship" with the sweetheart provoked an emotional disorder, which was what first made the patient aware of his own ego. Wherever there is a collision, we tend primarily to perceive not the objective cause of the disturbance but the impact on the subject. However, the ego stage proved insufficient in our patient's case because the ego was unable to enforce its will – the attainment of the sweetheart. On the contrary, any attempt in this direction aggravated the disorder. Therefore, the patient, or rather his ego, had to accept the limits of his possibilities and strength in the encounter with what thwarted him. First of all, he encountered what he did not want to be, the shadow. Secondly he met his own psychic "not-I," the archetype of the collective unconscious. And thirdly, he encountered what *he* was not, but the other was: the individual reality of the "Thou." His shadow was the disturbed individual, the psychiatric case he did not want to be. Through the re-collection of the anima projection, achieved through his illness, he encountered the archetype whose partly irrational, fairylike, emotional image he had to carry within himself, though he had yet to make the distinction between his ego and that emotion. He had, as it were, *to learn to talk with his emotions.* And then, not overnight, but after some time, he also had the possibility of approaching the individual reality of the sweetheart, freed from the confusion with the anima projection. The patient was able to meet the woman in an atmosphere no longer poisoned by the partial identification of his inner reality with the external object, and to see her more objectively. This led to an amicable separation. With that, a conscious stage beyond the ego stage was achieved, one that established a living, conscious relationship in place of the primitive, archaic identity of a part of the subject with the object. Identity was replaced not with a rift but with a unifying relationship that said, There is no light without shadow, no consciousness without unconsciousness, no I without Thou. When the doctor rejected the patient's supposed illusion that he had to get to his sweetheart as soon as possible, even to marry her, the rapport with the patient was obviously interrupted. The simultaneous disorientation and impoverishment of the patient's ego in the *abaissement du niveau mental* shows that the patient's contact with the unconscious was also interrupted. The normal personality – which has no *abaissement* – receives impulse and vitality through the constant stream of energy flowing in from the unconscious in the form of plans, ideas, moods, and so on, in other words, of psychic contents that are only in small part rationally produced. The rapport with the doctor has to be maintained not least so that the patient does not lose contact with the unconscious.

It follows from this that it cannot be for the doctor to give rational advice. After all, we know too little of the individual circumstances to give precisely the piece of advice that is needed in a difficult case. But above all, we should not dismiss the irrational experiences of the patient – generally, the patient is all too inclined to do that himself. We ought rather to take the content of the irrational experiences seriously in psychological terms and to try to understand it; in that way we may facilitate the patient's progress towards the wholeness that encompasses both consciousness and the unconscious.

All the same, the ego and the unconscious should not be brought into contact too early. Clinically, as the two cases we have looked at so far suggest, the condition defined as a lack of contact between ego and unconscious is for the patient, at least subjectively and almost always objectively too, a severe state of helplessness and loss of energy, for example, a chronically distracted depression. If this state arises spontaneously and if it has been going on for some time, it is important to respect the separation of consciousness and the unconscious, particularly when the patient displays strong resistance to the contents of the unconscious coupled with fear. In such cases it is to be assumed that there is a risk of consciousness being flooded, in clinical terms, therefore, of psychosis. The weaker consciousness is, the greater this danger, and the temporary separation of consciousness and the unconscious has to be seen as a necessary defense mechanism. In general, it seems to be the rule that the weakness of the conscious standpoint – evidenced, for example, by panic-stricken clinging to unfounded hypochondriac ideas – is proportional to the strength of the resistance. Active steps such as dream analysis or the activation of fantasies are to be advised against; you have to wait until the patient feels able spontaneously to allow the unconscious contents to surface. Narcoanalysis may seem a good way of forcing access to the unconscious. My personal view is that this method is permissible only when it is not simply a means of avoiding total commitment to the case and responsible discussion with the patient. There is the further risk in cases where consciousness is threatened by unconscious contents, which nearly always belong to the collective sphere, that through the physical means (narcotics) the invading energy can, under certain circumstances, be partly diverted into the body, endangering the patient's life (emotional excitement with a risk of heart attack, etc). Extreme caution is called for in dealing with older patients or those with any form of toxic damage (e.g., from alcohol) as soon as the resistance is seen to be considerable, or if there are signs of panic. In many cases of loss of contact with the unconscious, it will be impossible to avoid exposure to the transference phenomenon. By carefully acknowledging the patient's conscious standpoint, the therapist will try to win and retain the patient's trust. The success of such an attempt assumes, as we have already seen, the spontaneous reaction of sympathy, which in both partners is essentially irrational and unconscious. In other words, there are not just *two* of you, there are *four* of you: Besides the consciousness of doctor and patient, there is also, often as an increasingly decisive factor, the unconscious of both doctor and patient. In showing a willing concern for the patient's mental and emotional distress, the doctor exposes himself to the troubling unconscious contents and so makes himself vulnerable to their induction effect. This gives rise to projections on both sides, and doctor and patient find themselves involved not only in a relationship on the conscious level, but also in one based on shared unconsciousness. The latter creates a peculiar, unreal-seeming *intimacy*, familiar to every psychotherapist, the affective, all too often incestuous nature of which is appropriately characterized in the *Rosarium Philosophorum* as a "left-handed encounter" (the persons to be joined together touch each other with the left hand; left is dark, sinister, clumsy, unconscious). The enactment of this encounter "in the flesh" has poisoned more than one transference situation; it should only ever become reality "in spirit." It often seems as if the role of establishing contact with the unconscious has been transferred from the patient's ego directly onto the doctor. He then has to try to understand the situation and, as far as possible, the patient's symptoms too. It is not a question of interpreting, but rather of caring and under-standing.

Despite the greatest care, the invasion of an unconscious content, overpowering and flooding consciousness, can occur spontaneously, causing actual possession: psychosis. Suicidal impulses and potentially fatal physical illness are common side effects. A good rapport with the doctor – as we have described it – can be a great help, precisely in such situations, and can help ensure that the flooding of consciousness by the unconscious does not lead to devastation, but to fertilization and renewal, "just as the annual flooding of the Nile makes Egypt's soil fertile" (Jung).

A case example will make this clearer:

Case 3. A fifty-five-year-old English painter, daughter of a priest with strict morals, became increasingly depressive and anxious, slept badly, and suffered from gastrointestinal disorders and frequent panic states. Since the woman was clinically on the edge of psychosis, what was called for was a patient, more or less palliative therapy. But things got rapidly worse until the patient herself felt that something had to happen and admitted to the therapist that for several years she had been doing what she herself described as "filthy homosexual things." A few hours later she began to get more and more agitated and the next day was in a severe, agitated, catatonic state, so that she had to be transferred from the open ward of the sanatorium to the closed ward.

Homosexuality, which in her case was a physical urge, was all the more of a problem for her in that the highly moral world of her father, the world she grew up in, could only deliver a negative judgment on it. Clearly, the patient at that moment was not equal to the conflict; as a result, consciousness was almost extinguished. In a dream that she recounted to the doctor a week before the catatonic phase, the approaching dangerous collision of the op-posites contained in the conflict was indicated: "I am standing on a lovely riverbank. In the distance I see a gigantic column of water, flowing from top to bottom and from bottom to top at the same time and approaching threateningly." The collision, but also the unification of opposites was getting closer. The opposites were represented in very general terms as the water "above" and the water "below" (compare this with the second day of creation in the biblical story, when God separates the waters above the vault from those below). During this phase, which lasted several weeks, the patient's only utterances were more like cries of fear. Discussing these cries with her was out of the question. Nevertheless, I discussed them in her presence with my colleagues and tried to understand them – as in a clinical lecture. This had a curiously calming effect on the patient; probably, she was still in a position to grasp that an understanding was being sought and could be found. Later, she had a complete amnesia.

The first exclamation was, "The atom bomb is going to go off!" Obviously the opposites have met; this is where it gets dangerous. Then, "Just keep the lid on the pot!" It seems as if, in the sickness, something was being, as it were, cooked that had to be held together in the pot – precisely so that the opposites could be united. During this phase of the illness, the patient suffered from pneumonia and was treated with penicillin; at times she was drip-fed. The "pot" also referred to her body, which had to be looked after and protected against starvation and infection. Finally, she said, "There's a fire in the pigsty." Evidently, the things she had described as "filthy" were getting hot and so coming alive. In accordance with the unification of opposites that was taking place, the fire had a dual significance here: As the agent of destruction, the pigsty, or "filthy" habit, it was being incinerated and robbed of its dark, dirty character. But it was also the source of warmth and life: the burning pigsty or, in rational terms, the burning question of homosexuality had become a source of warmth, love, and feeling.

Following this episode, the patient emerged from her state of confusion and was able to return to her old room in the open ward of the sanatorium. In the first consultation after this transfer she said to me as if, since the original admission of homosexuality, nothing had happened: "Yes, well, homosexuality, it certainly wasn't decent. But I don't want to forget that it also brought me relationships with a lot of interesting women and endless intellectual stimulus." That is what the unification of opposites looks like in the light of rational consciousness, stripped of the emotional experience. The whole thing was boiled down, as one might say: a careful weighing up of for and against. A fortnight later the patient left the sanatorium, having replaced her boyish wardrobe with elegant, ladylike clothes. For the patient, the question of homosexuality had evidently become a complex, a "skeleton in the closet," concealing the conflict between her strict upbringing and her inner urges. The solution of the conflict, with its humane assessment of the darker side and its clear emphasis on intellectual values, corresponds to the alchemical *albedo* (whiteness) that emerges from the *nigredo* as a result of the union of opposites. "Whiten the blackness and tear up the books, so that your hearts may not be broken," we read in the *Turba,* a classic, alchemical authority of Arab origin. (At the same time, consistent with the stage of *albedo,* the opposites are still visible, though no longer irreconcilable as in the patient's formula of "indecent" and "intellectual stimulus.") The high intellectual estimation of female homosexuality presupposes indeed an act of "tearing up the books." This brings us up against a question that is collectively still largely unconscious, that is to say, the question of the creation of a specifically female consciousness. Today female consciousness is still often a poor imitation of male consciousness. In the development of female consciousness, however, homosexuality, properly understood, occupies a place similar to that of male homosexuality in the Greek schools that produced classical philosophy two thousand years ago. (Correspondingly, male homosexuality has, as a rule, a significantly more negative character; it is two thousand years older and corresponds to an attitude which is unaware of its own individuality in a way that is almost pathological for a man nowadays. On the other hand, I do not wish to deny that in principle, like any other psychic symptom, male homosexuality today may conceal a prospective tendency with a goal as yet unknown. Perhaps man's consciousness of his own individuality, such as can develop within the framework of modern culture based as it is on classical culture, is superseded, so that what we are seeing is the reemergence of the old questions in a new guise.)

It would have been completely pointless to try to make the patient see the intellectual aspects concealed in female homosexuality by explaining them to her; in the face of the approaching invasion from the unconscious, the attempt had to be made, but there was hardly any prospect of halting the irruption of the complex by those means. Intellectual enlightenment is powerless in such cases, and an answer can come only out of inner experience. When the patient is in a state of this kind, one that raises questions going far beyond the individual personality, the only useful response on the doctor's part is not to interpret, but with understanding to maintain intimate contact with all the difficulties of the case. Careful consideration of the social environment is extremely important, precisely with regard to the questions that exceed the limits of the personality. The attitude of the doctor can communicate itself not only to the nursing staff but also, above all, to the worried relatives, and in our case, of course, to the girlfriends, too, in a way that may perhaps be beneficial to the patient. Of course, the influence of the doctor in the transference situation should not be underestimated. When in her phase of severe illness, the patient was treated by a male doctor, one could not overlook the fact that she was for once under the influence of a man who was not her natural father. Accordingly, it may be that the declaration of the "burning question" that followed on the admission – though ineffective at the time – did have an effect after all. In that case, the intellectual attitude of the father was confronted with what the alchemists called the *aqua doctrinae* (literally, "water of the doctrine"), in other words, the intellectual attitude of the doctor, the carrier of the transference projection. This is where the (intellectual) waters from above and below meet; the meeting takes place in the patient. Of course, this meeting cannot be achieved consciously; it is a result of the phenomenon of rapport and in particular, as already mentioned, largely a result of the unconscious part of the rapport and a "left-handed" encounter.

In very general terms, though, the treatment of such cases requires close attention to the needs of the times; the *historical development of consciousness* should never be lost sight of. Frequently the patient falls ill because neither his upbringing nor his environment can provide an answer to his burning questions, and often the solution is found at the point where a future development of consciousness is about to emerge.

With regard to the interpretation of the psychological material, which influences the doctor's attitude and thus also his rapport with what is happening in the patient, it must be emphasized that, in contrast to the disorientation of the patient, the doctor's position has to be clearly defined. Hence the demand for a definite standpoint. The doctor must know what the patient's state means, he must grasp the important contents of the psychological material, using interpretations and ideas (*aquae doctrinae*) that do justice to the symbolism of the unconscious. To this end, the interpretation must itself, therefore, be metaphorical and symbolic. In the same way, by a stroke of genius, Freud called the disastrous desire of the son for the mother not the incest instinct, but the Oedipus complex, allowing the full mythical depth of the problem to emerge. The doctor's understanding of the unconscious has itself to come from the experience of unconscious contents; hence the – justified – requirement of a training analysis. Generally speaking, but particularly in dealing with clinical cases, the interpretation should not go off too far into abstract and theoretical considerations (it is best to keep to the traditional mythologems, e.g., religion, Christianity). That does not exclude the satisfaction of theoretical needs, but they should be kept *in usum medici* and *ad usum proprium*.

Medical psychiatric therapy always has its place in the context of a psychological relationship. I treated the last of the three cases I have described, at the peak of the catatonic phase, with insulin and electrotherapy. The psychological aspect of this treatment should not be overlooked, though naturally it cannot be more than a hypothesis. Here, as in analogous cases, I had the impression that the sudden entry of the complex into consciousness caused a blockage that brought the process of development to a halt. If we picture the confrontation of consciousness and unconscious as that between two opponents, then we could say that the two fighters are so tightly locked together that the fight has to be halted for a while. Shock treatment seems in general to stem the psychic energy, while consciousness, which usually reacts only mildly in a psycho-organic direction, is far less strongly affected than the invading complex, whose influence often suddenly disappears. Maybe the greater sensitivity of the complex has to do with its contents being historically younger than that of consciousness; in our case, the problem of female homosexuality is considerably younger than the opposing moral world of the father, which is thousands of years old. It is important, however, that shock treatment not be given in overdose, since that would not solve the conflict but only lead to undesirable repression. The therapeutic goal is not exorcism, but evolution and the synthesis of opposites. The opponent, the complex, is not supposed to be destroyed; one simply wants to ensure the further development of the conflict between consciousness and the unconscious. But the correct dosage of the shock therapy can only be found in close psychological rapport with the patient. It is interesting, in this respect, to note P. Rube's[10] observation that the success or failure of shock therapy depends on whether it is administered by the therapist in a mood of anticipation, as part of a psychotherapeutic treatment, or whether it is simply routine. Thus success is more than a lucky coincidence; the importance of the therapist's anticipation suggests that the unconscious rapport between doctor and patient is also crucial.

Needless to say, the dangerousness of an invasion of unconscious contents means that careful attention has to be paid to the somatic side of the case. Here, too, all theories about the curious relationship between soma and psyche are best kept for private discussion, whereas the therapeutic rapport in a clinical case is best guaranteed by orthodox medical diagnosis. Medical science is to the somatic level what the traditional mythologem is to the psychological level: the tried and tested remedy that provides orientation and so helps. The fact that, when there is an invasion of unconscious contents causing, for example, a catatonic phase, pneumonia is common and all the more dangerous, since the body's resistance is lowered, shows how great the tendency is for the individual (not consciousness!) to evade the solution of difficult questions. But it is not the moment to start speculating on the symbolism of the respiratory tracts. It is far more important to know that the white-cell count is rising long before the erythrocyte sinking reaction, the temperature rise, or an infiltrate is clinically evident; that chemotherapy must be started at an early stage and that, for that reason, the white-cell count must be checked constantly. The psychotherapist must seek out the vital energy where it appears, and confront it wherever energy and therefore danger occur. If this means he has to go outside his own special field, then – always bearing in mind his own ignorance on foreign territory, that is to say, his own partial unknowing – he should have no hesitation in seeking the advice and assistance of a specialist, for example a medical doctor. Only in that way can the rapport with the totality of the patient be maintained; and only that rapport can ensure that the most important task of psychotherapy is fulfilled, namely, establishing in the patient a rapport between consciousness and the unconscious, out of which a living relationship between ego and unconscious can grow.

In conclusion, I would like briefly to touch upon the question of the role of formal psychiatric diagnosis in therapy. We will discuss this question in greater detail in a later chapter (p. 171). But one thing must be said: Important though it is, on therapeutic grounds, to identify psychotic symptoms at an early stage, since the possible invasion of a complex has to be recognized in good time, it is equally important to beware of prejudicing, through the diagnosis, the course and prognosis. Besides, as M. Bleuler has demonstrated,[11] the theoretical foundations of psychiatric diagnosis have been shaken in recent years by new ideas. But he also reaffirms that, in the same period, the effectiveness of psychotherapy, even in cases of psychosis, has had striking confirmation.

Let me summarize: Taking the example of rapport, we have looked at the part psychotherapy has to play in the psychiatric clinic. Case 1 (depression) illustrated the affective side of rapport and its role in getting the psychic process moving. The importance of understanding the patient's "illusions" for the development of rapport and the course of therapy was discussed with reference to Case 2 (neurosis); in this context, we also talked about the position of the patient's ego and its rapport with the unconscious through the medium of the archetype (anima). In Case 3 we dealt with developments following the invasion of overpowering unconscious contents; here we also had an opportunity to discuss the place of shock therapy and medical treatment along with the importance of psychiatric diagnosis.

VI

PSYCHOLOGICAL-PSYCHIATRIC
FINDINGS AND THERAPY

One of the first fruits of the meeting of psychology and psychiatry was Eugen Bleuler's famous work on schizophrenia.[1] In the preface to the book Bleuler indicated that it was written with the collaboration of C. G. Jung. At that time Jung himself demonstrated how analytical thinking can help in understanding the strange utterances of the mentally ill; I am thinking among other things of his paper on the content of psychoses.[2]

C. G. Jung's subsequent work was concerned chiefly with the theory and practice of psychotherapy and psychology. Today it is reasonable to ask how the work of this pioneer in the study of psychosis contributed to the psychotherapeutic treatment of psychosis.

Nowadays many of Jung's basic principles have become common property in psychotherapy. Consider, for example, his statement on the theory of psychotherapy:[3]

> The great healing factor in psychotherapy is the doctor's personality, which is something not given at the start; it represents his performance at its highest and not a doctrinaire blueprint. Theories are to be avoided, except as mere auxiliaries. As soon as a dogma is made of them, it is evident that an inner doubt is being stifled. Very many theories are needed before we can get even a rough picture of the psyche's complexity. It is therefore quite wrong when people accuse psychotherapists of being unable to reach agreement on even their own theories. Agreement could only spell one-sidedness and dessication. One as little catch the psyche in a theory as one could catch

the world. Theories are not articles of faith, they are either instruments of knowledge and of therapy, or they are not good at all.

Besides such general principles, Jung also dealt with numerous questions of detail. The results of his work on their own will never be a sufficient basis for clinical psychiatric treatment. On the contrary, Jung called for proper clinical psychiatric groundwork as a basis for any clinical psychotherapy. The psychotherapeutic interest, that is, must not detract from medical, psychiatric responsibility.

Nor was Jung the founder of a psychotherapeutic method that could be used in the clinic as a therapeutic aid. He did not offer anything that could be introduced into the clinic, to compare with insulin treatment or group therapy. On the other hand, Jung's investigations provide the clinical psychiatrist and psychotherapist with knowledge. That knowledge enables us to add a psychological finding to the psychiatric finding, and the psychological finding can often vitalize therapy. I would like to deal with the problem of the psychological finding in cases of acute neurosis, and with the problem of the treatment of schizophrenia, on the basis of my own observations. My findings and the therapy I describe will highlight some of C. G. Jung's ideas.

The Psychological-Psychiatric Finding

Psychotherapy must begin with the admission of the patient into the clinic. It is not initially, however, a question of procedure or techniques of treatment, but is founded on the attitude of the doctor and nursing staff. When the patient first arrives in the clinic, we hardly know him. We have to get to know this person who is to us a stranger. He has to be accepted into the community of the clinic, not just into the building. The doctors will talk freely about the new guest both among themselves and with the nursing staff, as is natural in any community when a new person arrives. The patient should, as far as possible, be given the opportunity to express his views. He must be allowed to talk, and doctor and staff must listen to what he says, paying particular attention to the details. If the patient wants to write, if he wants to draw or even to make music, it is good that he be given the opportunity. That opportunity is often best provided by the nursing staff and without any specific psychotherapeutic objective. The doctor will be aware that every case is unpredictable and will wait to see what happens.

The first phase of treatment will last a few days, sometimes even a few weeks. Over this period, we will get to know the new arrival quite well. It is during this time that what Jung called constellation[4] takes place. Something manifests itself; what manifests itself has a bearing on fundamental questions affecting the patient's illness.

Psychosis shatters the unity of consciousness and the supremacy of the will. The something that manifests itself in constellation is the psychic factor (Jung called it a complex) that has created a disturbed state of consciousness by disrupting the order of consciousness. As a result, the patient suffers a loss of freedom that frequently corresponds in legal terms to diminished responsibility.[5]

The suspense felt on both sides is a crucial factor in the constellation. The therapist must be genuinely interested in what the patient has to say. Since evidence of such an interest encourages constellation in the patient, at the start of treatment there is a sort of experimental situation. However, what will happen is so vague and unpredictable that a proper clinical psychiatric framework is urgently needed, which could be described as the vessel in which the experiment is to take place.

The constellated contents are extremely varied. But one constantly comes across single motifs that recur in different cases. Freud emphasized the frequency of the Oedipus motif. Subsequently, Jung turned his particular attention to the study of such motifs.

By way of example, I would like to consider the psychological finding that Jung called the Medusa.[6] The Medusa has mythological and biological aspects. In mythology she is the mortal among the three daughters of Phorcys, known as the Gorgons. She has snakes for hair. Anyone who looks at her is turned into stone. Perseus succeeds in cutting off her head by not looking at her directly but instead catching her image in his gleaming, iron shield.[7] In the context of biology, a medusa is a sea creature with neither shell nor backbone. It belongs to the group of nematophores and has tentacles containing poisonous stinging capsules; it uses the poison to kill its prey. The biological aspect of the medusa is further represented in patients' material by other sea creatures of a lower order that are related in form, such as the cephalopods (e.g., octopus) armed with tentacles, or the predatory starfish equipped with mobile arms.

I will now give a few clinical examples of this mythological and biological motif. In each case the pressure of a very considerable affect was involved, which so altered the patient's behavior that hospitalization was ordered. This does not necessarily imply a diagnosis of psychosis in the narrower sense of the term (cf. also the introductory remarks to this chapter).

Case 1. This case concerns a twenty-six-year-old student. For some time he had been making observations about himself, which he carefully noted down. He met a girl and established a friendly relationship with her, but then came into conflict with her with the result that she wanted to detach herself from him. The student was agitated and at a loss. He consulted a psychiatrist, but found no real rapport. Shortly after, he had an argument with a fellow student whom he suspected of having a relationship with his former girlfriend. This fellow student then got in touch with the patient's parents. At home letters had already come to light in which the patient explained that he felt inwardly wrecked. He was judged to be a danger to himself and was admitted to the clinic. In the clinic the patient was outwardly calm, though he admitted a certain suicidal leaning. Occasional nervous tachycardias indicated affective tension. In a detailed, written self-portrait he described the lost girlfriend as a *medusa*. When she left him, he had turned to stone; that was the "medusa effect, the panic." He maintained that, as a consequence of his inability to develop and sustain the relationship with his girlfriend, he had turned to stone for good. That was why for him she was a medusa, and why the effect she had on him was the *medusa effect*. He maintained that it had nothing to do with her own personality.

Let us contrast this self-portrait, and its strongly intellectual slant, with an acute psychotic condition.

Case 2. A twenty-seven-year-old man, also a student, fails his exams. Subsequently, he becomes increasingly convinced of his political importance, feels himself surrounded by spies, and is certified on grounds of paranoid symptoms. In the clinic, his condition becomes acutely catatonic after a few weeks. The patient believes his bed is on fire, feels burned all over, and has to be put in a cell. There he is frightened and agitated. What particularly horrifies him is that from the ceiling above his head hangs a giant *octopus* with alarming tentacles. He says he needs a doctor urgently, one who is half-doctor, half-veterinarian.

I have observed the image of the medusa – the boneless, tentacled sea monster – not only in intellectual formulations or hallucinations but also, in some cases, in pictures the patients drew. I will give three examples:

Case 3. A nineteen-year-old youth is undergoing clinical treatment on account of extremely undisciplined and dissipated behavior. After some time, an attempt is made to transfer the patient to an open ward. However, he very rapidly becomes manically distracted and finally so dissociated that he has to be transferred back to the closed clinical section. There, to occupy himself, he begins to draw. What he paints is an inferno, an underworld. The center of the underworld is ruled by a giant tentacled sea monster, a *starfish* (fig. 5).

Case 4. A forty-eight-year-old married woman has for years been suffering from depressive moods. Very gradually her state becomes manic and restless, eventually to a worrying degree. This leads to her being hospitalized. In the clinic, within only a few days, she gets into a state of considerable agitation. To calm her and distract her attention, a nurse allows her to draw. She draws an octopus with tentacles. Below the picture are the words "the *octopus,* the depths" (fig. 6).

Case 5. A twenty-five-year-old man makes himself conspicuous at his workplace. His colleagues, who see him toying with an axe in a strange and disturbing manner, speak of "mental derangement." He is admitted under observation. In the clinic the patient feels threatened by electrical tension and even by thunderbolts. In order to protect himself, he begins to paint the walls of his room. He claims this will shield him against dangerous rays (it is an advantage in such cases if the walls are painted with washable paint). One of the patient's paintings shows a completely empty landscape reflected in a lake. The mirror image, at the bottom of the picture and upside down, shows a living landscape with trees and houses. Right at the very bottom of the picture, a tentacled *starfish* is visible. It seems as if the starfish has pulled the living landscape down into the depths of the lake (fig. 7).

We have now described five clinical cases in which the medusa motif appears: once in an intellectual formulation, once as a hallucination, and three times in drawings. In all five cases it was clinically obvious that there was considerable affect. In all five cases, within a few days after the material took definite shape, whether through writing it down, telling the doctor about it, or painting it, the clinical condition became calmer. The patient was not yet in any sense cured, but was capable of behaving in a more or less ordered fashion again and was no longer a danger to him or herself. Jung notes[8] that in psychosis the dangerous *tremendum,* the excess of affect, can be warded off, or made less threatening and more familiar, by being captured in an image. This allows the patient's consciousness to return to some sort of order. In the last case cited, the patient himself emphasized how the image shielded him from danger.

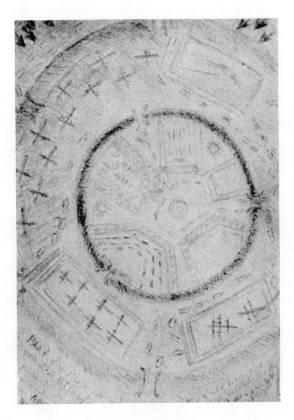

Fig. 1. Motif of the center. Town frozen in the Arctic: image of urbanization.

Notes on Figures 1–7.

The original format of figures 5 and 7 is 50 by 70 cm, that of the other pictures, 22 by 30 cm.

Pictures 1–4 were made by one patient during her emergence from chronic mental disorder (confusion). Their essential motif is that of the center and their character that of ordered arrangement.

Pictures 5–7 were made by three different patients in an acute state of excitement. They show the motif of the sea monster with tentacles (medusa) and have a shielding character.

134

Fig. 2. Motif of the center. Golden flower, on whose petals a child can sit: revival, rebirth.

Fig. 3. Motif of the center. Clock in the Jungle: ordered time reasserts itself.

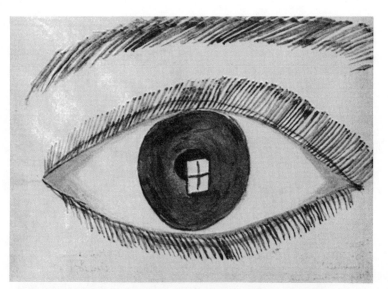

Fig. 4. Motif of the center. "An eye, a fish": as an eye, humanization, consciousness; as a fish, image of the self, of the whole personality.

Fig. 5. Motif of the medusa. Below, in the center, a starfish rules the inferno.

136

Fig. 6. Motif of the medusa. The octopus with its tentacles is identified with the depths.

Fig. 7. Motif of the medusa. The starfish has dragged the living landscape into the depths; above prevails Arctic abstraction.

Of course, the medusa motif is not something you come across every day in psychiatry; the cases I have observed date from the years 1951, 1955, 1957, 1960, and 1961. The number of cases, however, is such as to warrant an inquiry into the possible significance of the medusa motif. C. G. Jung devoted a study to this question.[9] He established that late medieval philosophy was extensively concerned with the medusa. The earliest mention of it (1593) runs: *Est in mari piscis rotundus, ossibus et corticibus carens* ("In the sea there is a round fish that has no bones and no shell"). Following late Hellenistic writings, this fish, the medusa, is understood symbolically. In 1623 Nicholas Caussinus wrote of it as *veri amoris vis inextinguibilis* ("the inextinguishable force of true love"). The medusa is described as fiery (one of our patients felt this fire very intensely in hallucination as a burning sensation). At the same time, many references in the literature suggest that medieval philosophy considered the medusa, the *stella maris,* as the source of *amor profanus,* sexuality. Again other citations, often from the same author, place the *stella maris* in the proximity of the Holy Spirit. With regard to the medusa motif, therefore, Jung's historical investigation can be seen to confirm in part Freud's view that the sexual character of the dangerous furnace in the depths cannot be overlooked. On the other hand, the spiritual aspect, which embraces the very highest things, is not secondary but the other side of the same coin.

Thus high and low appear as a pair of opposites in the image of the medusa. Jung wrote in 1912 [10] that there has to be a disruptive factor to separate the normally closely united opposites and to make them appear as separate tendencies. He cited La Rochefoucauld, who interestingly enough names a fish, the remora, as the disruptive factor and the origin of the most extreme "burning and malignant passion."[11] It can be shown that La Rochefoucauld was basing himself on Montaigne,[12] who in turn relied on the same late medieval sources that Jung cited in his work on the medusa.

The motif of the medusa reaches beyond the purely psychological level into the areas of biology and spirituality. Following

Eugen Bleuler,[13] Jung called these boundary areas of the psyche psychoid regions; Bleuler took the expression from Hans Driesch.[14] Wherever the psychoid regions are involved, a psychological diagnosis can be formulated only in the most general terms. Here we can say that the medusa corresponds to a very great affect. The medusa is a source of fire which can have a creative or a destructive effect;[15] for the weak it is lethal.

In order to understand a motif such as the medusa, purely scientific methods of thought are insufficient. Thus when Jung sought to gain understanding through images and comparisons, he was attempting to grasp the dramatic and poetic content of every psychic phenomenon. He was not alone in this. I am thinking, for example, of the magnificent way in which Freud represented the structure of the psyche in the image of the history of Rome,[16] or of L. Binswanger, whose beautiful words on true sympathy are based on Sophocles.[17]

Seen as an image, the medusa also provides clues about the biological and spiritual danger that it signifies. Seen biologically, it kills its prey with the poison in its tentacles. In a spiritual-mythological context, it is the snake-infested head of the Medusa that turns people to stone. It is reasonable to ask whether these aspects of the image also correspond to a clinical finding. Jung was of the opinion that the enormous affect associated with such images derives from toxic damage caused by metabolic disorders,[18] which blocks psychic development. In therapeutic terms, then, the neuroleptics of the chlorpromazine and rauwolfia groups, which are effective in schizophrenia, would be an antidote that could avert the threat of blockage or free a blockage if one has already occurred. The "poison of the medusa" needs an antidote; that is the biological aspect. With regard to the spiritual-mythological aspect, you will recall that Perseus overcomes the Medusa by not looking at her directly but catching her reflection in his shield. Thus the dangerous, panic-stricken fascination can be overcome through reflection. One of our patients also showed this reflection in his picture (Case 5, fig. 7); we emphasized that he felt it to be a protection. The reflection in Perseus' shield is an image of reflective understanding. C. G. Jung recommends, accordingly, that the doctor discuss the content of the psychosis thoroughly with the patient and provide him with the knowledge that will make it possible for him to understand.[19] In relation to the biological and the spiritual danger that arises when the motif of the medusa appears, therefore, an antidote to the metabolic poison and reflective understanding are both required to ward off panic. Psychological-psychiatric therapy thus demands close collaboration from pharmacotherapy and psychotherapy.

Psychological-Psychiatric Therapy

For the image of the medusa as a symptom of psychic excitement to manifest openly is a relatively rare occurrence. However, we can observe what our patient called the medusa effect relatively frequently: the victim is turned to stone, "burned out"; *médusé* ("petrified, paralyzed"), as the French describe it. The clinical picture is then unambiguously that of schizophrenia, more specifically of chronic schizophrenia (so-called schizophrenic dementia). We said that the medusa motif corresponds to very great affect. Such an affect is dangerous. If the danger is not averted and becomes reality, the result can be chronic schizophrenic psychosis.

When a person is *médusé,* it is a matter of luck whether he recovers from that state. But I would like to cite one case to show that modern psychiatric therapy has great potential in this respect. The findings obtained during the treatment are also of general psychological interest. These findings do not show the motif of the medusa (it is merely hinted at near the end of the development) but that of relatedness to a center.

A sixty-six-year-old woman, widowed, mother of two children, was booked in for clinical psychotherapy. The history was not very encouraging. The woman had been seriously ill for twenty-one years already. She had been in psychiatric care before on grounds of severe bewilderment, and neither insulin therapy nor electroshock had influenced the condition in any way. After twelve years of treatment in one hospital, she had been transferred to another one, to no avail. The patient was mute most of the time, occasionally grimacing and mumbling incomprehensibly in a mixture of German and English. Whenever she had the opportunity, she escaped from the hospital and had to be brought back by the police. Often she was found sitting on her wardrobe in an attitude of refusal, and she repeatedly smeared the walls of her room. She rolled the carpet, bedclothes, and linen together and threw them into a corner. Over the years, the patient lost nearly all her teeth and all her hair.

Curiously, the patient's family had gotten the idea that modern psychotherapy could help. At the family's insistence, we decided to accept the patient. She was brought to us by two nurses. The findings on admission were not unexpected – we knew the previous history – but hardly satisfactory all the same. It was impossible to talk with the patient; she immediately tried to run off, threw food around in her room, and again rolled up the bedclothes. We gave her 25 mg of chlorpromazine four times daily. Under this treatment the patient became somewhat calmer, but without changing in any other way.

After three weeks, the patient had at least become a familiar sight. We knew her idiosyncrasies, and now and then would risk letting her eat by herself. But then she immediately began to smear the walls with jam. And that was the beginning of psychotherapy.

It is a mistake in such cases to reject what the patient does as nonsense or as sick. An inspection of the smeared wall revealed that the patient was evidently trying to paint a face on the wall with the jam. In the presence of a nurse, I told the apparently completely distracted patient that it would perhaps be better to use paper and paints to draw with. At the same time I instructed the nurse to see that painting materials were provided.

Evidently, the patient felt herself understood. A few days later she had painted her first picture. The picture (fig. 1) shows a town plan with a central square; around the town are airplanes waiting to take off. The plan bears the caption "Part of a Plan of Heavenly Towns, Frozen a Long Time Ago in Arctic Waters."

The picture is what Jung called a mandala. Mandalas are, as Heinrich Zimmer has shown, traditional in Tibet.[20] They are a tool of contemplation depicting a centralized, symmetrical image. Together with Richard Wilhelm, Jung investigated the problem of the mandala in *The Secret of the Golden Flower*.[21] He came to the conclusion that a mandala of this sort is an image of an ordered (urbanized!) personality structure, and he also showed that such images occur as the spontaneous products of European patients.

I discussed the picture with colleagues in the presence of the still mute patient. The effect of the discussion was immediate. The patient began to write letters to numerous relatives and acquaintances. These letters were entirely normal, and spoke freely about life in the clinic and about nurses and doctors. We were even more amazed at this than the patient's family since for the family the letters, sent off after decades of silence, were merely proof of the expected success of psychotherapy. The aircraft waiting to take off in the patient's picture corresponded, it seems, to the letters about to be written, the resumption of contact with the external world.

The findings suggest that the patient's adjustment to society had been "frozen," as in chronic schizophrenia. The combined effect of pharmacotherapy and psychotherapy was to thaw out, as it were, the ordered personality structure. In the course of the following six months, the patient returned to normal behavior. She began to speak, very quietly at first, then in a normal voice and in German or English throughout (she was fluent in both languages). During that time, she received intensive human and psychological care from one of our nonmedical workers, an academic trained in psychotherapy. A nurse lacks the training for such difficult tasks. We must have people working with us who really know something about psychology and psychotherapy. A doctor who relies on his knowledge and ability, rather than on his prestige, has nothing to fear in the way of competition. The fact that, in this case, the nonmedical psychotherapist was a Catholic priest, while both the patient and myself were Protestant, never caused the least trouble. During this period we reduced the dose of chlorpromazine first to 25 mg three times daily, and later to one 25-mg tablet a day.

In the course of her readjustment, the patient drew three more pictures, which clearly illustrate her development. The first picture shows a large yellow flower (fig. 2). It is not for nothing that Jung and Wilhelm spoke of the "golden flower" as a living, human center. In contrast to the town, the flower not only showed the structure, but the structure is also alive. The patient's association with the picture was, "A child can sit on its petals." In other words, the new life that is developing is carried by the flower. As an image of rebirth, this motif is prominent in the Buddhist Amitabha meditation (424 A.D.): "You should imagine yourself to be born in the World of Highest Happiness in the western quarter, and to be seated, cross-legged, on a lotus-flower there." [22]

The second picture shows a clock in a jungle (fig. 3). Here measured time is reestablished and, with the moving hands of the clock, a centralized organization is also in motion. The clock says eleven: The patient did not have much time left if she wanted to return to life outside; she was already sixty-six years old. The image of the clock was extremely important to her – it is the only one that she kept. I just have a photograph of it.

The last picture shows an eye (fig. 4). Now the center is human; now there is conscious vision. The patient's association with the picture is curious: "A fish, an eye." Here beginning and end are one. The eye is the fish. The patient has overcome the dangerous power of that fish, the medusa; she has reached a new way of seeing. The eye, the purpose of which is to see the light and which is therefore to be allocated to consciousness, is an expression of the personality that lies above the ego, what Jung called the Self. The child sitting on the flower also represents this personality. Its appearance does not signify a dissociation of personality. On the contrary, it indicates unification.[23]

Her positive development in psychological and psychiatric terms did not solve all the patient's problems. Rather, the development itself demanded fresh psychotherapeutic work. Once the patient wanted to give up. She asked me, "Is there any point at all in going back out into life?" There was still a lot to be achieved. In part, there were simple things to be sorted out. The patient's baldness was concealed with a wig. Her teeth were laboriously repaired. A hearing aid was necessary to boost her reduced hearing. Her heart, weakened after years in the hospital, where no form of training was possible, had to be supported with digitalis. More important, though, was the attempt to clarify the patient's life story; for this purpose, dreams had to be taken into account. At first, the patient said she did not have any dreams; she only had images that flashed past in an instant. But then dreams began to occur. One of the first went as follows: "I am in a new house." That dream showed the patient's rebirth. But the next ran: "Behind the house is a lot of filthy rubbish." As analysis proceeded, the significance of the filthy rubbish emerged. Several questions concerning the patient's relationship with her family before her illness had to be discussed.

It was possible to discharge the patient after a treatment lasting fifteen and a half months. The certification imposed on account of the illness was lifted. Then "in order to enjoy life again," the patient traveled extensively to, among other places, Moscow and the United States.

It remains to emphasize the role of analytical psychological theory in psychological-psychiatric treatment, such as we have described it here. In the course of treatment we obtain psychological findings. The clinical psychotherapist is required to possess the knowledge necessary to understand such findings. If he has at his disposal a theory that mediates sufficient knowledge, the task of understanding will be made simpler. And if he demonstrates this understanding to the patient, it can contribute significantly to a positive development. Psychological theory is, therefore, in accordance with Jung's guiding principle, an instrument of therapy. It works as a catalyst to set the process of recovery in motion.

VII

THE ASSIMILATION OF THE INCOMPATIBLE COMPLEX IN ACUTE PSYCHOSIS

The systematizing psychiatry of the end of the nineteenth and the beginning of the twentieth centuries gave us refined methods of diagnosis, but was accompanied by marked pessimism with regard to the efficacy of therapy. The condition and the outcome of an illness were largely seen as inalterable fate. And every symptom was a negative factor that could only mean disorder or even destruction.

Those days of pessimistic psychiatry are gone. Increasingly the idea is gaining ground that the seed of a positive development can be found even in severe mental illness, and that psychiatry is called upon to foster the growth of that seed. Increasingly in the clinic, too, psychotherapy is coming to the fore. The starting point of psychotherapy has to be the search for the psychological understanding of mental processes, and this search has to be carried out in a scrupulous therapeutic spirit. Here as everywhere in the art of medicine, the care and attention of the doctor are vitally important to the patient.

When, therefore, we see cases with a favorable course, we must – as soon as we have an overall picture – consider the question of diagnostic assessment. A favorable course makes us inclined to classify the observed condition as neurosis, but if the condition is acute, to speak of acute neurosis; psychoses, then, would be only cases with an unfavorable course. However, we cannot ignore the fact that even cases that end in a complete cure can go through extremely acute psychotic states – to call them neuroses would be forcing the term. Basically it is a question of definitions, and the answer is largely determined by the scientific temperament of the individual. One person will say that even neuroses can go through very severe states which are almost indistinguishable from acute psychosis. Another will argue that the course of endogenous psychosis has for a long time been seen all too pessimistically and that precisely the most acute picture has, in fact, a favorable prognosis, presenting modern therapy with a worthwhile task.

Today we still have a long way to go before we will be able to offer a general theory or a statistical analysis regarding the questions just raised. What follows is more a description of the prevailing therapeutic climate than of the present state of knowledge. We still have to gather experience with individual cases; only the combined experience of many therapists can form the basis of a theory.

However, in order to gain experience with individual cases, some theoretical background is required, a perspective from which to order our experiences. The provisional nature of such a perspective affords us insight into its one-sidedness. We would do well to remember that any theoretical basis for the investigation of acute psychoses is as yet nothing more than a working hypothesis. Then, if the course is favorable and if the individual case appears comprehensible, there is at least a chance that the perspective adopted was adequate to the observed phenomenon; this revives the theoretical optimism we so badly need. For how can an undertaking succeed if one loses hope?

The working hypothesis that is to be tested against an individual case in this discussion is derived from the analytical psychology of C. G. Jung and runs as follows: Acute psychosis can be a process of self-healing. Prior to the onset of illness there is an inadequate, outworn mental attitude, a habitual attitude of consciousness that is no longer appropriate. But there is also difficulty in renewing consciousness, which is why the new factor that is to bring about the change takes the form of an autonomous complex in the unconscious. The complex draws psychic energy to itself, resulting in the undermining of consciousness, with a consequent loss of energy and confidence (*abaissement du niveau psychologique*, P. Janet). The weakening of consciousness in the *abaissement* allows the complex to enter consciousness. As a result the old order is overthrown, and in its place a disorder arises that clinically has the character of acute psychosis. The presenting symptoms have the character of daydreams, and have to be understood accordingly in symbolic terms. When the acute picture recedes, there follows a renewal of consciousness through the assimilation of the content of the complex. This can happen spontaneously, but often it seems necessary and possible to promote assimilation psychotherapeutically. The therapist will be all the more successful in fostering assimilation the better he has understood the symptoms of acute psychosis. It is only with the greatest possible understanding of all the determining factors of the illness that the nuances in the therapist's reaction can achieve the accuracy that is decisive in psychotherapy.

In view of what has just been said, it will be apparent why I have divided the course of the individual case that is to be discussed into a pre-acute phase, an acute phase, and a post-acute phase. The case concerns a young man, twenty-four years old at the onset of the illness. As an only child, he was spoiled by his mother. He lost his father when he was thirteen years old, supposedly as the result of an accident; this is a point we will return to later. There is a history of depression in the father's family: The father's mother and maternal grandmother and an aunt on the father's side are believed to have suffered from depressive attacks, though none ever received psychiatric treatment or was placed under care. The patient himself developed healthily, was a happy and alert youngster, and completed his education with top results to become an architect. The patient was Catholic and unmarried.

Pre-acute Phase

In the summer of 1952 the patient, who was English, joined the occupying forces in Germany as an officer (lieutenant) in an armored division. At first he did credit to himself in the way he carried out his duties, and was liked and respected by superiors and subordinates alike. He himself was enthusiastic about military service.

After a few weeks' duty, growing fatigue and gradually also a loss of self-confidence became apparent. The patient began to think of himself as a bad officer; increasingly he felt himself to be good for nothing, a bad person. He took his problem to the army medical officer, who referred him to a military psychiatrist. After conferring with the young man's superiors, the psychiatrist arranged the patient's discharge on medical grounds, giving a diagnosis of neurosis. Back home, the patient became restless and unable to concentrate. He was incapable of working. At the instigation of the local military medical authorities, he consulted a psychiatrist three times, but his condition grew visibly worse. Then the patient began to develop delusions: He thought he was syphilitic and that the psychiatrist treating him was in fact an examining magistrate who was preparing his arrest. Yet fatigue was still the dominant symptom.

This was the picture in the late autumn of 1952. The findings became rapidly more acute. The patient thought he was surrounded by spies; he believed there was no way out, that he was lost for the rest of his life. The patient's mother informed the director of a nearby sanatorium and nursing home, who advised that the patient be admitted immediately to the clinical section of Bellevue Sanatorium in Kreuzlingen. Since transporting the patient did not seem easy, the director took him there personally.

The beginning of this pre-acute phase illustrates in typical fashion how the energy available to consciousness is drained by the unconscious complex. At this initial stage, everyday consciousness is still more or less unaffected, but it becomes less and less able to cope with the demands of social adjustment. Subjectively the patient is acutely aware of a growing, genuine inferiority – in the form, on the one hand, of a reduced capacity for work, which he himself calls fatigue, and on the other, of an inability to concentrate. The lowering of the level of consciousness has the further, understandable consequence that the patient loses self-confidence. The fact that this state is in itself unsatisfactory is something the patient is acutely aware of. But the basically favorable prognosis of the *abaissement* is something he is naturally quite incapable of grasping, with the result that he judges his condition in moral terms and considers himself a good-for-nothing and a bad person.

Initial insights into the presenting problem emerge in purely symbolic form; they are not yet connected in any way with the acute consciousness, and so have the character of delusions. If the ideas that emerge are understood symbolically, some interesting questions arise. The patient believes he has venereal disease (syphilis). Could the illness have something to do with sex, i.e., possibly also with the family? Is there a hereditary problem? He thinks the doctor is an examining magistrate. This notion, properly understood, may not be so absurd either. Since the illness started during military service, the military psychiatrist who examined him (as well as the psychiatrist later, back home) was interested not only in the question of therapy; he also had to reach a decision regarding the young man's fitness for military service. Is a young officer who in peacetime service simply folds up fit to serve in the army at all? Might he not one day become a security risk? Here in unconscious, symbolic form, the patient has very neatly put his finger on something: It is questionable whether the discharge ordered by the military psychiatrist was the right thing under the circumstances. The delicate question of whether a soldier who suffers from a nervous disorder should simply be discharged and sent home, or whether he should not rather be hospitalized at the army's expense and at the same time invalided out in the interests of the army, was simply evaded, probably because the psychiatrist – and the patient – shied away from the idea of committing him to a psychiatric hospital. The circumstances, specifically the patient's being resident in a foreign country under occupation, make such a reaction understandable. Nor should one overlook the fact that it is very difficult to assess such cases accurately at the onset of the illness. Nonetheless, the psychiatrist's decision was wrong. He ought to have seen to it that, on the patient's return to his home country, the case was dealt with as directed. What we see here is a common phenomenon: The resistance of an already unsettled habitual consciousness ("I'm not really ill; I'm just a bit tired") exerts a suggestive influence on the doctor, so that the necessary conclusions are not drawn from the condition. Basically, the doctor participated in the repression that is also apparent on closer inspection of the patient's idea that he had syphilis. The patient realized that he was seriously ill, but did not want to believe it; for that reason precisely, the patient's insight into his illness could only take the form of a delusion. All the same, that delusion represented the illness as being serious and dangerous. So when the patient saw the psychiatrist who was giving him outpatient treatment at home as an examining magistrate, that could have meant: "This doctor should not be treating me as an outpatient, but should examine and assess my illness with regard to the need for hospitalization and fitness for military service, all the more so since the assessment up till now was wrong."

The idea of syphilis has a further subjective significance. The patient may be suffering from venereal disease in the sense that his personal sexuality, i.e., his manhood, is sick. Although he is already an officer, he is perhaps not yet a man. Emotionally he is perhaps still a boy. The question of fitness for military service, of the family situation (inheritance), and of personal manhood together form a sort of complex, the internal logic of which, however, we can only guess at. The interpretation of the first delusions, as given above, also seems generally quite risky. All the same, one should not be afraid to risk such interpretations, since we know that the interpretation is simply a sort of amplification or comparison, and is never intended to be the thing itself. On the other hand, faced with symptoms of this nature, we must always strive for understanding, since only understanding can give us access to the patient's problem. We can be open to new ideas at any time; opinions can always be revised naturally as the illness progresses. When the patient entered the sanatorium, I discussed these matters, not with the patient, but in part with the director of the institution; this provided an opportunity to establish right from the start a view of the patient and his problem.

The patient's fear of imprisonment, revealed in discussion with the psychiatrist whom he was seeing as an outpatient at home, also seems understandable. On the one hand, it reflects the distinct fear of commitment to an institution. On the other hand, the word "commitment" also contains the idea of "committing oneself." In a curious double sense, the patient has "committed himself" to the problem and cannot escape. Here too, perhaps, the objection that the ambiguity of "being committed" is not a proper basis for interpretation has some justification. But in cases where the unconscious is already close at hand or has even broken through into consciousness, puns of that sort are known to be common. So when the unconscious is at hand, it is legitimate to take the various connotations of a word into consideration in one's interpretation. Accordingly, in the case under discussion, which already shows clear schizophrenic symptoms, we must not be afraid, in making our interpretation, to speak in terms that are appropriate to the phenomenon.

The real problem is now looming closer and closer and is drawing off energy. Increasingly the condition, which at first was one of simple depression with pathological feelings of inferiority, becomes mixed with paranoid delusions. The complex begins to invade consciousness, without the patient's being able to understand what is happening. At the same time, he is all the more aware of the approaching "enemy." He feels he is surrounded by spies. The new perspective that is to overcome and transform the old, habitual attitude presses in on him from all sides. This also explains the patient's idea that he is lost. He is not lost, but since he is still wholly identified with his outgrown attitude, he cannot imagine its coming to an end as anything other than his own end. In this context it is very true to say that this is not an end, but a *Stirb und werde* ("Die and be reborn") in the Goethean sense, though what in the *West-östlicher Diwan* is poetry, is in human experience often full of anxiety and terror – and not everyone who encounters death also finds rebirth.

Therefore, the tendency of the complex to invade causes panic. It also gives rise to the tendency on the part of the patient to evade the dangers and the suffering he faces by turning the symbolic act of dying into a reality: the tendency towards suicide. Suicide seems the only way to avoid becoming committed to the complex. For that very reason, commitment – which provided the necessary conditions for inward calm – became inevitable.

Acute Phase

At the time that the patient was committed to psychiatric care, a very important fact emerged. As the psychosis came to a head, the patient's mother, before informing the director of the psychiatric institution, consulted her general practitioner. He agreed with her plan, but urged her to explain to the director about the circumstances of the father's death. The family doctor was the only person apart from the mother to know that the patient's father had not died in an accident, but by suicide. The father had been the owner of a respected firm of architects, inherited from his parents, though he himself was an active cavalry officer. When as a result of serious eye trouble, his career suddenly came to an end – he was at that time lieutenant-colonel – he succumbed to depression and shot himself with his army pistol. The mother and the family doctor then gave the death out as an accident, not least in consideration of the deceased's Catholic beliefs. Since the mother was afraid of telling the director about this hereditary taint, the family doctor did so himself; he felt that the record of suicide had to be made known to the psychiatrist for the case to be assessed properly. His action probably saved the patient's life, since it was that information above all that persuaded the director of the institution to accompany the patient to Kreuzlingen in person; it is doubtful whether the patient would ever have arrived safely without thoroughly competent supervision.

It is interesting to note that the patient himself had guessed the cause of his father's death years before and with almost complete accuracy. But because of his mother's reluctance to admit the fact, he never fully accepted it himself. He acknowledged it incidentally, as it were, and did not regard it in any way as a problem. But now at the moment of commitment, he sometimes thought that he could well end up like his father, which intensified his panic.

At the time of his admission into the clinic, the patient had a grasp of time and place, as well as of who he was. He was restless and gave a harassed impression; he spoke distractedly, though not really in a schizophrenic, dissociated manner, and was unable to concentrate in conversation. The degree of restlessness changed from minute to minute; calmer moments could be followed by states of open fear and panic, so that the immediate findings seemed critical, particularly with regard to the danger the patient might be to himself. The first task was to keep the patient under close observation and calm him down, for which purpose sedatives and soporifics were administered (small doses of tincture of opium, .5 to 1 gm diethylbarbiturate monosodium).

Needless to say, the blood was tested for syphilis (Wassermann reaction), and needless to say, the negative results neither reassured nor convinced the patient. The physical examination revealed a badly neglected infection of the left hand. A surgeon had to be called in, and it was pure luck that no bones were lost. Local or general infectious findings are common in acute psychosis, because on the one hand the body's resistance is lowered and on the other the patient also neglects himself. Often this physical danger is the greatest danger of all. In such cases it seems as if the body itself does not want to go on, and is ready to carry out the suicide of its own accord. The importance of the physical examination and care of acute psychoses is therefore plain to see. The psychiatrist is greatly helped in this task by the enormous progress that chemotherapy has brought to the treatment of physical illness. The appropriate medical and surgical response to the physical findings need not, however, prevent us from inquiring into the symbolic significance of the bodily disorder. Our patient has an infection on the left hand, and left is the side of the unconscious. It is reasonable to ask: Is the patient ill in that part of himself where he ought to act instinctively, from unconscious impulse? That would be understandable since, when a complex invades consciousness from the unconscious but cannot be assimilated, then the relationship between consciousness and unconscious is itself disturbed.

Yet in that case it is of the utmost interest to know why, from the point of view of habitual consciousness, the complex is so hard to assimilate. Here we touch on the difficulty the psychotic finds in renewing his consciousness. This difficulty explains why in cases of psychosis so much effort is needed for a mental and emotional readjustment which in another person might cause a slight upset or a passing headache.

In the first instance it is neither the complex nor habitual consciousness that causes the disturbance. It is above all the function which relates conscious and unconscious that is wrong. This function is emotional in nature and in men takes the form of a female inner counterpart. Considering its relatively independent nature in relation to consciousness, Jung personified this function in the form of the anima.

In accordance with the patient's age, the anima function is still projected onto the mother. But it is not the fact that the patient is an only child that makes the consequent attachment to the mother dangerous. Rather, it is the mother's attempt to conceal the truth, no doubt with the best of intentions, that is the danger. Her camouflaging of the father's suicide, and thus also of the father's true character, makes the complex we have tried to grasp in terms of sexuality (family, manhood) and the examining magistrate (judgment of fitness for military service) inaccessible. The anima is falsified. Even though the patient knows almost certainly about his father's suicide, under his mother's influence the father remains for him simply a "skeleton in the closet," in a *locked* closet! Somewhere in the structure of a psychosis there is always a falsification or concealment of facts that, for intellectual or moral reasons, are hard to accept. Here, too, lies the hidden reason for the incompatibility of the complex, i.e., for its incompatibility with the habitual point of view of consciousness.

In order, therefore, to calm the patient down, the mother had to be kept away. One might have expected that this task would be far from easy and that the mother would soon arrive and want to visit her dear, suffering son at all times of the day and night. And this was her intention. Her better self, however, saved her from that mistake by means of a "psychosomatic symptom." Every time she wanted to leave, she suffered heart spasms which stopped her from traveling. At a deeper, physical level she still knew what was right and, although she was annoyed to learn that the family doctor had betrayed the secret of her husband's suicide, the separation from her son had a beneficial influence, for her attitude grew rapidly more composed and reasonable. This development can be seen as a personal achievement if one considers how difficult it often is for a mother to relinquish the dominating and falsifying influence she has had on her son.

When the patient had calmed down a little, he was able to explain that the severe symptoms of fatigue and overexcitement had appeared when he tried to follow the advice of health books (*Live in Health and Happiness*, etc.). This, too, was an important symptom. Such books generally give instructions on how to combat an emotional crisis through strengthening habitual consciousness. In our patient's case, this was precisely the wrong course to take. The right course would have been, not to strengthen consciousness, but to weaken it so that the complex could enter; in such cases, the *abaissement* is not an illness (though it is a clinical state of illness) but a rescue. The inappropriate attempt to strengthen consciousness promptly caused the patient's mental state to react in the opposite direction, and the delusions of being spied upon were the first heralds of the invading complex.

Meanwhile it was 1953. In collaboration with the director of the institution, an application for exemption from military service had been applied for and the patient had to be told. All the same, in order not to provoke too violent a reaction on the spur of the moment, he had to be left the hope that, if the illness passed, later perhaps a revision of the judgment would be possible. The patient received the news that he was no longer to be an officer uncertainly, anxiously, with both relief and gloom. Apart from that, his clinical condition gradually stabilized; a markedly depressive and also quite apathetic pattern of behavior established itself, showing few ups and downs and giving the impression that the patient had somehow reached a dead end. In these circumstances, we decided on active psychiatric therapy. On January 6-8, January 13-15, and January 18-20, we gave him a triple sequence of electrotherapy (full shock); following that we gave small to medium doses of insulin (20 to 28 units; then from the middle of February, 40 units, without coma). Insofar as theoretical considerations beyond the purely empirical level are permitted, it should be added that the purpose of this treatment was not only to "unblock" the entrenched state with electrotherapy but also to calm the resulting nervous excitement with small doses of insulin. In any case, what took place after the nine sessions of electrotherapy can, without hesitation, be described as an "unblocking" (cf. on this subject also p. 122).

After the last of the nine shocks had been given on January 20, the patient was significantly less depressive until January 24, and also less apathetic. But it was the calm before the storm. On January 25, in the course of the day the patient grew increasingly agitated and suddenly started to maintain that a burglar had hidden under his bed. The motif of the burglar, which is often found in dreams too, corresponds to the invasion of the complex. Now the complex is no longer fragmented (spies); it is bunched together (one person) and is experienced as a strange (not yet assimilated), dangerous person who has the character of a real opponent. At the same time, the process of "breaking in" is projected entirely outwards and so is paranoid in nature.

The danger of the projection of the idea of the burglar is that instead of assimilation, identification with the complex (burglar) can take place. For the old consciousness in need of renewal, the complex bringing change is a dangerous enemy, a criminal. In identifying with the complex, the danger is that the patient will himself become a criminal, in other words, a danger to the public. The beginnings of identification were apparent in our patient insofar as the experienced nursing staff felt that he gave an increasingly threatening impression, while he himself thought that his hands were getting bigger and bigger and, eventually, enormously big and enormously strong. One can imagine the strength he would have displayed if there had been a sudden outburst of excitement! On the whole, both the relatives of patients and the general public have a very inadequate idea of the deadly serious and dangerous situations in which staff and doctors of a psychiatric institution often find themselves. This ignorance makes those concerned feel almost cynical. Consider, for example, the behavior of the press, which is supposed to be a responsible watchdog over conditions in mental institutions, but which never raises a finger to make sure that the directors of those institutions are given the means to carry out their difficult task.

The sensation of having "enormous fists" also, of course, represented the gain in strength that the patient's personality has received through the invading complex and the contact with the unconscious. The gain in strength from the unconscious was compensatory to the sense of weakness felt by consciousness. In this state the patient seemed so unpredictable to us (no one could know what direction the energy that emerged would take, possibly even against the patient himself) that we transferred him to the most secure ward in the sanatorium. There he grew so excited (afterwards he said that the big fists were at that time still growing) that an injection of morphine-scopolamine was prescribed.

It was the night of January 25-26. The two night nurses were unable to administer the injection, so they called the doctor. I went to the patient, who was lying in bed, tense with excitement, and who declared that he would let no one touch him. I sat down on the edge of the bed, wishing to take his hand; the patient jumped up and I drew back in alarm. At that, he smiled and said, "There's no need to be afraid, doctor, I won't do anything." At that moment the patient had realized that other people thought him dangerous. This realization was therapeutically decisive and was triggered by the doctor's instinctive counterreaction.

Important moments like these should be noted in psychiatric therapy, since they deserve closer investigation. It becomes apparent how important it is for the doctor to meet the patient personally at critical moments. We saw how at first the patient grew calmer when he was separated from his mother, the falsified carrier of the anima projection. But then, particularly after the electrotherapy, a new excitement began, triggered by the invading complex (burglar). As long as the complex is not assimilated, however, it constellates through its autonomy the other side of the patient, which is not feminine and emotional but masculine and aggressive: the shadow, in other words. At every moment there is the danger that the shadow contained in the burglar projection will become identical with the patient, and therefore also the possibility that the patient will become dangerous. In his anxious excitement, the patient is at first dominated by the projection. He is scared and excited; he will not let anyone touch him, because he is afraid of the nurses. The doctor, who is a figure of respect in the building, makes him even more frightened. But then when the doctor, whom he considered to be fearless and dangerous, jumps back in alarm, he sees who the really dangerous one is: himself. At that the projection is interrupted, the danger of identification disappears as well, and the patient makes an effort of his own accord to calm the situation: "There's no need to be afraid." The fact that the shadow contained in the complex could be dangerous is obvious. The complex seemed to have something to do with the warrior, and every warrior has the shadow of a murderer. Following his realization, the patient allowed the injection to be given quietly.

The episode I have just described displays a logical development. Once the detachment (separation) from the mother as first carrier of the anima has taken place, the anima is not as a rule and at the patient's age projected onto another object and so renewed immediately. More usually, psychic development proceeds, and new contact with the unconscious is established on the basis of the experience of the shadow; the new anima problem mostly comes later.

Once enactment (paranoid projection) and possession (identification) had been avoided through the realization described above, and following a quiet night, an event of the greatest psychological significance occurred. Clinically, the patient did not show any signs of particular excitement, but he seemed constantly absent to some extent. On January 29 he was noticeably more approachable, also more normàl affectively, and he made the following statement: "Now I can see the world as it really is again. At first, I had a central-heating radiator in my hands and was pulling and squeezing it like an accordion. Then suddenly there was a big bang, and I saw a very bright light. It seemed as if, before, I'd been surrounded by colored glass (like a bottle) in which I saw myself reflected as a bad person. But with the explosion, the glass shattered and I could see the world again. Only, I'm still not quite sure what my name is. And also, in 1925 (he pointed to the radio standing on his bedside table) they had completely different radios."

These statements encapsulate the peripeteia of the case. The withdrawal of the projection and the prevention of identification evidently created a state in which consciousness and the unconscious could meet and, in mutual contact, assimilation of the complex and renewal of the habitual frame of consciousness could take place. Before we discuss assimilation and renewal, however, the central experience as described above needs to be looked at more closely.

The use of the central-heating radiator as an accordion illustrates the enormous gain in strength that announces the approaching assimilation of the complex. Only a Titan could achieve that feat in reality. The instrument itself, a part of the central heating system, seems to have something to do with the "central fire," an inner warmth and vitality. It seems to become possible to convert this central warmth into music (feeling). The radiator, which gives out heat, is not the fire itself but a peculiar, technical device that probably has something to do with the psychic function of feeling. The schizoid, affectively defective rapport (danger of inner isolation) is replaced by a connection to the central fire and by the ability to play freely with the connecting instrument. The breakthrough of an emotional relationship to other people is anticipated by the patient's remark, "There's no need to be afraid, doctor." The activity of playing the accordion in itself shows an image of humanity in which the personality is not simply at the mercy of the powers of the unconscious, but there is an active and, in the act of playing, also a creative relationship between "I" (patient) and the unconscious (central fire).

Immediately after the establishment of this relationship, liberation comes with the force of an explosion. The patient's sensations are both acoustic and visual. A loud bang and flashes of light mark the moment when the complex enters consciousness, and for a few seconds consciousness and the unconscious are united. Normally the human psyche is split (dissociated) into conscious and unconscious. Precisely in psychotherapy, great efforts are needed to intensify and sustain the relationship between the two spheres. The ideal state of wholeness, the Self, is both a thing of the past and something yet to come, both the recollection of a lost paradise and hope in the Heavenly Jerusalem. Of the latter, the Book of Revelation says (21:11): "And its light was like that of the brightest gem, of a bright jasper." In individual experience there are probably, in rare cases, moments when the separation of conscious and unconscious falls away, moments experienced typically as a vision of light. Jung described this phenomenon as "a detachment of consciousness."[1] One could also say, perhaps, that it is simultaneously a conscious unconscious and an unconscious consciousness, the paradoxical reality of wholeness. There is a classic example of such an experience of light in the memoirs of Benvenuto Cellini:[2] After long incarceration, Cellini had a vision of a sun, pure gold without rays, a pure and clear disc. The vision then brings liberation through the apparently fortuitous concurrence of favorable circumstances. Cellini's Catholic and dogmatic interpretation of the vision is quite a different matter (though we will return to one particular detail later), likewise the self-glorification to which Cellini felt he had a right: "Since that time a halo has remained about my head, visible to all, though I showed it only to a few."

In the case of our patient, the vision of light, which along with the accompanying explosion recalls the short-circuiting of two poles with opposite electrical charges, results in the smashing of the schizophrenic barrier to the world. Before, he had been cut off from the world behind a sheet of colored glass, as if he were in a bottle. He saw himself reflected in the glass, an accurate expression of schizophrenic autism. The colored glass, which the patient did not describe in further detail, reminds one perhaps of crystal, which in turn makes one think of the student Anselm, in E. T. A. Hoffmann's *The Golden Pot*. In that book, the student is imprisoned inside a bottle by a magic spell, and an evil old woman, a shrunken woman's face, shouts at him, "Into the crystal you go and there you must stay!" But the student replies, "You're to blame for everything." Thus in our patient's case, too, it will have been the mother who spun a web around him, but whose power is now broken. Now he looks out into the actual world again.

Two other parallels to the experience of imprisonment and breakthrough into the real world are worth a brief mention. First, the patient's entry into the clinic signals the transfer of the maternal function to the clinic. There he is, as it were, in an intrauterine prison, and the breakthrough is then also the vision of rebirth which anticipates his eventual release from the clinic. Second, the image of a person in a bottle is also found in Goethe's *Faust* where, as the *homunculus*, his function is to show the way to the deeper layers of the unconscious in the classical Walpurgisnacht. In our case the patient is his own *homunculus*, the human core of the alchemical operation. The smashing of the glass that accompanies the vision of light brings the transformation. In *Faust* it is Proteus, the spirit of transformation, who causes the bursting of the glass: "It is *homunculus*, seduced by Proteus ... He'll be smashed to pieces ... Long live the fire, long live this strange adventure!" (V 8469, 8472, 8482-83).

At first, the new consciousness is uncertain about the simplest things. The patient is not even sure of his own name. His last remark, though, about the different radios they had in 1925, is not so easy to interpret. In conversation it emerged that he did not in fact mean 1925, but the time of his stay at the clinic; in other words, 1952, the previous year. The inversion of the last two figures can be seen to reflect the uncertainty in time that almost always prevails in close proximity to the unconscious. The alteration of the radio indicates a new quality of reception. The receiver (the radio) is different from what it was at the time of the patient's admission into the clinic. This characterizes the importance of the change very well. The change is not an end in itself, however. The true meaning of this change lies in the new possibilities for receiving natural and intellectual things, events, and movements, just as a radio receives signals. Jung noted the existence of reception phenomena. Probably almost every insight is the result of the reception of otherwise intangible facts or processes. But the receiver is our own habitual consciousness; and when our consciousness changes, the world changes for us, too.

The entire core experience has the character of an "illumination," and it will become apparent that it also has a religious aspect.

Post-Acute Phase

The patient's statement, "I'm still not quite sure what my name is" shows that, through the transformation, he has lost his awareness of personal identity and must regain it. The new personality that is to grow from the new attitude of consciousness is still as helpless as a newborn child.

Initially, therefore, treatment continued in the form of nursing. The fact that on February 1-2 a further dose of electrotherapy was administered was an exception. Not only before but also, to a lesser extent, after the invasion of a complex, there is a danger that the psychic process will become blocked and – insofar as the clinical picture indicates the necessity – this danger has to be actively met with preventive, therapeutic measures. As part of the general treatment, we continued to give small to medium doses of insulin until the middle of March; the hormone insulin probably has a certain relaxing effect on the psychic structure. Along with the insulin we administered a medium-strength sleeping pill. At the center of treatment, however, was the reconstruction of social behavior. Regular walks were followed by occupational therapy in a bookbinding studio, and the two were fitted into a proper daily program of activity. The uncertainty with regard to time that accompanies an invasion of the unconscious (1925 instead of 1952!) must be countered with a precise organization of the daily routine. After the occupational therapy, work therapy was undertaken in the form of gardening in a group.

The importance of a daily routine and work therapy in this phase of treatment cannot be exaggerated. It is of absolutely central importance in the reshaping of a personality after the invasion of a complex. Integration into a working group is also vital, since the personality that is taking shape has to fit into the structure of society and find its proper place there.

Work therapy and a daily routine are psychotherapeutic measures. During this phase of treatment, psychotherapy in the narrower sense was restricted, aside from support and encouragement, to making sure that the fact that the patient had been judged unfit for military service was not forgotten. The events described and investigated in the course of the pre-acute and the acute phases were never discussed with the patient. Nevertheless, it is not unimportant in treating such cases that you try to achieve understanding. Even though they cannot provide material for theoretical discussions with the patient, it is still useful for the therapist to keep in mind the images that have come to light, and to look for their meaning. If one keeps the images in mind and finds a meaning for them, one is more likely to take the right attitude towards the patient. For that reason, the psychotherapeutic treatment of real psychosis requires not only a capacity for understanding but also the will to carry out exact and conscientious observation of the phenomena. However, the doctor is not on his own when it comes to making observations. A trained staff that is under orders to report in writing on each case and to make accurate notes on the patients' verbal utterances and behavior can be very helpful. In general, clinical psychiatric work is not the task of the doctor alone, but of many people in collaboration. Of course, the doctor must in some sense be the leader, which is often the basis for transference. We have already seen the shadow transference and the withdrawal of the projection in the acute phase ("you needn't be afraid, doctor"). Then in the post-acute phase, the doctor has more the role of a fatherly friend. This position had to be carefully sustained in everyday contact with the patient, e.g., in organizing the daily routine and work therapy, in order to oppose a more positive father image to the partly disturbed image (suicide) that came to light in the course of the illness. Paternal guidance was to occupy a very important place at the end of the treatment.

On March 18 we transferred the patient from the clinical to the open ward of the sanatorium. He was still rather timid and weak, but completely uninhibited and natural in his dealings with fellow patients. At the end of March, we gave him a week's leave to visit a Swiss town, where his mother was staying on holiday. During this vacation the sleeping pills were stopped completely.

On his return from holiday, the patient seemed pleasantly relaxed and eventempered. We gave him leave again on April 14, when we also allowed him to drive a car. We asked him to come back as an outpatient on April 23, and finally discharged him to return home for good.

Before the second leave on April 14, and on the occasion of the outpatient checkup, we gave the patient his only two proper psychotherapeutic consultations, each about an hour long.

In the first consultation, the problem of the father was discussed. The result was as follows: If you have a father who as an officer shot himself with his army weapon, then you do not necessarily have to want to be an officer in the army, too. You can simply adopt the position that the suicide was a purely private affair of your father and represents, for the son, neither a cause for guilt nor a responsibility. If nevertheless you decide not to put on your father's military uniform, that is not cowardly but quite natural. I told the patient: "My own father was an enthusiastic mountain climber. Imagine that he fell on the Matterhorn. Even if it were none of my concern, no one could see anything wrong in it if I for my part did not want to climb the Matterhorn, but declared that I would rather go for a walk in the woods." You do not always have to challenge the gods. And it is possible that the patient's family was not in fact particularly suited to military life. At least, the father left behind tasks of a very different nature. What about the family firm of architects?

It turned out that the firm had in the meantime fallen into other hands and that it was not going to be easy for the patient to find his rightful place in it. It would certainly require a great deal of humility, and determination as well, before the patient as his father's successor would be the boss (father) there himself. I told him: "Here you have a task in civilian life. You're not an officer on the career ladder yet, but you're qualified as an employee like an NCO, and you should also see to it that you get some further training." I added that it was no longer so important nowadays whether you were a soldier or not, since in a real war it was open to question who needed more courage, the soldier in the field or the civilian in the towns under bombardment.

While taking his leave to go on holiday, the patient met another doctor from the sanatorium in my presence. The doctor wished him all the best and then said: "And what are we going to do about our working groups? We're losing our best NCO." That hit home at once deliberately and unintentionally. We can see in this casual, meaningful remark the effect of *synchronicity,* whose often invisible influence is what probably makes the successful treatment of such cases possible. In a clinic governed by under-standing, the doctors do not talk past each other. Not the fantasy of the officer, taken over from the father and proved wrong by his suicide, but integration into civilian work at the humble rank of NCO was the patient's task. Thus he could find a way of one day himself becoming a boss (father), which would then correspond to complete assimilation.

The reference to civilian duty was a paternal word of advice, so to speak, which also contained something the patient had missed in his youth: the paternal reminder of duty, responsibility, and position in the world. That sort of paternal educative function is all the more effective the more you show the patient, where appropriate, not only love but also trust. That is why, as a proof of our trust, we allowed the patient to drive a car.

In the course of the final consultation, on the occasion of the outpatient checkup, the patient quite unexpectedly and spontaneously raised the question of religion. The vision of light in the core experience, which as an illumination also touched on the question of the divine, made that understandable. In the case of Benvenuto Cellini, for example, the vision of light turned into a vision of Christ on the cross.[3] In our patient's case, the experience of light was not consciously dealt with later, but the religious sphere appears to have been affected and set in motion. The patient said that what had always caused him inner difficulties was that, in religious instruction at school, the priest had condemned all other denominations and religions and had described the fate of all those with a different faith in the most lurid colors. He had never really been able to understand this. He wanted to be a good Catholic, but other people who were not Catholic were probably good people, too. And now he had been helped through a difficult period precisely by non-Catholics.

We told him that his being Catholic was fine. You cannot change your denomination the way you change your clothes, and it is almost always better to keep it, just as it is also better, for example, to keep your nationality and your ancestors. You can only try to understand them better. No doubt it is true that from the point of view of Catholicism all other teachings are false. This is why that statement is also true for Catholics. If religious life were subject to general, public rules, such as civil and criminal law, living together with people of other faiths would give rise to serious conflict. Genuine religious experience, however, is not of a general, public nature. It is individual and part of the individual personality. My truth does not have to be another person's truth. But the fact that this truth of mine is not a private game, but a real truth, is something you can only know when you have been saved out of great need. Then you know that that is the way you are, and this knowledge is not "subjective," but the beginning of a process of individuation. You have to let the other person be and yet not give yourself up, for there are differences between people. So as not to give yourself up, though, you need a very stable point of view. A church that set other teachings on a level with its own in a spirit of freethinking and relativism would put itself at risk and undermine the standpoint of its individual members. It is possible that the priest did not express himself very well towards the patient in religious instruction classes all those years ago. But it was quite logical that he should have presented the teachings of his church as the only true teachings; otherwise, he would not have been able to communicate any firm standpoint at all. Every truth is both individual and general, and this individual-general truth is, for the individual, absolute truth. But only someone who has had real experience can appreciate that. The paradox of religious life – like that of life itself – cannot be learned at school; it has to be experienced.

After his final discharge the patient first went home and then soon after began further training with a German firm of architects. Clinically at the time of his release he was healthy.

The fact that the illness was cured does not in itself say anything about the prognosis. The actual anima problem could perhaps prove very simple for the patient later on. Behind the patient's father lay his depressive female antecedents, and the psychological importance of that burden was still far from clear. But anyone who has come through once can hope that he will come through again.

Finally, I would like to emphasize as a matter of principle that a psychological, psychotherapeutic point of view does not exclude the use of whatever other means of treatment are available; this ought to have become apparent in our case. On the contrary, one-sidedness is to be avoided. Faced with an acute psychosis, the doctor must use whatever means he has at his disposal, and all schematism is misplaced. Electrotherapy and insulin treatment, especially, demand that the doctor be alive to the psychic reality of the patient. It is not the choice of means, but the spirit in which the means are applied that is the task. One has to recognize that what is taking place in acute psychosis is a process of psychic development of the greatest importance and dramatic significance, a process that will reach its goal all the sooner the better it is understood psychologically. If one understands, then – God willing – the task can be achieved.

In conclusion, let me give a summary of the observations we have made. The experience of patient and doctor in the course of an acute psychosis has been described on the basis of the analytical psychology of C. G. Jung and with reference to an individual case (a twenty-four-year-old man). A distinction was made between pre-acute, acute, and post-acute phases of the illness. In the pre-acute phase, consciousness was affected by a loss of energy (*abaissement du niveau psychologique*), while psychic contents that could bring about a reorientation of consciousness took the form of delusions. The acute phase began with the exposure of the parental problem (the father's suicide, hushed up by the mother). In connection with electrotherapy and insulin treatment, a central experience occurred, which among other things had the character of an illumination. The resulting reorientation of consciousness was understood on the basis of the material as a new possibility of reception towards psychic contents. In the post-acute phase, the development that followed from the reorientation of consciousness took shape. The importance of transference and the great value of work therapy were emphasized. The overall course of the illness showed the invasion of consciousness by a complex which at first, owing to the parental problem, was incompatible, but which in connection with the central experience was nevertheless assimilated. It was stressed that such a process of development is more likely to succeed the better the doctor understands it psychologically.

VIII

MEANING IN MADNESS

> Since I am not alone in the world, since
> each of us is, at the bottom of his being,
> not only himself, but also everyone else
> at the same time, my dreams, fears, and
> obsessions are not mine alone; they are
> an inheritance handed down by my an-
> cestors, an age-old possession and com-
> mon property.
>
> Eugène Ionesco[1]

If we talk of meaning in madness, of the meaning of madness, it is
because we want to understand madness. We want to understand
it in context, to find coherence.[2] Where coherence is lacking, we
speak of nonsense. As we know, there is a tendency to think of
madness as nonsensical and incomprehensible, and our inquiry
into the meaning of madness could therefore be considered nothing short of paradoxical.

In addition, it will be assumed that we cannot begin to answer
our question until we know what madness is. On the face of it,
that is easy enough, since doctors learn to define it as part of their
training; there are explanations in every textbook. In 1889 Emil
Kraepelin, the famous Munich psychiatrist, described madness as
a pathologically distorted imagination.[3] In 1916 Eugen Bleuler of
Zurich said: "Delusions are incorrect ideas that are not the product of an error of logic, but of an inner need. They always follow
a particular direction, corresponding to the patient's affect, and
are not accessible to correction through fresh experience or

instruction as long as the condition that gave rise to them per-sists".[4] In 1959 Gottfried Ewald of Göttingen emphasized that madness, with its affective alteration of reality, leads to a completely *altered attitude towards the environment*.[5]

In fact, understanding madness is not so easy, as I discovered in my first term as a student of psychiatry. I was practising as a medical candidate in 1936 at the Charité Hospital in Berlin. The Berlin Olympics were over, and the führer's empire was flourishing. Christmas was approaching, and on the radio you heard the staccato singing of the Hitler youth celebrating the equinox. The doyen of German psychiatry, Privy Councilor Karl Bonhoeffer, introduced us in clinic to a paranoiac, a white-haired old man who suffered from a persecution mania. The councilor, a kindly old gentleman, sat the white-haired old man next to him and drew him into conversation. With great dignity the patient turned to the professor and said, "Yes indeed, Councilor, Germany has yet to clean out its Augean stables, and not only in this world, but also in the next." I will never forget the two old men sitting there side by side on their chairs. I knew that one was a professor; I could hear that the other was speaking the truth. And I realized that the question of what is madness is a difficult one. Of course, the old man's words were somehow strange, even oracular. And yet his oracle needed no interpretation.

It need hardly be said that the question of madness becomes especially difficult when the madman, with his (as Ewald put it) altered attitude towards the environment, lives in a world such as that of Hitler's Germany. One could argue that it is easier to say what madness is when the environment is not as a rule as disturbed as it was in Berlin in 1936. Is the environment, then, not disturbed as a rule? What is it like as a rule? It is hard to see just what it is like when you are living in it along with the madmen; after all, in 1936, I had arrived in Berlin from abroad.

All the same, let us see what observations can be made regarding madness and the environment in a civilized, modern country.

We live in a community. Marriage, parents, and children constitute the family. Larger communities are the responsibility of the municipality and the state. The community teaches its members in educational establishments, administering religion in the church and defense in the army. To serve the good of all, there are hospitals, old people's homes, welfare services for surviving dependents, insurance, and also sports facilities. The cinema and the circus provide entertainment, and culture is offered in concert halls, theaters, and museums; both culture and entertainment are also brought into the home through radio, television, and records. Nearly everyone has a job and goes to work every day; trams and railroads, cars and airplanes help speed things along, all according to the exact divisions of each day.

In this community even madness has its place, which is called a psychiatric hospital, or in plain English, a lunatic asylum. The asylum, everywhere one of the largest public institutions, is evidently necessary, although everyone who can avoids it. To have to go there is a misfortune, to be there, a misery; the asylum is feared, and no one likes to think of it.

But the lunatic asylum is a social institution that was developed at the same time as the schools, railroads, sports grounds, and museums were beginning to be built. In times past the mentally ill were put in chains; they languished on beds of moldy straw and were even thought to be possessed by evil spirits. In the early and mid-nineteenth century, treatment of the mentally ill was reformed and organized. People suffering from madness were housed in monasteries that had fallen into disuse; many buildings, particularly from the baroque era, were available for that purpose. Where none existed, new buildings like army barracks were erected and given pretty names that evoked woods, pastures, alpine meadows, and beautiful views. The patients received discipline, cleanliness, food, and occupation, and their guardian, the nurse, was raised from the rank of a surly warder to that of a specialist.

Then the management of these institutions was put into the hands of scientifically trained doctors, who investigated madness in the way that a geologist examines rocks, a forester, trees and woods, and a linguist, language. Thus these doctors became specialists, namely psychiatrists. They erected a truly impressive scientific structure. Esquirol, working in Paris, listed findings; Kraepelin in Dorpat and Munich sorted them into a system; Eugen Bleuler in Zurich elucidated the system with psychological knowledge. The patient was no longer simply insane. In fact, he *wasn't* anything anymore; instead, he *possessed* and *had* things. He possessed centripetal functions such as sensations and perceptions, concepts, ideas and associations, memory, orientation and affectivity, attention and suggestibility, and where applicable a dereistic (apathetic and nonfactual) way of thinking, a personality, and an ego. Then there were centrifugal functions such as aspirations, decisions, will, and drives. Such was the psychological overview in Bleuler's textbook, and I should add that I find his overview excellent.

In addition to possessing all these things, the sick person could also have a lot of other things: for example, an organic psychosyndrome, dementia paralytica, oligophrenia, toxicomania, epilepsy, or even an endogenous psychosis. One is almost tempted to say that whoever had nothing else at least had a neurosis.

Like a Gothic cathedral, the doctors' scientific edifice grew and became more and more ramified. A distinction was made between manic-depressive and schizophrenic; the schizophrenic subgroups catatonia, hebephrenia, paranoia, and schizophrenia simplex were identified; the patient had holothymic and catathymic reactions; he was mutistic, negativistic, and cataleptic; and all of this was subject to secret rules. Hence it was known that a psychopath could not be psychotic, that senility was incurable, that the schizophrenic burned himself out, and that the epileptic reached a bottom level. Moreover, all of this happened to be true; any reasonable observer had to agree, which meant that the nursing staff, too, had to acquire the basics of the discipline together with all the right Greek and Latin terms.

The patient, meanwhile, continued to live his own life within the framework of this new psychiatry. Julien Green reports in his diary[6] how a gifted Englishwoman spent several months in 1922 in an English clinic. Certainly, she said, during her illness she had experienced moments of extreme happiness as well as deep religious feelings. She had not been badly treated, but she had suffered from the chilly atmosphere. The patients spoke their own language. The doctors were obviously totally unaware of this fact, since their ignorance of what was going on inside the patients was considerable.

Nor should we pretend that the scientific-psychiatric edifice lessened the public's fear of the lunatic asylum. Although people generally did not doubt that the psychiatrists were highly educated and humane doctors, they feared their judgment because anyone who had once been given the label schizophrenic or oligophrenic was unlikely to lose it easily. These designations were all the more useful in public life. Courts of law and the relevant authorities could call on expert scientific reports to find out what was wrong with a patient; and extensive experience made it possible to connect a psychiatric diagnosis with clear, decisive conclusions, so that you knew where you were.

In no way do I consider the imposing edifice of scientific or so-called school psychiatry worthless. If I nevertheless find it unsatisfactory, I know my feeling is shared by many colleagues. The edifice is besieged by raiders who instill doubt into even new ideas. The doubters focus on the truth of the edifice. Sorting mental disorders into a system on the basis of psychological knowledge had the peculiar, practically unavoidable consequence that the original concepts were hypostatized. In other words, originally a psychological concept was a sort of shorthand way of referring to the results of observation. But soon the concept became confused with the thing that the patient "had." The doctor met a patient. He observed that the patient thought and behaved in a curiously two-track fashion, and that it was impossible to form a normal relationship with him. So he called what he saw schizophrenic. But then the patient became a schizophrenic; he had schizophrenia. And the doctor no longer felt that he had a difficult relationship with the patient; it was the patient who had a bad affective rapport. Putting facts in order with the help of concepts is justifiable, but hypostatizing the concepts, turning them into things that a person can "have" is indefensible and wrong.

Today when there is a case of madness, the well-ordered, civilized world we live in perceives it largely through the medium of psychiatric concepts; those responsible for the concepts are the psychiatrists. Increasingly, there are psychiatrists who are asking: Even if we do not hypostatize, even if it is perfectly clear to us that we are handling concepts, not things, do we still see things as they really are when we use psychiatric concepts? Do they help us understand what happens in madness? And there are voices calling for a renewal of psychiatry. That any such renewal concerns the civilized world at large is something I intend to demonstrate.

In order to get a better grasp of the subject, I would like to give three examples. They concern three cases of paranoid schizophrenia, in other words, of the particular subform of mental illness named schizophrenia that is characterized by delusions. This is, so to speak, the classic form of madness. I should add that in all three cases the diagnosis was made, independently of myself, by two or more specialists in psychiatry. These examples will help us see what really happens when civilized society has to have a person taken away to the place where madness is at home – to the lunatic asylum. One thing we know already, and that is that whatever happens is crucially important for the future of the individual concerned.

Case 1. A thirty-three-year-old man, a dairy worker, became increasingly taciturn and eccentric. Then he began to feel himself persecuted. Consequently, in the village where he lived he became violent, began to rave, and was eventually taken off to the asylum in chains by the police. Not long before that, he had undergone treatment for two months in a different institution. His family assumed that the illness had arisen on that occasion in connection with an unhappy engagement and a series of mishaps in moving house. From the case history at the other asylum I learned that *"depuis trois jours, avant l'entrée, le malade présenta un état d'agitation qui s'aggrava rapidement. Il présenta en outre des idées délirantes qui deviennent de plus en plus intenses."* One can see that that sort of conceptualization tells us little about what is happening. But for four weeks I learned nothing from the patient himself either. He was completely mute – mutistic, as we call it; only once he spoke briefly: "It's the end of the world." He was clearly extremely distrustful.

Gradually it began to seem as if something ought to be done for the patient. A gifted nurse offered to see what he could do with him. He then explained to the patient that it was essential that he write down for the doctor what was actually wrong with him, and pressed paper and pen into his hand. The patient responded immediately and wrote the following:

We had a contract saying that whoever withdrew from the contract had to pay an additional five thousand francs. I had put down five thousand francs as a deposit. Stocktaking was to be on August 4. So we did the moving on the last day of July. The moving van left on its own and my parents knew nothing about it. We drove to the owner of the place where my fiancée and her mother [*sic*]. He was selling the house and drove to his brother, who owned a factory making domestic ovens. There we looked at a beautiful oven. A wood-burning electric oven. We loaded it onto the trailer. Then we drove (of course we went back to the flat first). He has a son and a daughter. There we drank tea and chatted. Time went quickly and we had to be on our way. When we arrived, the moving van was already there. We set about unloading. Only, with just the two of us we couldn't work very fast and it was hard work. Last of all came the oven, weighing about 250 kg. Between us we carried it up the narrow staircase. That was too much. Something in me went, anyway it was too much. After that we worked day and night almost. Putting lining paper into cupboards and nothing to eat. In the kitchen we had an electric stove. The gas stove was still connected and we only had electric pans. We were getting low on cash, too, I think. We worked until twelve o'clock at night, and already at three in the morning I could hear the kneading machine in the bakery close by. In the mornings I drove

with Mr. Cheval to the wholesale market. Sometimes you had to
wade your way through it. One Greek grocer had whole crates of
aubergines; the customers would come and test them and crush them
and they went moldy. There was a grocer selling vegetables for soup
there. A small dealer among the big importers. He said to me, watch
out, that Mr. Cheval is a rogue. So on Saturday we drove to the
owner of the block. He was sitting in his office. And then he said to
me, look, you've got to put down another five thousand francs
deposit. That was when it really started. I rang home. They told me
to postpone taking over the flat until everything had been sorted out
in the contract with the landlord. By now things were heating up. He
came up into the flat every day and made a scene. My father had
underwritten the contract. Then on top of everything, my fiancée's
mother accidentally made the bathroom door fall over and smashed
the glass by the bath. The bottles and everything smashed. Then my
condition got worse. I wanted to get away on holiday somewhere.
My fiancée lost her head, didn't know what to do, and in the night
from Sunday to Monday turned on the gas tap. I heard it and ran to
turn it off. On Monday we walked to the hospital. There I held my
head under the water tap for about two hours. Then I think a nurse
wanted to take me away. Then I bit her. And after that I was taken to
the asylum.

Now we can see more of what happened. In clumsy but
strangely vivid language, the man describes the course of events.
The account seems almost surrealistic, and yet it is completely
realistic. James Joyce has shown us broadly what can be said in
such language in his novel *Ulysses*. Our patient reports that the
move itself was somehow hasty, the purchase of the heavy stove
perhaps a mistake, the moving badly organized, and on top of all
that the strange town with the dishonest Greek tradesman con-
fusing. Then they try to cheat him over the flat. To add to his
misfortunes, the bathroom door falls over; the disorder is too
much for him, and he wants to get away. And then his fiancée
makes a suicide attempt. That is the last straw. He loses control,
biting the nurse at the hospital and ending up in the asylum. But
he cannot get over it. It drains him, persecutes him, until he

finally realizes he is being persecuted, and the world comes to an end. Desperately he tries to break free; he hits out and once more ends up in chains in the asylum.

Is this madness the symptom of an illness? No, it is the encounter with an event. That event is called persecution by the overwhelming force of experience; it is called "the end of the world." How easy it is after hearing Bruckner's Ninth Symphony to say, "It was overwhelming." Or, as they say on the film posters, "breathtaking, fascinating." And how shallow all that seems in contrast to this encounter with breathtaking persecution, overwhelming experience, the end of a world. Here it is reality, not an allegory, when the man is persecuted by his inability to cope.

As far as the course of the illness is concerned, we can say the following: Reflective consideration of the sequence of events through writing them down proved a release. In discussion it emerged that the two themes – "being cheated over the flat" and "the fiancée's suicide attempt" – had to be dealt with separately, since the man was not up to coping with the two events in combination. Today, several years after the illness, the man runs his own business and is the father of a family.

As far as the madness is concerned, we can say that the diagnosis "paranoid schizophrenic" is not to be rejected. It served its purpose as far as the biological side of the case was concerned. The levopromazine we prescribed probably had a beneficial effect on the excessive fascination with affect; one of the most important indications for this medicine is paranoia. But the psychiatric diagnosis is completely inadequate for grasping the problem as a whole. It has to be understood that the observed persecution mania is a primal event which is true. Understanding, in this context, also means being impressed by the force with which the event overtakes a person and holds him prisoner. The person is no longer free; he is possessed, in the possession or power of something stronger than himself.

Case 2. Truth, however, is not the only thing we discover in such cases. A thirty-one-year-old man, a carpenter, seems to doctors and staff in the clinic to be agitated. He gives the impression of being dangerous. Furthermore, he has acquired a large, strangely shaped piece of wood, which he carries around with him in a sinister fashion. As a precaution he is put into a cell, before which he is searched. A note is found explaining the strange piece of wood:

> I have decided to reveal yet another secret! God is living on the 11 balls in the mist again. If a man takes a plank of wood and makes 12 holes and marks each hole, the 11th with 11/0, then stands the board on the ground, looks through the 12th hole, then looks up, thinks 12-24, while the woman – who must lie half to the left of the man – sees an apple, then it is possible that a child of God will be born. This has to be done in the woods, since you don't get the right contact with life indoors.

Here, too, there is an event. Everyone else drives to work and works, looks after the fields, maybe goes to church on Sunday to serve a religion that stood by helplessly during two world wars. Here, though, is someone with something else on his mind. By his own efforts he wants to conceive a child of God. He has already got hold of the plank of wood with twelve holes that he wrote about. And the woman who sees the apple recalls Eve, the first woman. To be sure, the man is in the place where madness is at home, in the lunatic asylum. And yet, can the world be hopelessly lost as long as there is one among us who longs for the child of God? The event we see here is of a spiritual nature. And it is living religion. The child of God has been the hope of mankind for two thousand years, and to be a child of God has been its greatest longing. As a child of God, this child differs from the concrete experience "child" precisely by virtue of its divine, nonhuman aspect. As a means of expressing a spiritual state, it testifies to original truth; anyone who, whether deliberately out of ambition or involuntarily through unfavorable force of circumstance, becomes separated from his original character, is reminded by the child of his origin, of the roots he has lost. Let me also quote C. G. Jung here:[7] "In view of the fact that men have not yet ceased to make statements about the child god, we may perhaps extend the individual analogy to the life of mankind and say in conclusion that humanity, too, probably always comes into conflict with its childhood conditions, that is, with its original, unconscious, and instinctive state..." The child of God reminds us of the original condition of mankind in order that the connection may not be broken. Thus the child of God has a dual aspect, an earthly and a divine aspect. The actual ceremony of our man with the twelve holes in the piece of wood is a development of this duality. He maintained that originally there were two holes; he knew of a stone with two holes in it that had survived from the Bronze Age. What is signified here is the dual birth of human beings, the earthly and the divine. In Swiss German as in English, this is beautifully expressed in the baptism: Each person has a father and a mother, but also a godfather and a godmother. With that in mind, our man wrote, "Only then can children come into the world the way they ought to come if man is not to remain an animal." The development from the two to the twelve corresponds to the development of the human-divine contrast in Western culture, as commonly encountered in the prevalence of the second number, from the dozen to the twelve hours, the twelve apostles.

There are just two further points to be mentioned. First, the man wants to participate actively in the advent of the child of God through preparation and his own effort; he wants to be genuinely creative. And second, his note is addressed, curiously enough, to a respected publisher; it was found in a properly addressed envelope. What he does, in other words, is of concern to the general public.

The creative and the public dimensions will become clearer when we consider the third case.

Case 3. A thirty-three-year-old man got into a highly dangerous state of excitement. He had to be overpowered by six men and was transported to an asylum. With sedatives it was possible to calm him down. Soon after his release, however, he became agitated again. His doctor asked me if I would take over the case because the man had some very peculiar ideas which someone really ought to discuss with him; in a large clinic it was unlikely that anyone would have the time to do that. His arrival at our clinic turned out to be quite dramatic: The man was completely beside himself, and it was only with the greatest difficulty that he was led to the clinical department without a fight. There, however, he became relatively amenable, but saw and heard ghosts everywhere, which he described very vaguely. Occasionally he also felt electric currents. It was only after a long time that we were able to learn that before his illness he had gone on a skiing holiday with a young woman, his fiancée. The girl broke her leg on the tour. She was taken to a hospital, where a few days later she died, probably as a result of an embolism. In the hospital, though, it was also discovered that the young woman was pregnant; our patient was convinced that he was the one who had made her pregnant. He developed the idea that the fatal embolism after the broken leg could only have occurred because she was pregnant. So it seemed logical to him that if he was guilty of making the girl pregnant, he was guilty of her death.

The patient was still plagued by ghosts even after having recounted this story. But then he began to draft a document that he held to be extremely important. I would like to give some excerpts from the document, which comprised twenty typewritten pages:

"Blessed Are the Poor in Spirit"

Darwin's theories were politically misused during the Nazi period. They wanted to shake Western culture to the foundations by maintaining that man was descended from an apelike creature, Neanderthal man. The Neanderthals lived in the Stone Age. Nazi theologians maintained that mankind had developed stage by stage, and that an ape had turned into a man. Where man had got his mind and his soul from was something they were careful to keep quiet about; it did not interest them either. Darwin and his successors, on the other hand, claimed only that all life came originally from the sea. In the deep sea there are, as Piccard has demonstrated, minute living creatures, the atoms of life. These atoms of life can give rise to all manner of living creatures. So you do not have to believe that all forms of life derive from fishes. The human embryo is more closely related to the creatures of the ocean depths than to any fish. When nature needs a living creature, those minute atoms are there. So in the earliest period of history, the sea could have washed all sorts of embryos up on the dry land, and man and the animals are descended from them. One should not forget that, although man resembles the animals in physical appearance and life-style, he is also emphatically different in other ways. That is to say, he has understanding and an immortal spirit, or soul, which animals do not have. Therefore, one should not forget that God gave man spirit and soul and made him different from the animals. The Nazi ancestor, the Neanderthal, is thus more a cross between an ape and a human than the ancestor of all human beings. Humans are humans, whether they are black, yellow, or white. It would be wrong and discriminatory to continue to tell our children in school that the Neanderthals are our ancestors.

Who were Adam and Eve? Adam and Eve do not have to have been the first human beings ever; they were just the first to believe in God. I do not believe that man has developed over the course of the millennia, but rather that we have a creative act of God to thank for our humanity, just like the stars. Since the creation there have always been man and the one that apes man, the ape. Maybe the Creator wanted to let human creatures see right from the start what a difference there was between themselves and the animal that most resembled them: Man can think, speak, and create meaning, whereas animals can only vegetate as their instinct dictates. The Bible is the only book that tells us about the time when mankind was born. I have not yet found the Bible to tell lies in any respect. At most it suppresses discrete details. It does not say, for example, where Cain went when he was banished after the first fratricide. I would suggest that Cain was rejected by all the women of his tribe and for that reason took an ape for a wife, and that that is where the Neanderthals come from.

It appears that the Neanderthals did not last very long. Apparently they were an inferior race that soon died out. Since they have so far only been found in Neanderthal, that would seem a fair assumption. But are there not also among our generation descendants of Cain and the ape? Was the moon perhaps inhabited by humans in the dim and distant past? Were there always oceans on our planet? Was the earth once pear-shaped and not round as it is now? What I am writing here is pure fantasy, anyone who does not believe it will not be deceived, but I for my part do not believe what geologists say about the birth of the planet either; it is all speculation, since there was no one on earth billions of years ago, and so there was no one to write it all down.

I do not know whether the weapon that could destroy the earth's entire atmosphere through a chain reaction has already been invented. But one day it will be invented. If that weapon were ever used, it would be the end of life and vegetation on this planet for good. Maybe a few ants would survive. That would be the total Communist victory, since ants have a Communistic state on the Soviet model. And either I am the biggest swine on earth or the ants will win the final victory; they are cleverer and do not eat each other.

Are we the first or the last people in the universe? Both are possible. But God would be a complete idiot if there were no death in our world. Because then, the world would have been annihilated long ago.

What is Communism? Many people refuse to understand the word because it was falsified by the Neanderthal Stalin. The first Communist was not Marx, but Jesus Christ. He established the communion. And he said, "Love your neighbor as yourself." Since without love it is impossible for the universe and life to continue to exist in him. Anyone who skipped school and never learned about the Communist world revolution that took place two thousand years ago will not understand, and ought to go back home with his bad marks in history and leave thinking to horses, since they have bigger heads. Why should it not be possible for us humans to build a new sun? The universe will never be finished as long as there are people who want to work and build on it. When we stop wanting that, we can withdraw into death, the spirit world, and spectatorship.

I imagine that in its original form the earth was a pear-shaped body. Because of its abnormal shape, the earth followed an eccentric path. That way it collided with other stars and over millions of years was scraped round. Most normal people's thoughts seem mad to a second person, and particularly the thoughts of a witty person, because in the mad rush of life nowadays his thoughts get confused. And when the dead think of him, he goes mad and has to be brought back into line with the general way of thinking. Only good psychotherapists can do that. But you cannot force inner peace on a person without robbing him of his personal freedom. The pig-headed and the obstinate have always been the hardest cases. Yet only stupidity is incurable.

Thus reads the patient's document as excerpted. Following the writing of the first draft – a fair copy was written out later – another ghost appeared to the man. This time it was clearly delineated. It was the dead fiancée, and the man had the impression that she had appeared to him to let him know that she was happy in the other world.

We have here a highly individual creation story, which also deals with religious problems and the current political situation in the world. The arguments may not always be very well supported, but the language is forceful; it has enthusiasm, even humor. The dark side of man, the deformed creature conceived by Cain and born of the ape, is starkly depicted. The patient also drew pictures showing how the earth was made round ("a fixed star has just brushed the earth and is moving away") and of "the sun that we can build" (figs. 1-2). The idea that the earth was originally pear-shaped and was ground down to become round is, interestingly enough, one that others besides our patient have had. Professor de Ajuriaguerra, director of the Geneva psychiatric clinic, pointed out to me that the French poet Henri Michaux, who was completely unknown to our patient, in his book *Equador* makes the remarkable claim, *"La terre n'est pas ronde, il faut la faire ronde."* Finally, the creative individual who builds new suns is a last step before the curious conclusion of the document which represents, as it were, a theory of the clinical condition. Thoughts are disturbed by the mad rush of life. And because the dead think of a person, he becomes mad. The cure, bringing the madman back into line with normality, is effected by the good psychotherapist, who robs the person of his personal freedom and forces inner peace on him.

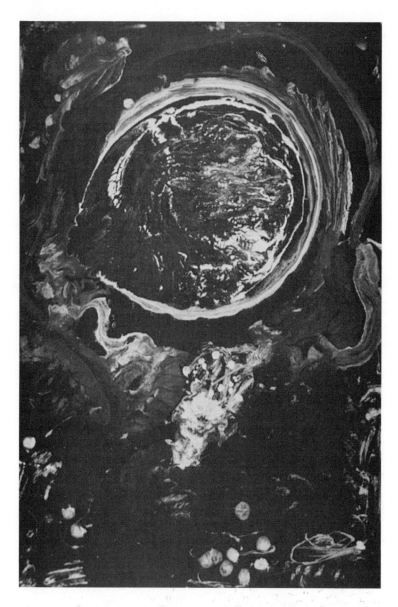

Fig. 1: "A fixed star has brushed the earth"

Fig. 2: "The sun that we can build"

Forcing peace on the patient as the goal of psychotherapy may seem a strange idea. Anyone who met the man could see that there really was a Neanderthal in him that had to be tamed; for in the final analysis, the words of Johann Tschallener, spoken 120 years ago, are as true today as they were then: "To each should be given as he gives to others; to each his own."

As a whole our document is a creative event. A broken world is reconstructed. And just as that old man in Berlin in 1936 demanded that we act not only in this world but also in the next, the reconstruction of the world in our patient's case likewise extends to the other world: The lost fiancée is reconciled and released.

In the treatment of this case, too, as in that of the man who longed for the child of God, the patient's fascination with affectively charged, mythical ideas was countered pharmacologically with levopromazine. We have already discussed the complementary relationship of pharmacotherapy and psychological understanding in a previous chapter (p. 136). I will only emphasize again that pharmacotherapy and psychotherapy are not mutually exclusive, but must work hand in hand in clinical psychiatric therapy. The patient who wanted to create a world and the patient who sought the child of God did not, it must be said, become clinically healthy after the formulation of their views and plans. Although they led an ordered life and were socially well-adjusted afterwards, they were not psychologically or psychiatrically stable, since there is usually a long way to go from the moment of conceiving a plan to the moment of accomplishing it. Nor should we be trying to understand what the patient has expressed primarily in order to "cure" him with it, but rather to share in his life and so to share with him the experience of being human. This is not therapy, but the basis of therapy.

For this patient who wanted to create a world, the creation myth that we read about in books came to life. It became active in the life of an individual. In this connection, we may recall that the first to demonstrate the *continuing vitality of myth* was Sigmund Freud, when he referred to the Oedipus myth in *The Interpreta-*

tion of Dreams. The first to give expression to his emotion at this colossal discovery was C. G. Jung. In the introduction to *Symbols of Transformation,* he wrote:[8] "The impression made by this simple remark may be likened to the uncanny feeling which would steal over us if, amid the noise and bustle of a modern city street, we were suddenly to come upon an ancient relic – say the Corinthian capital of a long-immured column, or a fragment of an inscription. A moment ago, we were completely absorbed in the hectic, ephemeral life of the present; then, the next moment, something very remote and strange flashes upon us, which directs our gaze to a different order things. We turn away from the vast confusion of the present to glimpse the higher continuity of history. Suddenly we remember that on this spot where we now hasten to and fro about our business, a similar scene of life and activity prevailed two thousand years ago in slightly different forms; similar passions moved mankind, and people were just as convinced as we are of the uniqueness of their lives."

This man's individual world creation as well as the other man's search for a child of God are mythical monuments; Jung's words highlight the contrast between them and the ordered, busy world we live in. And it is equally important to both men that man is different from the animals. The man who wrote the creation myth approached me with the request that I publish his writing. And the man in search of the child of God also turned to a publisher. It appears that both men thought that what concerned them concerned the general public, too. Certainly it cannot be a matter of indifference to the general public that such monumental events should take place in the midst of its "hectic, ephemeral life." Primal events of that sort are of an archetypal nature, and they always affect both the individual and society. So it is not surprising that I should have come across the need to make public so-called madness, which is a myth, on numerous occasions.

No doubt it is also important to know that it is not only the privilege of certain heroes of the mind, of poets and thinkers, to encounter the primal event, but that this can happen to anyone. Publication in book form is not necessarily the best solution, though. The world would be submerged in even more paper than it already is. A solution that takes into consideration both the individual and society should also be simpler and more convincing. It ought to follow naturally from the present encounter between man and primal event.

It is characteristic of this modern-day encounter that the individual wants to be active. The seeker after the child of God wants to lie down on his mythical piece of wood so that the child can be conceived. And the world creator would like to build new suns. This activity is clearly a modern phenomenon. People nowadays do not want to wait for salvation to arrive. They will not be patient until grace is bestowed on them; they want to do something. The modern nature of activity was expressed very nicely by Bertolt Brecht:[9] "But one thing has become clear: The world of today is only describable to the people of today if it is described as a changeable world. For people nowadays, questions are worthwhile because of the answers. People nowadays are interested in conditions and events they can do something about."

In active participation, however, man comes worryingly close to the primal event. C. G. Jung clearly identified the danger that arises when many individuals encounter the primal event:[10] "The question then arises whether these many are all complete Godmen. Such a transformation would lead to insufferable collisions between them, to say nothing of the unavoidable inflation to which the ordinary mortal, who is not freed from original sin, would instantly succumb."

And that inflation, that overestimation of one's own ego in the encounter with the primal event, is a very frequent phenomenon. It leads directly to the "disagreeable collisions" that Jung so feared. Overestimation of one's own ego leads to grand, unconcerned, godlike behavior, which can be disturbing and threatening in the ephemeral but ordered world of society. That is why society has the troublesome God-persons taken away to the asylum.

To the observer this seems a thoroughly reasonable step. Because one thing is certain: If a person failed to achieve the necessary humility when in the primal encounter he became a God-man, then in the asylum he finds himself in a place of impotence. In the asylum the doctors and nurses are in charge, not the guests; freedom of action and self-determination are largely taken away, and many who set out to shake the universe end up incapacitated and subject to a guardian. Such things put a stop to the power of ego inflation, which is greatly to be welcomed.

The aspects of mental care that are less welcome were mentioned at the beginning of the chapter. Of course, since the time that Julien Green's gifted English lady was under treatment in 1922, a lot has changed. But the ignorance she complained about among the doctors is still something we have to overcome. It is no doubt commendable that new drugs and new psychotherapeutic methods have been introduced into psychiatric clinics today. But there is still too little emphasis on the simple need to open one's eyes and ears to find out about the event that the patient has encountered. It is not interpretation that is needed, but eyes to see and ears to hear. And the argument that lack of staff makes it impossible to try to understand the patients properly can only have been thought up by the blind and the deaf.

To repeat what I said before: Imposing discipline on the inflated ego, on the illegitimate God-man, is necessary. The humility required of the individual concerned has been formulated by C. G. Jung as follows:[11] "Even the enlightened person remains what he is, and is never more than his own limited ego before the One who dwells within him, whose form has no knowable boundaries..." But for the purpose of understanding what can happen to a person in such situations, a purely medical point of view is not enough.

Just how unsatisfactory it can become is shown in a striking manner by a formulation of Eugen Bleuler's. Bleuler pointed out[12] that a mistake can be corrected but a delusion cannot. And he continued, "The physiological analogy of delusion, therefore, is not error, but faith." This sentence is doubly misleading. If the analogy to madness that we find when we look at ordinary life is said to be physiological, our ideas are steered in the wrong direction. Certainly, "physiological" originally also meant "natural," yet one thinks automatically of something physical, of physiology in fact. Madness, however, touches precisely not on physical, but on mental or even spiritual questions. Furthermore, the parallel to error is clearly not faith, but false belief. It seems that, for the academic in the age of science, the difference between belief and false belief is no longer significant. So although it is not actually wrong, Bleuler's view is formulated in such a way that it does nothing to help us understand madness.

Bleuler was nevertheless an important man. For that reason, a closer look at his formulation can help reveal a crucial point. In madness every individual is a heretic who experiences the presence of myth without regard to faith or denomination. That would be a way of describing figuratively the "inner need" which – according to Bleuler – is the source of madness. It is no coincidence that the mentally disturbed should in earlier times have often enough ended at the stake.

That is the way it is. In such situations ego inflation can lead to "disagreeable collisions." What is required is, as the world-creator patient put it, that the individual concerned be brought back into line with the general way of thinking. And a problem, or task, of that nature is not something that can be tackled by a single faculty. No one will dispute that madness raises medical questions, but there are legal, philosophical, and theological questions, too. The problem of madness as a whole is not a matter for a single faculty, nor is it an academic problem. At bottom it is a problem that concerns everyone, in accordance with Ionesco's words: "Every one of us at the bottom of his being is not only himself, but everyone else as well."

This truth ought to be acknowledged publicly. It is in this sense that madness concerns everyone. The barrier which separates the world of society from the place where madness is at home, the asylum, and which has been strengthened by rigid medical terminology, must fall. This should not be taken to mean that the doors of the asylums should be opened and the insane let loose on the general public. What it means is much more likely to become clear if you visit an institution housed in one of the old baroque monasteries. Because they were monasteries, their architecture breathes an atmosphere of form and spirit. There was no unauthorized admission, and the inhabitants were only allowed out of the building under the strictest regulations. And yet these institutions were not cut off from the rest of society. It is true that only a few people knew the details of their organization, but people knew about the spiritual values that they fostered.

Today these buildings serve new purposes; and new buildings have been added. But the institutions they house should not be isolated from the rest of society. Society should know that a person can be overwhelmed by the primal event, and that life then becomes difficult for him. And it should also know that the fact of being overwhelmed is a sign of the vitality of the human soul. Because that vitality concerns all of us. That is the meaning of madness. We know that the mentally ill never want to believe in their illness. The one-sided understanding of madness as an illness prevents the content of the primal event from being recognized. But if the doctors try to understand, if those affected by madness face not an illness but a living task, and if the efforts of both are morally supported by the public, then it will be possible to see madness in its true meaning. And then the asylum will really become a place where people are cured.

Now, society at large is bound to be affected if it accepts the primal event, madness. What that means can be best described if we consider the particular meaning of madness that we find encapsulated in the literal sense of the word. There is a verb derived from the German word for madness (*Wahn*). If we think of someone in passing, and we say what we are thinking, we call this mentioning them (*erwähnen*). We also have the simple verb, *wähnen,* which means to "suppose" or "fantasize." So "madness" is the German word for fantasy. And for society to recognize madness means for it to acknowledge fantasy, creative fantasy. This means recognizing that it is not the material world but the world of the mind, of creative fantasy, that determines the development of mankind. Such an admission would be bound to have a decisive influence on our still largely materialistic world.

It would mean that the encounter with creative fantasy is not – as is widely assumed – the task of a select few, but that everyone is given this possibility and responsibility. That being the case, we would do well – with all due regard for social discipline – not rashly and casually to dismiss something as nonsensical simply because we do not understand it. Society's acceptance of madness can help us to see the creative element in the community and to let it grow.

IX

THE ATTITUDE OF THE DOCTOR IN PSYCHOTHERAPY

The claim that, in principle, only medical doctors should practice psychotherapy is heard more and more frequently nowadays. And yet it is not at all easy to show why, in principle, that claim is justified. Of one thing we can be certain, however: that the high value placed on a medical standpoint does not imply that every doctor practicing psychotherapy does so from a medical standpoint. It is not just the doctor's degree that counts, we know that much. Nor do I dispute the view that a layman, given training and experience, could reach a point where he, too, would be able to practice psychotherapy from a medical standpoint. One could also argue that there are several other professions besides that of the doctor which fulfill the conditions for successful therapy in the field of the soul. I am thinking of teachers, psychotechnicians, theologians, maybe even lawyers – in fact any profession whose task it is to educate, judge, or guide people, or to stand by them in times of trouble.

The question we have to consider, therefore, is what, in very general terms, are the distinguishing characteristics of a doctor's attitude towards human problems. The medical attitude, like any other professional attitude, is in large part acquired, following strict rules laid down by the collectivity, the state. The prospective doctor is trained, first at a university and later in the hospital, to observe clinical pictures. He has to get to know all the plants and vertebrates; he has to study the chemical and physical structure of living things; in anatomy and pathology and in the clinic, he has to learn about the condition and functions of the healthy and the sick individual alike.

Finally, he has to be able to relate his observations to the sum of medical experience by making a diagnosis of the observed condition. That diagnosis then forms the basis for therapy. Therapy is always based on observations and experience passed along by doctors past and present; sometimes it is also influenced by the doctor's own ideas, but in most cases it is ultimately determined by the rules of medical science and art. Anyone who does not follow the rule that practical experience and practical knowledge must dictate what a doctor does is not a real doctor at all.

But this training also imparts something else, something that makes a doctor the sort of person people come to for advice and confide in. He has learned to look at whatever he sees completely objectively. He respects the task the patient has given him, the task of removing a disorder, but he does not judge that disorder in any way. And even if he does judge it privately, the question of whether the disorder is right or wrong does not influence his actions as a doctor.

Let me give two simple examples: A housewife with seven children and a drunken husband, clearly oppressed by the circumstances in which she has to live, contracts pneumonia. She goes to the hospital where she is looked after and treated. To all appearances the illness is a blessing for the woman since now at last she has time for herself.

A young musician, who is about to take his final exams, also falls ill with pneumonia. His studies are interrupted, he gets out of practice, misses his exams at the conservatory, and in the end loses a year, as a result of which his already hard-pressed father has to make further financial sacrifices. Obviously for him the illness is a disaster. The doctor, however, does not ask himself whether illness is either a blessing or a disaster. He deals with both cases according to the rules of his art. He takes things as they come and, if he does say anything on a personal level, he limits himself to words of encouragement and comfort and listens to what the patient has to say, knowing that he has to keep everything to himself in accordance with the rule of confidentiality.

This attitude is extremely important, at least at the beginning of treatment, and particularly in psychotherapy. Let me give another example: A married woman without children suffers from an abdominal complaint which, after repeated specialist examination, is recognized as purely psychological. In the psychotherapeutic interview she explains that she is deeply upset by the indifferent and unfeeling attitude of her husband. Although he gives her presents of jewelry and precious stones, and is always buying her flowers, he will not grant her one wish – to have a little dog.

The doctor naturally suspects that this seemingly harmless wish conceals a deeper psychological problem. He may feel inclined to have the husband come and see him, and to make it as clear as possible to the fellow that he should see to it that he buys his wife a dog without delay because if he does not he is a scoundrel. But this is where the doctor must not forget that he is not supposed to make value judgments regarding the clinical picture. He cannot know what the significance of the dispute might be for the couple. Why exactly does the woman want a little dog, a living creature, to relate to, when we know that what matters for a woman is the relationship in itself; the object could just as well be a piece of furniture, a chest of drawers, for example. What is it that this man has been unable to give his wife that now makes it impossible for him to give her the dog? Why then is the marriage childless? Is it that the husband is psychogenically impotent? For the doctor simply to demand that the wife's wish be fulfilled would, if he were unlucky, be like putting a bare, undisinfected hand into an open wound. It could cause a catastrophe. A tragic conflict which is on the whole well compensated and which has so far caused only mild symptoms of disorder in the wife, would be laid open with all its destructive potential, without the doctor having any guarantee that he would be able to close the wound again. All that the doctor can do in such circumstances is simply to take note of the situation as it is described to him by the patient. Bearing in mind the element of paradox, the ambivalence predominant in every conflict situation, he will pass no judgment. He must know that he has to follow that line consistently – and the patient will expect that knowledge from him, too. This is precisely why the patient decided to consult a medical doctor and not a teacher, lawyer, or theologian, who would have judged the situation in terms of principles or ideals. Otherwise, she would hardly have had the courage to speak about such matters, so dangerous are they and so charged with ambivalent tension. And it is only when the doctor does nothing, when he simply listens to the patient and acknowledges her conflict as a clinical picture, that there is a chance – as long as the existing solution is not the best that can be achieved under the circumstances – that things will gradually start moving and that the conflict will begin to develop in ways we cannot at first foresee.

The fact that the conflict is acknowledged by the doctor as a clinical picture means that, even if the doctor does nothing but watch and listen, something very important takes place. Whether the doctor intends it or not, the conflict is completely reevaluated. Until now the patient has always thought that, while he was perfectly all right as a person, he was unlucky enough to suffer from this stupid, disgusting disorder. But now, with the doctor, the disorder becomes the center of attention. It becomes so worthy of attention that even a scientifically trained person finds it perfectly right and proper that it should be looked at. Apparently the disorder might even be interesting – otherwise the doctor would be bored to death with such patients, which does not seem to be the case (and is sometimes explicitly denied). It is also assumed that the doctor might know something about this supposedly stupid and meaningless disorder, something that is important and could somehow put an end to the disorder. Simply through the patient's having consulted a doctor, then, the disorder is seen in a new light. At the same time, the notion that what until now seemed a meaningless and disgusting business could be important and possibly even in some way understandable casts doubt on existing attitudes, on the patient's current outlook. Thus the seed of a new, revised outlook and of the devaluation of the old, superseded outlook is sown, since it was from the perspective of the old outlook that the disorder was judged to be stupid and incomprehensible. It is essential to remember in all of this that the impulse for such a development does not come from the doctor; rather the development begins the moment the patient decides to consult the doctor. In this situation, therefore, the doctor is merely an instrument and, in accordance with his role as an instrument, all he has to do is watch what happens and react as the rules of his art dictate. It is not advisable for a doctor to attempt more, to feel called upon to lead people or indeed to shape their lives. If he does, sooner or later he will have to pay for his presumption, a presumption that is thoroughly detrimental to his own spiritual hygiene. The sight of a would-be leader of men reduced to helplessness and despair by his own conflicts is one of the most tragic things I have ever experienced. I cannot help but think of Dr. Faustus in the medieval puppet plays, mercilessly crushed by the powers to which he had sold his soul.

I would like to try to explain how a new development can emerge from the changed situation resulting from the doctor's acknowledgment of the clinical picture with the help of one final example: A hitherto successful industrialist, manager of a large firm, is bewildered and dismayed to find that he is beginning to lose his ability to tackle decisions and his spirit of enterprise. Even the simplest decisions begin to pose a problem. He is scarcely capable of writing a letter, because the consequences of even the most trivial action now seem unforeseeable and uncertain to him. As a result, he suffers from a considerable state of anxiety, feels depressed to the point of utter despair, and considers suicide. It is only with the greatest effort that he succeeds in keeping up appearances. It is in this state that he goes to see the doctor. He explains that he used to be the center of energy in his firm. His energy flowed into everything that went on. Thinking back, it seems to him that he was like a miniature sun and all his colleagues and employees were like planets orbiting around him, deriving warmth and impetus from his initiative. Now unfortunately, at a time when he feels exhausted, powerless, and frankly eclipsed, his firm is facing a crisis, brought on by the aftermath of the war, which really demands his full attention.

The simple fact that the patient thus describes his state, while the doctor listens in silence, means that the most important step has already been taken: The patient has admitted that he is not at all like the sun, does not radiate energy, does not foresee or initiate anything. Through that act alone his almost superhuman qualities are reduced to human proportions. In fact, it would be fair to say that his earlier state of mind was at least as abnormal as his present one, since we know that no one is like the sun, and we also know that our decisions and actions are only to a limited extent our own; innumerable coincidences and imponderables often play a decisive role that we fail to notice and are even less able to control. Anyone who insisted on knowing with certainty whether what he planned to do was right and would succeed, before actually doing it, would eventually (if he were clear in his own mind about what he wanted) never leave his room. You might meet someone by chance and that meeting could disrupt all your plans completely. But there is really no need to aim for such perfection. It is enough to have a clear perception of life's difficulties, to weigh up the possibilities, and to make your decision as best you can. Then all that remains is – paradoxically, you might almost say – for you to take full personal responsibility for the decision, even though it is only partly your own. Because taking that responsibility means quite simply that you have decided to stand by your fate and thus also yourself.

In the case under discussion, the patient's condition seems particularly meaningful. Not only does it form the transition to a better understanding of life, it also intervenes in the existing situation to regulate it. The crisis in the firm where the patient is a manager calls for some fundamental new decisions, decisions so new that it is impossible at the moment to guess what they might be. It might even be better if the patient were to give up as general manager altogether and start a new life. In any case, his present situation prevents him from doing anything precipitate. Whether he likes it or not, he is forced to accept the situation, to take things as they come, and so he has the possibility of discovering something really new, i.e., something of which he has been completely unaware. Before, he seemed to himself to be almost omniscient, an attitude that automatically prevented any genuine reorientation.

The task of accompanying the patient through the difficult period naturally leads beyond simply acknowledging the clinical picture. It is a matter of working together with the patient to recognize that his present condition has a meaning and should be accepted as an important part of life. Exactly how this is to happen can only be decided in the light of later developments. In states of this kind, which in their rigor and atmosphere of fear are comparable to the experiences of ancient mystery cults, a person's entire life comes to a head. A fundamental transformation of the personality is in preparation. The transformation is already hinted at in the motif of the old sun that has lost its brightness; meanwhile the patient has to wait in darkness for the return of the bright star on the other horizon, in other words, for the reemergence of psychic energy from a new source. Questions of guilt and atonement are raised, everything is subjected to revision, and all human relationships are altered. The doctor will constantly seek to understand the patient by making observations and comparisons as he has been trained to do. He will constantly try to show his understanding and, insofar as possible, communicate it to the patient.

While the simple task of acknowledging the clinical picture is not for the psychiatrist alone, but has always been part of every doctor's job – and in particular that of the family doctor – the task of understanding the more complicated psychic disorders demands a special training. Generally it needs more than basic common sense to understand such cases. But we should not forget that statements about the mind always have to be understood figuratively, because psychic reality is beyond rational description. Therefore, it is not surprising that psychotherapy can be practiced from a variety of very different points of view and is divided into numerous schools. Each of these alternatives has its justification, since each can enable the psychotherapist to adopt a specific position from which to tackle the difficult situations that he has to deal with. Whatever happens, though, he will be careful not to intervene in a conflict situation prematurely, because it is in such a situation that the patient experiences himself as well as the powers that are stronger than himself and stronger than the doctor. There is a concentration of energy which no one should interfere with and which is likely to burn more than just one's fingers. The danger of overhasty judgment and intervention is superbly described by Jeremias Gotthelf in *Anna Babi Jowager* (vol. 2, chap. 11) where, following the death of her nephew, the curate feels obliged to give Anna Babi some foolish theological advice on saving her immortal soul:

> "He had no idea that he had done any damage... It is possible that some young cannibal of a doctor or pietist might say to himself that, when it's a question of saving souls, whether some poor individual loses his mind or not is neither here nor there; you have to be ruthless – go right ahead, they would say. It is possible that some would talk like that, but only medical and pietistic cannibals, that's for sure... Anna Babi screamed out loud as if she had been stabbed. And she had in fact been stabbed with a dagger, a spiritual dagger... A priest should not drive the red-hot blade of conscience into a heart he does not know, any more than a doctor should stick a kitchen knife into a person's eye when he wants to touch a cataract."

It is a different matter if the conflict raises questions that concern the therapist himself. If that happens, not only is the therapist what I would like to call the human mirror of the patient, but the patient is also the mirror of the therapist. Often one finds intellectual stimulus, often one is annoyed or otherwise emotionally affected. Then, it seems to me, it is not right for the psychotherapist as a person to hide behind the façade of the impassive psychiatrist or psychoanalyst. On the contrary, he should not hesitate to show his reactions and to stand by them. Of course, the therapist has to react in the right way. For that reason, anyone who wants to work as a specialist in treating the more complicated forms of mental illness should not only possess a thorough knowledge of psychology in general, but should also have worked seriously on his own psyche. It is not for nothing that all schools of psychotherapy insist on a training analysis. After all, the doctor has to find the spiritual knife with which to touch the patient's cataract within himself. He is himself the instrument of therapy, and if he wishes to be properly equipped, he must first of all deal with himself. But given that preparation, he can afford to react when necessary. And in doing so, like a catalyst, he will exert a therapeutic influence. But he will also have to acknowledge in all humility that in fact the patient has just as much psychological influence on the therapist as the therapist has on the patient. Thus there arises between the two people a relationship that may well contribute more to solving social problems than any number of cleverly devised plans.

To summarize: The attitude instilled into medical doctors through their training is equally valid in psychotherapy. It provides a standpoint from which the therapist can observe the clinical picture and where possible, understand it without making judgments or acting rashly. One could say that, to begin with, the therapist should take what he sees and hears in the spirit of what Kipling called a "just-so" story. That is enough to start with and is effective therapeutically. Human conflicts should not be interfered with – that would be too dangerous. But where the therapist himself is affected, he should react. It is only through his being affected that there can be further developments that are beneficial and right.

X

MEDICAL AND PSYCHIATRIC DIAGNOSIS

When in a psychiatric examination a medical diagnosis is made, two specialized branches of medicine come face to face. In such an encounter, the facts are illuminated from two different points of view and, consequently, there may emerge something of fundamental importance.

I propose here to describe a case which is in itself neither out of the ordinary nor new; it is intended to give practical interest to the discussion.

In the spring of 1956, I was consulted by a thirty-year-old woman, an academic. At that time she had been married to a respected official in Stuttgart for a year and did not yet have any children. Because for some days she had been feeling persecuted, she had taken refuge with relatives in Kreuzlingen. There were spies lurking everywhere, she felt, and red cars belonging to the Gestapo were patrolling the streets, ready to take her to prison. She had refused hospitalization when her husband suggested it, assuming that any such suggestion could only be a trap to lure her into a state-owned building where she would then be arrested. But since she was hardly sleeping and was becoming more and more panicky, her relatives decided to take her to see a neurologist.

The relatives, and eventually the patient too, lived in fear of learning that this was the onset of a long-term mental illness. In the examination the patient presented the picture of subacute paranoid schizophrenia. Physically she was a woman in full bloom, whose shining eyes with a slight exophthalmos immediately suggested exophthalmic goiter; there was also a swelling of the thyroid glands, a fine tremor when the hands were out-stretched, and a pulse of 104, as well as a history of supposedly significant, but indeterminate, weight loss. In view of the patient's state of panic, compulsory hospitalization seemed inhuman, and a more exact clarification of the medical side of the problem in a clinic equipped for that purpose also seemed impractical. The technical details of a determination of basal metabolic rate, for example, would no doubt have been seen by the patient as an attempt to gas her. It is not unusual in outpatient psychiatry to find that it is impossible to obtain a more accurate medical diagnosis. The patient, often desperate and in a panic, wants help immediately, while a more thorough examination, perhaps in a laboratory where there might be "sinister" pieces of apparatus or even the feared "rays" (x-ray), is out of the question, and so the physical diagnosis often has to be made purely clinically and on the spot.

I diagnosed a thyreotoxic psychosis and prescribed 0.05 gm of 4-methylthiouracil three times daily as well as one tablet of cyclobarbitone calcium for the night. After five days the pulse was down to 80, the tremor had disappeared and the panic was greatly reduced, even though there were still very occasionally delusions. A reduction of the thiouracil dose to 0.025 gm twice daily proved premature; the symptoms returned with greater severity, but then lessened again on a dose of 0.05/0.025/0.05 gm thiouracil daily. The white-cell count after two weeks was 7200. After a month of treatment – I had seen the patient seven times as an outpatient – the condition was stable, with a pulse of 78. However, the patient still felt listless. All the same she decided to return home with her husband, who had meanwhile come to Kreuzlingen, and to start looking after their home again. Before she returned to Stuttgart, I had the patient examined by Professor Dr. L. Heilmeyer at the university hospital in Freiburg im Breis-gau. He found not only an iodine avidity of the thyroid paren-chyma but also an increased iodine metabolism, which made the concentration of protein-bound radio-iodine in the plasma climb to twice the normal level. The patient was referred to a medical specialist who would continue treatment in her home town.

In view of what has been said so far, the situation seems simple enough. An incipient psychosis has been recognized as a thyreotoxic psychosis and treated accordingly. However, looking more critically at the diagnosis, the situation seems considerably less simple than that. It is particularly important to ask oneself whether thyreotoxic psychosis exists as an illness in the first place, one that a person can "have" and is clearly defined. What, for example, do the old masters of psychiatry and neurology, Eugen Bleuler and Robert Bing, have to say on the subject? E. Bleuler[1] found it impossible, in cases of goiter (either those he read about or those he treated himself) to distinguish with confidence between psychosis and schizophrenic states. R. Bing[2] believed that thyreotoxic madness does not exist and that the connection between goiter and psychosis is coincidental. For my part, I am convinced that a psychiatrist can achieve successful results with the diagnostic and therapeutic procedure I have described (I myself have treated three severe and several minor cases of a similar nature), but that one should beware of being too hasty in confirming the diagnosis or claiming to have found a "disease." It only needs a slightly more detailed history, and the case can appear in a different light. As I mentioned, the patient was collected by her husband. On that occasion he stated that since their marriage his wife had been suffering from vaginitis. In addition, for the past few months she had been feeling generally tired. They had then decided to consult a gynecologist. But although they had an appointment, they never got to the consultation since, two days beforehand, the psychosis had started and the wife had run away from home. The husband assumed that his wife had a neurosis which, in the panic caused by the imminent gynecological examination, had led to psychosis.

In any case it is once again undecided whether what we are dealing with here is a neurosis, possibly even a psychosis as the relatives and the patient herself clearly supposed, or a hormonal disorder as the psychiatric examination seemed to show. It is easy to understand why clinicians such as Bing and Bleuler should have been cautious in their attitude towards the question of thyreotoxic psychosis; that the former should have denied its existence, and the latter – more wisely, perhaps – should have considered a differential diagnosis to schizophrenia impossible. When in a case such as ours, there is a search for the "cause of the illness," it immediately becomes apparent just how dubious such causal explanations often are, and to what extent the demonstration of the supposed causal link merely reflects the point of view of the doctor examining the case. Granted, at the time of the examination, goiter was present; that much is certain and was proved in Freiburg. But whether the psychosis that brought the patient to the doctor was caused by the goiter, or whether a long-standing neurosis led to a panic situation which triggered a hormonal disorder which then in turn intensified the psychic symptoms, is something each has to decide for himself. One could say, for example, that the woman had already had hyperthyreosis for a long time. The hormonal disorder manifested itself in fatigue and a nervous strain resulting in vaginitis. But fortunately, before an inappropriate – gynecological – examination could take place, the hormonal finding became accentuated to the point where psychiatric symptoms also appeared; these then led to an appropriate form of treatment being given. But one could also say that the woman had long been neurotic. The fatigue she complained of is consistent with a subdepressive loss of energy, and the vaginitis suggests that the neurosis may had have something to do with the sexual sphere. The patient's sexual phobia became apparent in the panic that overcame her shortly before the gynecological   examination. The neurosis became acute and led to secondary hormonal disorders. It is possible that the secondary goiter accentuated the psychiatric symptoms so that, when the metabolism was brought under control with the thiouracil, the psychiatric symptoms also receded a little. Far more important, though, was the fact that the thiouracil medication gave consistency and continuity to the treatment, so that the patient was guided and calmed through suggestion. The choice of medicine may not even have been so important. "A good doctor can cure his patient simply with water" is an old Russian proverb.[3]

Accordingly, it is impossible to decide whether in the case under consideration a panic caused the goiter or the goiter was the cause of the panic. Both views are possible and arguable, and neither of them can be proved. The fact that these two contrasting points of view are equally possible does not mean, however, that the treatment prescribed in our case was wrong. It only means that the diagnosis of thyreotoxic psychosis does not imply anything about what the illness actually *is* or what the patient *has*. The diagnosis, then, indicates the choice of a point of view from which to examine and treat the case. And that choice of a point of view is not an insight into the true state of affairs, which is often far more complicated, but a *therapeutic act.*

The dual aspect of a borderline psychiatric-medical case of this sort is also important for the prognosis, and in particular for the future continuation of therapy. Whether the goiter is the cause of a psychotic disorder or a psychosis is the cause of the goiter, either way the case is far from simple. It is doubtful, therefore, whether the treatment I have described – whether it is thiouracil or guidance and suggestion – can achieve a satisfactory compensation in the long term. Medically, the doctor will have to decide whether a strumectomy is needed to stabilize the condition once and for all. On the psychological-psychiatric side, he will need to consider whether there should not be a more thoroughgoing course of psychotherapy later. In a final consultation with the patient and her husband, I cautiously touched on both possibilities and equally cautiously left both options open. It was not for me to anticipate the therapeutic decision of any colleague who might happen to see the patient later, whether to pursue the chosen somatic approach (operation) or to change to a different approach (psychotherapy); I had to allow for both possibilities. Because, however important it may be in such cases to take a position on one side or the other and to follow a clear line of treatment, it is equally fundamental that you should not lose sight of the dual aspect, there being two possible points of view. That is the only way you can strike the right balance in your dealings with the patient; and it is the only way to avoid prejudicing possible future developments.

It is very important to avoid prejudicing those developments. It is obvious that the doctor's decisions, particularly in cases of this sort, can sometimes change the course of a person's life. From a psychiatric point of view, for example, the choice of medication or surgery as a form of treatment in the case I have described represents a conservative therapy. In other words, an attempt is made through external measures to compensate the situation in such a way that the conflicts (here the sexual conflict) do not erupt into the open. This is also known as social compensation (e.g., patching up a marriage). In psychotherapeutic treatment, on the other hand, the conflicts are liable to come to the surface, even endangering the marriage. In our case, the decision was that, for the time being, the best thing was to try to relieve the symptoms through medical diagnosis and therapy; any attempt to unwrap the psychological problem would have been inappropriate. Naturally, to a large extent that decision can be put down to the state of relations between doctor and patient at the time and to the temperament of the doctor. But precisely for that reason future decisions should not be prejudiced. At a later stage the state of relations may be different and, in particular, any colleague handling the case must retain the right to act in a way that fits his nature. I realize that, in saying this, I am implying that patients usually do not choose their doctors in a random fashion but rather in a meaningful way. That assumption is not unjustified, though, when one considers that the patient often weighs his or her choice of doctor far more carefully than we doctors imagine.

Having examined a psychiatric-medical case in some detail, we might now ask whether there is also a similar dual aspect to conditions that are either clearly psychiatric or clearly medical. This is best seen in highly acute psychiatric or medical conditions. Through the excess of emotion, acute delirious catatonic schizophrenia lowers the resistance to infection, in particular to acute pneumonia, to such a degree that an infection can take hold with sudden and overwhelming force. On the other hand, acute pneumonia can also cause toxic delirium. If pneumonia can cause delirium and delirium can cause pneumonia, not only do you have a mirror-image situation; you also find that, whichever point of view you adopt, you often discover features that are almost indistinguishable. I have seen patients in medical and psychiatric clinics who demonstrated identical clinical symptoms: findings of pneumonia with corresponding temperature, pulse, and blood count; and anxiety-ridden, agitated hallucinosis with visions of fire and massive hallucinations of medium intensity (e.g., of animals). The distinction between the clinical-psychiatric and medical points of view is similarly blurred in the choice of treatment. The circulation requires clinical supervision first and foremost; the course of the infection is monitored on the basis of temperature control and blood count. Cardiac drugs and chemo-therapy or, alternatively, antibiotics play a vital role. And the agitation has to be countered with sedatives so that breathing is not at risk.

Meanwhile, the doctor knows that he can only bring the patient through this critical stage if he sees the clinical event as a crisis in the life of his patient. He has to relate to the patient and his milieu (his relatives, for example); otherwise, he will not meet the needs of the moment and will not be acting from a deep bond with his patient. If there is no bond, he cannot act with the sureness of instinct. He has to see his patient's illness not only as a clinician sees it, but also in the way that a poet might describe it when he is recounting a person's life. In *Effi Briest* Theodor Fontane de-scribes the sufferings of a young woman who dies of tuberculosis. No one would suggest that Effi's illness could be seen simply with x-rays, or that it could be explained solely in terms of droplet infection and Koch's bacillus. No one would suggest that a case like hers could nowadays be cured simply with streptomycin, for example. Anyone who believes it could is blind.

A good doctor knows this. In his memoirs the great French surgeon René Leriche gives us the following account of his method of clinical examination:[4]

À partir du moment où j'ai eu quelque expérience, c'est-à-dire vers la quarantaine, je me suis dépouillé des plis rigides de la méthode scolaire que l'éducation impose justement à tous. Je m'en suis affranchi, n'y revenant que quand la complexité l'exigeait. Sans calcul, je devins spontané, instinctif, m'adaptant à l'état d'âme que je percevais... Spontanément, j'agissais de façon que le malade se sentit compris *dans sa vérité* et pris en charge tel qu'il était. Ce n'était pas du cancer de M. Durand que je m'occupais, mais de M. Durand tout entier, avec ses angoisses et ses soucis.

Leriche demonstrates magnificently how the response to the clinical findings during the examination and interest in the patient as a person can be fused into one. He does, of course, examine the patient, and he also reserves the right to go back to textbook methods of examination in complicated cases. But for the most part he acts spontaneously and instinctively, as his personality prompts him, and relates to the mental and emotional state of his patient, to his fears and worries. Thus he finds access to the truth of the patient through spontaneous action. Whereas, with the case described at the beginning, we said that diagnosis and therapy also depend to some extent on the immediate state of relations between patient and doctor and on the temperament of the doctor. Leriche would add that whoever acts spontaneously, in harmony with that relationship and his own temperament, will reach a diagnosis and prescribe a therapy that is no longer simply a matter of discretion but part of the truth of his patient. That he must first have learned the textbook method is something Leriche quite rightly stresses.

If in both borderline and highly acute cases medicine and psychiatry are to collaborate because a "dual standpoint" is needed, then we have to ask ourselves whether a similar approach is not called for in all cases, even in less complicated or less dramatic ones.

For the medical specialist this would mean that he would constantly have to ask himself whether, alongside the medical diagnosis and therapy, he has paid sufficient attention to the place the illness occupies in his patient's life. Especially when the situation gets difficult, for example, when the patient fails to follow the doctor's orders properly or the relatives put obstacles in his path, it is good for the doctor perhaps to widen his perspective in that direction. The psychiatrist, by contrast, will constantly have to examine whether, in addition to the psychotherapy and psychagogy, he has paid sufficient attention to actual infectious or hormonal disorders. He will have to think in terms of purely preventive measures and look ahead, warn of physical risks, and protect against them, not forgetting either that the physical risks include the risk of accident (e.g., when a patient in a submanic state decides to go mountain climbing or driving). When a doctor claims that the patient could have been helped if he had not died first, it is evident not only that an essential factor has been neglected but also that the treatment has been one-sided and one-track, which indicates a lack of spontaneous rapport with the patient.

From what has been said, it might seem to follow that even a doctor with specialist training should go back to something like the attitude traditionally adopted by a good family doctor. As we all know, that conclusion is not quite correct; at least, it is too simple. It is too vague, too emotional, and filled with nostalgia for the old days. What is missing is any mention of how an approach that deals with the whole person can be combined with highly specialized methods of diagnosis and therapy.

In this investigation I have tried to show how every specialist diagnosis and therapy is in itself one-sided. This one-sidedness, however, is no cause for criticism. On the contrary, the treatment of a case from a single, specialist point of view is itself a therapeutic act. It is positively required that a doctor take a clear position and pursue a clear policy. At the same time, he has to be aware that in doing so he gives a one-sided account of the illness and its course. If he is aware of that one-sidedness, he will not forget the other possibilities. If he is a master of his art, like Leriche, he will know how to combine both possibilities without abandoning his own point of view. If he sees his own one-sidedness, then he will be able when necessary, as was demonstrated by the case described at the beginning of this chapter, to change his diagnostic and therapeutic standpoint, which is again a therapeutic act.

The requirement that in diagnosis and therapy a case be seen from two different points of view, and that one should nevertheless clearly commit oneself to a single point of view, does not seem all that complicated. But anyone who considers how great the tendency to one-sidedness is in most people, knows that it is not easy to meet.

Postscript: As indicated at the beginning of the chapter, the case chosen as an example was examined and treated in 1956. My reflections on the diagnosis were noted down at the end of that year. Later I was able to carry out a catamnesis, which threw a revealing light on the question of the therapist's change of standpoint. In 1958 the patient's delusions recurred and were successfully treated in her home town with rauwolfia preparations. In 1960 the patient entered a state of agitation colored by paranoia, in which she constantly demanded that her husband, from whom she still had had no children, be examined by a specialist. Then she came back to me for treatment, since a second course of rauwolfia had brought no improvement and had led to strange attacks of trembling; these attacks, lasting from two to three hours, were characterized by trembling affecting the entire body. My impression was that features of Parkinson's disease, brought on by prolonged use of rauwolfia, had combined with a goiter-related tremor to produce a peculiar symptom. On discontinuing the rauwolfia, the attacks soon stopped. With thiouracil and melleril, the psychic state also grew calmer. The patient then went to Italy with her husband on holiday.

On the face of it the diagnosis of thyreotoxic psychosis was still justified. On their return from holiday, the husband and the wife came back for a review. This time, strangely enough, the husband appeared paranoid. He claimed that his wife was deliberately trying to annoy him by using southern German turns of phrase (he himself was from North Germany); and then to really get him worked up, she would for example, slam the car door a second time when it did not shut properly the first time. Meanwhile, in the patient the symptoms of exophthalmic goiter had increased once more, so she stayed with us for further treatment.

It emerged that the psychic disturbance – in this case the paranoid symptoms – had not disappeared as a result of the anti-goiter treatment, but had been transferred to the husband. In the patient the finds of exophthalmic goiter were not consolidated, so at the end of 1960, we had a strumectomy carried out; histologically, the surgical specimen was identified as diffuse goiter. At Christmas 1960, the patient went back home to her husband in a sound state.

Once again, the somatic point of view seemed to have been proved right. The psychic disturbance in the patient's husband, however, left a question mark hanging over it.

Only four months later the patient was back. Everything, even the tiniest thing the husband did, seemed to her an affront. There were no symptoms of goiter. After consultation with the husband as well as with the patient's close relatives, it became evident that the affective relationship between the patient and her husband was hopelessly wrecked. It was decided, therefore, that the patient should not go back to her husband. This led to a stabilization of the psychic findings, and the paranoid symptoms receded.

In the course of the year 1962 divorce proceedings were started. When the decree was announced, the patient presented short-term depressive symptoms of a typically endogenous character, without any paranoid features.

Thus at the third attempt, the psychiatric-psychological point of view could no longer be avoided.

XI

THE CLINICAL IMPLICATIONS
OF EXTRAVERSION AND INTROVERSION

The concept of an individual's constitution implies that all people are not the same, that they are different. Yet they are not infinitely different. Some people are similar in disposition. Thus it is possible to identify constitutional types.

Extraversion and introversion are typical constitutional attitudes. The primary interest of the extravert lies in the object, that of the introvert, in the subject. Interest, in this context, means conscious presence; it is where the center of our attention is.

In order to investigate the consequences of the two possible attitudes, that of the extravert and that of the introvert, we first have to identify the moment at which the distinction between object and subject arises. Object and subject are intended as concepts that describe human experience.

Object and subject emerge as separate entities whenever the relationships obtaining in a *participation mystique* (Lévy-Bruhl) are subjected to criticism. In the *participation,* as in paradise, all things are woven into one. Criticism marks the dubious birth of a consciousness that makes distinctions, symbolized by the taking of the apple from the tree of knowledge. Criticism generates consciousness, and then what was previously one becomes two: object and subject. This is an event, a dynamic phenomenon with significant consequences. The archangel Gabriel was the one who enforced them. Psychologically it is an event that can affect the whole personality, for example, in a small child or in largely unconscious, primitive people. It brings with it differentiation; it is bound up with intellect and is an unnatural act; and the consequences are responsibility and the seed of guilt.

But even in a differentiated adult there is still a sector that is not yet developed, still some degree of unconsciousness, and so sometimes there are conflicts that arouse criticism and dissolve a surviving *participation mystique*.

Conflict means that two people who are in a relationship do not harmonize fully with one another. If an individual experiences such a disturbance of harmony, he is as the experiencing person the subject. To him, the partner with whom there is conflict becomes an object. Conflict becomes a source of consciousness if it is worked through. If, on the other hand, the antagonists resort to fighting, what they are trying to do is forcibly to push aside the task facing them.

At such moments of disturbance, the following changes can be observed in a person: affect is generated, which means that innervation and the flow of ideas are disrupted; there are frequent conspicuous gestures, and calm judgment is replaced by over- or underestimation. There is also the anima/animus problem. Under the influence of affect, a woman becomes the caricature of a man, full of opinions that are really prejudices, whereas a man becomes the caricature of a woman, full of emotions that would be better described as moods. In that way, though, affect becomes the first step towards completeness, since it activates the contrasexual possibility that every person has within him. Under the influence of affect, a person experiences difficulty in adjusting to the environment, now seen as an object, which in turn arouses affect in others. Here we see the problem of the shadow. In situations of conflict, one's actions often have the opposite result from what was expected. The agitated mother, for example, thinking that she is caring, is often for the child a dangerous, suffocating mother.

The classic example of the way conflict and affect expand consciousness is that of growing children when they discover that their parents are not as perfect as they had thought. This leads to anger at the parents, affect, and to problems of adjustment, troublesome behavior. Now the way is open for the child to ask, "Who am I?" And also, "Who are my parents?" And then, too,

"What is meant by 'I'? What is meant by 'father,' 'mother'?"
Thus subject and object are born. A distinction is made between
"I" and "Thou." And we know how quickly the archetype ("father" and "mother") then emerges. The image of father and
mother is linked in the original *participation* with something great
and comprehensive, extending as far as God the Father and the
Great Mother. When anything on that all-encompassing scale
encounters criticism, the affect that is generated is considerable.

Wherever a *participation mystique* is dissolved, everyone
faces the same problem. The problem is of a general nature; it is
the subject of general psychology. However, the manner in which
each individual tackles the problem varies according to whether
primary interest is directed towards the subject or towards the
object. The concepts "introverted" and "extroverted" thus belong
to a special branch of psychology that investigates the different
forms in which a general process is manifested. The way in which
an individual deals with the dissolution of the *participation,*
therefore, indicates his or her constitutional type.

The introvert focuses primarily on the subject. In a conflict
situation, he becomes conscious of whatever it is in the subject
that is causing the disturbance, that is to say, the affect. His
concern is to pacify the affect, and he sets about this task with a
will by looking for a new, more calming attitude. Little or no
attention is paid to the external cause of the disturbance, the
object. He tends to a mild degree of autism, because he is not
much interested in what others might think. Thus the introvert
soon comes to resemble his shadow (e.g., to become odd, cranky,
arrogant, or even nasty). This difficulty is not met with raised
consciousness, that is to say, with insight, but with evasion. An
introvert can systematically limit his circle of friends, and by
picking and choosing avoid difficult choices. The reduction of
contact with others is often the first sign of an incipient developmental disorder in the introvert. Often, however, the introvert
comes up against the external world which everywhere besieges
him. He can find himself a victim of the "malice of the object"; he
can be unlucky. The bad luck that follows the hero of F. T.

Fischer's *Auch Einer,* for example, with his "evil eye," has no end; he is the one who talks of the malice of the object. An introvert can easily break a leg on the stairs, even a young person. He does not watch out for the steps because he is too busy dealing with his feelings of anger at the fact that the runner is such an ugly red (in order to be able to say, "It doesn't matter what color runners are," or perhaps, "I don't like that red because it's not my color"). In that way he pacifies his affect, but becomes outwardly a shadow, in this case, for example, uncertain. The emotion recedes, and so he is spared any nervous metabolic disorders. External disturbance – breaking a leg, for example – is more likely; everywhere he goes he bumps into things, and so he will probably have more contact with the surgeon, though mostly in the area of minor and medium surgery. So far, the attitude of the introvert seems to entail certain problems, but not yet a crisis. It seems, at this stage of development, as if the spirit were being satisfied but the instincts were being neglected. Intellectually superior, as it were, but unworldly, the introvert comes into collision with the world; generally his life is not at risk, though. There is perhaps the worry of whether – in order to stay calm and avoid contact with the world – the introvert does not suffer from inadequate and constrained breathing so that he is relatively susceptible to tuberculosis of the lungs. If the constriction to the patient's breathing is legitimated by making it an obligation for him to lie down, then the outcome can be favorable; in any case, the rest cure, as the classic form of treatment, meets the introvert's need for withdrawal from the dangerous world.

The extravert focuses primarily on the object. He wants to organize his relationship to the object. He devotes himself to it and does not seem at all shadowy. He overlooks the fact that something is going forward inside him, that something inside him has been set in motion. And that fact sometimes becomes apparent to an observer, despite the extravert's good adjustment to the object. The ignored affect manifests itself in occasional changes of mood, which can easily take on a shade of animosity. Thus, for example, an extraverted boss is well adjusted "so long as you're careful how you treat him"; it remains questionable, though, whether you do him a service by treating him carefully! The affect that the extravert fails to recognize can have an effect on his metabolism; liver complaints are typical. The heart can also be affected. Spas recommended for the metabolism and the heart are therefore popular with extraverts. At this stage of development, the extravert is more likely to come into contact with the medical specialist than with the surgeon. As a rule, though, his life is not at risk while he obeys instinct, as it were, but neglects the spirit. Here, too, there is a problem but not yet a crisis.

It is curious to note that, so long as there is only a *problem,* the introvert needs external medicine, surgery, whereas the extravert needs internal medicine. That is because the inferiority of the introvert lies on the side of the external world, that of the extravert on the side of the internal world.

But the first stage of development is followed by a second. The introvert's outward maladjustment can increase. Despite all efforts at evasion and despite the attempt to limit the number of objects through selectivity, there may occur a collision with the world that makes it impossible to ignore the reality of the object. And then the affect can no longer be satisfied; it manifests itself, and the introvert is filled with animosity. And in fact he is usually noticeably more venomous than a harmless extravert. When the introvert turns his attention to the external world, he is animated by a sense of inferiority, and can often seem something of a malcontent, or even paranoid.

The extravert, on the other hand, reaches a point where his affect screams for satisfaction. Then the affect breaks through violently, adjustment to the external world is destroyed, and a very dark shadow emerges. The extravert is confronted with the question of the subject, of his own reality as a person. He turns inward with a sense of inferiority and becomes self-tormenting or hypochondriacal.

In this situation, the introvert should be more extraverted and show an interest in the object; and the extravert should be more introverted and pay more attention to his own little self, the subject. The inferior typological opposite, therefore, sets a task. If the task is not accepted, there are clinical consequences; the individual follows a path that veers off into illness. In such cases, it is fair to say that "whoever strays from the path of God falls into the hands of doctors" (Jes. Sirach 38:15)!

The individual clings one-sidedly and frantically to the original constitutional type. But it is already superseded and has lost energy to the opposite attitude; now it finds itself in an *abaissement* (P. Janet). Janet describes vividly how in such cases the intellectual level is liable to spontaneous oscillations, so that the individual can still appear intelligent at times but is usually extremely foolish. The originally superior attitude is no longer functioning reliably; it has become inferior. The originally inferior attitude, however, has not yet established itself, so that the old attitude seems devalued while the new one seems undeveloped. Accordingly, the existing system threatens to collapse. The effects of the collapse, if it occurs, are apparent right down to the physical level.

The introvert becomes susceptible to sudden infections that can be dangerous. Excessive affect can disturb his metabolism to such a degree that the situation becomes critical. The danger now comes from within; the introvert needs the help of a medical specialist, for his life is in danger. Because his resistance to infection is low, highly acute pneumonia can appear, particularly in schizoid individuals, who are normally resistant to infections. The metabolic disorder conditioned by the affect can also in some cases lead to intellectual death (schizophrenic dementia) (cf. p. 139).

The danger facing the extravert is no less considerable if he tries to maintain his superseded primary attitude. His adjustment to the external world no longer functions reliably; now he is susceptible to accidents and is likely to need a surgeon. The surgeon, however, is often called upon to carry out major surgery, because the accidents of the "decompensated extravert" tend to be serious (e.g., road accidents, mountaineering accidents). It is tragic to see the once so active extravert a cripple, laboriously sewn back together by the surgeon. But it is not always the surgeon who is called upon to help. Often the problem assumes a legal dimension. Blindness to the subjective side and the dark shadow can lead to bankruptcies, fraud, and other forensic matters. Thus the extravert can put his own life at risk through accident or foolish crime. One does not need the death penalty to destroy a life; prison can destroy a life, too. Here intellectual death takes the form of a death by shame.

At this second, critical stage, therefore, the introvert needs the help of a medical specialist, the extravert, that of a surgeon. As a crisis, this stage is an alarming condition that presses towards a change. The alarm makes the individual look for a way out. But evasion only succeeds if personal development is completely suspended; therefore, evasion means suicide. The introvert commits suicide in a burst of affect, as a panic reaction to the affect he so hates for destroying his subjective peace and calm. And to think that there was a time when the problem of affect could be solved so cleverly. The extravert, too, can evade the problem through suicide. He devotes much sinister thought to planning it and so manages not to have to work through the loss of object security. And he uses the adjustment that once helped his success purposefully to destroy himself.

In the moment of *crisis,* therefore, the introvert displays the symptoms of the extravert, but on a more threatening scale. Precisely when he refuses to accept extraversion, it manifests itself of its own accord in an archaic form and with a malignant character. Clinically the disruptive affect forces him, not to visit a spa, but to accept hospitalization. The more dangerous disorders can be treated much more successfully nowadays than even twenty years ago. Infections can be treated with antibiotics, and metabolic disorders can be controlled with drugs such as rauwolfia and chlorpromazine. However, the danger of physical death (collapse of the body's defense mechanisms under the pressure of excessive affect) and of intellectual death (metabolic disorder brought on by the affect) has not yet been overcome. The danger comes from within. All the same, the progress achieved in the treatment of the crisis of the introvert over the past twenty years is astounding; of particular importance in this respect is the progress that psychotherapy has brought in its treatment of "intellectual death."

The extravert, for his part, when he reaches the crisis point, displays the symptoms of the introvert in exaggerated form. Latent introversion manifests itself in a threatening, archaic form. The collision with the world is no longer restricted to the "malice of the object"; it is a catastrophe. If the extravert collides with the external world through an accident, modern surgery with its improved technology and refined techniques of anesthesia can achieve a great deal; orthopedic surgery can help people who have been crippled to resume active life. The two world wars, collective catastrophes of the Western world, brought unimagined progress in surgery. If the collision with the world has legal consequences, there is always the fact that the death penalty has been largely abolished and that a movement is under way to make imprisonment less a means of destroying the criminal and more one of educating him. However, we still have a long way to go in the field of the psychological care of offenders. Besides, the extravert also faces the risk of death. The danger comes from outside: death by accident or social destruction.

The inferiority of the introvert's extraversion can also be observed formally, for example, in perception: Fascinated by the external world, he can intuit things, but his intuition is inferior. And so possibilities that would be seen by a developed intuition are not seen, while what the introvert does see amounts to "impossible possibilities." It is only a small step from this to persecution mania with delusions. When the external world is perceived through the function of sensation, it is not grasped in any order but in a scattered fashion. Here, too, the findings are often quite pathological. Thus on a formal plane, we find not only the problem of the constitutional types but also that of the psychic functions – intuition, sensation, feeling, and thinking – which can equally be either superior or inferior. An investigation of the problem of the functions would have to include a detailed description of the pathological forms of thought and behavior; however, too little work has been done in this field.

The inferior introversion of the extravert shows itself in the fact that, although attention is now concentrated on the subject, the effort of concentration often degenerates into helpless self-torment. This is above all because the extravert fails to make adequate distinctions. In criticizing himself, the extravert mistakes a part for the whole. The whole person is rejected on account of a single error. Feelings of guilt, even delusions of sinfulness, can be the result. The autonomy of personal development is also very clearly recognized, but it is perceived as a catastrophe. It is always striking how the decompensated extravert is filled with a mixture of astonishment and panic when he perceives his own inner dynamic. On the whole, the result is a depressive picture. Occasionally the fascination with the subject fades, and then all that remains is the original extraversion, now inferior, in the form of a mania.

Thus the crisis of the constitutional type leads beyond the sphere of dangerous physical disorders into the sphere of psychiatry. One could say that in the case of the introvert the inferior attitude produces schizophrenic symptoms, whereas in the case of the extravert it causes manic-depressive symptoms. If the psychotic symptoms are pronounced, the constellation of the inferior attitude can be observed particularly clearly. In major psychiatry the fundamentals are often obvious. One just has to listen to what the person says. An introvert can, when he turns his attention to the external world, display a paranoid reaction. Then a bizarre fascination with the object emerges, and the individual says, "He did such-and-such, he may, he may not, he ought to, he wants to." At the same time, the inferiority of the extraversion is projected onto the object. Accordingly, the other person in the encounter is seen as evil, foolish, or reprehensible. In any case, what interests the introvert is the "He"; interest is transferred from the subject to the object. If in the opposite case, an extravert who ought to be more introverted becomes melancholic, what we find is that his thoughts circle exclusively around the subject. He says, "I have done such-and-such, I ought to, I am." And the inferiority of the introversion is unloaded onto the subject. As a consequence, the extraverted depressive thinks himself guilty, unworthy, weak and impoverished.

The following psychiatric experience is also worth mentioning in relation to constitutional types. Generally psychiatrists recommend that schizophrenics be discharged from hospital as soon as possible (the so-called early discharge). In the case of manic-depressives, on the other hand, a late discharge is called for. In view of what has been said about the problem of the inferior opposite attitude, one could say that the schizophrenic who is primarily introverted, but shows signs of a developing extraversion, should return to normal life as early as possible in order to practice his extraversion. The manic-depressive, however, who is extraverted by nature, should remain in the clinic long enough to practice his still undeveloped introversion. In making this observation, we are following an essential principle of modern psychology: It is not always necessary to use psychotherapeutic methods when we want to get closer to the patient psychologically. It is often better to follow the rule of classical psychiatric medicine, although at the same time the patient's condition has to be carefully observed and assessed psychologically. The question we then must ask ourselves is this: "What does the condition want from the patient? Where is it leading him?"

Although psychopathological cases illustrate certain problems very clearly, they are not of course the norm. Normally the problem of the inferior opposite attitude marks the transition to the second half of life. Not infrequently, the first symptoms are marital conflicts or other difficulties in social life. In pathological cases the problem often appears much earlier. One reason for this may be that familial or environmental influences have falsified a person at an early age. It can happen, for example, that a constitutional extravert is imbued with an introverted attitude which is foreign to him and from which the original tendency strives to release him as soon as possible. The clash of a healthy but underdeveloped extraversion with a falsified, inappropriate habitual consciousness that is introverted can lead to very complex, often pathological findings. An introvert can experience the same falsification. I believe that the falsification of a constitutional type by the environment is an important cause of the psychotic symptoms of so-called psychopathies. Experience with younger patients, using psychotherapy to treat psychosis, has shown again and again that environmental factors in early youth have a tendency to falsify the patient's character.

The ideal case, then, would be one in which the development of the opposite attitude proceeded without interruption. As always in medicine, though, and particularly in psychology, such cases are far from easy to observe precisely because there is no call for observation. When disorders do arise, however, one finds all possible gradations, and it hardly seems feasible to arrange all the observations systematically. Nevertheless, the following details are perhaps worth recording: The introvert who needs to develop his extraversion is relatively prone to stomach and duodenal ulcers. In the case of the extravert who needs to develop his introversion, the danger in my experience is rather that of early arteriosclerosis. The fact that psychotherapy can help in the treatment of stomach ulcers is well enough known. What is perhaps less well known is that even relatively serious arteriosclerotic findings can show a surprising degree of improvement under appropriate psychotherapeutic treatment, quite contrary to the defeatist psychiatric prognosis given in every textbook. Particularly, therefore, in cases where an extravert needs to work on the opposite attitude and is at worst depressive, the importance of arteriosclerotic symptoms should not be overestimated in making the prognosis; psychotherapy should not be neglected on their account. In fact, generally, pessimism based on organic findings is to be avoided. The effects of the organic findings, even their development, depends not least on how fit the individual concerned is psychologically.

From what has been said, the following overall conclusions can be drawn regarding the implications of the typical constitutional attitudes in clinical practice: The introvert aims first and foremost to satisfy affect, and comes into collision with the external world. He risks injury in minor and semi-serious accidents. The extravert adjusts to the external world and ignores affect. In his case it is metabolism and circulation that are at risk. To that extent there is a problem.

Sooner or later, both types face the task of developing the inferior opposite attitude. If this task is not achieved satisfactorily, disorders can occur that are usually severe and sometimes even fatal. In the case of the introvert, infections or pernicious metabolic disorders can take hold. The extravert is at risk of serious accident, sometimes of criminal behavior. The introvert is furthermore prone to ulcers of the stomach and duodenum, the extravert to arteriosclerosis. What we see here is *the crisis resulting from the inferiority of the originally superior primary attitude.* The crisis is *somatic,* in some cases *social.*

During the crisis, the introvert's fascination with the outside world manifests itself in paranoid-schizophrenic symptoms, and the extravert's fascination with the inner world, in melancholic symptoms. *The crisis resulting from an overwhelming fascination with the originally inferior opposite attitude is psychic.*

With regard to the psychiatric aspect just mentioned, it should be emphasized that, even during the crisis, the spontaneous, original primary attitude remains visible (alongside the physical constitution, masterfully described by Kretschmer). When an *asthenic* schizophrenic turns to the external world, his spontaneous interest is in the subject. Accordingly, his affective rapport with the external world is poor. What characterizes the pathological extraversion of the introvert, therefore, is bad affectivity corresponding to the introversion. When a *pyknic* melancholic, on the other hand, turns to the internal world, his spontaneous interest lies in the object. So his affective rapport is good; and this good affectivity is maintained even in the context of the extravert's pathological introversion.

It is striking how – against all the resistance of habitual consciousness – the psychosis helps the inferior opposite attitude to break through. The introverted schizophrenic is brought into contact with the external world by an eruption of aggressivity. And the extraverted melancholic shuts himself off from the world, with the idea that no one understands him and no one can help him; in that way he is thrown back on himself. Accordingly, the pathological symptoms in cases of psychosis are often a sign that the opposite attitude is demanding to be realized; it is important for therapy that that fact is recognized.

We now have to consider the demands that a modern medical understanding of the problem of constitutional types ought to satisfy. In very general terms, it is obvious that any medical, surgical, and psychiatric complications that arise in the course of the development have to be treated in accordance with the rules of medical experience and the doctor's art. Beyond that, however, it is often important to establish the diagnosis that the patient is a person who needs to work through this crisis in order to realize his inferior opposite attitude. For this method of typological diagnosis, it is useful to listen very carefully to what the patient says and to consider what physical type he belongs to. It is also essential to remember that the crisis in which the patient finds himself creates added dangers. The situation has its own dynamic, and is moving towards a turning point that is both fearful and fruitful. The therapist must, therefore, be particularly careful and attentive. If, for example, the inner stability of the introvert collapses, an infection can take hold extremely swiftly. Antibiotics must be administered promptly. In case of doubt, the white blood cells must be counted regularly; it is not enough just to check pulse and temperature. If the white-cell count goes above 10,000, antibiotic treatment should be started (cf. also p. 124). If, on the other hand, the outward adjustment of the extravert collapses, the increased risk of accident has to be considered. Risky outings in the mountains, even driving a car, should be strictly forbidden.

Besides a clear medical viewpoint, what is also required is an understanding of the psychological content of the symptoms, whether physical or psychological. Pathological symptoms are eccentric and inferior. What we have to recognize in their eccentricity and inferiority is the individual's effort to deal with the inferior opposite attitude. In that sense the medical symptoms are to be seen positively, that is, not as a pathological aberration, but as a way towards personal wholeness.

The goal of development, then, would be the merging of introversion and extraversion in the same individual. A state would have been achieved in which the division of the world into subject and object is replaced by a living relationship in a new unity. Such development thus aims to reunite what is divided.

XII

FEAR, TRUTH AND CONFIDENCE:
LIVING WITH CANCER

> [The doctor] knows that the sick, suf-
> fering, or helpless patient standing be-
> fore him is not the public but is Mr. or
> Mrs. X, and that the doctor has to put
> something tangible and helpful on the
> table or else he is no doctor.
>
> C. G. Jung[1]

My contribution to this subject takes the form of a study based on
personal experience; what I would like to do is look at the facts
and see what insights can be gained if we confront them squarely.

But first, so that we know what we are talking about, I will
describe the disease of cancer. Originally, cancer meant the crab,
the hard and – when cooked – red shell of the familiar clawed
crustacean that is supposed to walk backwards. Hard and red, like
the shell of a crab, is also how the entire thorax of a woman
becomes if a cancerous tumor of the breast is not treated and is
totally neglected. It is a deplorable sight that has become very
rare nowadays, since it rarely happens any more that such a
serious illness is allowed to take its natural, destructive course.
The last time I saw the, so to speak, classic picture of cancer was
in 1934. My teacher in surgery, Professor Henschen at Basel,
showed us students two Alsatian peasant women. In their rural,
ignorant surroundings the disease had developed unchecked.
They had been sent to hospital in a hopeless condition, emaciated

and squashed up inside the hard, red, tumorous shell, to be looked after through the final stages. Even in those days such findings were a rarity.

The possibility of operating at an early stage, and afterwards perhaps of checking the development of the disease through radiation treatment or growth-inhibiting drugs, has made pictures such as that just described almost a thing of the past. Cancer, however, has still not been defeated. On the contrary, the problem of cancer has become more urgent. Thanks to the general progress of medicine, people now live longer, and more and more people reach the age where cancer can develop; cancer is incomparably more common among older people than among the young.

In principle, the development of cancer is always the same. The animal organism is a harmonious association of cells. Every cell respects the functioning of the others. When a cell divides, the genetic material contained in the cell nucleus is also carefully divided. In that way the organism as a whole and every part of it always has the basic qualities that are characteristic of the individual. And cell metabolism with its step-by-step method of breaking down food ensures that the organism derives the maximum benefit in terms of nutritional energy. Cancer is a disruption of this harmony. A group of cells – perhaps at first a single cell – drops all consideration for the organism as a whole. That is anarchy. The anarchistic cancer cells forego the careful division of the genetic material so that way they can multiply rapidly. They no longer try to fit into the organism as a whole; they form an independent tumor, ruthlessly invading other organs, forming metastases, and spreading along the pathways of the bodily fluids. Through their egoistic, simplified metabolism, they squander the body's food energy and so eat away at the substance of the healthy cells. Thus the unharmonious, unscrupulously greedy tumor grows, while the harmonious cells of the body dwindle. Mostly this process is accompanied by pain, because the tumor also eats into sensitive nerve fibers.

The cellular anarchy of cancer is justly described as a malignant tumor. The best treatment is the complete extermination of the focus of the anarchy, removal by operation. Where radical surgery is not possible or proves unsuccessful, radiation therapy and medication can be used. Medication offers the best hope for the future. Because the cancer cell differs from a healthy cell in its metabolism and its method of reproduction (through division), it ought in principle to be possible to find an agent that will destroy the cancer cell without damaging the healthy cell. Unfortunately, we are not yet that far ahead. Radiation treatment and medication often help considerably, but they do not yet offer any certainty.

With cancer, therefore, patient and doctor are in a situation that is dangerous and full of uncertainty. Cancer creates a crisis; in other words, the situation gives cause for concern, and the way out is called "change." Will things change for the better or the worse?

Such situations easily give rise to considerable emotion, or what we call affect. Cancer is a disease the very name of which is charged with emotion. The forces of destruction that we have just described are familiar not only to the pathological anatomist, but also to every lay person. Accordingly, the patient is alarmed when he hears the word "cancer" spoken. The doctor is not unaffected either. Any doctor who has examined the first x-rays after an early operation to remove a cancer of the breast and has discovered the small black spot that was the first metastasis, anyone who has examined a patient with a supposed irritable bowel and has felt the coarse tumor that makes an already extensive cancer all too probable, knows about the affect the doctor, too, experiences.

The affect, the emotion aroused by the diagnosis of cancer, has the same qualities as affect in general. Innervation and thought processes are disturbed. Restless, distracted, gesticulating behavior can be a consequence; this behavior is accompanied by a tendency to make false judgments, overestimating some things and underestimating others.

In a critical situation such as arises when the diagnosis is cancer, disturbed behavior and thinking are obviously dangerous.

The shock caused by the discovery of the disaster can prevent doctor and patient from finding the right solution. They may panic; they may become afraid. And a person who is afraid cannot act. "In fear a person shrinks back, which is of course not the same as flight, but a spellbound immobility." That is how Heidegger (*What is Metaphysics?* 1929) describes what I would like to call the state of being transfixed by the hypnotic gaze of danger.

The reason for the fear, however, is not the affect alone. The reason for the fear lies rather in the fact that the person whose emotions are aroused in the moment of crisis lacks orientation. If he had an orientation, he would not be spellbound, because then he would have a goal and he would be able to act.

In order to orient ourselves, we have to be able to assess the situation. And our assessment must reflect the actual circumstances. An assessment which does that, we say, is true.[2] Accordingly, truth can overcome fear and lay the basis for orientation.

We have said that an assessment is true if it reflects the actual circumstances. We might question whether such an assessment is of any use to doctor or patient in the case of cancer. I believe it is, but the question has to be looked at more closely.

First of all, what is cancer? Cancer is not in any sense a fact, an actual circumstance. Cancer is a medical concept. The fact we encounter is not cancer; the fact we encounter is the particular person, the individual who is sick with cancer. As a living person, the individual has many other attributes. He has his character, job, family, and position in society; he has his field of vision, convictions, outlook on life, passion, and love; he also has a life story. And this individual finds himself in danger; the way out is uncertain. In order to banish fear, in order to find the way forward, we need to find the truth. And to that end, we have to investigate the actual circumstances of the patient. How else could anyone interpret them accurately and find the right, true assessment?

Cancer is a threat to the whole person; it is a matter of life and death. Statistics cannot help in dealing with an individual case, a person afflicted with cancer. Because even if I know that for a given type of cancer there is a 75 percent chance of a cure, I still have no idea whether the present case is one of the 75 percent that are cured or whether it belongs to the 25 percent that are not cured; so I am no wiser than I was before. Or even if I try to see the problem from an intellectual angle and take my cue, for example, from the fine observation of the psychosomatic specialist A. Jores[3] – "Illness has its role to play in the passage to maturity" – I still have not begun to understand the case in hand.

Thus in dealing with a serious and dangerous illness such as cancer, there is no way around it: One has to investigate the actual circumstances such as they are in the case at hand. If you then order them correctly, you may discover a truth that, despite the variety of manifestations, affords fundamental insights.

Having many such fundamental insights can be called experience. A person cannot be said to have experience if he simply comes across the same thing time and time again. Experience is what a person acquires if he always finds something new in familiar situations. Anyone who has traveled the stretch from the outskirts of a town to its center on the local train a thousand times is by no means an experienced traveler. But whoever keeps his eyes open will be able to gain experience of travel without having to sail around the world, because he will see a variety of actual circumstances.

Therefore, although I am by no means a round-the-world yachtsman in the field of cancer research, I will have to write about what I have seen if I want to talk about truth in relation to cancer. I would like to make it clear in advance that the material I intend to present is almost exclusively concerned with patients who are not resident in Switzerland, and that – likewise on grounds of medical discretion – I will give only brief details of personal matters. Even so we will see that there are many sides to the problem.

Case 1. I was consulted – twelve years ago now – by a forty-five-year-old Swede, married, a doctor of medicine and dentistry, and ambitious and successful in his job. He said that he would like to recuperate a little in Switzerland after a bout of "flu" and that all he wanted from me was some information on an unimportant professional matter. In the course of our conversation I discovered that, in order to treat an angina which had still not quite subsided, he had been giving himself daily injections of penicillin. This prompted me to carry out a physical examination, which he said was wholly unnecessary. I found that one of the pharyngeal tonsils was swollen to the size of a nut and hard. Therefore, I sent the man to a surgeon, who carried out an exploratory excision. The following day my secretary reported that the Swede wanted to speak to me urgently and was completely beside himself. It emerged that the surgeon's office had inadvertently telephoned the result of the excised tissue directly to the Swede, instead of to me. The result stated that he had a malignant tumor (sarcoma) of the lymph tissue. I realized that the man was in a dangerous panic, and so I asked the surgeon to get in touch with the anatomist who had examined the tissue immediately. The anatomist agreed to write a report of the examination that could be shown to the patient; he wrote that the microscope findings showed a tubercular tumor of the pharyngeal tonsils, a dangerous but not malignant condition. The Swede allowed himself to be persuaded and reassured. Filled with fresh hope, he said: "That means I will be able to go to Finland again this year as usual for my elk hunting." But the situation still gave cause for concern, and I must admit that even then I associated the elk-hunting trip vividly in my own mind with the idea that the man was unconsciously, but revealingly, referring to the "happy hunting grounds" that were waiting for him. The tumor, of course, needed treatment – specifically, radiation treatment. We managed to convince the Swede that it was standard practice here to start treatment of any such tuberculosis with radiation treatment. Under radiation the cancerous tissue melts like snow in the sun and has already disappeared by the second dose. (Lymph sarcomas usually respond well to radiation treatment.) Two months later, however, the Swede visited me again. He told me that, two months before, he had arrived at the clinic for the second dose of radiation rather too early and had gone straight into the radiology room. There on the doctor's table, he had seen the pathological anatomist's real findings, and had realized that he was in fact suffering from a malignant tumor. But by then he had overcome the shock and was able to accept the truth. Previously it had been different. If we had not succeeded, immediately following the disastrous telephone call from the surgeon's office, in convincing him, even if only for a few days, that he was not in fact suffering from a malignant tumor, he would have shot himself that same night; he had already obtained a revolver for the purpose.

Shortly after that conversation, the patient traveled to Finland to hunt elks!

So we see, one should not necessarily tell a patient that he has cancer, even when the diagnosis has been made, because the patient's fears regarding the hopelessness of treatment and the disease itself are often exaggerated. Even – or above all – a patient with medical training can see things all too pessimistically. And anyway, it is almost always a mistake to confront a person with a difficult situation so abruptly and without careful preparation. It is good to remember Jores's dictum: "You can kill a person even with the truth."[4] The short-term deception of the patient was not a lie, but a life-saving medical intervention. The truth in this case was not what the patient thought: "I've got cancer; I've had it and it's going to be torture." The truth began to emerge only in the course of treatment: The disease was surprisingly harmless and completely curable. One bold question remains: Is it possible that the patient's great burst of emotion, his affect, which suddenly turned from fear to hope and in which according to our physiological knowledge his nervous system (especially the vegetative system) and hormone metabolism played an important part, also influenced the curiously successful course of the illness? I can only pose the question; I cannot answer it, but I will come back to it later in this discussion.

Here I would like to touch on two rather important side issues. Even a medically trained person should not treat himself with drugs, such as penicillin, that require a clear indication. The danger of making a false diagnosis and giving the wrong treatment is too great. And second, every doctor, whatever his specialization, should consider every finding that appears. In this case, the psychiatrist had to recognize the physical danger, and the surgeon and the pathological anatomist had to help overcome the threat to the patient's life that lay in his psychological reaction.

However, the patient's mental reaction is not always the same by any means. In order to know what measures are right psychologically, one needs not only a physical diagnosis but also a psychological diagnosis.

Case 2. Not so long ago I was treating a respected and skillful Belgian lawyer. The gifted sixty-year-old had, over the past several years, slid into the habit of alcohol abuse. Besides the impairment arising from frequent drunkenness, he also demonstrated typical symptoms of alcohol damage, including superficial thinking and other signs of brain damage. In addition, he was insanely possessive of his wife, a feature common among alcoholics. After several weeks of abstinence, he recovered somewhat. There remained, however, a childish, quarrelsome attitude which made him see faults in others while remaining blind to his own shortcomings; in other words, he was the sort of unreasonable and troublesome addict who is so difficult to treat. In the course of a wave of flu in the sanatorium, it was found that he was running a temperature every evening rising to 38 degrees Celsius by six o'clock and falling back to normal again by ten. When these daily oscillations remained constant for a week, we sent the patient for a fluoroscopic examination and an x-ray of the thorax. The patient declared that the examination was ridiculous, and that anyway he had better doctors in Belgium than there were in the canton of Thurgau. The x-ray picture showed a shadow in the area of the apex of the right lung, which could only be interpreted as a pleural effusion. Apex pleurisy on one side only is extremely unusual. There has to be an irritation at the site to explain so unexpected a finding. In view of the patient's age, therefore, lung cancer was a possibility. With this patient I said right away that I thought there might be a carcinoma and would have to transfer him without delay to a hospital for examination and treatment. I then transferred him to a Belgian clinic where at first, under antibiotic treatment, the temperatures disappeared. The specialist examination revealed an apparently still undeveloped bronchial carcinoma in the upper part of the right lung. The patient was therefore lobectomized, that is, the upper part of the right lung was removed.

As soon as the patient knew of the danger he was in, his behavior changed dramatically. He pulled himself together. He became calm, assured, and polite. His original gift for dealing with people and his cultivated personality, which had once helped him in his career, reasserted themselves; he radiated warmth and friendship. He faced up to his illness with manly resolution and at the same time with quiet submission. When the patient returned to his home country – a week after the diagnosis had been established with all probability as carcinoma – he did not leave the sanatorium as a desolate alcoholic, nor did he leave with everybody glad to see him go. Instead, he left as a friend, and both doctors and patients realized that they had gotten to know a man of character. The letter the patient sent to his friends in the Swiss sanatorium before the lobectomy is a true document of humanity: open and full of love for others, its author facing what lay ahead with exemplary resolution.

The encounter with the diagnosis of carcinoma transformed that person. It finally confronted him with reality, when for so long he had sought refuge from any sort of emotion in intoxication. As a result, he reverted to his genuine and true self and was once again the valuable person he had been originally.

The two cases I have discussed so far show that the question of whether one should inform the cancer victim of his condition is wrongly put. You cannot ask what anyone ought or ought not to tell a cancer patient. "Cancer patient" is a concept, too. What we actually see is the individual with cancer, a person who is sick and in danger, a different person every time, each one an individual. It is a matter of knowing and sensing *what* you can and must say to *whom*. The task is to find what the great French

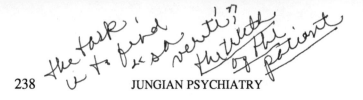
the task is to find it; to use so verité; the truth of the patient

surgeon Leriche called "the truth of the patient": *sa vérité* [5] (cf. also p. 210). If you speak to the patient, if you see him as a human being, as a brother, it is possible to find that truth, because, as Nietzsche says, "Truth begins when two people come together."[6]

One should not rely on the patient's explanation when it comes to finding out the truth. Of course, there are statistics. In 1955 in the state of Indiana, for example, of the 477 healthy people who were asked, 96.6 percent wanted to be told the whole truth about cancer.[7] But who can be confident that he would accept the truth if it came to the crunch? Not many, I suspect. Therefore, the responsibility should not be palmed off on the patient. The doctor himself has to come to a decision based on his knowledge of the patient. And then he has to talk responsibly with the patient. A doctor who fails to do so shows, as Singeisen so aptly put it, "a lack of courage."[8]

In our second case, too, there is a side issue to be discussed. For that patient, blindly prescribing antibiotics would have been especially dangerous. In the Belgian clinic the patient's temperature disappeared immediately under such treatment; obviously, it derived from a secondary infection of the irritated lung. If it had been treated with antibiotics immediately in Switzerland, most probably everyone would have stopped worrying about it, and the carcinoma would not have been diagnosed. The possibility of cancer, therefore, requires that the medical principle be rigorously upheld: first the diagnosis, and then the treatment.

In both the cases we have looked at so far, it was a matter, on the physical level, of making a diagnosis of cancer in good time and then of carrying out the most promising form of treatment. But the situation is by no means that simple in all cases. You cannot always expect, especially not with cancer, to arrive at a cure by straightforward means; often the treatment follows an erratic path.

Case 3. A highly regarded specialist in internal medicine referred to me from Germany a fifty-five-year-old director of a medium-sized industrial enterprise and father of two children, for psychotherapy. For over six months the man had been suffering from a curious deglutition spasm; he constantly had the impression that food was getting stuck in his throat. A thorough physical examination had revealed no pathological findings. Also, there seemed to be considerable potential conflict in the management of his firm. It was natural to assume, therefore, that the man was suffering from a nervous disorder. The German doctor sent me the negative stomach x-rays and, in his accompanying report, recorded the diagnosis as "neurosis." In the psychotherapeutic consultation, the patient was open and willing to talk; he was interested in finding out himself what the source of his neurosis might be. He insisted that his complaints were real, and I was able to judge for myself (since I had accepted him as an inpatient). It was evident, as soon as he began to eat, that a spasm was making it extremely difficult for him to swallow. At the same time, however, I noticed that the patient showed visible alarm when the spasm occurred. The contrast with his relaxed and uninhibited behavior in the psychotherapeutic consultation was very striking. Somehow it seemed to me unlikely that this man, who seemed psychologically so well balanced, should be suffering from any such neurosis. So I decided to settle the matter by having further x-ray pictures taken. Since there had already been a number of x-rays taken with no positive finding, we had to think of a new basis for the examination to see if there were, after all, some hidden disorder. Therefore, an x-ray of the patient's stomach was taken with the patient standing on his head. The picture showed a tumor the size of a fist at the entrance to the stomach, a cardia carcinoma that was already beyond the stage where we could have operated.

I had been lucky with my diagnosis. This also illustrates how wrong it is to diagnose a neurosis simply by exclusion, that is, to classify the patient's symptoms as neurotic simply because there are no physical findings to explain them. The neurosis must also be diagnosed positively, which requires that the personality of the patient be considered as a whole. The supposedly neurotic symptoms should then be assessed in the context of that whole. It is extremely helpful if you can observe the symptoms yourself and not, as is often the case in dealing with outpatients, merely have them described to you by the patient. My German colleague acted quite properly. His diagnosis of neurosis prompted him (since the treatment of neuroses lay outside his competence) to refer the patient to a psychiatrist. And then, when the diagnosis of neurosis could not be confirmed psychiatrically and we therefore decided to proceed with a physical examination, it was all in the normal course of events. After all, the first step for every specialist in treating a new patient is to decide whether the case belongs to his field of competence. That is one more reason, and not the least important, why every specialist should have a general medical training.

Unfortunately in our patient's case, making the right diagnosis was not a triumph. I found myself in a challenging situation: *Hic Rhodos, hic salta!* In other words, you say you are a psychotherapist, now show what you can do. It was too late for physical treatment, so the only hope was that psychological influence might affect the course of the illness. It was brought home to me on that occasion that a psychotherapist does not demonstrate his skill as a specialist by working his way towards a physical diagnosis with the help of a skilled colleague in the radiology department, but by giving successful psychotherapy. The distress of that realization was probably the reason why, in this difficult case, I was lucky a second time. The basis of a doctor's work is not scientific superiority, but the urgency of the patient's need.

First I told the patient that the x-ray had shown an organic irritation that definitely needed attention. After that I discussed the general situation with him. Clearly, there were a lot of difficulties. There were things that needed seeing to, both within the firm and within the family. In particular the patient's son, who was neglecting his studies, had to be put back on the right track. After that interview, I prescribed for the patient a light diet and, before every meal, a pinch of Bourget powder, a refined form of sodium bicarbonate.

With that, interestingly enough, the therapy was completed. The patient was immediately relieved of his symptoms. He became extremely active, asserted his authority in the firm, and had a serious talk with his son. In that way he put things in order. No further symptoms appeared. Three weeks after the diagnosis had been established, that is, after the last x-ray, the patient died suddenly in his bed; the cardia carcinoma had perforated. He had done his duty as a father, and his life's work had been brought to a close. Thus his exit, while distressing, was not tragic.

It was partly the effect of the Bourget powder. The deglutition spasm probably did not come from the tumor as such, but from the ulcerated and sensitive mucous membrane on the surface of the tumor; the powder had a soothing effect on the sensitivity of the mucous membrane, making the spasm disappear. The fact that the course of the illness then remained favorable – not for long, but for long enough! – is attributable, I believe, to the patient's having turned his attention to where his personal problems lay. Very often it is wrong to let oneself be fascinated by the idea of death and to say, "This man is ill; he is going to die." We all have to die some time. And for the time being the patient is still alive; he is not yet dead. He has duties and responsibilities which no doctor can relieve him of, as if the doctor were an army medical officer and life a form of military service. No one can stay at home; everyone has to live his life. Yet deeds that give life meaning make symptoms recede in cases not only of neurosis but also of physical illness.

It is remarkable, for example, how a man such as the American secretary of state Dulles could be so filled with a sense of his political duty that, for a long time, he was able to rise above his carcinoma. In our patient's case, it is not unlikely that he felt death approaching. Otherwise, he would perhaps not have thrown himself with such energy into the task of putting his house in order. And when I spurred him on to it, I did so knowing how things stood with him. I never spoke to him of death – only of life – because that was where his truth lay, the path he had fearlessly to follow. Death then came quietly in the night.

That man was lucky. Unfortunately, inoperable cancer usually ends differently. Sooner or later the cancer becomes obvious. Then the patient, his relatives, and the doctor can find themselves in situations that are among the most difficult in cancer treatment. One reason for the complication is the question of whether to use painkillers such as morphine, which is addictive.

In such cases the treatment has to be organized with subtlety, circumspection, and firmness. By subtlety, I mean a sympathetic awareness of the condition, a balancing of medicines one against the other, and a careful regulation of doses. Circumspection implies that the physical and mental state of the patient should be observed very carefully. Only in that way can we reach the right choice of painkiller, one that is effective and yet changes the patient's mental state as little as possible. A small additional shot has to be given, for example, at the right moment and in the right way; the combination of painkillers with neuroleptics of the chlorpromazine and rauwolfia groups is often useful. The patient has to be told what is going on tactfully, clearly, and always in such a way that he can see that the doctor has not given up on him, that he still wants to help him. By firmness, I mean that the doctor and the staff must realize that the doctor has a definite plan, which he is not going to abandon. And relatives of the patient who try to interfere in the treatment have to be dealt with firmly. At the same time, it should be recognized that the reason for the relatives' unreasonableness is often their love for the patient, their fear of losing him.

Psychologically, it is good in such cases to investigate where the patient's living problem lies. Especially with inoperable carcinomas, the problem may rest in the patient's environment; for a loving husband, for a wife, the presence of the patient can mean everything, so life can be extremely meaningful for the patient's relatives.

In severe cases of cancer, there can be no question of setting up general rules. It can only be a question of approaching the case with humility, of taking all the circumstances into consideration, of paying attention to every detail, and of combining the resources of physiology, pharmacology, and psychology. Then it will be possible to find the individual solution that corresponds to the particular case. A solution of that sort can be significantly more fruitful than you would expect if you simply considered the pathological, anatomical picture of the cancer, its extent, and its probable growth. I know patients who were told by a respectable doctor that they did not have long to live but who, under the right treatment, remained active in their own circles for years. The doctor as clairvoyant is something else again. People are all too keen to misuse doctors as prophets; but giving dates in cases of cancer is almost ruled out. Particularly with inoperable carcinomas there is also the question, mentioned above, of whether the mental state of the patient is connected with the course of the illness. I believe it is possible – though unproven – that a favorable affective state, in other words a favorable emotional reaction, elicits a favorable reaction from the nervous system and hormonal sphere. As a result of the action of the glands with their hormonal secretions, a form of endogenous hormone-treatment may take place naturally. Occasionally one is struck by how rapidly a cancer patient deteriorates when he loses hope. There is no reason to lose hope, though, since even in severe cases meaningful treatment is still possible.

The question of hope also deserves consideration on a higher plane. There are patients who themselves have no hope and who are wholly dominated by the thought, "I am lost; I am going to die." One has to remember that such talk can never be more than half-truth. The idea of being lost and having to die generates fear. But there are others who react differently. Others in the same situation of incurable, fatal illness say to themselves: "I am not lost, because Christ is my savior. And I am not going to die, because I am going to enter eternal life." Such people have no fear. Whose truth is correct? Which view corresponds to the actual circumstances?

Perhaps science can contribute to finding an answer to that question. Modern physics, as founded by Einstein and Planck with the relativity and quantum theories, shows that our picture of space and time does not correspond to reality. So it is also open to doubt whether our physical existence in space and time is the last word about human nature. And modern psychology, founded

by Freud and Jung, can show through the analysis of the unconscious that important psychological factors are dependent on
space and time; therefore, the soul must be something that goes
beyond the body, which itself is subject to space and time. For
these reasons it would seem that the religious view represents the
truth, the actual circumstances, more accurately than the materialistic outlook derived from a superseded mechanistic world-
view.

As a doctor, one has to bear this in mind when one is treating a
fatally ill patient who has lost hope. Generally, one tries with
gentle hints to remind the patient that there is hope beyond our
present life. Once I spoke to a patient, a critically ill business-
woman from St. Gallen, quite openly: I explained how I understood the end of our life, with reference to modern physics and
modern psychology. She replied: "Now at last I can stop worrying. Why did no one ever explain that to me, not even the priest?"
In such situations every doctor will act in accordance with his
general understanding of the world. But it is always essential for
a doctor who wants to help someone facing death without hope to
have clearly thought-out views on the matter of life and death.
Only then will he be able to help the patient find his own truth and
so overcome fear.

As we have seen, the problem of cancer and cancer treatment
has many different aspects. It is impossible to set up simplified
guidelines for medical procedure; each case has to be looked at
afresh both as a clinical picture and as a whole person. The basic
principles of the doctor's activity, however, must remain the
same: a clear diagnosis of the physical illness, an assessment of
the patient's mental state, efforts to instill hope, and a clearly
thought-out program of therapy. Physical diagnosis and therapy
encompass wide areas of surgery and medicine. Psychological
diagnosis asks: "How should I talk to this unique individual? Are
the main problems located in the sphere of outward responsibility
or in that of inner development? Or are they perhaps located in
the nature and character development of a person in the environment of the patient?" Especially with critically ill patients, it is

often forgotten that they are still alive and still have the responsibilities of life.

Sometimes, however, it is not the problems of living that oppress the patient, but the problems of dying. A doctor has to understand the human necessity of not giving up hope. People's longing for hope is at bottom the knowledge that human existence has a meaning that goes beyond physical existence. All the same, hope in life has to be maintained until a higher hope appears. Otherwise, a state of hopelessness takes over in which the knowledge of the meaning of human existence is lost. So long as the patient clings with all his hope to this life, his problems relate to actual responsibilities. Those responsibilities call out to be fulfilled; and if they are, even serious cases can often take a favorable course. For life demands fulfillment. Once the responsibilities of this life have been fulfilled, there is time to think about things beyond this life. It would probably be fair to say that the patient's problem lies in this life, but it may also lie in the next life. This, too, can become a question of psychological diagnosis.

The doctor who deals with a cancer patient must consider the whole personality of the patient. He must recognize what questions have to be asked with regard to the physical and mental condition of the patient. In this way he arrives at a picture of the actual circumstances. The questions that arise have to be answered. Thus the doctor reaches an assessment that matches the actual circumstances. By the method of question and answer, the doctor finds the truth of the patient. On the basis of this truth he is able to help the patient, and then there is no cause for fear. Because *truth overcomes fear and inspires confidence.*

If truth overcomes fear and inspires confidence, there is spiritual harmony. And that spiritual harmony counterbalances the biological disharmony of the cancer that has invaded the body. To achieve this end, knowledge and skill, seeing and doing, have to become one, for the doctor's task is neither erudition nor technique; it is the practice of an art – the art of medicine.

In conclusion, I would like to make explicit the idea on which the present chapter is based. We described the therapeutic procedure in cases of physical illness. We considered the anatomical picture of the physical illness in structural terms, here in the case of cancer, as a disharmony. That structure in the physical sphere has to be confronted with the opposite structure in the psychological sphere – in this case, harmony. In 1906, at the Burghölzli Clinic in Zurich, it was demonstrated that in functional disorders the effects of the psychological difficulty can be felt even in the body and that the psychological difficulty is the cause of the disease.[9] With physical illnesses, however, the scope of the problem exceeds the merely psychological and vegetative level and reaches the areas that Eugen Bleuler (following Hans Driesch) called the "psychoid unconscious."[10] By that is meant, on the one hand, the genuinely physical, organic aspect of man and, on the other, the spiritual aspect.[11] The attempt to establish a relationship between mind and body is no theory; rather, as a working hypothesis it contributes to a form of therapy that seeks to understand man, who is both body and soul, as a unity.

XIII

MEDICINE AND SPIRITUAL WELFARE

The doctor sees in his patient not only the illness but also the individual. For that person *the illness* is also *an experience* that confronts him with *spiritual difficulties*. Dealing with those difficulties is in the first instance the concern of the theologian or pastor. But the doctor cannot simply ignore his patient's spiritual difficulties, and so is liable to find himself facing questions he would perhaps rather have left to the pastor. As a rule, of course, the doctor is consulted about quite different problems from the pastor. He is called when people think that what they have is an illness, that is, a pathological disorder that intervenes in a person's life; and what they expect from him is that he fight to remove the disorder, or at least put things in order. But the first thing the doctor does is to establish the facts, the findings. Then he will take appropriate measures, whether in the form of a course of antibiotic treatment in a case of pneumonia or, after a road accident, the transport of the injured to hospital once the appropriate dressings have been applied, or compulsory hospitalization in a case of mental illness, or a rest cure in the mountains in a case of tuberculosis. Nonetheless, the doctor will not simply ignore the spiritual distress associated with an illness. The longer one has had to deal with sick people and illnesses, the more evident it becomes that falling ill and being ill represent, for the person concerned, the *invasion of a sinister power* that seizes hold of him and, along with him, his relatives. Through the illness, which is stronger than human will, something is forced upon those involved, something that is initially quite contrary to their wishes and intentions and that obeys laws all its own. Let us consider the

examples just mentioned: a serious road accident or a sudden
attack of madness can transform the picture of a family for
decades. The simple discovery on an x-ray of a tubercular lung
disease can throw an ambitious young man out of his career and
condemn him to years of lying in a sanatorium; inner conflicts
extending to the point of despair are almost unavoidable. "Does it
have to be this way?" we ask ourselves. And, "Why does it have
to be this way?" The medical point of view is unlikely to be able
to answer these questions. It is more apt to take the opposite line,
namely: Whether it has to be this way, we cannot say. Why it has
to be this way is even more impossible to say. But there is one
thing we do know and that is that it *is* this way; that is a fact that
no amount of clever reasoning can wish away. This becomes
especially apparent in a case of purely psychic illness, when it
seems as if some underhanded power coming out of the blue
wants to throw the person off course. I am thinking of a young
man who, while he was walking along a busy street in a big city,
was suddenly seized with great fear and weakness. He had to be
taken home in a state of panic, and needed months before he once
again dared to go out among other people and had regained
initiative for everyday affairs. I am thinking of another who was
so troubled by restlessness at night that he eventually started to
believe there were mysterious rays coming out of the earth. Filled
with alarm, he constantly rearranged the beds of his wife and
children in the deceptive hope that this would enable him to
escape the strange, completely irrational influence that had burst
in on him.

Wherever illness occurs, it is perceived by those concerned as
an intrusion into human plans and intentions. Here, if anywhere,
modern man has to admit that he is subject to forces that are
stronger than he is. And while the doctor's first concern is with
the practical measures the situation demands, he must also be
open to the human suffering and the difficult spiritual experience
involved; otherwise, he has no proper relationship to his patients,
finds no rapport, and his orders and interventions generally remain
useless. But in order for a proper human relationship to exist

between doctor and patient, the doctor does not simply need empathy. He also needs a point of view. One thing, at least, follows from his position as a doctor: While the patient finds the invasion of the irrational in the form of illness incomprehensible and often cannot accept it, the doctor finds it completely natural and normal that illnesses should occur (in the case of some doctors, it has to be said, only so long as they themselves stay healthy!). As I have already suggested, sometimes one gets the impression that the force that compels people to change the direction of their lives against their will is most often experienced nowadays in the form of illness (as long as we do not have any war!). Some time ago I was on a hill above Basel and looked down onto the city stretching out across the Rhine plain. Basel is dominated by two buildings: on the left, the Gothic minster, built by medieval people in the service of religion, and on the right, the new municipal hospital built by the modern residents of Basel at enormous cost – two temples from two different ages.

Since we are now on the subject of history, perhaps I may be permitted a historical digression to help define my own position. The emphatic *experience of the irrational* that you see in every new patient raises the question, "How have people responded to this experience through the ages?" The first thing you notice is an undeniable tendency to personify, or at least to materialize, the invading force. Primitive fetishists have always suspected that the spiritual power of a tree, a stone, a leopard, or an evil wizard lies behind whatever it is that is troubling or hurting them. Such ideas are widespread even now, especially in the countryside; there is still much secret pagan talk of magic.

The primitive's understanding of the irrational powers clings to nature and the supernatural. People and things are included in what the French researcher Lévy-Bruhl called *participation mystique*. Turning to the ancient Greek world-view, we find a higher level of thought. The invisible powers are likewise personified. They are the various gods who intervene decisively in people's lives. Together they form a family, the mighty Zeus, his noble and jealous wife Hera, the radiant children Apollo, Athene, slender Artemis, changeable Hermes, and all the rest of them. This conception is no longer primitive insofar as it represents a world-view which, while symbolic, is also spiritual and abstract. The divinity may well live in a tree or a bush, but it is not identical with it. The conception remains pagan in that the divine is internally divided: Homer's epics show how the gods are forever challenging one another and how each wants to destroy the other's favorite. The fact that during the same period the Germanic races developed a notion of the irrational that differs in principle only slightly from the Greco-Roman image suggests that the idea of a suprapersonal, anthropomorphic family of gods was appropriate to that particular stage of culture.

Nevertheless, in its own time that stage had already been superseded by the Jews. Measured against these pagan images, the Jewish idea represented an enormous step forward: The irrational is to be seen as a single entity ("thou shalt have no other gods beside me"), and it exceeds the capacity of human imagination ("thou shalt not make any image or comparison"). But Jewish tradition also shows us something else that is perhaps just as important: It shows how our ideas about the irrational-divine come into being. Anyone who reads the Old Testament will realize that he is not reading a philosophical structure of ideas. The prophets of the one, abstract God are not thinkers and scholars; they are people possessed, who are guided and driven on by a higher power. The irrational power of which they speak is the same irrational power that inspires them to speak. What we see here is not science or philosophy, but what is rightly called "revelation."

However, the Jewish God has one thing in common with the gods of Greece and Rome: He is an unpredictable, cruel, irascible god. He permits Job to suffer, for example. He calls the devil to account for it. And then he lets Job suffer again. It is said that one old priest wrote in the margin of his Bible at that point, "If it wasn't written in the Bible, it would scarcely be credited." That the Lord should create human beings only to let them commit sin so as, finally, to drown them all (with the exception of Noah and his ark) strikes one as very peculiar behavior. A human father who did the same would be risking the intervention of the local authorities and a psychiatric report.

One has to bear in mind the element of terror and unpredictability that the Jewish God has in common with the pagan gods if one wants to understand what Christian redemption meant for antiquity and all subsequent ages. At this point, we have digressed so far from the field of medicine and find ourselves on such slippery ground that we hardly dare to proceed any further. Just one more observation perhaps: In Christian life there is the constantly renewed attempt to accept what seems incomprehensible and burdensome, and to acknowledge it as the working of a wise and good God (one must bear one's cross). And the heavy task of accepting that paradox is made possible for the Christian by the great paradox of the death of the Son of God: An inconceivably bad and sad event – the crucifixion of Christ – is possible, and its consequences are quite unexpected. The greatest disaster and injustice in world history does not lead to the end of the world but, miraculously, to the redemption of the world.

Having defined my position from a historical perspective, I would like to make a personal observation. In conversation with theologians, I have found now and again that they were almost astonished that I, as a scientist, should accept the divine power as a reality. In this respect my views have been decisively influenced on the one hand by the psychology of the unconscious discovered by Sigmund Freud and developed in significant respects by C. G. Jung, and on the other by the theory of relativity established by Einstein. The problems encountered in this connection have already been mentioned in chapter 12 (p. 243).

What, then, does the doctor find when he attempts to take account of the spiritual events that come into play with any illness? In the first place what he finds is this: In situations where a person is suffering, where a person is in despair, where he is at odds with his fate, that person is also *the focus of the effects of the irrational*. Something that is stronger than the human will intervenes in his life with overwhelming force and forces him to change course. The first thing to be done is to pay that force the respect due to it. And the experience that the force imposes on the individual has to be given the importance it deserves. In practical terms this means that you have to know what the patient is suffering, and let the patient know that you know. You have to say quite clearly that it is difficult, that it is sad, and you have to say this before you say anything else. You should not speak of "God's will" or speculate that everything has a deeper meaning (unless you can say what that deeper meaning is). Empty phrases can at best seem like mockery. In fact, as a doctor, you should not mention religion at all unless it is specifically brought up. Anyway, the patient has firsthand experience of the effects of the higher power; there is no need for a commentary from the doctor. All that matters to begin with is the experience. And you should let the patient see that, too, by not disparaging his experience – by never saying, "It's only..." or "It's senseless" – and never encouraging the patient's own tendency to belittle his experience. But the knowledge that, in his suffering, he encounters a higher power is a knowledge that emerges from the patient's own experience; it is not something the doctor can teach. Such knowledge is more than just knowing something as a fact; it is a knowledge that comes from living, a knowledge that is often etched in deep lines into a person's face. Suffering undergone in conflict with internal or external reality can, for example, form curious folds on the upper eyelid known as Veraguthian folds, after the neurologist Veraguth, which give a person an owlish look. He becomes singular, truly himself, and yet an oddball, a "strange old bird," and he comes to resemble the owl, the emblem of Athens and of wisdom. And he seems to possess a wisdom that he did not get from the doctor or from the priest, that he did not think up himself, that through experience of life has made him a stronger person. The most important thing is that you know there is a meaning in bitter experience and that, knowing this, you can give encouragement to the disheartened.

But it is not only respect for the patient's experience that forces restraint on the doctor. It is also presumptuous to want to interfere in a slowly developing situation, and it is usually impossible to foresee what lies behind seemingly trivial details. To give an example from my own experience: A forty-year-old man was seriously ill with heart disease. The usual treatment with intravenous injections of strophantin brought considerable improvement, but the patient still displayed a marked tendency towards anxiety-related breathing difficulties, which seemed to me to have a clear nervous component. I thought it best to tell him he would have to learn to live with his condition, which at that moment was not too serious, and to forego his extensive business trips in Europe. The result was astonishing: Shortly afterwards I met his wife, an attractive young woman, who was visibly distraught. Hesitatingly she told me that her husband was sitting in his room at home in tears. She herself had suddenly developed an itchy rash that was driving her to despair. Her expression said, "This is all your fault." The rash resisted all forms of treatment. It was localized in the lower part of the body, where it was growing worse and worse. Not knowing what to do, I turned for advice to an old medical book from the year 1918 and read that the itch this illness causes in women can become so severe as to drive the patient to suicide. The only treatment that can help is psychotherapy. But since, as is usually the case with such advice, nothing was said about how that psychotherapy might be carried out, I stuck to the rule, "If you do not know what to do, you should do nothing." When the patient came again, I sat down in front of her without saying a word and waited to see what would happen. After a few minutes of silence, the spell was broken. The woman told me the story of her husband's affliction: For twenty years her husband, a lively, active person, had been suffering from a form of sexual impotence that had led him to diverse psychiatrists. No treatment had been of any avail; each attempt had led him only deeper into despair. Now at last he had turned his attention outwards, and through tireless effort had created a firm that extended across the whole of Europe. It gave him a form of compensation and a purpose in life. His heart condition, however, had taken that compensation away from him, and my advice to accept the way things were had, in a quite unintentionally cruel way, thrust him back on the old problem of impotence and shameful defeat; it had made his whole achievement as a businessman seem a self-deception, an escape from himself. This had led him to despair. Carefully and without touching on the background, I discussed the matter again with the patient. In this way at least I managed to restore the balance. Strangely enough, three hours after she had unburdened herself to me, the woman's rash had completely disappeared. I would not like to say that I made a mistake in this case; rather the opposite, in fact. I only wish to show how often, concealed behind apparently minor details, a person's whole life may be hanging in the balance, and how now and again when you notice that fact, you feel like the horseman who tried to ride across Lake Constance.

Besides respect for the experience of the higher power that forces itself upon us with every patient, there is another reason for caution that should not be underestimated – and that is self-protection. When a person or a group of people find themselves in a force field that is stronger than human strength, then one has to remember that what is at work is also stronger than the doctor, and that overhasty intervention or overhasty assessment could easily become dangerous for the doctor, too. The psychological dimension in a situation of conflict is still ambivalent, paradoxical; it is good and evil at the same time, a good and a bad thing. But to what extent the psychological development that is set in train when a person falls seriously ill is also good, desirable, and fruitful can only emerge spontaneously in the course of the illness; and anyone who passes judgment runs the risk of destroying what is most important and will pay for it one way or another. Particular attention should be paid to the nature of the ambivalence in the personal conflicts that often come the doctor's way. One should not feel that because a husband describes his wife as a slut, a father his son as wayward, or a woman her friend as bossy, one must intervene immediately or call on someone else to do so, or that one must judge and condemn right away. Often what is described is just the other, so far hidden, side, and all one needs to do is listen and look. Anyone who acts too hastily can easily find that the dirt he wanted to clean up clings to his own hands and clothes – and it is not always only dirt, either; it can sometimes be blood. Every personal conflict is not primarily something that should be removed, but a form of experience. In conflict with others, a person comes to know himself, and he also comes to know the higher power. Thus others serve as a mirror in which he sees himself reflected and through which the powerful rays of eternity shine.

As everyone knows, it is all too easy to spot the faults in others. It is easy to take offense at them, and it is tempting to make them a target – until suddenly you yourself are hurt deep inside, and you feel as if the ground were swaying beneath your feet. Suddenly you see the weaknesses, mistakes, or inabilities in yourself that you never wanted or were never able to see, and that are difficult to acknowledge. Frequently, the person concerned is not in a position to see the weak point in himself. It is anyway extremely difficult to see yourself objectively, because you are also the one who has to do the seeing, so that without a good mirror there is often no way of doing it. Or to put it another way, the white spot where the optical nerve enters the back of the eye is also a blind spot. Therefore, painful conflict with other people, the source of self-knowledge, does not lead to knowledge immediately. On the contrary, the immediate reaction is mostly panic, a great sense of weakness, often physical illness. Only with time, through the consequences of the development that has been set in train, can anything meaningful take shape.

However hard personal conflict often is to tolerate and endure, it seems important to me that it should be *endured in earnest and with a will*. All too often we succumb to the temptation simply to project everything. Hardly have we met the person with whom we have a disagreement when, besides all the faults we so keenly observe in him, we have already pinned on him all the faults we have ourselves and that we ought, through him, to recognize in ourselves. When a person, deliberately or not, touches our weak or even our evil side (which we all have, since the angels are in heaven and the saints died long ago), we immediately think, he is hurting me, and that proves that he must be a particularly nasty person. – "But no, he can't be good, because he is hurting me," as the humorist Wilhelm Busch puts it. The fact that it hurts not because the other person is cruel, but because he hit me where I am vulnerable, is overlooked. And it is only with difficulty that we can ever see this, because we like to think of ourselves as good people and always hope that we are not vulnerable. Thus the task of examining objectively the mostly exaggerated, but mostly also justified, accusations that our opponent makes against us is successfully avoided through projection. But the truth that is evaded on a small scale constantly reappears on a larger and larger scale, until eventually millions of people stand on either side of the conflict, seeing only the bright side in themselves and only the dark side in the others, so that finally the only way out is for them to kill each other in the vain hope of thus getting rid of their own shadow. We have two such "heroic" attempts to our credit, and live in fear of the third.

The other danger in personal conflict, a danger not to be underestimated, is the *virtuous attempt to avoid* the inevitable conflict through thoroughly correct behavior. I once had to treat a lawyer who, in a personal quarrel, had scrupulously avoided any unfairness in a way that was quite touching. He had done the right thing in a systematic way, so to speak, and in a very clever way, too, which really demanded a legal training to accomplish. But then he broke down, because he still could not make his opponent listen to reason. Ignoring the proverb "Even the Gods are no match for stupidity," he had attempted nevertheless to achieve the impossible, and it had been a nasty experience. It would perhaps have been better if his own "stupidity" had shown through a little bit more; he might then have behaved in a more human way. A show of emotion, for example, even perhaps a show of emotion that – heaven forbid! – could have put him just a little bit in the wrong, would probably have had a far more conciliatory effect than his exasperating loyalty. Here, too, we can draw lessons from recent history, when a policy of appeasement produced highly undesirable results. It is a strange thing, but all that is evil, stupid, and false in the world cannot be argued away with legal tricks, however cleverly devised; yet if instead you confront it boldly, this can often prove surprisingly and incomprehensibly fruitful. Often it would be only too understandable if someone were to say that doing wrong is just as useful as doing good: understandable, that is, if it were not for the moral conflict which constantly reminds us of the fact that bad is bad and right is right. That is something else we cannot avoid.

A particularly familiar example of personal conflict is the *generation conflict,* which can sometimes be quite severe. When a father, deeply wounded by the uncaring and dissolute behavior of his son, exclaims, "I would never have acted that way towards my own father!" one thinks to oneself: That just basically proves that the son acts differently because he is a different person from his father, and the father ought to realize that he is not the same as his own father either. He ought to realize that he cannot be a loving father, as his own father was in his day, but an angry father who says that he does not understand what is going on anymore; and the son has to see to it that he earns his own pocket money for once. Maybe it occurs to us that this is how every generation learns to distinguish itself from the previous one and to stand on its own two feet. But we have to be careful about saying these things. If they are to have any positive effect, these insights have to be gained by those concerned through their own experience. If we were to leap in with our value judgments, those value judgments would be perceived as uncaring and lacking in understanding. And if they were understood, all that might happen in some instances is that the argument would be replaced with a superficial intellectual understanding and the whole development would be brought to a halt. Here, too, the main thing is the conflict, not the commentary, and a conflict that is both biologically inevitable and culturally determined. Morality demands that we be at peace with one another; human nature, on the other hand, demands that we have vehement quarrels now and then. Perhaps we ought to quarrel more often. After all, we are supposed to love our enemies. It does not say anywhere that we are not to have any, or that we are to ignore them. Only we must never forget that the neighbor, who is so important to us, is a human being not a saint, and we ourselves are not angels, not by any means.

A corresponding situation can, of course, arise at any moment in the human encounter between patient and doctor; somehow it is always constellated. But the knowledge of the higher power in the patient's conflict, and the recognition of the possibility that one could oneself at any moment become – and basically always is – an instrument of the higher power, forces one to make careful *distinctions*. One has to make distinctions in two respects.

First, I carry *in front of me,* facing the patient and the world at large, what in the case of a doctor might be called the "doctor façade" (doctor persona). Every profession has its façade as an important tool of adjustment to the world. A priest, for example, who thought he could behave like a lorry driver or a member of Parliament, would cause general astonishment and throw his parish into confusion. And a general who behaves like a tailor is not an elevating spectacle.

However, my façade is not identical with my self. It is the work of generations of doctors, of legions of scientists, and it is closely bound up with the social context. And the patient has a right to that façade. He has a right to be treated by a doctor who behaves like a doctor, who shows sympathy, who makes appropriate use of medicines, and who avoids mistakes as far as humanly possible. That façade is no more a lie or a farce than my trying to make sure that I shave before my consultations is just a silly performance. Anyone who fails to distinguish between himself and his façade falls victim to a fundamentally absurd inflation of the ego, and anyone who fails to cultivate his façade makes himself just as ridiculous and is more of a hindrance than a help. A doctor's duty to help is properly regarded as a noble duty. But even if I strive as best I can to fulfill that duty, this does not mean that I, too, am a noble person. That in itself is rather unlikely. The duty is noble – not the individual.

The *second* distinction relates to what is, as it were, *behind me*. I ought not to imagine that I can change, improve, or cure people. In the words of the famous sixteenth-century French surgeon Ambroise Paré, *"Je le pansais, Dieu le guarist"* ("I dressed his wounds, God healed them"). In the field of the soul, it is best to *do* as little as possible. Enough happens as it is. We have our obsessions that can lead us astray. We make mistakes. Or alternatively, we may quite inadvertently say the right thing. But was it "we" who did this? Were we not rather the tools of stronger (archetypal) forces?

Nevertheless, notwithstanding the second important distinction between ourselves and what lies "behind" us and works through us, we will take the consequences upon ourselves, acknowledge both our mistakes and our insights, and press on courageously, knowing that even in the encounter between doctor and patient another hand guides us.

In rare cases, religious themes may come up in conversation. Not that we should touch on the subject ourselves, and so risk hurting the patient more than we help him. On the contrary, results are achieved not when we touch on anything, but when we ourselves are touched. Once a woman recounted to me her sad life and the tragic experience of her sister who, through her own fault and that of others, had landed in deep misery. The woman despaired of herself and of the whole world. She told me: "I had got to the point where I wanted to jump out of the window of my flat, which is on the fifth floor. I had already climbed onto the windowsill. Then suddenly, I felt a strong hand pulling me back, and I stepped back into the room." Almost involuntarily, the question slipped out, "And whom did that hand belong to then?" At first the woman looked at me in astonishment, then gave a quick "Oh!" – and left the consulting room. We can see from this example how essential it is at such moments that you have a definite point of view to help place the manifestations of the irrational.

These observations of mine would not be complete if I did not make it clear that their main purpose has been to describe what the care of souls, in the Christian sense, means for a doctor. Beyond that, we find in practice that the most urgent needs of the sick soul are often shockingly unchristian, at least unchristian as measured against traditional, historical Christianity. Frequently we have to rely on whatever the power that is stronger than human strength can achieve. Frequently, what is written in Holy Scripture is of secondary importance by comparison, and often it is all too clear that what comes out of it all is more a curse of the devil than a gift of God. Heinrich Pestalozzi once asked in his enlightened way: "Will men be forever blind? Will they never discover what it is that shatters our spirit, destroys our innocence, ruins our strength, and condemns us to a life of frustration and thousands of us to death in the hospitals and to raving insanity?" He saw the only way out of this pitiful condition in the "cultivation of human nature."[1] But when we see what happens when a human being really follows his nature, we realize that that idea sounds much better in theory than it often works out in practice. And yet we have to follow our nature, otherwise we end up in a bitter struggle with ourselves which can only be fruitless and senseless. There is a great truth in the idea of the imitation of Christ. But as a doctor one always has to remember that Christ is an example to us primarily in the way he lived up to and remained true to what *he* was, drinking the bitter cup to the dregs. It is surprising how often one can see an identification with the son of God in what people say of themselves, for example, "No one has ever suffered as I am suffering." It would be nice, too, to be a second Christ. What is far more difficult, though, and more useful, too, is to find out what an ordinary, natural person one is oneself, and then to live it because one has no other choice. Then it is time to give up many illusions one has about oneself and the world, and yet still to look forward rather than backward.

The way forward is simple and yet difficult. When a doctor encounters serious illness, whether psychological or physical, he finds a person who is compelled by forces stronger than himself to change the direction of his life. The doctor will acknowledge the reality of the stronger force, and he will see that it requires the person to change. In this way he can help the person to accept the future. And then the doctor can quote the words of the poet: [2]

> So you want to be saved!
> And saved you can be,
> But not made a new man.
> What you once were is no more,
> And what you have it in you to be –
> Will you take it upon yourself?

XIV

PSYCHOLOGICAL-PSYCHIATRIC DIAGNOSIS: DREAMS, RESISTANCE AND WHOLENESS

> Dreams are democratic and benevolent,
> since everyone can dream, rich and poor
> alike. By the time you are twenty-five,
> you should have learned how to handle
> your dreams. Write them down – keep a
> *Diary of Your Nights.* Writing down
> dreams is also good for developing skill
> with words.
>
> *Synesius of Cyrene,* A.D. 400

We shall be discussing the subject of dreams in the context of C. G. Jung's analytical psychology. In 1914 Jung founded his own school or branch of psychology; he declares as much in his editorial preface to the first volume of *Psychologische Abhandlungen* (Psychological Essays).[1] But applying Jungian ideas does not mean expounding a dogma. Jung himself consistently refused to offer anything in the way of a definitive doctrine. On the contrary, he held to his view that "it is ... quite wrong when people accuse psychotherapists of being unable to reach agreement on even their own theories. Agreement could only spell one-sidedness and desiccation."[2] Accordingly, we cannot argue the case for analytical psychology here, nor can we prove that other points of view are wrong. What we aim to show is how Jung's analytical psychology understands dreams in the context of resistance and wholeness. It need hardly be mentioned that the author's personal views also play a role.

For the purposes of our discussion, a dream is to be defined as a spontaneous fantasy that occurs during sleep and is remembered. Of course, there are dreams that are not remembered (one only knows that one was dreaming, or one may not even know that much); and there are also daydreams that occur in the waking, often somewhat drowsy state. But to include these aspects of dreaming would lead us too far. We will be concerned only with remembered dreams, as encountered in analytical practice.

It is in itself a remarkable phenomenon that during sleep there can occur a conscious experience that is remembered. If we observe dream material, we find that as a rule things are seen and experienced differently in dreams than during the day, when we are fully conscious. In the rare cases where simple events of the previous day recur unambiguously in a dream, it can be assumed that the dreamer has given too little attention to the simple tasks of the day, so that they come back to him during sleep. To dismiss these dreams as unimportant and banal is resistance – and, on the analyst's part, counterresistance! Such dreams are, on the contrary, generally very important, and the first step towards wholeness in these cases is to obey the call to take one's daily duties more seriously.

On the whole, though, dreams show us a different world from that of everyday. This otherness is important. Through the influence of family, society, personal history, and also personal mental constitution as described by Jung[3] in his psychological typology, a person develops a habitual, relatively constant consciousness. This consciousness is also bound up with an ego that is experienced as continuously identical. "It's strange that I'm always me," as a young six-year-old once told me. The child was describing the fact that already, at the age of six, the continuously identical ego was established and with it – in my experience – the basis of habitual consciousness, too. Conditioned by the standpoint of this habitual consciousness, the encounter with the world in the form of experience and action is one-sided, often appropriately but sometimes inappropriately, too. This is where the, as it were, fairy-tale world of dreams can provide a valuable balance.

Clearly, dreams are composed of the contents of consciousness: the father, the dog, the tree, the abyss, the music or the catastrophe that appear in a dream are familiar to consciousness. But these contents are used in the dream to construct a fantasy that gives new facets to experience. Those new facets are best acknowledged in analysis by considering and appreciating the dream as a whole. It is good to recall, in this context, the words of H. Bergson:[4] "It is indisputable that every psychological state, simply because it belongs to a particular person, reflects the whole of a personality." (Bergson, 1859-1941, received the Nobel Prize in 1927). The dream as a whole reveals the nature of the dreamer. But it shows it in a very different light from that of habitual consciousness. In the form of fantasy, dreams respond to experience and the world in precisely the way that habitual consciousness is unable to. So, for example, an intellectual, practically and realistically oriented person might have confused, fantastic, and emotional dreams, because that side of the person is also in him and strives for consciousness; it wants to be seen. (Other people may have seen that side of the dreamer long ago but, because it was unconscious, they saw it in a more negative, archaic form.) In this sense dreams are compensatory, balancing out the one-sidedness and limitations of the daytime attitude. Looking at and appreciating dreams as a whole shows the nature of the personality in a new and often necessary light. I know people who take great pleasure in the sheer inventiveness of their dream life and who, without necessarily risking an interpretation, feel enriched by it. One of the first concerns of the psychotherapist, when he encounters the dream phenomenon in his work, must be to help the patient discover this enrichment by paying attention to and reflecting on his dreams.

As an enrichment of the possibilities of experience, the study of dreams brings with it an expansion of habitual consciousness. Where the inner balance of a personality is disturbed, such an expansion of consciousness is often urgently needed. The forms of experience made available in the dream fantasy have to be seen and linked to the patient's consciousness. The lack of this counterbalancing form of experience is often the most important source of mental disorder, and is what C. G. Carus[5] in 1846 called "unconsciousness" (not "the unconscious"!). "If it were absolutely impossible," he wrote, "to find the unconscious [here he uses the word "unconscious"!] in consciousness, we would have to despair of ever attaining a knowledge of our own souls, that is, true self-knowledge." The study of dreams helps us towards this healing self-knowledge by bringing new forms of experience to consciousness.

The direct healing power of dreams was known to the ancient Greeks; it lay at the heart of the cult of Asclepios (Epidauros, Kos, etc.). C. A. Meier[6] has devoted detailed studies to the connections between this "incubation" and modern psychotherapy.

There is no doubt that something previously unknown is an unconsciousness. To what extent it can more exactly and more positively be called "the unconscious" is a question we shall come back to in the course of this discussion.

A common form of resistance is the tendency to focus too soon on the details of a dream, interpreting and amplifying them without paying sufficient attention to the dream as a whole, as a drama. The discussion is then about details, whereas it is the mood and attitude of the analysand as aspects of his general state of mind that are the immediate problem and that point the way to wholeness. Resistance thus becomes direct evasion, with unconsciousness as the overall attitude. It is clear that the analyst, too, whether as a result of his own attitude or under the influence of the analysand, can also make the same mistake. Counterresistance is just as important and common as resistance. This is something which is often forgotten.

Of course, simple passive acknowledgment of the dream is not always enough. At the beginning of this century in his pioneering work *The Interpretation of Dreams,* Freud showed that it was both possible and necessary to understand the content of dreams in detail by learning to speak the fantasy language of dreams. Whatever one's views on this work of Freud's – some would have major reservations, others only minor ones – one thing is certain: A psychotherapist who has not read the book reveals a serious gap in his education, and probably one due to resistance!

We could call the understanding of dream language the interpretation of dreams. I would like to give some examples of how dreams can be interpreted within the framework of Jungian analytical psychology. It goes without saying that many of the fundamental ideas of Freud and other scientists cannot simply be thrown overboard, since any psychology that wishes to be taken seriously is based on the work of many individuals and cannot be merely an exercise in apologetics on behalf of some prophet. The latter, apologetics, was characterized by Jung[7] himself in his book *The Relations between the Ego and the Unconscious* as a regressive development. Apologetics is resistance; it shows a lack of wholeness in the analyst, and it leads the analysand away from wholeness. Naturally, that is very convenient for many analysands, since it is more comfortable to read Jung, for example, than to meet their own stupid or vulgar shadows.

The Interpretation of Dreams

An example of how something that happened during the day can recur in a dream to remind us that our everyday duties need to be taken seriously has already been given.

In the same connection, let me quote from the *Diary* of Samuel Pepys,[8] famed as one of the great books of seventeenth-century English literature. The entry for November 1660 reads:

> At night to bed, and my wife and I did not fall out about the dog's being put down into the cellar, which I had a mind to have done because of his fouling the house, and I would have my will, and so we went to bed and lay all night in a quarrel. This night I was troubled all night with a dream that my wife was dead, which made me that I slept ill all night.

But the next day, his wife was still alive. So what does the dream mean? It says in effect: If, in a quarrel with your wife, you

simply assert your authority, if you cannot see that to your wife –
and to many women! – locking a dog in the cellar is an act of
cruelty, then you are losing touch with your spouse. Mrs. Pepys
herself is not dead. But what you call "my wife," your partner,
she is dead.

The dream's warning is obvious. The unease associated with
the dream and emphasized by the dreamer produced spontaneous
results. Just nine days later, on November 15, Pepys, who was
Secretary to the Admiralty, presented his wife to the Second Lord
of the Admiralty, which, he wrote, was "the first time he ever did
take notice of her as my wife, and did seem to have a just esteem
for her." (Evidently, Pepys had previously regarded the fact that
he had a wife as a *quantité négligeable*.) Pepys thus reacted to the
dream by giving his wife her proper dignity. By doing so, he once
again made her what he could legitimately call "my wife."

Pepys' dream shows how it is possible for a psychologist
directly to understand a dream if he knows the language of
dreams. It also shows how a dream can produce in the dreamer an
affect – Pepys speaks of unease – that prompts self-regulation
and leads to the situation's being put right. Naturally, this event
represents only one step in the development of Pepys' marriage.
Further steps can be glimpsed here and there in his *Diary*. A
marriage needs to develop constantly. It is impossible, for example, to overlook the fact that, although Pepys gave his wife
back her rights, his resistance led to his not only advancing her
but also, so to speak, advancing her "out of his way." In effect, he
left her alone with his lordship and simply went away. Psychologically this phenomenon is not uncommon: Although the dream
intervenes to bring about self-regulation, the false attitude is
liable – because of the resistance – to turn into its opposite, and a
satisfactory midpoint corresponding to wholeness is reached only
slowly, with swings in either direction.

The next dream demands more detailed interpretation. A
young psychiatrist undergoing his training analysis is completing
a year in a clinic for internal medicine. His plans are to become a
psychotherapist, but at the moment he is under the influence of

the personality of the senior consultant he is working for. He dreams: "I am standing in front of an x-ray unit. Suddenly my consultant appears from behind the apparatus. He has a very large head, but is only fifty centimeters tall. I am astonished at his sudden appearance and his small size."

One might interpret this dream on several different levels. On the first, immediate, everyday level the dream says:

a) Objectively,[9] i.e., when the figure of the consultant who appears in the dream is seen in relation to the real person: Your boss, with his large head, is certainly not insignificant; all the same, he is not what you would call a great man.

b) Subjectively,[10] i.e., when the person appearing in the dream is seen in relation to the subjective state of the dreamer: Your medical training (represented by the senior consultant) is coming along, but it is not completed; you still have a lot to learn.

Dreams, whose images are always appropriate, usually have something to say on both the objective and the subjective levels. Because of the resistance associated with his one-sided habitual consciousness, the dreamer is always less keen to see the level that it would do him good to see, in this case, the subjective level, the still-incomplete medical training.

On a second, symbolic level the dream says: Internal medicine (the senior consultant) is also a form of introspection, perhaps even of meditation. As such, it cannot be mastered by technical means; for the x-ray apparatus, the little man standing on the floor would be too low to even register. Introspection, which also has a leading role to play (the consultant is the boss), has to be encountered directly. It may appear small and insignificant, but it is very important for you. And also for your consciousness (the consultant has a large head).

The dream also reveals a third, mythological level. There is no such thing as a senior consultant fifty centimeters tall. A senior consultant like that is a mythical creature, a dwarf. The mythical dwarf is of a chthonic, phallic nature; he is earthy and creative. In order to do justice to the significance of this mythical dwarf in analysis, it would be necessary to draw on parallels from history to illuminate the character and activity of the dwarf from various points of view. This procedure, which Jung called amplification, assists our understanding of the dream figure. In the present case amplification would reveal, among other things, that the dwarf possesses qualities otherwise ascribed in fairy tales or folk imagination to godlike creatures. The encounter with this earth god also constitutes an intervention in the dreamer's destiny. From various points of view – outwardly as clinical medicine, inwardly as meditation (introspection), physically also as sexuality – the sudden encounter with the dwarf not only points a direction but also indicates future developments in the dreamer's life.

Formally understood, the dream is a little drama:

a) *Exposition:* The young doctor stands in front of the x-ray unit; he believes that he has to learn by recognizing and seeing through things.

b) *Climax:* The dwarf-consultant appears; the dreamer learns that essential truth, the diverse aspects of which we outlined above, is only to be found through direct experience.

c) *Lysis:* He is astonished; for the dreamer this is something unexpected, new, and therefore important.

This way of studying a dream with regard to its dramatic structure can often be very helpful in understanding more complicated dreams. It can also ensure that a resistance does not obscure an important aspect of the dream; in this case, for example, anyone who looks at the exposition (with the x-ray unit) sees clearly that the dreamer thinks the way to progress is by "seeing through" things. Or anyone who appreciates the lysis, with the dreamer's astonishment, realizes that the dream points to something new and therefore important.

The young doctor had the dream before he started analysis. But the analysis was already planned, so the dreamer was able to dream about the transference aspect in advance. That aspect could be translated as follows: "You think the analyst is a great man. That need not be so. He may be small, but he is still important for you." The phallic side of the figure (dwarf) also shows the analyst as a partner who stimulates a new departure.

On the question regarding the extent to which the simple acknowledgment and appreciation of a dream – which may be followed by a thorough examination at a later stage – is effective, I will give the following revealing example:

More than twenty years ago, a patient was referred to me from a state-run clinic with the request to attempt clinical psychotherapy with her. The patient was difficult and very aggressive. The therapy, which was psychiatric, including medication, support, guidance, and personal contact between patient and therapist, lasted for four years and was in no sense analytical. Towards the end of the fourth year, the patient spontaneously wrote down a dream. It began with an eclipse of the sun during the night and ended when, to the delight of the dreamer, a sun appeared in a clear sky at the same time as a wonderful, shining moon, without being in the least artificial. The patient handed me the dream in a carefully bound volume. The dream showed how mental darkness (the light [the sun] is at night) was superseded (eclipsed) and replaced by a daytime sun and a daytime moon. Now there was both a clear consciousness (sun) and a conscious womanhood (daytime moon). Following the occurrence of this dream, the handing over of which was evidently very important for her, the patient was soon able to be discharged.

The entire dream, bound in a booklet, consisted of seventeen pages of minute handwriting. It was not until months after the patient had been discharged, during my holidays, that I found time to decipher the document. But before I could go into the dream in detail, I first had to have the seventeen pages typed out by a secretary, since it was scarcely possible to gain an overview of the dream from the manuscript. Then I had to wait for my next holidays to work through this psychologically extremely interesting document, which described in great detail the transformation "from night to light." Nearly two years passed after the patient was discharged before I was able to study and appreciate the dream properly. Nevertheless, I did manage it eventually.

The manner in which the patient handed me the dream and the circumstances showed that she knew I would be able to appreciate it. In other words, it is frequently not the act of appreciation in itself that is effective. What is more important is that the patient find a therapist who has in his own personality the ability to understand the patient's material, and who is therefore also able to understand the totality of the patient's personality (cf. the remark of Henri Bergson quoted above). Because then the encounter between patient and therapist is genuinely human and positively therapeutic. The seed of understanding is present from the outset in the encounter and therefore also effective. Whether this understanding is complemented with a detailed appreciation by the therapist of the dream and its contents immediately or not until later is, in some cases, not the most important thing.

Now once again we turn our attention to dreams in general, as a phenomenon, in order to study in more detail an aspect of resistance and wholeness that is encountered in many multi-layered dreams and is not at all easy to describe. So far we have been looking at dreams as fantasies in search of the unknown, as unconsciousness in Carus's sense. Something that is not known, or not available, can have considerable effects. The lack of gasoline, for example, can be fatal for a driver in the desert, despite the fact that lack of gasoline is merely a concept, a lack, something you do not have; in other words, "nothing"! The same applies to a consciousness that lacks something. We have to ask, though, whether dreams are not also produced by a region of the psyche which, although it is not conscious, nevertheless leads a life of its own. If that were so, then unconsciousness would also deserve the title of "the unconscious," which Carus himself used on occasion. G. T. Fechner (1801–87) wrote in his work *Elements of Psychophysics,* (1860): "In the state of unconsciousness, something in us disappears."[11] Freud's account of repression shows that conscious material can become unconscious and still be there nonetheless, and that it can play comical or tragic tricks on us, in the form of slip-ups and errors, for example. Observations made during analysis, and in particular the study of dream sequences, suggest that many things develop first of all on an unconscious level and then, when the time is ripe, enter consciousness in the form of dreams or also of sudden ideas and inspirations.

In addition, when consciousness is suffering under the impact of the unconscious, it is possible to observe in people a tendency to see things in a mythical light and to experience and act in a typical, mythical manner. Freud showed convincingly that the myth of Oedipus, who murdered his father and committed incest with his mother, lives on at an unconscious level in people of our own time and is constantly being experienced and undergone anew. Jung[12] pointed out that the tendency to react to crisis in the form of a myth is not limited to the Oedipus myth, but encompasses a wide variety of general, mythological situations. He called these situations the "world of the archetypes." The biologist A. Portmann[13] says on this subject, "The need for form is given in our genetic structure." Dreams, too, as the example of the chthonic, phallic dwarf illustrates, are determined by this unconscious human tendency to create typical forms of a mythical nature. In that sense, dreams are a symptom not only of unconsciousness but also of the unconscious.

The mythical contents of the unconscious which, as Fechner himself knew, have their own autonomy and which, as a result of the inherited need for form, lead to typical forms of behavior – of acting and reacting – are also associated with a considerable affect; this is apparent from Jung's association experiment. To the extent that the resistance, whether in the analysand or in the analyst, is conditioned by such affect-laden, archetypal factors, it can no longer be seen reductively as a mistake. Resistance that is conditioned by archetypal factors is also a trickster; it has a mercurial, creative character. In analysis it is often very difficult to get the right emphasis, to recognize, for example, where the subjective level is important and where the objective level is important, or where a dream image has to be seen as a symbol or even as an actual myth. Often the emphasis shifts from consultation to consultation. If the emphasis is wrong, this may be due to a resistance. But if the resistance is conditioned wholly or in part by archetypal contents, it can often triumph despite all the analyst's skill, thanks to the high energy of the archetype, which is expressed in affect. The form in which it triumphs depends on the mental structure of the analysand and the analyst. The result is that the analysis deviates from the theoretically desirable course and acquires a particular slant, which is a symptom of the relationship between that one analysand and that one analyst. A further consequence is that the analysand develops into a person who fails to achieve an ideal, conscious wholeness free from resistances but who, while partly conscious in a way that is characteristic both for him and for his analysis, still retains the shadow that Goethe[14] so aptly called *der Erdenrest*. Thus in effect, the archetypally conditioned resistance has intervened in a creative sense as a trickster to ensure that the development does not go too far. Development that deviates from the ideal of wholeness is called the process of individuation, since the ideal itself is collective, not individual, whereas we are individual precisely insofar as we are imperfect and therefore personal. Incidentally, the well-known truth that every analyst has his own typical counterresistance and that it is therefore easy to recognize by whom a person has been analyzed is not a bad thing. After all, analysis is not a technical handicraft, but a humanistic enterprise in which human and all-too-human factors have their rightful place. Of course, acknowledgment of the fact that resistance and counterresistance can sometimes, in a mercurial, creative way, lead to the right kind of wholeness, should not be used by analysts as an alibi for their own mistakes. Rather, it should remind them of how devilishly difficult (like a trickster, in other words) the problem of resistance in analysis can often be. Then they will be humble and realize that Tyche, too, the goddess of luck, must have her say if the task is to succeed.

Finally, I would like to discuss a special feature of certain dreams. The dream fantasy that occurs during sleep does not always seem to be tied to time and space in the way we experience them when we are awake. Schopenhauer,[15] in his essay "On the Appearance of Purposefulness in the Destiny of the Individual" (1851) remarked on this curious fact; he referred to his thoughts on the subject as "the mere ventilation of a very obscure matter."(!) In 1952 Jung coined the term "synchronicity" to describe these phenomena, and in his essay on the subject[16] records the following case: An Englishman, J. W. Dunne, dreamed in 1902 during the Boer War in South Africa that he was standing on an island that he knew to be immediately threatened by a catastrophic volcanic eruption. He tried to persuade the French (!) authorities immediately to mobilize all available vessels for a rescue mission to save the four thousand inhabitants of the island. A few days later he received a copy of a newspaper in which he read that before the dream – but before he could have known about it – the volcano Mont Pele on Martinique had erupted, killing forty thousand people. In exceptional cases dreams can, so to speak, see beyond the boundaries of space and time and display telepathic or prophetic traits. A typical feature of this example is the inaccuracy of the figures. The dream says four thousand, whereas in reality there were forty thousand victims. But then, on the other hand, there is the accuracy of the nationality. The Englishman Dunne tried to persuade the French authorities; and Martinique, of course, belongs to the French.

This aspect of dreams is often particularly difficult to judge in relation to resistance in analysis. Of course, there are some such dreams that are necessary, as it were, in that they convey meaningful messages. But telepathic or prophetic dreams of this sort can also be a sign that the only reason the unconscious knows so much is that consciousness knows far too little, and that consciousness does not want to know anything because the first thing to become conscious would be the realization that one is completely insignificant and uninteresting. With such dreams, though, one is at least still worthy of interest. In other cases, however, even for people who need them, dreams of this type can mediate contact with irrational or even religious regions, against which there is resistance of a rational nature. In those cases, the dream breaks through the resistance to beneficial effect. In order to work out what is what with telepathic or prophetic dreams, a careful analysis of consciousness is called for. But the analysis has to be carried out with tact and kindness because of the possibility that the analysand might come face to face with his own nothingness. Kindness above all is important – a person who is accepted in a spirit of kindness does not feel like a nobody.

In conclusion, we can say that in practice dreams first have to be appreciated as a whole. Analysis of the dream and thus also analysis of the resistance are to be carried out if and when necessary. The emphasis is of course to be placed in a way that corresponds to the associations and situation of the analysand. And at this point, we have to say one more important, last thing about resistance.

If the analysis brings to light certain duties and responsibilities, they have to be carried out in real life, too. Without that "translation," what has been gained through the analysis is effectively squandered and remains ephemeral. Wholeness is gambled away like a precious stone that you once had in your possession, indeed held in your hands, and then lost again.

The resistance that is the danger here is sloth. It is the sloth which – like the inertia of physical mass – resists any change. Of this sloth, La Rochefoucauld[17] says (1665): *"La paresse, cette béatitude de l'âme, c'est le plus grand vice."* And he continued, interestingly, "It is the remora." He got the concept of the remora from Montaigne (1580) who, for his part, found it in the same alchemical writings that Jung[18] discusses in the chapter on the fish in *Aion*. This fish, which blocks development – the ancients said that a little fish could hold fast great ocean-going ships – was cited by Jung with reference to La Rochefoucauld in 1912 in *Symbols of Transformation* as the great sloth that tries to hold onto the past and fastens the libido to childhood objects. But it is also, as Jung shows in *Aion,* a symbol of the Self that is constellated in the unconscious.[19] The impulse to break free from the past can come from an ethical insight (conscience) or from a creative urge to shape one's own life. But suffering, too, in the form of conflict, neurosis, or general malaise, can drive a person to liberate himself. And then, for the person who seeks freedom and not infantile dependence, the remora – inertia – will not have a crippling effect; instead, as resistance, it will be a spur that leads to development and to wholeness.

XV

DIAGNOSIS OF THE INDIVIDUATION PROCESS IN ANALYSIS: THE LAMBSPRING FIGURES

Lambspring's figures are a sequence of fifteen pictures with accompanying texts. They are an alchemical example of the problem of opposites in the process of individuation. The title page of the original edition reads as follows: "Lambspring is a masterly German treatise on the philosophers' stone, written some years ago by a German philosopher of noble blood called Lampert Spring, with beautiful figures. Frankfurt am Main, Luca Jennis. Anno 1625."

In the *Hermetic Museum* (Frankfurt am Main, 1678), there is a Latin translation of the German text with the same pictures. The *Museum*, edited by Hermann A. Sande, is a collection of important alchemical writings of the time. The Lambspring translation is dated 1667 and bears the title, *"Lambsprinck nobilis germani philosophi antiqui libellus De Lapide Philosophico, E germanico versu Latine redditus per Nicolaum Barnaudum, Delphinatem Medicum."* There is also an English translation of the Latin text, published by Arthur Edward Waite.[1] Aniela Jaffé[2] published the pictures of the German edition in 1955 in the German magazine *Du* with a short commentary to the effect that the figures represent problems of opposition.

By means of figures and text Lambspring illustrates a spiritual development. In *Psychology and Alchemy*, C. G. Jung showed that in alchemy the dynamic of the soul is described with terminology we no longer understand today. Modern science attempts to describe the soul with coined phrases that are often rooted in

Latin or Greek; it uses concepts such as ego, unconscious, motivation, dissociability, and tension. In alchemy, by contrast, the diagnosis of the mental state and of the process of spiritual development is represented with the help of pictures in which every detail has its meaning, and the pictures are accompanied by a symbolic text. Together, the pictures and the text speak a language such as we find in people's dreams and fantasy life. Sigmund Freud showed in his *Interpretation of Dreams* that the language of dreams can be understood. Ever since Jung's analytical psychology opened our eyes to alchemy, we have never ceased to be impressed by how the "old philosophers" could develop a psychological science which, in a responsible manner and on a high level of culture, provided direct access to the foundations of inner life. It is fair to ask whether the alchemists did not describe important aspects of man's spiritual tension and the development it gives rise to better, and in a way that comes closer to reality, than modern science with its words and concepts.

Despite the help given us by Jung, alchemical writings are not easy to read or understand. We need some knowledge of the meaning of the symbols we find in the text, and we also need experience in the observation of the human soul. In attempting here to give a commentary on Lambspring's figures, I am not claiming in any way to be a specialist. What I can talk about, though, is the result of the practical application of the figures in my analytical and psychotherapeutic work.

It is now more than twenty years ago since I first realized how accurately the mental state of one of my patients was expressed by one of Lambspring's figures (the third). I was greatly fascinated and began to use the figures more often in practice. I compared the patients' dream material with the figures, and I also tried to understand the patients' behavior better with the help of the figures. Step by step I became acquainted with the figures, and was able to set about reading the text and seeing the internally coherent sequence of pictures in my own way. The result of my studies is more a personal encounter with this "masterly German treatise" than a purely scientific essay. But personal encounter is probably the right way to an understanding of alchemy – since, for the alchemists, there was no science without personal participation in the observed phenomena.

For my commentary on the figures I will use the Latin version, because that is the one that always accompanied me as an analyst. The quotations, too, are translated from the Latin. Of course, one ought to discuss every sentence in the text and every detail of the pictures, but that would require a work of encyclopedic proportions and would also exceed my capacity as a scholar. I would like nevertheless to emphasize certain basic principles. If we want to understand Lambspring's work, we must not only read the text accompanying the pictures. We must also study the pictures with an analytical eye, and try to "read" them as an analyst reads the "pictures from the unconscious." At this point, however, we have to be quite clear that Lambspring's pictures do not come from the unconscious. On the contrary, they were drawn quite consciously on the basis of the alchemist's knowledge of the soul. Lambspring expressed his insight into human nature both poetically (the pictures are also works of art) and in the form of ideas. He also showed that, as a rule in the life of the soul, the image comes first and words come later. And that is true; that is the way we see and think.

Lambspring's work consists of a title page with a figure followed by a coat of arms with a lamb, a foreword of three pages, and fifteen figures, each of which has a page of commentary text.

The Figure on the Title Page

Here the author is represented in the full regalia of a knight of the Holy Roman Empire. He is standing next to his alchemical oven. The figure shows that the development to be described is of general or "official" importance, hence the official regalia. The process is bound up with the oven, in which fire is kindled for both human and scientific purposes. As an image, the oven holds the fire (our affects) together and contains them; this means that we have to control our affects and try not to explode. We should work on our affects, and so confront our own reality and the reality of the external world. The latter, the world, is represented as a beautiful landscape with mountains and castles in the background.

Foreword

With the coat of arms that precedes the foreword, as in the figure on the title page, Lambspring introduces himself to the reader. He begins, "My name is Lambspring and I come from a noble family." The process that he describes is of general importance, but we also have to know the man who writes the description. Although the description is very general, it cannot, according to the principles of alchemy, be dissociated from the author. It is even true to say that the more general a description is, the more it is also a personal work of creative experience. Lambspring continues, "I have read and understood philosophy in depth." In other words, a work of this kind demands careful scientific preparation. "I have studied the profound knowledge of my teachers exhaustively." That is to say, before you can be a master, you have to be a pupil: First learn the science under the guidance of the teacher; you can still become a genius later. Lambspring then thanks God for "giving him the desire to understand the science." In other words, the science is not just a question of insight; it also requires affect and feeling. In general terms he says of his work, "As yet (God be praised) I have forgotten my own humble self in it," that is, he is aware of the necessary and unavoidable subjectivity of all science. He also knows that it is a blessing that it should be so; and he knows that it is a blessing, not a merit, that he is aware of the fact. All too frequently nowadays we come upon works in which the author has not seen the subjective factor at all, which then leads to false results.

Lambspring advises the reader to study his book again and again. In other words, a complicated scientific description cannot simply be read like a novel; it needs working through thoroughly.

Then he states, "There is only one substance, in which every-thing else is concealed," that is, it is true that all of existence is a unity, a whole. Consciousness breaks or destroys that unity. But a valid human development has to find a path which does not allow the original wholeness to be forgotten, and yet leads to a mean-ingful insight. With regard to that path, Lambspring advises, "Therefore, be sure of your heart." He means, as long as you respect your feelings and affects, you are not lost.

For the right way of the heart you need "mild" cooking, time, and patience. Time and effort should be given with "gladness," not as a sacrifice; it goes without saying that we will need time and patience, and that no development can take place without effort. Remember, too, that in alchemy one's own affects have to be "processed" in the "oven." Mild cooking with the oven is a process that corresponds to the French method of *bain-marie*. The inventor of this method is sometimes said to have been the legendary alchemist Maria Prophetissa.[3] The cooking does not take place inside the oven; rather, a pot of water is placed on top of the oven and in it is put a second pot with the substance to be produced. Thus the substance can never get too hot. Lambspring also speaks of "gentle" cooking, that is, we must be gentle and careful in the way we treat our affects if the result is to be good. And as we have said, the attitude during the work should be one of gladness, since a dark mood is in itself destructive. If one is too serious, one is cramped and achieves nothing.

The substance to be prepared in the "gentle cooking" is "the seed and the metals." The alchemist's "seed" is the origin of the process and a center. The alchemical "metals" are "living metals." They are the result of the process. Like the metals ascribed to the planets in astrology, they show the possibilities of human devel-opment and the appropriate forms of behavior. The spectrum of metals develops out of the seed, and that spectrum in turn defines the center, the seed. Both possibilities – the seed that produces the metals, and the metals that constitute the seed – are aspects of the process of individuation. If, as a young person perhaps, you feel and evaluate your personal possibilities and fulfill what you see as your vocation in everything you do and say, then it is the seed that creates the metals. If, on the other hand, you know life and also know what you are and what you do and are looking for an inner center that can provide a balance, then it is the metals that show you the seed. The center constitutes the circle, and the circle constitutes the center. Of course, both possibilities are constellated at every stage of life; in fact, both usually work together and are, from the alchemist's point of view, the same thing. The nature of such a unity in duality is described by Thomas Norton, also in the *Hermetic Museum*, as follows:[4] "Imagine two twelve-year-old children, a boy and a girl, both dressed the same. You would not be able to tell them apart. As soon as they take off their clothes, you see." Seed and metals are simultaneously one and separate. For the alchemist, the seed that calls the metals (actions) into being is active and masculine. If the core of the personality is to be found by contemplative means on the basis of completed actions (metals), that for the alchemist is feminine.

Lambspring's description of the seed and the metals tells me, know your inner center and grow into what you are to be. If you are something, be aware of your actions and behavior. If your actions are related to the core of your personality, the center, you will retain an inner balance. Endure your affects when you encounter yourself and the world. Avoid outbursts of affect. Treat the affects gently so that you learn what they signify; learn to talk with them. Give yourself time for this; have patience, stay cheerful, even though the work itself is not always easy. You will probably get further if you can laugh about yourself. If you have no sense of humor, you will get nowhere.

The importance of the inner center is strikingly revealed in the observation of the human soul that we mentioned at the beginning of our discussion. Whenever the soul is not balanced and is not related to the center, there appear in dreams, fantasies, and everyday experience the symbols that Jung – comparing them to the Tibetan images used in contemplation – called "mandalas": the circle, the quaternity, also the sun, all of them images that show an equilibrium with a clear geometrical center. These images remind the person of the center, and in fact often correct the maladjustment spontaneously.

Lambspring continues, "The task (the gentle cooking of the seed and the metals) seems impossible to most people, although it is a pleasant and enjoyable undertaking." And indeed, to the intellectual mind which, as Hamlet says, is "sicklied o'er by the pale cast of thought," the unification of the opposites seems impossible. And yet it takes place every day as a perfectly natural phenomenon. In a genuine democracy, completely opposite points of view can work together to make the state live. Anyone who watches his own actions or those of others constantly sees how our actions are often determined by quite contrary motives, which does not by any means lead to our being unable to act, but rather makes our actions human. In relation to psychic development, however, this tension of opposites is in Lambspring's opinion a somewhat sensitive matter.

"If we showed it to the outside world, we would be laughed at by men, women, and children." The fact is that a real psychic development is a private, esoteric affair that other people do not understand. "Tell no one but the wise; the crowd will straightaway mock," as Goethe wrote.[5]

At the end of his foreword, Lambspring gives another extraordinarily important piece of advice: "And remember your duty to your neighbor and to God." The fact that the individuation process demands something akin to a religious attitude is well known and self-evident. What is important, though, is that Lambspring mentions the duty to one's neighbor first. Individuation does not mean withdrawal into an ivory tower; on the contrary, social responsibility is a crucial element of individuation. You only have a balanced personality if you are ready to help others and live in contact with your fellow human beings.

In conclusion Lambspring says, "And now follows the first figure."

286

Title Page

Fig. 1

Fig. 2

Fig. 3

Est summum portentum
Ex duobus leonibus unum fieri.

QUARTA FIGURA.

Spiritus & Anima sunt conjungendi & redigendi
ad corpus suum.

Xx 5   Alexan-

Fig. 4

Lupus & Canis sunt in una domo.
Postremo tamen ex his unum fit.

QVINTA FIGURA.

Mensicatio, & albificatio, corporis conjunctusque
cum Anima & Spiritu imbibitio

Herren-

Fig. 5

Hoc verè est magnum miraculum & cita fraus,
In venenoso Dracone summam medicinam inesse.

SEXTA FIGVRA.

Mercurius rectè & chymicè præcipitatus vel sublimatus, in
sua propria Aqua resolutus & rursum coa-
gulatus.

Yy   Nidus

Fig. 6

Duæ aves in sylva nominantur,
Cùm tamen saltem una intelligatur.

SEPTIMA FIGURA.

Mercurius sæpius sublimatus, tandem figitur, ut non amplius au-
fugere & avolare per vim ignis possit; Toties enim sublima-
tio reiteranda, quo usque fixus fiat.

Yy 2   Sept-

Fig. 7

288

◄ (357) ►

Dux aves funt nobiles & magni pretii,
Corpus & Spiritus, alterum consumit.

OCTAVA FIGURA.

Corpus iterum ponatur pro digestione in fimum equinum vel balneum, superfuso suo aere vel spiritu à corpore olim subtracto. Corpus factum est per operationem album, Spiritus verò rubiet arte. Entium opus tendit ad perfectionem, praeparaturque, sic Lapis Philosophorum.   Yy 3   Nunc

Fig. 8

◄ (359) ►

Dominus sylvarum potitus est suo regno,
Et ab infimo ad supremum gradum conscendit.

NONA FIGVRA.

Si fortuna volet, fies ex Rhetore Consul.
Si volet haec eadem, fies ex Consule Rhetor.
Intellige primum Gradum Tincturae verè apparuisse.
   Omnes

Fig. 9

◄ (361) ►

Salamandra vivit in igne,
Ignisque hanc mutavit in optimum colorem.

DECIMA FIGURA.

Reiteratio, gradatio & melioratio Tincturae, vel Lapidis Philosophorum Augmentatio potius intelligitur.
   Zz   Seben

Fig. 10

◄ (363) ►

Pater, Filius, cum ductore sibi sunt juncti manibus,
Corpus, Spiritus & Anima, hic subintelligitur,

UNDECIMA FIGURA.

Zz 2   Hic

Fig. 11

⊷ (365) ⊷

Alius mons Indiæ in vase jacet,
Quem Spiritus & Anima, utpote filius & dux, con-
scenderunt.

DVODECIMA FIGVRA.

Fig. 12

⊷ (367) ⊷

Hic Pater devorat Filium:
Anima & Spiritus è corpore promanant.

DECIMATERTIA FIGURA.

Hic

Fig. 13

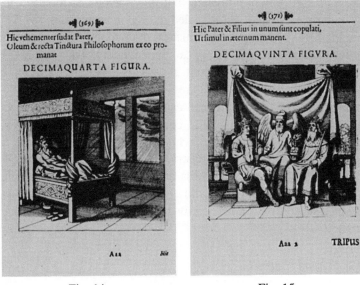

⊷ (369) ⊷

Hic vehementer sudat Pater,
Oleum & recta Tinctura Philosophorum ex eo pro-
manat

DECIMAQUARTA FIGURA.

Aa

Hic

Fig. 14

⊷ (371) ⊷

Hic Pater & Filius in unum sunt copulati,
Ut simul in æternum manent.

DECIMAQVINTA FIGURA.

Aaa 3

TRIPUS

Fig. 15

The First Figure

"Two Fishes Swim in Our Sea"

The sea is a well-known symbol for the unconscious. For the alchemist, however, it is "our sea"; it concerns everyone as well as each one individually, which means that it is an archetypal sea. A content of the unconscious, the fish, comes to the surface. But already there is a tension of opposites: There are two fish. While they are identical in appearance, they are facing in opposite directions. Lambspring reminds us that all of this is at the same time (as is also the case in the following figures) an original unity. He says, "The two fishes become the great sea, and the wise man knows that the two fishes are one and not two." Lambspring also knows that just as the sea is symbolic, so the fish are symbolic, too: "They are fish without flesh and bones."

The sea is calm, and a few trading vessels are sailing on it. But on the sea a complex (fish) with a dual aspect is constellated. It is the sort of psychic situation we find in people who are completely normal, kind, often cultivated, but unconscious of themselves. The complex has not yet revealed its true inner tension; the fish are identical. If in a psychic situation of this kind the complex is touched on, it generally disappears immediately, like a fish in the sea. All the same, it does not always disappear. The psychic situation described in this figure therefore demands that the experienced investigator proceed cautiously. Anyone who knows about the constellation of the complex, Lambspring believes, should "hide his knowledge to his own advantage." Because if you are not careful, the tension of the opposites can emerge unexpectedly into consciousness, and suddenly the "kind" people can become very dangerous and aggressive. Two world wars that erupted senselessly on the "cultivated" European continent prove that.

The Second Figure

"The Fight with the Dragon"

This figure describes the dangerous outburst of affect, of which Lambspring warned at the end of the discussion of the first figure. The fight takes place in a forest, which is also a symbol of the unconscious but which, as living nature, is closer to consciousness than the sea. The battle has to end in triumph; otherwise, all possibility of development is destroyed. *Putrefactio* is the figure's warning subtitle. Anyone who knows people knows how dangerous it is to touch an unconscious complex. When a sore point is touched in yourself, you should recognize the affect, endure it and, without being overcome by it, wrestle with it. Then evil can show its good side: "The blackness of the dragon will disappear and a clear white will appear." Seeing the brighter side of dark qualities and affects is, of course, a very personal matter and should not be talked about too much. Lambspring says, "You should not tell it to any foolish people." A foolish person will think that the possibility of a brighter side to dark qualities simply means that any form of immoral behavior is permitted. The right path is best not expressed too clearly in words. Lambspring says, "Even the wise do not talk completely openly about it in their writings." Anyone who knows what is at issue also knows that an overt description of the good that is in evil can easily seem flattering, somehow false or even ridiculous. We can see this today if we read good case histories of analytical psychotherapy. Even in the best account the central point of the analysis escapes definition and, if one tries to describe it, one is usually misunderstood.

The Third Figure

"The Unicorn and the Stag"

Once we have dealt with the first great outburst of affect – many fall at this first hurdle – the situation becomes calmer. We are still in the forest, where the unconscious predominates. But now the affect displays two sides in the proper sense, since now we see two *different* animals. Lambspring makes it quite clear that the image and the animals are symbolic: "Thus we can apply this

symbolic image to our own art." The unicorn with its phallic horn
is masculine and aggressive; the stag is on the whole a rather shy
creature, and if you meet it in the forest it swiftly disappears. The
result of the battle with the first dangerous affect is still a com-
plex-personality. We all know people of this sort; they are sensitive and shy, but can also become unexpectedly very aggressive.
Such people can be termed neurotic. Nonetheless, this attitude of
mind represents progress compared with the seemingly normal
attitude (first figure), which conceals a murderous affect (second
figure). According to Lambspring, the unicorn has a more spiritual, intellectual aspect, whereas the stag has to do with soul
(feeling). Here we see a contrast, which for the alchemist is also
male-female (intellect-soul). At the same time, it is the same
contrast as was discussed with the seed and the metals. The
unicorn, like the center, has a single horn; the stag's antlers have
many branches, just as there are many metals.

The Fourth Figure

"Two Strong Lions"

We are still in the unconscious, in the forest. But after further
work the two sides of the affect have achieved good collaboration.
Until now they have been represented in formal alchemical terms
as seed and metals, male and female. Here they are clearly
pictured as a lion and lioness. They accompany one another
calmly and peacefully. They must also, as Lambspring says, unite
to become one creature. This means that, once we are able to
pacify our sensitivity (stag) and control our aggressivity (unicorn),
our affects can be a help to us and give us strength. Both sides of
the affect must work together. Lambspring puts it as follows:
"Whoever can master them with wisdom, but also with skill, and
lead them in the *same* forest is on the right path." One could say,
without affect there is no real strength. A teacher, for example,
who is overemotional is often helpless in front of his class. But a
teacher who can deal with his affect is capable of educating his
pupils, often with humor and enthusiasm, perhaps with grim

laughter, too, and if necessary with sharp reprimands. Lambspring sets great value on the collaboration of the tension of opposites in affect; he calls it a "great miracle." It is also a first important step in the development of the personality; others will follow.

The Fifth Figure

"The Fight of the Wolf and the Dog"

So far, the encounter of opposites has been natural – first in the water, then in the forest. Here the two animals are seen in a new situation, in open country, which clearly indicates a more conscious problem. This problem emerges when a person reaches the limits of the development of his natural being. Lambspring says at this point, "Alexander writes from Persia." "Alexander in Persia" is the alchemical formula for a human state that has reached its limits. In this situation the problem of self-knowledge and culture arises. Here the opposites are the natural, wild wolf and the domesticated dog. "The wolf comes from the East, the dog from the West." Thus the natural element comes from the beginning of the development (sunrise), and the domesticated element stands for its end (sunset). Lambspring says that the two kill one another and in the process (work) are transformed into a single creature. The emotional problem that is confronted with culture and civilization can be seen, for example, in the sexual problem. At some level we, too, are wild animals, and sexuality is a natural aggressive drive: a wolf. On the other hand, we are also human, civilized beings; for us, love is also eros on a cultivated level: a dog. There is, therefore, in sexuality and in eros a conflict between nature and culture. There are beautiful erotic feelings that overlook sexuality, and there is sexual aggression that forgets love. "The one kills the other," says Lambspring. Accordingly, we have to work at the problem in such a way that sexuality will be a part of love and, if we are human, there will be no true sexuality without love. Of course, there are many other areas of life in which the contrast between nature and culture can be seen. An important step has been taken in the development.

The Sixth Figure

"The Serpent-Dragon Biting Its Own Tail"

Before the development can proceed, we encounter an extraordinarily difficult problem. The development is no longer a matter of dealing with a state, but becomes a forward development through transformation. Accordingly, the intellectual principle is no longer called *spiritus* but rather Mercurius, in line with the alchemical idea of transformation. The beginning of this development returns us to the unconscious, to the forest. The dragon-serpent is the familiar uroboros, symbol of circulation. As Lambspring says, it is "extremely poisonous." But the author also adds that, if we deal with the problem, "the poison becomes a great medicine." The circulation of the uroboros corresponds to the theorem of the alchemist Maria Prophetissa, whom we have already met in connection with the "gentle cooking." It runs as follows: "The one becomes two and the two become three, and from the three comes the one – as the fourth." This can be understood as follows: The first is the ego, the second is the problem that the ego encounters, and the third is the consequent affect. By coming to terms with the affect (the fourth) we return to the starting point. But it could be that we are then no further than we were before and so the circulation can start all over again. Such a solution is unsatisfactory and dangerous. It corresponds to the poison of which Lambspring speaks. What it means is that after every burst of affect one simply calms down again. The calming down becomes a habit, and in place of a development comes a sterile attitude that is unfortunately all too widespread. A colleague once said to me, quite accurately, "Most people just vegetate after the age of forty."

I would like to show with a negative example what is really at issue if the poison is to acquire healing power. Goethe, who had an excellent knowledge of alchemy, describes in *Faust* the rejuvenation of Doctor Faust which is to initiate a new development. A witch hands Faust the rejuvenating potion. At the same time, she pronounces the axiom of Maria Prophetissa in an altered form, saying, "From one make two and two is three, lose the four." (This quotation is abbreviated; the rest of it refers to the higher alchemical numerical sequence from one to ten.) The further development of Faust shows how destructive the loss of the four is. Faust destroys Gretchen, and loses Helena and his son Euphorion; he even has the ancestors Philemon and Baucis murdered. He is still full of feeling, but completely lacking in insight.

So when Lambspring talks about the transformation of the poison into a medicine, it is the content of the "four" that is at issue. The four must not be lost by allowing it to become one again without further commentary, or by simply "losing" it (leaving it out). This means that the affect experienced in the encounter with the world or with oneself should not be dealt with simply by calming down again, or by neglecting to deal with it at all (Faust). It has to be dealt with in such a way that the four remains in existence, which means that you learn something from the emotion that you have experienced. Only when Maria's axiom brings progress in terms of insight and knowledge of the soul is it positive. In Lambspring's picture this positive possibility is shown in a very subtle way. The dragon-serpent does not bite the end of its tail, but a point slightly above it, while the end of the tail curls in an extension of the circle; and the hook at the end of the tail indicates that something new has to be sought.

The Seventh Figure

"Two Birds"

This picture, like the preceding one, is also a picture of development in the sense of Mercurius. As creatures of the air, birds indicate *intellectual* progress. The birds are still in the forest, though at the edge of it in the picture. One of the birds is flying away; the second is sitting quietly in the nest. The development, which is still largely natural and spontaneous (forest), is one-sided to begin with. Only one bird flies away. This represents an important principle of spiritual development. Although the elements described by Lambspring are always seen in relation to the problem of opposites, here one side is, so to speak, immobilized: The second bird stays in the nest. In practical terms this means that, despite all the contradictoriness in knowledge, it is necessary for any intellectual development first to acquire a clear attitude through careful work, even if it is temporary and one-sided. For example, in psychiatry or in any school of psychology, a student has to apply himself conscientiously and completely to acquiring the teachings of his science, although naturally these can only give a one-sided picture of psychological problems. But the student has to know where he stands and has to be thoroughly trained in this respect. The fact that the acquired doctrine reflects a one-sided point of view (obviously, since the second bird stays in the nest) can be brought up later. This thorough training calls for care and patience. Below on the ground is a snail – not an overhasty creature, as we know.

The Eighth Figure

"The Fight of the Two Birds"

The form of one-sided intellectual development in the previous picture also corresponds to the one-sided nature and temperament of the individual concerned. The fight of the two birds, the encounter of the opposites, is the logical consequence, and in that sense it is not a Mercurial transformation. The ruling spirit is once again referred to as *spiritus*. On the other hand, the encounter of the opposites leads to an expansion of the existing horizon. The previous limits were called "Alexander in *Persia* " (fifth figure). Here, however, the encounter extends beyond those limits. Accordingly, using alchemical terms Lambspring says, "The battle takes place in *India*." It is also significant that the fight is supposed to take place "in *horse manure*." This means that precisely what is commonly regarded as "filthy muck" is the basis for the encounter. Muck is not just filth; it also fosters growth. The person who has found his own point of view now has to come to terms with what, until now, he has regarded as false, senseless, and worthless. Our own point of view is much better defined by people who have a different point of view from ours than by those who agree with us. A definite and recognizable opinion can only exist if there are people who have a different opinion. A trained analyst, for example, knows the teachings and rules of his own school, but he also recognizes the limitations of his views and is ready to discuss them with another whose views may appear to him eccentric or even absurd, although the other is obviously neither stupid nor insane.

The Ninth Figure

"The Master of the Forest"

With the ninth figure, we leave the forest. The development has led to the point where the king of the forest arises and sits as ruler in his throne room. His feet rest on the now submissive dragon, the tamed affect. The master of the forest is the ruler of human nature and its cultural origin. He represents the general conditions determining the individual's attitude of mind, of which most people are completely unconscious. Even when they think and act as they believe is right, they do not know that this applies only to their country, their social group, their family, or even just themselves. There is absolutely nothing wrong with being ruled by a given condition, but the alchemist deems it necessary to develop a consciousness of this determining condition. His view is that true development consists in a creative transformation of the existing mental attitudes. This requires that the existing mental conditions be recognized. Making these conditions conscious is the task which Lambspring has been describing so far and which is completed when the ruler of the forest (the unconscious) appears in person as a king on his throne. As was indicated in some of the previous figures, the task is only possible if the affects are brought under control. Thus the tamed dragon is shown lying under the feet of the ruler. Lambspring considers the development up to the appearance of the master of the forest to be fundamentally right. He states, "Now we have reached the first grade [i.e., the first step]."

Evidently this step is valuable. An analyst, for example, who is aware of his own intellectual assumptions can usually (not always!) avoid unconsciously influencing the analysand with his own prejudices.

The Tenth Figure

"The Author Working with the Salamander in the Fire"

The knowledge of his own intellectual background is not enough to enable the adept to take a genuine step forward and achieve an individual development and transformation. That knowledge is static, not dynamic. For the dynamic transformation of the intellectual background, complete personal devotion is needed.

In Lambspring's work, the author himself appears twice, the first time on the title page in the formal dress of a knight of the empire. In the figures themselves he only appears once, in this tenth figure, which indicates its importance. Here Lambspring is naked, that is, he dedicates his whole being to the work of the alchemist, which is always symbolic. This is the beginning of the second grade (second step). In the first step, the task was to endure the affects. In the second step, where the personal intellectual background is to be developed further, one has to work with the affects; and that work must be emotional work. Lambspring is working on the salamander, which is itself in the fire, with the trident. If we compare it with the preceding pictures, we see that the salamander is a milder, tamed form of the dragon, the great affect. Not only is it held in the fire, it is also born in its true, effective form out of the fire, because the salamander is the creature of transformation that arises in fiery affect within the fire. It is not easy to describe this event. It is always a very moving, critical period in a person's life, in which he has to commit himself wholly and "nakedly" to the task, and in which he is also "naked" in the sense of being unprotected and exposed. I will try to give an example from analytical psychology. *Symbols of Transformation* was the work in which Jung set out on a new path which departed from that of Freud. The book opens emotionally, enthusiastically celebrating Freud's discovery of the Oedipus complex and its mythical dimension. In the continuation of the work, Jung encounters his affect over the existence of myth in the human soul. He responds to the affect in an openly emotional way. Reading the book, one is fascinated by the wealth of ideas and by Jung's language, which is simultaneously inspired and poetic. It could be said that Jung was working emotionally with his emotion. I heard from his own mouth how gripped and moved he was at that time. The result was a book on the libido and its transformations. But it was not an outstanding account of the libido as Freud understood it; it presented a new picture of the libido as comprehensive psychic energy, whereas Freud restricted the libido to the sexual sphere. A new chapter in the history of analysis had begun and, as Jung himself said, a new analytical school or direction had been founded. The event was archetypal, that is, of both general and individual significance. It was a new beginning, the beginning of the second step in analytical psychology; but for Jung it was also a crucial personal event.

The Eleventh Figure

"Father, Son, and Wise Leader"

In this figure, the result of the work described in the tenth figure becomes visible. The alchemist undertook the work in the tenth figure because something new had to come. Next to the old "king of the forest," the old attitude, walks a son, a young king. At the same time, in the work with the salamander in the fire, the principle of insight, already mentioned in our discussion of the oroboros, has taken shape as a clearly defined figure, that is, a definite principle. As the principle of insight, it is the archetype of the wise old man. In the alchemical process this is a pronouncedly intellectual guide, a leader with angel's wings, a psychopomp. Its task is to ensure that the tension of opposites between the old king and the young king (father and son), in other words between the old and the new attitude, does not cause destruction, but is fruitful.

From this figure onwards the proportions are reorganized. The events take place in the open or in the king's palace. Only human beings appear in the pictures since, once the master of the forest has appeared as the old attitude, the unconscious in the shape of water or forest no longer plays a role, and the stage of the "animal-soul" has been accomplished, too. The old king, who is evidently the master of the forest, is as father the condition for the future development and is called "body" (*corpus*). The young, newly arrived king, who is to bring about the continuation of the development, is a fertilizing agent and is called "spirit" (*spiritus*). The guide of the soul, who governs the whole development, is called "soul" (*anima*). But in contrast to the same principle as it appeared in the first step, this is an anima on a higher level, which as a psychopomp also includes the Mercurial principle of trans-formation.

The Twelfth Figure

"The Wise Old Man and the Son on the High Mountain"

This figure offers advice of great wisdom which is valid for the individual but also for other areas, including science and politics. The young king, the new attitude, has to change the world of the old king. But before he does that, he must get to know the world of the old king and its existing structure generally and thorough-ly. If he wants to change things, he first has to know *what* should be changed. Accompanied by the philosopher, he has made his way to the top of a high mountain outside the old king's country. It is only from a point outside that one can have a proper view of an area. That is why Lambspring calls the mountain "a mountain in *India*." From there, engaged in earnest conversation and pointing in various directions (look at the position of the arms), the two survey the empire that is to be taken over. The need to consider everything also from a general point of view is empha-sized by the starry sky, in which sun and moon prevail. This means, everything has to be seen *sub specie aeternitatis*, too. We can see an example of what the picture expresses in the development of psychiatry in the twentieth century. The introduction of psychology (the young king) into psychiatry led to tension. But then, far too early, psychology set itself up in opposition to psychiatry and failed in the eyes of existing medical psychiatry. This led to sometimes sharp opposition between psychiatry and analysis, which was not to the benefit of the patients. The opposition is being worked on today step by step, but still has not been completely resolved.

The Thirteenth Figure

"The Father Swallows the Son"

In the presence of the philosopher, the old king is about to swallow the young king. While the new element is expected to acquire an understanding of the realm of the old, the old element, too, has to make its contribution to the development. The old attitude knows that it needs rejuvenation. Before he starts swallowing the son, the old king says, "My son, I was dead without you and was living in great danger." The old attitude must be ready to incorporate the new attitude. Here, too, we can refer to our example of psychiatry. Of course, analysis did not understand psychiatry sufficiently, but psychiatry was also not ready to accept analysis and thus to gain a further development.

The Fourteenth Figure

"The Father Sweats on Account of the Son"

The old king has swallowed the young one. This causes him great discomfort and sickness. He is lying in bed, visibly suffering, and also has a rash. He is well looked after; chamber pot and slippers are at hand. Here the old king is alone; not even the philosopher can stand by him. Wisdom can prepare the assimilation of the new by the old, but the assimilation itself is a spontaneous process that we have to endure patiently. As Lambspring says, the poor king "earnestly begs God for help." And God does help by sending a fertilizing silver rain in through the open windows, which expose the king even to storms. Generally, the picture shows that we can assist progress with our efforts and also find a new attitude. True acceptance of the new, however, takes place through suffering and, if the suffering is fruitful, we can call it luck or the grace of God.

Everywhere we look in the world today, we see how new tendencies are shaking existing structures; we see that many people suffer as a result, and we hope that something good will come of it. But that will only be if we are lucky. In this we can briefly extend the psychiatric example. The introduction of analysis into clinical psychiatry in particular is not at all easy. The dynamics of transference and countertransference, such as we encounter them in analysis, are for a clinic often tied up with the risk of very considerable disorder. Some clinics have been obliged to break off the "psychotherapeutic experiment," though possibly with a view to taking it up again later.

The Fifteenth Figure

"The Father and the Son Are Now United"

The two are united by the winged wise old man. They rule jointly. There is neither suppression of the new principle nor destruction of the old one. This is not revolution, but *evolution* (organic development). The goal of the development is not the dethronement of the old element by the new, but rather their joint rule in a synthesis.

The whole process that Lambspring describes is an archetype, a typical form of attitude and emotional behavior. The practical examples given in the course of the description of the figures were just isolated instances intended to throw light on the meaning of the figure. The development that the sequence of figures illustrates can be seen as a problem and a task on many different levels. A young person, for example, who is getting married has to adopt a new attitude; yet he must not lose himself and must remain the person he really is. Or a doctor who is training to be a specialist must always remain a doctor and a faithful pupil of

Hippocrates. On the social level a democracy has to serve greater and greater social needs, but not at the cost of democratic freedom. Likewise, a person should accept and assimilate his dark side, but not devalue his good side. The rule is always the same: "Know who you are, even if it means agitation or even shame. Go to meet the new experience that is coming your way with insight and understanding, and if you change, do not destroy anything, but develop and grow." In this sense, Lambspring calls the goal of the development "improvement" and "increase." But with his fourteenth figure, he also shows us that even the best preparation cannot spare us the attendant suffering.

Lambspring published his work in 1625. The Latin translation appeared in 1677. Those were very critical years for the Holy Roman Empire, of which he called himself a knight. During the Thirty Years War (1618–48), Germany was largely destroyed; misery was everywhere. The destruction of the empire called forth a countermovement. People like Lambspring sought and described in a very personal and beautiful way the true nature of man and his cultural possibilities. They also showed how conflicts ought to be resolved. We can assume that people understood what he had to say to them, since the book was received with great interest. Just how important his figures and text were considered is shown by the fact that his work was translated into Latin and incorporated into the *Hermetic Museum*, which was published in a very large edition. In this way, Lambspring was able to help when people needed his spiritual guidance. For us, confronted with the conflicts of *our* time, it is again of benefit to read his work and give ear to his knowledge.

It is remarkable how soon after Lambspring this knowledge about direct observation of inner states was lost. A reorientation was already under way in Lambspring's own time. René Descartes (1596–1650), who might be called the father of modern rational thought, was his contemporary. The last person to support Lambspring's view was Goethe, whose knowledge of alchemy we have already mentioned. In his theory of color, he single-handedly defended a theory that is far more alchemical than scientific. Slowly this is receiving recognition today; the Zurich writer Adolf Muschg[6] drew attention to it in the context of the Goethe Year (1981).

XVI

PSYCHOLOGICAL-PSYCHIATRIC THERAPY: THE PSYCHOTHERAPEUTIC CLINIC

Psychotherapeutic clinics are set up to treat disorders that are psychologically conditioned. The disorder usually rests on mental dissociation, the state of not being at one with oneself, which means that a person is not living and experiencing things in the way that he ought to. A person may think he wants one thing but then, without being properly aware of it, do something quite different. The result can be a mental disorder, or sometimes a physical disorder.

The treatment of mental, or even physical, disorders by psychological means is called psychotherapy, a term introduced by the Bernese doctor Dubois. Over the course of the past eighty years, under the influence of Sigmund Freud, C. G. Jung, Alfred Adler, and many others, psychotherapy has been developed into a whole treatment procedure. There are analysis sessions at regular intervals. Mistakes or omissions are exposed, and the so-called blind spot is discovered. In psychotherapy the patient at last expresses himself the way he is, and in the encounter with the therapist he experiences himself as a new person. The influence of mutual emotions is considerable; nighttime fantasies or dreams can bring fresh insights; and finally, the carefully guarded daydreams are also discussed. Jung has shown that daydreams can also be actively shaped using a method that he called "active imagination." By this means, and also in suitable cases through creative activity, the creative side of the personality can be vitalized and so lead to new forms of life.

At present, in contrast to outpatient psychotherapy, clinical psychotherapy is considerably less well developed. The circumstances are somewhat different. It is certainly possible to adopt the procedure of regular analytical sessions in hospital. But there this procedure is only one aid among others. Perhaps the most effective aspect of the hospital is the surroundings, which in themselves are a challenge to old, entrenched habits of behavior and thought. In addition, it is more usual in hospital than in outpatient care to combine psychotherapy with medical treatment.

Since it is such an important factor, the nature of the hospital environment demands careful thought. Psychiatric hospitals today are mostly much too big, so that it is not possible to give the patient the degree of personal attention he needs. And the better class of private clinics are often too much like hotels: comfortable, certainly, but sterile. What we should be aiming for is a small-scale unit in which the patient, too, can have a say. Having a say can be a way of discovering new self-confidence and a sense of community. At last the patient is doing something again, and at last he is doing something for someone else. Needless to say, this should not become a routine. There are people who first have to learn just to do nothing for once.

In a family atmosphere it becomes obvious how questionable the value of single rooms is. Through lack of initiative the patient is often completely incapable of "filling out" a single room all by himself. A single room can also foster his inability to find contact. Thus, in effect, the private room that many wealthy patients in particular feel they have to have can become a "golden cage," which sustains and fosters the mental disorder particularly effectively. The most satisfactory system in clinical practice has proved to be the three-bed room, since it prevents any patient from being psychologically dominated by another.

The patients should have a say in the day-to-day running of the clinic, for example, in the provision of meals or the arrangement of rooms. Beyond that, the demand for communal care also means that some patients cannot be cared for exclusively by nurses while other patients look on as spectators. It should be self-evident in a psychotherapeutic clinic that the patients also care for one another. Very often, patients show greater sensitivity in caregiving and greater foresight in carrying out supervisory duties.

The communal ideal of the psychotherapeutic clinic would also suggest that some of the beds should be reserved for suitable patients who have no financial means.

The basic phenomenon that determines clinical psychotherapy in very general terms is constellation. Gradually you get to know the new patient. A stranger at first, within days or sometimes within weeks, he soon becomes a familiar person. At the same time, the problem typical for that particular patient also becomes apparent. And the emotionality bound up with that problem emerges. It is essential to know this. The emergence of emotionality at the start of treatment can sometimes lead to what seems like a deterioration in the patient's condition, although in fact it is very positive.

Apart from individual psychotherapy, which usually takes place in hourly sessions, the whole atmosphere of the psychotherapeutic clinic should be underpinned by an analytical psychological attitude. This attitude is fostered by group sessions in which mutual "family" relationships are consciously cultivated. Of course, people will not talk to one another as in most real families, where everyone usually lies to everyone else, but with conscious analytical openness. Sometimes you can use psychodrama (Moreno), a method of treatment that some extraverts often respond to astonishingly well.

A further important factor is the pursuit of gymnastics and sport. The mentally ill often have a particularly bad relationship to their bodies.

In the workshop that is part of the psychotherapeutic clinic, senseless routine is to be avoided. Patiently and calmly the staff should let what the patient does and makes take shape at its own pace. Even doing nothing in the workshop, at first, can produce results later on.

On the whole, though, the patients should not be given too much active encouragement to take part in activities or in psychotherapy. There are those who are then only too inclined to abuse the situation in the clinic, and especially in psychotherapy, in order to run away from themselves.

In the hospital there will be occasions for what we call "major psychotherapy." This can take place in individual consultations or in the psychotherapeutic environment of the hospital. The difficulties it brings with it have to be accepted. The extent of its success can become a measure of the psychological competence of the hospital.

As a rule in the psychotherapeutic clinic, the physical examination is not restricted to the simple physical state, but is carried out with all the aids of modern medicine. A psychotherapist knows that the physical findings are an important aspect of the overall state of the patient and often reveal vital facts. But he also knows that those findings often go deep and are by no means restricted simply to so-called vegetative disorders.

Medical treatment, in particular the treatment of psychosis with neuroleptics, will also be given in the psychotherapeutic clinic. But experience shows that simultaneous psychotherapy is also important in such cases. The medicine helps to shield the patient from overpowering affect. Then psychological problems become apparent relatively quickly, at an early stage, as it were; accordingly, they have to be carefully observed and continuously worked on.

The work of the hospital also involves contact with the patient's relatives. For a clinical psychotherapist the relatives are not simply a nuisance. They are extremely important, since it is through contact with them that it becomes possible to approach questions concerning the patient's past. Sometimes there is advantage to be gained from involving the relatives in the patient's therapy. The same can be said of the patient's employer. It is also useful for an appreciation of the patient's background to have the cooperation of the family doctor.

In the present state of psychotherapy it is possible, wherever psychotherapists are available, to treat cases of low to medium severity as outpatients. The hospital should deal with serious cases (endogenous or organic psychoses) or cases with attendant high risk, such as suicidal states or addiction. This means that the hospital will have an open and a closed section; and that its psychiatrists will not rely on innovation, but on the tried and tested rules of the art of medicine. Such guidelines provide a clear framework ("vessel") which with the right psychological attitude can be beneficial in itself, and in which it is possible to endure even the more turbulent phases of clinical psychotherapy. Thus the psychotherapeutic clinic is itself an instrument of clinical psychotherapy.

XVII

PSYCHOTHERAPY
IN THE TREATMENT OF DEPRESSION

It is widely assumed that psychotherapy cannot be used to treat severe depressive disorders. This is not the case. The psychotherapeutic treatment of depression requires a procedure that is specially adapted to the circumstances we meet; it will differ from the usual analytical and psychotherapeutic method in several details.

Depression is characterized by typical psychiatric findings. These findings prompt the therapist to think along certain lines and to take certain measures. An awareness and psychological analysis of the findings form the essential basis for the psychotherapeutic treatment of depression. Similarly, the therapeutic considerations and measures that come to mind should also be subjected to analysis.

Analytical reflection starts with the simple *description* of the depressive state: The patient is not just sad, he has lost hope. Evidently, on the basis of the existing mental attitude, there is no scope for fruitful development.

– The patient feels weak, even to the point where the subjective feeling of physical weakness persists despite the absence of physical malfunction. He feels a lack of concentration and attributes it to the onset of senility. Furthermore, there is a lack of willpower and initiative. Clearly, energy has been withdrawn from active consciousness; it has been diverted "into the unconscious."

– There is insomnia. The contact between consciousness and the unconscious is disturbed, which means that the natural transition from the conscious to the unconscious state, in other words, going to sleep is made difficult.

– Metabolic disorders (liver or, in some cases, sugar metabolism) can occur, indicating the presence of considerable affect associated with the depression.

– Ideas of impoverishment and sinfulness indicate that the existing mental state is undermined and that a release from this state is needed, although it appears impossible.

– Suicidal tendencies show the need for a fundamental change. The existing state of things has to die away so that something new can take its place. It is the Goethean idea of *"Stirb und werde!"* ("Die and be reborn!"). But the depressive sees only the first part of the phrase!

Needless to say, the psychological nature of the observed findings does not excuse us from the duty to carry out a *medical differential diagnosis,* since physical illnesses can begin with depressive symptoms. Those to be considered in this context are nephritis with suburaemia, diabetes mellitus, heart disease, carbon disulphide poisoning (e.g., in the artificial silk industry), and other toxic disorders; then there are incipient cerebro-organic diseases, such as arteriosclerosis, Parkinson's disease, brain tumor, or multiple sclerosis. On the other hand, however, the fact that the depressive state disappears with the improvement or cure of a physical condition does not prove that the observed depression did not have any psychological aspects. Such depressions often have a dual origin, so to speak. Under the pressure of a physical disorder, it may emerge that there was a lot wrong with the patient psychologically; the physical disorder led to the decompensation of a psyche that was in any case far from stable. The disappearance of the physical disorder then leads to the renewed compensation of the psyche, which does not mean, however, that everything is as it should be psychologically. A psychological attitude would therefore require *that, despite the physical components, the presenting depressive symptoms be carefully noted and their contents taken seriously.*

A great difficulty for the psychologically oriented therapist is psychiatric differential diagnosis. The better you get to know a patient, the more difficult it becomes to see the dividing line, for example, between "psychogenic" and "endogenous" depression. It may be more accurate to say that in severe depressions presenting the classical clinical picture of "melancholia" (with inhibition and retardation of thought processes, marked suicidal tendency, an absence of purely external causes of illness, an occasional tendency to delusions and also with repeated depressive phases), the psychological aspect is characterized by the *absence from consciousness* of an often seemingly insignificant *principle,* but one that is important for the patient. The absence of this principle is probably conditioned by circumstances associated with the milieu from which the patient comes. Earlier depressive phases may correspond to the vain attempt to solve the problem associated with a psychic situation of that nature. The practical examples I shall give in the course of our discussion to illustrate what is said here are all, in that sense, cases of severe depression.

The *psychiatric treatment* of severe cases obviously has to follow known rules. There are also *important psychological considerations* attached to those rules:

– The patient must be calmed; usually treatment is best given in hospital. For the patient this helps to clarify the situation. It is made clear to him that he is depressive and that he does not have to be anything else; and it is made clear that the situation can be organized in a meaningful way. If you compare this organization with the agitated helplessness from which the patient and his relatives were suffering before the start of treatment, then the value of such a clarification becomes apparent.

– During the treatment a daily program should be established, if possible in tandem with occupational therapy. In his unstructured depression the patient has fallen "outside of time," as it were, which is why the hours that divide up the day have to be made visible again.

– The patient must be examined repeatedly, and the observed symptoms should be described and explained to him again and again. For example, if the patient discovers that the therapist

knows how physically weak depressives can feel, he feels understood. In general, through examination and explanations, one
should try to let the patient see the common and typical aspects of
his condition, since he feels threatened by something strange and
incomprehensible.

– The therapist's patience and sense of responsibility should
also come from the knowledge that the patient, who after all has
no hope, does not need the arrogant attitude of a would-be healer
in whom he can have no faith, but the warmth and support of a
therapist who is there to help a fellow human being.

In the therapeutic situation, patient and therapist come closer
to one another; as a result, the therapeutic event that Jung called
constellation becomes a possibility.[1] What is constellated in this
quasi-experimental situation is the factor that is absent from
consciousness and the absence of which has given rise to the
disorder. The circumstances we find in depression are shown in
Jung's investigation of the fish in alchemy, and in particular in
Jung's discussion of an anonymous alchemical tract from the
seventeenth century.[2] The inhibiting factor (complex) is represented in that tract as a small fish, called a remora, which can
"hold back the proud vessel of the great Ocean sea." There is, in
reality, a fish called a "remora"; it is a type of mackerel that
clings to the bottom of ships with its dorsal fin, which functions
as a sucker. In antiquity it was believed that these fish could
immobilize large vessels. In the text cited by Jung, though, the
feat of holding ships fast is obviously intended symbolically.
What it describes is a seemingly tiny complex that can give rise to
a serious inhibition and block in consciousness. In the tract, it is
claimed that the fish could, of course, be caught naturally, quickly,
and easily with the help of the "philosophers' magnet." The
inhibition would then be lifted.

Accordingly, the therapist should have a store of knowledge
corresponding to the "philosophers' magnet." The attitude of a
fisherman who is ready to wait patiently and quietly is a very apt
image for the attitude that is needed. It is that attitude which
makes constellation possible. In treating depression, we also have

to take seriously the alchemist's demand that the fish be caught "naturally." We have to observe without preconceptions, think in an uncomplicated manner, and above all, listen very carefully. Paracelsus described this therapeutic principle very beautifully. In his essay "Labyrinthus Medicorum"[3] he says, "If a doctor cannot see right away what is wrong, he gets lost in a labyrinth, misleading himself and others, *since he has proof of it from the patient's mouth and it is there for eyes to see and ears to hear.*"

No psychiatrist will deny that modern *pharmacotherapy* has made the treatment of depression considerably easier and faster. However, it has not made psychotherapy superfluous. If a depression is treated simply with drugs, the patient often feels degraded as a person. He suffers as a person, so when the treatment consists simply of pills and injections, he gets the impression that he is not being treated by doctors at all, but has fallen into the hands of veterinarians (a phrase used by Manfred Bleuler at a symposium held at the psychiatric hospital at the University of Zurich). Moreover, the psychological problem tied up with the depression is not solved with drugs, but often simply suppressed, which naturally cannot be good for the prognosis in the long term. Accordingly, the acceleration of treatment through medication demands particular *care and attention on the part of the therapist.* When the depression recedes, the psychological problem (the "little fish") can emerge very suddenly, but it can also disappear again equally suddenly. That is why you have to keep in mind the Hippocratic principle "The art is long, but the moment is transient."

In contrast to pharmacotherapy, *electroshock therapy* is very dangerous in cases of depression. The treatment is harmless enough in itself; the "shock" is simply an artificial epileptic fit, and if it is carried out properly, the treatment is painless and safe. Electroshock treatment can be startlingly successful in putting an end to depression. And then the doctor says proudly, "Now we can cut the length of stay of depressive patients by more than half," which is precisely why it is dangerous. As early as 1951, Herbert Lewrenz in Hamburg showed from a sample of 595 cases that electroshock therapy does not cure or shorten the phase of illness, but only interrupts it. Cases of complete cure, so-called, were ones that were treated at the end of the phase.[4] If electroshock therapy is administered in the middle of the phase, the depression may after a certain period (from a few months to a year) reassert its hold on a person who thought himself cured. Such an attack takes place in a matter of minutes in the form of severe depression: The person suddenly feels quite lost and, before anyone else notices anything, he has committed suicide. In this sense, the use of electroshock therapy in cases of depression can put life at risk. It is also a sign of impatience, which is inappropriate to depression.

We know that the treatment of depression not only demands the patience of a fisherman, but that one must also constantly give the patient hope. In that way, the patient is shown that a turn for the better is anticipated at the end of a development. This highlights the *psychic process.*

The incomprehensible, overwhelming nature of the depression has to be discussed with the patient in a way that makes the *autonomy of the psyche* apparent. This autonomy has to be trusted, since in the autonomous psyche there is a constant resurgence of self-healing forces. The attitude of patience that is required while one waits for the psychic process to appear recalls the sort of psychological advice given, for example, in the literature of the eighteenth century, where it is said that in times of need one should wait "for God's springs to start flowing again."

The therapist should also bear in mind the overwhelming influence the depression can have on himself. The patient's death wish can be so intense that it *blinds* the therapist and leads him to act foolishly – in a way that provokes suicide. On three occasions, I have known an experienced psychiatrist of the utmost competence to explain to a depressive patient that he was suicidal and would therefore have to be admitted to a secure hospital within the next few days. By that time the patient was dead. It is characteristic, too, that these were experienced doctors: *Wherever the unconscious exercises its power of suggestion, there is a reversal;* and the experienced person turns out to be more inexperienced than someone without experience.

Of particular importance in the psychology of depression is the patient's conviction, best formulated as follows, *"that no one has ever suffered as I am suffering."* In reacting to this conviction, the therapist should see that it has two sides. On the one hand, it is impossible to dispute the truth of the statement in a purely formal sense. In depression the patient experiences his completely personal, unmistakable problems, and so he alone suffers in precisely the way that he is suffering. The therapist should acknowledge this aspect of the depression, that is to say, the depression as part of the process of individuation. On the other hand, though, the insistence on "unique suffering" is also inflationary; it shows a tendency to feel oneself to be someone special on account of one's suffering, exalted, like Christ, above other mortals. This inflationary aspect of the conviction can be met through a thorough and repeated discussion of the depressive symptoms. The discussion will show that the "unique suffering" has certain common features familiar to every psychiatrist, so that there can be no question of uniqueness in that sense. Thus precisely by this discussion, it is possible to demonstrate an essential characteristic of the *process of individuation:* Subjectively the process is unique, but objectively it is a universal human experience, since it is the particular experience of a perfectly ordinary person.

What follows are *practical examples* which should help to elucidate what has been said so far. Needless to say, they cannot possibly give a systematic demonstration of all or even a majority of the ideas mentioned. It is well known that such a demonstration is only possible by doing violence to the observed material. However, the examples can illustrate how the therapeutic encounter with the depressive patient develops when the therapy proceeds on the basis of the *attitude* described above. Each of the cases outlined below deserves a detailed case history; but here I will limit myself to a few essential points.

Case 1

A sixty-year-old man was receiving hospital treatment for depression accompanied by helplessness and despair. At that time, circumstances meant that as a rule I did not treat any patients personally, but supervised the work of the hospital instead. My colleagues were unanimous in the opinion that psychotherapy was impossible with that particular patient because "he always said the same thing every day and was incredibly boring." This prompted me to take over the treatment myself after all. I saw the patient every day, and it had to be admitted that he always said the same thing. All the same, I decided to keep an exact record of everything he said. Then it became possible to detect slight nuances in what he said; it was also possible to say in what personal, unmistakable manner that person was "unoriginal." In that way, to me at least, he became a familiar and simple, but likable figure. When after ten days the depression lifted, the patient ascribed it to the psychotherapy. Admittedly the case may not have been very interesting, but when you see in how many different ways people can be "uninteresting," and when you study the particular manifestation of that in the case you are dealing with, the patient can be helped to regain self-confidence and a sense of personal worth. What is *individual* about a person is expressed in everything he says and does. In this connection, I am always reminded of a motto dedicated to one of my ancestors by Johann Caspar Lavater: "What poise there is in a man, what gestures and movements, what variety of ways of lying and sitting and standing!"

Case 2

A sixty-three-year-old English psychiatrist, director of a big institution, was treated by me for nine months – it was before the days of modern pharmacotherapy – for suicidal depression. I saw the patient for an hour every day. He himself was completely convinced that his illness was endogenous and that psychotherapy would have no effect. But he was also convinced that I knew that, too, which led him to the conclusion that I was a quite outstanding psychotherapist. For if I did not come to "cure" him, it was clear that I came to him because of who he was, and that *sympathy* was the reason for my behavior. After nine months the depression faded. It was interesting that the patient's deputy, who was in charge of the hospital in the latter's absence and who was known as an opponent of psychotherapy, wrote me a friendly letter thanking me for curing his colleague with psychotherapy! The case had an interesting sequel. During the nine months of treatment, I had discussed all kinds of professional psychological matters with the patient, as a colleague, and much of what I had said was new to him as a purely clinically oriented psychiatrist. When he retired a few years after the treatment, having previously worked only as an institutional psychiatrist, he opened an outpatient practice which soon grew successful. After all, he had undergone a nine-month training analysis beforehand! So we see that we can never know when and how our psychotherapeutic efforts will be rewarded; if we have a serious attitude, the encounter with the patient will be important one way or another in the patient's life history.

Case 3

I observed this case many years ago. A woman of over seventy years lost her husband after fifty years of happy marriage. Following his death, she fell into a highly erethismic, suicidal depression and had to be kept under constant supervision. The family doctor consulted C. G. Jung, who prescribed tincture of opium (following Kraepelin) and thought that probably the weather was having a detrimental effect at that particular time. When the condition failed to improve, Jung was again consulted. He altered the dose of opium and said that the weather still seemed to be unfavorable. Not long after this second consultation, the patient asked to be given writing materials and composed a document that ran over several sides. The facts were as follows: The woman had originally been Catholic. Her fiancé, a Protestant and at bottom an atheist, was prepared to receive instruction from the Catholic bishop, but refused to be converted. In these circumstances the woman went over to Protestantism before her marriage. She also accepted the philosophical and atheistic point of view of her beloved husband. The document she composed during her depression, after her husband's death, was a very personal confession of faith, which struck an interesting balance between a Lutheran attitude on the one hand and Catholicism on the other. With this writing down of her confession of faith, the depression came to an end. The woman lived a few months more and then died suddenly in her bed of a heart attack. The woman's confession of faith was clearly "born" out of the depression. In the confession she found her way back to the intellectual independence she had renounced in favor of the attitude of her husband. But half a century spent at the side of an atheistic philosopher could not fail to leave an impression. Accordingly, a return to her original Catholicism was not possible, and the woman had to make a conscious effort to find her personal religious position. Through a purely passive stance, Jung had aided this intellectual achievement. One has to appreciate that the appearance of this famous psychotherapist had aroused high expectations in the patient and those around her. The fact that the expected "pearls of wisdom" failed to materialize *threw the woman back on herself,* and the intellectual potential she had within her was *powerfully constellated.* Thus it is not just what is said that is important, but the effect of what is said also depends on the personality of the therapist.

Case 4

A fifty-two-year-old man suffering from depression developed depressive ideas of persecution. He thought the police were after him because he had run into an old man with his car. Although extensive inquiries failed to bring the supposed victim to light, the patient grew firmer in the conviction that he would be taken to court, that he would be convicted, and that he would have to go to prison for many years, to the disgrace of himself and his family. Having gone over this question with him at length and in all its details, I was suddenly seized by an *emotional counterreaction.* I said to the patient: "I don't believe that you will go to prison. But what do you think of your own attitude? Guilty or not guilty – there is such a thing as a miscarriage of justice – and it can happen to anyone. Haven't you got any philosophy or religion that would help you to face this?" The patient leapt up and replied, "That's it, that's just the point!" He explained how the milieu from which he came had provided him with nothing in the way of higher ideas, and how the European experience of the Second World War had finally robbed him of all spiritual guidelines. We then went on to discuss man's relationship to himself, to the world, and to the irrational against the background of the patient's life. The treatment was lengthy. But right from the beginning of the discussion – from the moment when the patient said "That's it!" – delusion and depression had disappeared.

Case 5

A sixty-year-old depressive undergoing hospital treatment wanted to speak to me urgently one day. He told me that he had discovered the reason for his illness. He was a great sinner. He also told me his sin: Once at a dance, when he was seventeen, he had almost put his hand "under a waitress's skirt and touched her leg." That meant that he had as good as done so, since simply having such an intention showed him to be a completely depraved person. The man had led a blameless life as an honest employee and faithful husband; he had even been one of the volunteers to keep the church clean. To all appearances his self-reproach was completely ridiculous. But it only seemed so, because that reproach revealed the *problem of sin*. For him at the end of his life, this problem was crucial. Evidently after a spotless life, he had great difficulty in finding a wrong deed that could pose the problem of "sin" (even the absence of guilt can represent spiritual poverty!). Therefore, this distant, trivial incident had to be taken very seriously, and there was every reason to be glad that it was possible to find an event around which to develop a discussion of the psychological and philosophical questions of guilt and salvation. Of course, guilt is bad, but sometimes it seems even worse to have to be a Pharisee!

Case 6

A forty-eight-year-old lawyer received hospital treatment for severe depression. He believed not only that he was beyond hope, but sometimes also that he was suffering from incurable venereal disease (syphilis), even though there were no indications of lues. The treatment was at first under my supervision. The first therapist, a Freudian (there is of course no judgment on the psychoanalytic method intended here!), declared that psychotherapy was impossible in this case because the patient's sole topic of conversation was the fact that cars ought to have a right-hand drive rather than a left-hand drive. Apart from these eccentric rationalistic digressions, it was impossible to get anything personal, let alone psychological, out of him. The treatment was then taken over by a Jungian (see the note above!). He discussed the symbolic meaning of "right-hand drive" and "left-hand drive" with the patient and explained that "right" tended to indicate the conscious attitude and "left," the unconscious attitude. The patient answered that that interpretation did not seem meaningless to him, for he admitted that he probably ought to declare his views more consciously at work and in the family. But that would in no way provide a solution to his problem. He was not speaking of a symbol, but meant quite plainly and practically that a right-hand drive in cars was less dangerous and that that fact ought to be officially confirmed and acted on. Then partly on organizational grounds, I took over the treatment. I discussed the advantages and disadvantages of right- and left-hand drives with him in detail, at which he soon became highly excited. He had already collected a great deal of material on the subject. I also discovered that he had for a long time been talking of going public with his arguments, but that both his relatives and his professional friends laughed at him and described his plans as nonsense. In the course of therapy, the patient finally decided to publish his thoughts in print; and indeed, a corresponding voluminous manifesto appeared some time later. This activity resolved the depression. The principle that was elaborated in the course of treatment could be formulated as follows: *"An honest man stands by his views in public even when everyone else laughs at him."* This principle also shows the symbolic significance of the delusion regarding venereal disease, since for the patient the principle was decidedly "masculine," and as long as he did not demonstrate his adherence to it, his "sex," his attitude as a man, was indeed sick. It was evident that the patient was able to demonstrate his adherence to the principle only when he had found at least one person – the therapist – who did not laugh at him!

Case 7

A fifty-year-old managing director had been in a state of severe suicidal depression for over a year. He had previously suffered for years from intellectual doubt. Intensive study of Eastern philosophy and Western psychology had not gotten him any further. Once he even consulted Jung, who apparently simply told him, "You are too high up in the clouds; you should come down to earth." I treated the patient for several months in the hospital. When for many weeks he had been telling me he was incurably ill and would end up in the third class of a state institution, I decided to try a "psychotherapeutic operation." I said to the patient: "What makes you think that that couldn't happen to you? Every day around the world people are admitted to psychiatric institutions and stay there as incurable cases, and almost all are housed in the most basic class. Do you think that destiny has issued you with a special diploma which excludes the possibility of long-term hospitalization? *That sort of thing can happen to anyone,* even to you." The patient responded very angrily (obviously, there was a reawakening of energy!). He told me I was a heartless and mean psychiatrist, got in touch with his wife, and got her to take him home immediately. His angry uplift, however, was short-lived. After a week, the patient was so depressive that the director of his local state hospital (!) was consulted, and the patient was admitted to the first-class section of the hospital. In the following weeks, the patient put such pressure on the doctors and on his family with delusions of impoverishment that he was transferred first to the second-class section of the hospital, and finally to the third class on grounds of cost. Now he was where he had been afraid of going; he was with the incurable cases. Having taken this burden on himself, which required two weeks, he noticed to his astonishment that the depression had gone. Soon he received permission from the doctors to go out on his own, and then was discharged. Thus as a result of an unconscious and spontaneous development, the patient had accepted precisely what I had said to him: namely, that he had no "diploma" that excused him from the possibility of ending up a permanent inmate in the third class of an institution. By accepting that, he had "gone down to the ordinary people," which is what Jung had recommended, too. In his factory also he became "one of the ordinary people." Before the depression he had held an almost dictatorial position as director. As a result of his absence, his colleagues had gained influence and, to their surprise, when the patient returned he accepted his new role as senior member of a team. The fact that this development had been set in train by my "psychotherapeutic operation" was something the patient himself felt and documented. He sent us a twenty-two-page account of his descent to the third-class section of the state institution. In it he wrote that the development had brought about what I had wanted to bring about on that previous occasion; with my observation, I had – like a dentist who touches a raw nerve – come upon a layer that was still capable of reacting.

Case 8

Whereas in the previous case the "depressive delusion" was, so to speak, lived out in the external world, in this case there was a differentiated attempt to come to terms with the depressive loss of energy, which is experienced as weakness. The case concerns a thirty-year-old man, senior assistant at a university institute, who was hospitalized on account of acute depression. Although other doctors and a psychologist were also trying to help him, he

thought I was the only one who understood him, probably because I listened to his depressive tales with great interest. A very
interesting development occurred, in which there were three
quite simple dreams. I saw the patient daily. He complained of
weakness with apparent monotony. At first he expressed himself
in very general terms: "There's this weakness." After a week he
began to say, "I've got a weakness." So he had already recognized
the weakness as something that belonged to him. After a further
week he said, "I'm weak." Now he no longer described the
condition with a noun, as a concept, but simply recognized that
he was weak. During this development, in which step by step he
came to an acceptance of his weakness, he dreamed repeatedly,
"I am fighting with animals." Correspondingly, the conflict was
carried out on an animal and biological basis, formulated as the
problem of a lack of strength. Having reached the realization "I
am weak," the patient suddenly decided to pay a visit to his
university institute. He returned in indignation because his boss
had complained about his long absence, which he felt was heartless. But after a second visit he developed the insight that his
absence was, after all, very difficult for his boss, who had only
recently taken up the position. So he was able, in the encounter
with his colleague, to see the other's point of view and problems,
too, and not just to think of himself. During this period of
development he repeatedly dreamed, "I am fighting with people."
Here he met conflict with fellow humans. Clinically the patient
was now no longer depressive. But he himself did not know how
to judge his condition, and asked me what I thought of his being
discharged. To my counterquestion, "What do *you* think about it?"
he reacted angrily and declared loudly, "I have no right to think
anything about it!" Then I was able to discuss with him his duty
to face up to his condition and so to himself, and eventually to
form his own personal judgment. During this period of self-
encounter he repeatedly dreamed, "I am fighting with relatives."
The "relatives" – as often emerges in dream analysis – were inner
psychic factors ("endogenous relationships": brother as shadow,
i.e., his own dark side; sister as anima, i.e., his own emotionality).

Having accepted this confrontation with himself as a necessity, the patient left the clinic and returned to work. With regard to the problem that he had *"not only a right but also a duty to think about himself,"* he told me on leaving, "That is going to be important for me for the next forty years." His remark can be understood to mean that in the depression he had encountered his personal task for the second half of his life, which gave his life a new direction.

Case 9

In the therapeutic encounter with a depressive, the problem can be constellated in completely unexpected, peculiar ways. For months we treated a fifty-three-year-old English woman without success. Electroshock therapy had been tried previously in a different hospital; we tried pharmacotherapy. Detailed discussion of the case history and of numerous dreams produced some interesting points in connection with the patient's earlier relationships with men, but the clinical condition remained unchanged. One February evening the patient asked me whether there was any hope, and whether I was not at all in a position to name a date for the cure. As she was completely desperate, I could not bring myself to give the usual – and correct – stalling response, and said, "The cure is coming at the end of May, on the thirty-first." I told myself I would have to get myself out of trouble later, and anyway the patient would know that my claim was very bold. However, the patient started with emotion and cried, "How do you know that?" It was her greatest wish, she explained, to be back home on the first of June of that year because that was her husband's sixtieth birthday, which she would like to celebrate with him. This strange, so to speak, synchronistic coincidence of dates made me take the situation seriously. I immediately booked the patient's flight home to London for May 31 and simply noted that she would travel on that day. Her condition did not change in the least as a result of this, and at the end of May the patient was still as depressive as before. But in a reaction I could hardly justify on rational grounds,

I did not depart from the plan, and on May 31, I had the woman taken to the airport still in a depressive state, from where she flew alone to London. When she arrived in London, the depression had disappeared; and the birthday celebrations became at the same time a celebration of her recovery. What the patient had needed was to find somebody who was prepared *to build on a completely irrational event* – the synchronicity mentioned above – and to draw all the necessary consequences. As a result, her own irrationality, her "faith," was revived. No other theory was needed. Only this perhaps: Some years later the patient stopped at the clinic while passing through. She visited all the therapists and nurses who had taken care of her at that time. She also came to me. She greeted me, shook hands, and then said, "Well, I'll be on my way now; with you, a second is enough."

From the examples given above, which show a wide spectrum of human encounters, it is evident that the application of psychotherapy to cases of depression requires an open and uninhibited attitude on the part of the therapist. The right attitude means that the clinical symptoms are appreciated from both a medical and a psychological point of view; it also means that the patient's condition is received with an attentive ear and personal reactions. Since it is frequently the dark sides (shadow) of the patient that are constellated, the *attitude* of the therapist should be more that of a *brotherly companion* ("brother" would be the appropriate transference figure) than a caring mother or a guiding father, which would only lead the patient into an infantile regression. Schizophrenics, who have to be searched out and confronted in their infantility, often need parental transference figures. Depressives usually have more "grown-up" problems. The transference is not a purely spontaneous event; it is also, within limits, influenced by the behavior of the therapist. Sometimes, of course, the pressure of the transference from the side of the patient is so strong that he governs the situation. See also the example involving the risk of suicide (case 7)!

One might be inclined to think that the practice of psychotherapy in cases of depression demands certain special, for example, intuitive abilities. That is not the case. An experienced psychiatrist or psychotherapist will know that one cannot learn the details of psychotherapy from books, since every case raises new, individual questions. What one can describe, though, is a therapeutic attitude which is appropriate to depression. However well thought-out it may be, this attitude should remain simple and natural. It is what Paracelsus called *theoria*, which ought to be "free and easy." On the basis of this attitude, there can be an encounter with the patient, and questions can be answered. As our examples showed, the questions are quite various, which is not to say that they are particularly difficult. In order to answer them, the therapist of course needs extensive *knowledge,* knowledge that encompasses the world and life, history and the present time. A philosophical or religious point of view is also important. This means that psychotherapy in such cases requires what has always been known as a liberal education; it is no coincidence that the leading psychotherapists are also humanists. Their humanism is what the ancients called *philosophia*. For them *philosophia* was never a book, but always personal knowledge of what is essential. In this sense Paracelsus would have said that in the treatment of depression *theoria* and *philosophia* should become one. The unity of *theoria* and *philosophia* would then be the philosophers' magnet, which catches the little fish (the complex) and so answers the patient's vital question.

XVIII

POSSESSION BY THE MOTHER ARCHETYPE

Possession is a state to which people can succumb. In the state of possession a person is changed. Gone are self-criticism, level-headedness, and acquired manners. The ability to enter into a discussion is lacking. What you then see in that person is a great affect. The cause of the affect is a foreign something that has taken possession of that person and assumed control. That is when you ask yourself: What has got into him?

The something that takes control of a person in the state of possession is an archetype. That is to say, a typical pattern of behavior of general significance dominates one-sidedly and tolerates no competition. At the same time, the person who is possessed develops ideas of a universal, mythological nature, which he considers all-important. Both these aspects show the high energy with which an archetype can invade and take control.

The high energy of the archetype can be dangerous for the individual and for those around him, giving rise to what we call a psychiatric emergency. Cases of this sort are always instructive, since the archetype is not only a threat but can also teach us a lot, though its language is not always easy to understand.

I would like to present a case as a contribution to the diagnosis and treatment of possession. First I shall give the actual findings at the start of treatment.

A twenty-year-old girl was admitted to the clinic. She had to be brought by ambulance on a journey of several hours and, despite a sedative injection, was so agitated during the journey that a doctor had to give her another sedative injection. On admission, however, she appeared extremely restless. The parents, who accompanied her and were evidently educated people, were shocked by their daughter's wild behavior. She had hardly set foot inside the clinic when she started screaming and thrashing around, so that she had to be restrained by several people. The possession, in which levelheadedness and manners had disappeared, was plain to see. After a third sedative injection, the patient finally became calmer.

After a few hours the situation livened up again. I went to see the patient. She was able to speak to me hastily and often quietly, and then sometimes too loudly, but in a more or less ordered way. The patient's Christian name was Maria. She said, "A voice told me that I am now Holy Mary and that I am going to go to heaven with you, and die and be immortal." The patient was also worried by "the big sun out there"; it was not clear whether she was seeing the sun in the room or through the window.

We now have to examine the actual findings at the start of treatment to discover what they mean. From there we can proceed to an understanding of the case as a whole and arrive at the right therapeutic attitude.

The findings are dominated by the "great light," the "big sun out there." This light is a common finding in critical states. The light could mean extreme consciousness, but the consciousness it represents is not in the power of the individual; it is "out there." Light is an attribute not of the ego, but of the Self. It is in the form of light, too, that the great energy which bursts in on people from archetypal regions is perceived. A striking example of this phenomenon is presented in the *Memoirs* of Benvenuto Cellini. In prison, at a time of great distress, Cellini experienced the light phenomenon as something divine. The fact that Cellini later believed in all seriousness that, since that experience, he had had a halo was part of his arrogant Renaissance attitude; he claimed that the halo was clearly visible in the evening and that it appeared on the head of his shadow.

A tragic case was experienced by Dr. Ohm, prison chaplain in Moabit/Berlin during the war. An innocent German woman was arrested and beheaded in the aftermath of the assassination attempt against Hitler on 20 July 1944, as a result of intrigues. Dr. Ohm was present at the execution. A few seconds before the guillotine fell, the woman called out to Dr. Ohm, "Father, I can see a great light!" That is the light of eternal life.

Interestingly, this intense and total sense perception is experienced not only visually but also in rare cases through other sense organs. Dr. Schuerch, former editor-in-chief of the newspaper *Bund* in Bern, reports how he was saved purely by chance from an avalanche. Lying in the snow, close to death, he heard beautiful, unearthly, and very intense music. And a friend of mine, as a child, was driven out into the middle of Lake Constance by a great storm in an open rowboat; but then he ceased to be aware of the storm and danger, hearing only beautiful music. The child was later found in the harbor near where he lived, unharmed and asleep in the bottom of the boat. It seems as if these optical and acoustic phenomena not only signal danger but also provide protection. Once, I remember, an old woman who was physically ill and dying told me that she could smell exquisite scents, sweeter than the scent of roses.

The "great light," therefore, shows that the moment is important and critical. All the more reason to take what our patient says seriously. She is Holy Mary, and she is going to go to heaven with the therapist. Also, she is going to die. We will now try to understand these statements.

The idea of dying is relatively easy to understand. There is a very real aspect to it. The state of possession is often a danger to the patient's life. In his turmoil, he may have an accident, he may commit suicide, or he may get so excited that circulation and metabolism break down and death ensues from a collapse. In the latter case, the collapse is not amenable to medication. On the other hand, though, there is also a symbolic aspect. A person does not emerge from such a crisis unchanged; after it he is a *renatus*, a person reborn. So we can apply the Goethean motto *Stirb und werde* ("Die and be reborn") again here, though at the beginning of the crisis it is the motif of death that predominates.

In the present case, the metamorphosis consists in the patient's going to heaven as Holy Mary together with the therapist. Evidently the patient has immediately formed a relationship to the therapist, and she has plans for a great undertaking with him. What those plans are in detail is not yet apparent. But it must be something fundamental that she has in mind, since in heaven eternal laws apply. A crisis is always also an occasion to define one's position, and the two who are supposed to ascend into heaven will perhaps discover one of the laws. The laws themselves are often not at all complicated, but on the contrary very simple. However, some people will believe in them only when they have experienced their force.

For the moment we are not yet very far. The actual findings demand immediate treatment. In particular, steps have to be taken to protect against the danger threatening the patient. Careful nursing and supervision go without saying. But it is especially important to prevent a collapse. The introduction of the neuroleptics, such as chlorpromazine, has brought great improvements in the treatment of these cases. Our patient became considerably more calm and orderly under treatment with nozinan (levopromazine, Spezia/Paris).

While this pharmacological treatment was proceeding, we were able to obtain from the relatives and later from the patient herself information that enabled us to go beyond the current findings to establish a history. In that way it was possible to see how the possession had developed.

We learned from the patient's father that she had always been healthy. She did not like theoretical subjects at school, but loved music and showed a developed sense of the comic and the grotesque. In company she was confident and open, although lately there had been a certain aloofness in her behavior. She began to dress in a boyish way and showed no interest in fashion. Two weeks before the illness, on her own initiative, she accepted a position in a home for "problem" children. There were four hundred children in the home. The atmosphere was puritanical and very religious, which the patient did not like at all. She clashed with the other members of staff and then rang her father, sounding so upset that he immediately took her home. Back home she explained meaningfully that she now knew why she had been baptized as Maria. She demanded immediate interviews with Ernst Jünger, the pope, and the philosopher Heidegger. Then she got her parents to arrange for her to play the piano in front of a concert pianist – in view of her coming "big concert." But the occasion became a heart-rending Ophelia scene, since apparently the patient seemed megalomaniacal and ill in equal proportions. Within a matter of hours her excitement grew to such a pitch that she had to be hospitalized immediately.

What the patient herself told me was the most important thing. It formed the basis for an analysis of the case history. In order to achieve the necessary rapport with the patient, it was important to proceed cautiously, since she recoiled from the idea of systematic psychotherapy. Accordingly, the first conversations with the patient were limited to everyday matters. Then after eleven weeks of treatment, she decided of her own accord to give an account of the circumstances of her illness in the form of a written report. The report related exclusively to the time when she was working in the home for "problem" children. It comprised thirty-three handwritten sides; I will give a résumé:

One afternoon, when I had charge of the girls' group, two children came to ask me whether they could go roller-skating. I said they could and went with them into the yard, since they were only allowed to roller-skate under supervision. If two want to roller-skate, all the others want to roller-skate, too; otherwise they feel they are missing something (although they soon get bored, as I had found out a few days before). So when a couple of other children came along and wanted to roller-skate, too, I would not let them and suggested other things they could do, also explaining why I would not let them roller-skate. They went away swearing at me. At that time, one particular little girl was feeling excluded by the others from their games and conversations; she stood around by herself and did not know what to do. I took her to my room, gave her a jump rope, and told her that she could have it. The little girl did not put the rope down all day and was happy to have something all to herself for once. Naturally children are envious when one of them has something new, and the one who has something new will not let go of it on any account. Evidently I had shown preference towards the little girl, although at other times it would be somebody else who got to do a special job, or whatever; it depended on the occasion.

In this first section, the writer describes her first experiences as a teacher and also draws simple theoretical conclusions from her experiences. She continues:

At meals you had to keep strict order; otherwise, it was chaos. There was one girl, for example, who ate disgustingly and fidgeted in her chair. Of course, the others immediately had to say something. I told them they would do better to look after their own manners. I noticed that they only ate properly for me (as in school, where most children learn for the teacher – if I ever learned anything, I always did it for the teacher). It takes a long time before children learn and begin to sense what is good for them and what is not. The other teacher, who had very good control of the group, had gone on holiday; the children's first reaction was to run riot and to take advantage of the new teacher [i.e., our patient] for all they were worth. Children will try anything: They cheat, quarrel, tell tales, and so on.

Gradually, we see difficulties appearing. They soon become obvious.

In the evening they were terribly boisterous; their heads were so exhausted by the unaccustomed thinking they had been doing during the day that they were completely beside themselves. Noisiest of all was Karin, who is one of the older ones, already almost fourteen years old, and always in high spirits. I let the children shout and scream as much as they liked; I would not have got far with shouting at them, nor by being particularly kind. Suddenly Karin wanted to jump out of the window. I did not say anything. She expected me to forbid it, of course. She was already sitting on the window ledge. I stood just behind her; all the children came from their bedrooms to watch. So there she sat, and I even said: "Do you think you can do it? Do you really think you can?" At the same time, I kept telling myself, "I can't let anything happen." After some hesitation, she jumped out (about two meters). Down at the bottom she rushed around like a lunatic, screaming: "I'm free! I can scream as much as I like!!" etc. That was the point where I felt that there had definitely been enough. Fairly strictly I ordered the children back to bed, and off they all went. Karin could not climb back up, so I had to go all the way around the outside of the building to fetch her. When we got back, she was still not satisfied. I told her she could come for a walk with me, which she was enthusiastic about. She got dressed quickly, and we went outside. Soon, however, she realized that it was not such fun to go for a walk in the dark with me after all (that was predictable enough) and was longing to get back to her bed; I could see that.

We had just come in the door; inside there was chaos. It was all to do with Edda, who was crying. She told me her father drank a lot and used to hit her mother. I sat by her bed, with the other children (who had also frightened her by telling her she would be getting a stepfather) listening in the background. There is no limit to children's imaginations. You cannot blame them for it. They have no idea how it feels to be Edda, though you can try to explain to them what the consequences of their teasing might be. You can never prepare the explanation in advance; it always depends on the immediate circumstances. Edda kept groaning and saying, "Why doesn't my mother come?" I took her to another room and sat by her bed for a long time. Very slowly it got better. I took her back to her bed, where she immediately fell asleep.

The writer has clearly mastered the difficulties (not without considerable wear on her nerves, but in the end very skillfully), and in the final scene she gives motherly attention to little Edda, as a mother substitute. Thus her self-confidence grows, and at the next opportunity she voices criticism of the home:

A girl about twelve years old, with a broad, good-natured face, was sitting on a bench in the corridor all alone, her eyes swollen from crying. She could not go to school, because that day she had to go to a closed institution, for her a prison. Why? The doctor who tests the children had found that she was incapable of living together with the

other children. I do not know what else he said about her. I only
know that the woman in charge of the group told me that it was not
quite right. The girl had described all the terrible experiences she had
been through with her stepfather, which aroused disgust and loathing
in the other children. She did not have an easy time, but no one
thought to tell the children openly what it was all about. I think that
every child who has been through something as terrible as that has to
get rid of it somehow, and here it was happening in an unpleasant
way. I asked the girl if she in fact knew why she had to go away; she
shook her head. Someone should at least have explained to her that
the new home was better for her, and not just have left it to her
imagination. She then told me in tears that she had not got back her
album, which the others had all written in. Although the children
were so nasty to her, she still wanted the album as a keepsake.

What is happening to this girl is deeply upsetting. Our patient
now begins to act. She has heard that the medical report on the
child is still under discussion at a meeting in the director's office.
She writes:

I knew that the discussion was going on, with the director of the
home present. My self-control was almost at an end. All the same, I
burst in on the middle of the meeting. The session was suspended on
my account and, when I had steadied myself again, I began to talk.
They always found objections, and I always found an answer. When
I told the story about Edda, I was told that she had only been
playacting. And I noticed, too, in the short time I was there, that
children always try to lead you around by the nose and fool you
whenever they can. But if you know the children individually, you
soon notice what is genuine and what isn't. Children quickly see
through grown-ups, particularly when they have been through what
those children have been through. But teachers who let themselves
be fooled and do not understand the children have a very hard time of
it.

Our patient's appearing before the governing tribunal, like
Michael Kohlhass, to fight for what is right achieves nothing. Her
anger grows, and soon she voices criticism at everything:

A teacher came in and said one of her boys had scratched her new cupboard – that it was disgraceful and what were they going to do with him? The discussion went this way and that. No one stopped to think what could have put the idea into the boy's head, or what form of punishment he could be given that might be of some use. Instead, he had to stay in over the Whitsun holidays, and probably got into more trouble stuck inside for all that time. In the end it is the director's decision, I think. But generally, I got the impression they were talking about the boy as if he were a piece of wood. In the same tone of voice they talked about the holiday in Italy, how nice it had been to go there, and so on. So I just said everything I had been thinking while they were talking, and also what I would have done.

So much for the patient's account of events. To start with, as we saw, everything went well. A lot was new to her; she constantly had to deal with difficult, wearing situations, and yet she could still cope as long as her deeper feelings were not involved. But when she sat on Edda's bed like a mother and also acted like a mother, it was no longer possible for her to adjust. It is not that the patient's thinking became wrong. On the contrary, one suspects that she saw the children's problems very correctly. But her bursting into the director's meeting and handing out advice to the board, as a beginner who had only been working there for a fortnight, was quite unacceptable. And the way she then arrogantly hurled her opinions in the faces of the long-standing, experienced members of the staff shows that she had already reached the state of possession, in which acquired forms of behavior are lost. The possession then grew rapidly. The extent to which megalomania had set in is clearly demonstrated by the planned "big concert." Equally megalomaniacal was her intention of holding discussions with three great men. The fact that this German (Protestant, not Catholic) Holy Mary chose as great men the poet Ernst Jünger, the pope, and the philosopher Heidegger shows wit; the patient does not seem to have lost her sense of the comical. But we also see here a paternal "Areopagus" of a curiously nebulous composition; this indicates a very unclear father image. The question of the father archetype became relevant at a later stage.

Writing down the recent history that led to the possession was very useful for the treatment of the condition. An objectivation of that kind encourages a reorientation. However, one must wait for the patient to undertake the written account of his own accord. One can aid the development if one is extremely restrained in therapy and abstains as a matter of principle from questioning. Any question will always prejudice the answer, which is not good. The essential contribution has to come spontaneously from the patient. Precisely when questions are not asked, the patient can with time begin to feel the need to explain the circumstances to the therapist, who does not suggest what he knows by asking questions.

The patient's document then had to be studied diagnostically and, in conversation with her, therapeutically. The fact that this aloof, boyish girl was not equal to the maternal reaction the situation suddenly demanded of her is not so difficult to understand. The disorder began when, at Edda's bedside, she took the place of the girl's mother and so was exposed to the transference. As a result, the mother archetype was constellated in her, leading first to an inflation and then to possession, which went as far as identification. You have to ask, though, why the reversal was so sudden and so dangerous, despite the fact that the patient's educational views were not obviously wrong at any stage.

I concentrated on this question in my discussions with the patient. I had to point out that institutional reform needed more than the spontaneous reaction of a gifted young girl. In order to bring about reform, you must work for years to build up a position from which you can exercise influence. And you have to learn not just to have right ideas, but also to represent those ideas with both determination and tact. This applies in many fields. In every country there are a lot of people who know better than the leader of the government but, even if they do know better, that is not enough to produce better government. Anyone who wants to exercise influence has to have influence in the first place. And as surely as every soldier carries the marshal's baton in his knapsack, no one becomes a marshal without working his way up through the ranks. A beginner cannot reform an institution by bursting into a board meeting uninvited and giving those present a lecture which may be full of right ideas, but which is also unclear and excited; it is not that simple.

In elaborating these fundamental ideas together with the patient, I found myself in the position of a father, contrasting with the position of the mother. The order of life, and considerations of career and influence, are paternal interests. The patient was obviously hopelessly naive and ignorant in these respects so that, the moment she was approached by the mother archetype, she lost her head and, possessed, became megalomaniacal.

The conclusion that emerged from our discussion was that the maternal pattern of behavior could be productive only if it were coupled with paternal order. With that, the analysis of the initial, immediate findings was complete. The patient had to die, that is, she had to stop being naive and be reborn as a wiser person. And having experienced the general principles of maternal love, she had to accept the principles of paternal order from the therapist. The problem needed to be discussed in fundamental terms and on a general, higher level. That is why the patient had to "ascend into heaven with the therapist." "Heaven," in other words, represented a general, higher level of intellectual consideration.

In purely formal terms, the problem to be discussed and solved in this case was relatively simple. And it should not be forgotten that archetypal problems in particular are not characterized simply by importance and depth, but are also at the same time thoroughly banal. In the initial findings, though, the aspect of importance was emphasized by the "big sun," the great light. Mother archetype and father archetype form a pair of opposites, which demand a productive relationship. When, as in our patient's case, the mother archetype predominates and the principles of the father archetype are lacking, the balance can be upset with disastrous consequences. Possession rushes in like an avalanche, and the individual is shattered by the force of the archetypal energy. It then becomes an urgent priority to restore the balance of the opposition, since only then is further development possible.

As can be gathered from the case we have been studying, situations of possession like this require a special psychotherapeutic technique. An analysis carried out methodically with regular consultations, is usually quite inappropriate as well as impossible. The best thing is to deal with such cases in a completely uninhibited way in medical, human, and nursing terms and, as far as psychotherapy is concerned, simply to keep one's eyes and ears open, being ready when an opportunity arises for a discussion with the patient. What is required, in other words, is careful and patient attention. Insofar as possible, any psychic material that arises should not be interpreted, but understood directly through the application of psychological knowledge. Only such understanding can break the spell of possession and establish contact with the patient.

The question then arises whether this sort of therapy can bring about a new compensation, or whether a legitimate step along the path of individuation can be achieved. Here we have to beware of schematic thinking, which likes to make a distinction between compensation successes on the one hand and individuation successes on the other. We can say straightaway that neither the healthy individual nor the individual who has undergone systematic analysis is anything other than compensated, since for both there is always the danger of archetypal inundation; a person who was not at risk would be like a god. A different criterion is probably more important. Many cases of possession gradually calm down spontaneously and without psychotherapy. One has to see whether in the course of the crisis the patient has discovered an important new perspective. If not, then the whole thing was "much ado about nothing," and the prognosis is not likely to be especially hopeful. But if the crisis gave birth to a fresh insight which really concerns the patient, then a step along the path of individuation has been achieved. One then has the right to hope: "We've gotten this far, so – with luck and God willing – we'll manage next time."

Finally, it is of some theoretical interest whether a state of possession such as that just described can be accommodated within the framework of conventional psychiatry. The findings at the start of treatment lead one almost inevitably to suppose schizophrenia. On the other hand, the simple proportions of the development of the illness and the psychotherapy could suggest rather a neurosis. One gets a clearer idea if one considers the psychological development of the condition with regard to content. It is neurotic if a girl becomes too aloof and boyish. It is also neurotic if a girl cannot cope with the maternal behavior that the situation demands of her. And if, owing to the absence of an ordering, paternal perspective, the maternal behavior becomes megalomaniacal, then one practically has a psychosis, or perhaps an acute neurosis. In any case, there is seriously disturbed behavior and a very dangerous dissociation. This dissociation became plainly visible when the patient, preparing for her "big concert," played for a concert pianist. There was a dangerous gap between the girl's actual insignificance and her idea of her own importance; the result was a heart-rending Ophelia scene. Such states of acute neurotic dissociation demand immediate treatment; the way back is still not too difficult. Here, for example, it was possible to compensate the situation by opposing the father archetype to the mother archetype. However, if one does not succeed in counteracting the possession to restore the balance, an unfavorable development with fixated dissociation can soon set in, leading to a longer-term, decidedly schizophrenic-psychotic state. The assumption that psychosis is a process which inexorably invades a person's life is false in this formulation. What invades is not a process, but an archetype with typical behavior and corresponding mythical ideas. If an archetype invades, if it takes possession of a person, appropriate psychotherapy is an urgent necessity and often decisive. In itself, the acute psychopathological picture of possession is not psychosis; it lies between neurosis and psychosis. If understanding and treatment are successful, there has been a step forward in the process of individuation. If the circumstances are unfavorable, the first stage in a psychotic process has been reached. Thus one can say, when an archetype invades, a process begins. It is then the task of psychotherapy to help ensure that the path followed is that of individuation rather than psychosis. This is the meaning of the "great light": What is aimed for is not mental darkness, but enlightenment (consciousness).

XIX

PSYCHOTHERAPY AND THE SHADOW

The shadow, the dark side of the personality, is an urgent problem in psychotherapy through its relationship to the fundamental pairs of opposites: light and darkness, good and evil, high and low. Since the dark side of an individual who encounters it is often largely unconscious, it is often first experienced in the form of a projection. The way the individual responds in that encounter is of fundamental importance. At the same time, certain typical images appear in the consciousness of the individual. The constellation of the question of basic behavior and the appearance of typical images identify the shadow as an archetype. In clinical terms, this means that the shadow often constellates a very considerable affect, which may be reflected in a correspondingly pronounced psychiatric picture.

The dark side of the personality, projection, behavior, experienced images, and the clinical aspect of affect in the psychiatric clinical picture are all phenomena which can only be observed in the individual. Psychotherapy affords the opportunity to perceive such phenomena at close range. In that respect it is almost a refined form of psychiatric exploration. Of course, the relationship of the therapist to the patient's experience often makes it nearly impossible to objectify that experience; vital moments can usually only be recorded afterwards. The difficulty in getting a record of the facts is more than compensated by the human contact and interaction in psychotherapeutic experience. Generally, the findings obtained in psychotherapy are in no way less clear than those provided by psychiatric exploration. But they are always individual, and usually they are not static but rather stages in a development.

Despite their individual nature, psychotherapeutic findings are of general importance because, in critical situations, people tend to show typical forms of behavior and at the same time to develop images of a general and typical nature. It is on this fact that C. G. Jung based his concept of the archetype, the first outline of which he gave in his discourse "Instinct and the Unconscious" at Bedford College in 1919.[1]

The individual case I wish to focus on here is one I treated for a year, from mid-April 1947 to mid-April 1948. I have a catamnesis up to the year 1981. The case concerns a married woman born in 1902, with two daughters. The treatment took place on a semiclinical basis, that is, the patient spent part of the time during treatment in an open sanatorium with some nursing care, while at other times she lived together with a nurse in a hotel. As a rule, I saw the patient three or four times a week, mostly for about one hour. I visited her in the sanatorium or hotel; she rarely came to my consulting room. I made no notes during the consultations, but wrote down the essential details of each consultation immediately afterwards. In the way I dealt with the patient, the treatment never resembled outpatient psychotherapy. Rather, it was clinical psychotherapy in which the human encounter in every gesture, in the fact of being together as such, is as important as the spoken word.

The patient and her family resided in the south of the United States of America. On account of her illness, the patient traveled to Switzerland, accompanied by one of her daughters. They hoped to find treatment for her in Switzerland and consulted first of all a general practitioner. He referred the patient to me for psychotherapy. He also took responsibility for looking after her during the short periods when I was away on holiday or for military service. During those absences he sometimes prescribed sedatives, which were stopped on my return since I was carrying out the therapy without the help of medicines. It is not that I was against medicines on principle. But it became apparent that, with psychological supervision, the developing clinical picture did not call for medicines.

The daughter, who on my advice returned home after our discussion, told me the following facts. The patient came from a psychiatrically healthy family. Her one brother, whom she loved, had died in an accident (a fall at a building site) when she herself was eighteen. Around the age of twenty-five, she had been in low spirits for a few months without anyone at that time suspecting any illness, let alone calling a doctor. The present illness had been going for five and a half years. First there had been depressive symptoms. The patient did not want to leave the house – she shunned strangers. Although she was a very good piano player, she avoided all music. She slept badly, lacked initiative, and expressed fear and despair. While her condition deteriorated steadily, the various treatments that are often tried before psychotherapy were tried: stimulating and calming injections, vitamin injections, vegetarian and salt-free diets, gymnastics, baths, and two courses of electrotherapy. In the past two years new symptoms had appeared. Not only did the patient's movements become inhibited so that she mostly just sat stiffly or, if standing, just stood motionless; she could also hardly speak. There were only two things she could still do: She ate compulsively, developing a true eating compulsion, and while she was eating her fear diminished. And whenever possible, she washed her hands, spraying water around the whole room. As these two compulsive symptoms increased, the physical appearance of the patient changed. In the past two years she had gone from 128 pounds to 172 pounds. And although she washed her hands, she neglected the rest of her body completely, as often happens with compulsive washing. She was dirty, very badly dressed, and her teeth in particular, a row of black stumps broken by gaps, were in a dismal state.

At our first meeting the patient initially said nothing at all. Since I assumed that any overhasty activity on my part could prevent the constellation of the psychic contents and so make psychotherapy impossible, I was silent too. After fifty minutes the patient said, "I'm suffering." I simply replied, "Aha." There was not much else I could say, since I did not know what the suffering meant.

Over the following eight weeks a discussion developed on the subject of suffering. In a fragmentary way the patient told me how disgusting all the eating was just to calm the fear for a few moments. And how excruciating it was constantly to have to wash her hands. But she suffered particularly from the degeneration in her exterior personality, her ugliness, and the impossibility of talking to other people. For my part I could not but express my sympathy with the patient. That was all that was forthcoming for the moment, and the patient's condition did not alter. The seriousness of the case, however, was sufficient reason not to lose patience too early.

There were other problems involved in the case. The patient's treatment in the sanatorium had to be organized. With the help of the matron and chambermaids, the patient's clothes were cleaned and mended. As with all compulsive neurotic symptoms, a certain degree of discipline was possible, which was important particularly with regard to the compulsive washing, since having the room flooded regularly would have aroused resistance in the staff and could also have damaged the building. Now and then the patient was taken for a walk by one of the nurses, which seemed to me a necessity of hygiene. All this created a lot of work on a small scale and demanded both firmness and tact.

Imperceptibly during this period, in the psychotherapeutic consultations and through having to deal with the questions of organization, a first step was taken. A relationship took shape between myself and the patient. We got to know one another. The patient's regular visits became part of my day; she was in my mind, and I had also become important for her. In conversation with her there gradually developed – despite all her inhibitions – the almost familiar atmosphere that is a sure sign of the incipient transference situation. The seed of this development was planted at the point where the patient aroused my sympathy. The effect the patient has on the therapist gives him a point of contact (in this case, sympathy) and links him with the patient's personal problem, which is the subject of the therapy. So the effect of the patient on the therapist is the starting point of psychotherapy.

After eight weeks of treatment, the contact between patient and therapist had become so close that the patient was prepared to risk talking about the psychological and emotional background of her illness. Her story was remarkably simple. The illness had manifested itself in the course of a summer. It was preceded by an experience the patient had had at Christmas of the year before. The patient's husband was managing director of a machine tool factory; the firm itself was a joint-stock company. Every year the patient, as the wife of the managing director, gave a small present to the wife of the president of the company board. The employee who delivered the present, a vase with some flowers, on leaving the house heard the lady make a disparaging remark to a third person who was standing in the hallway: "This isn't the sort of thing you give your superiors!" She promptly reported this remark to the patient.

The patient assured me that it was a perfectly normal, quite acceptable present. She could not, however, entirely dispel my suspicion that she had chosen a slightly tasteless or otherwise unsuitable present in order to express a certain animosity towards her "superior." In her mind the other woman was the epitome of presumption and arrogance, "an evil, nasty woman." The experience tormented her, but she could find no connection between her present illness and the trauma she described. She told me about the experience only because she thought you had to tell everything that meant anything to you if you wanted to get any further. After all, she said, the illness had not started until months after that.

The latter fact, precisely, suddenly threw light on one of her symptoms – the compulsive eating. She could have gotten angry and reacted in her anger. "I got a bit angry," is what people would say in ordinary speech. And she could have risked a conflict. But the patient had no access to that sort of behavior. She was too well brought up and too educated; in her circles you were "always nice," never angry. And so she swallowed her own black anger. At first it may have been right to do so. Affects have to be worked through; hitting out immediately is often foolish. Months of brooding over her anger led in the patient's case, however, not to action, but to resignation. She wanted to "just let the whole thing be forgotten." That is where the psychological disorder set in. The affect was not overcome – the process of swallowing the anger had not been completed. Not realizing this, the patient began to give physical expression to the swallowing process. She repressed the connection between the trauma and the psychic disorder. But she could banish the fear, which was fear of the affective act in real life, only by eating. Then she was still in the "brooding" stage and so was legitimized and free of fear. Here we can see clearly the origin of the symptom: Swallowing the affect was originally justified in order to avoid ill-considered behavior. When, despite months of brooding, no action followed, and, on the contrary, the conflict was laid aside ("let the whole thing be forgotten"), the inner process was replaced by a physical, symbolic act: compulsive eating. And since it is legitimate that an affect should be dealt with before proceeding to act, and since that gives a temporary dispensation from the need to act, eating ("I'm still eating; maybe action will come later") had the effect of ensuring inner balance; at least at the moment of eating, the fear was banished.

Where, then, was the evil rage that was boiling inside the patient? It had been projected. The only evil person was that woman who, with her careless and tactless remark, had triggered the anger in the first place. This is not to say that the patient did not also look for blame in herself. She asked herself whether her present had not been in some way inappropriate. But she could detect no failure in herself. However, one cannot help wondering whether the present did not, as we suggested above, contain some hidden spite. Whichever way it was, the patient ought to have confronted her own aggressiveness and anger. Repressing it left the shadow in the projected state, attributed to the opponent, who from then on was thoroughly evil and bad.

Having let a long time go by without using it to gain self-knowledge, the patient then began symbolically to express the problem of self-cleansing and of her own dark side, too: She began ceaselessly to wash her hands. The hands represent action. A person who washes his hands wants to act without getting his hands dirty. The washing compulsion, though, expresses this thought: "You would like to be pure in your actions. But no water is pure or strong enough to make your hands completely clean. There is always a spot of dirt left." Anyone who acts can never act completely in the light; he has to act partly in the dark. But our patient shrank back from the darkness implicit in every action, and so she never stopped washing her hands.

It is interesting how much time can go by in psychotherapy before some important past event is discussed. There are always certain sore points that cannot be touched on until the psychotherapist has won the patient's confidence. The trauma in the present case seems almost ridiculously trivial; yet when it comes to the inner life, the tiniest things can sometimes have the greatest consequences. The fact that this seemingly minor detail concealed a considerable practical problem came to light only much later. Generally speaking, the patient's experience showed all the characteristics of trauma as defined by Freud: "We give the name trauma to an experience which in a very short time gives such a stimulus to inner life that it proves impossible to cope or come to terms with it in the usual way, which necessarily results in lasting disorders in the internal economy."[2] The origin of mental disorder "through the incapacity to deal with an overwhelming emotionally charged experience" was also emphasized by Breuer and Freud in 1893/95.[3]

I discussed the trauma and its ramifications with the patient. As was to be expected, the clinical picture did not change in the least as a result, let alone improve. Gradually she began to recognize the connections. But she was still far from achieving the ability to act, the knowledge of the right thing to do. That knowledge, as Freud said, has to come from "an inner transformation within the patient."[4] And there was still a long way to go before such a transformation was completed.

Nor was anything gained by a brave, but purely intellectual, attempt at a solution. With great difficulty the patient wrote a letter to the woman in America, in which she accused the woman of arrogance and bad character. The letter merely aroused astonishment in America, where no one could remember what happened at Christmas six years ago. For a few days the patient was happy about the letter. Then the fear returned. The compulsive eating and washing had not stopped for a moment. The most important thing about the letter was perhaps that its composition showed to what extent the therapist was already involved in the patient's thoughts and actions. I helped her write the letter, and I encouraged her, a type of behavior I was in theory strictly opposed to. ("The therapist should never do what the patient ought to do; he should never act on the patient's behalf.") The infringement of principles is always a clear sign of the mutual dependence of patient and therapist in the transference situation. And it is at this point that something starts to happen.

This dependence, which developed further as time went by, showed itself in the patient by her speaking less and less well. Often she could still manage to speak in my presence, but she only spoke well when I let her read aloud. I let her read some short stories by Gottfried Keller. Originally her family was from Germany, and she herself spoke good German, but she lacked contact with German cultural circles. It is perfectly permissible in longer-term courses of psychotherapy to spend time enriching and so reinforcing consciousness. The patient herself liked reading aloud because she enjoyed speaking fluently for a change, and also because the content of the reading disrupted the monotony of her illness.

Outwardly, the clinical picture deteriorated over the following months, the compulsive eating and washing increased, and the patient's weight, originally 128 pounds and at the start of the treatment 172 pounds, rose to 211 pounds. Toothless, swollen, and ill-kempt, the patient gave the curious impression of an old Indian woman. The encounter with the dark side of the personality also constellates the primitive side of one's own origin. In this connection, I have always been struck by the fact that the span of possibilities is particularly wide in America, where "moderate" possibilities tend to lose importance; a patient in regression can thus sink relatively quickly to a very primitive level. What you see then is the negative aspect of primitivity; the patient presented the image not of a wise, but of a drunken, degenerate Indian.

It is obvious that the deterioration of the clinical picture was no reason to change the treatment. There is no going back in severe cases like this; the patient has to go through the development of the condition.

After half a year of treatment, the patient began to recount dreams. With great difficulty she described short dream sequences. It proved impossible to elicit further associations to the dreams. Therefore – as often in psychotic or near-psychotic cases – the dreams had to be understood directly from the images they contained, rather than interpreted. The therapist's behavior towards the patient and also what he says to the patient can be colored or even guided as a result. And when the dreams are emphasized and shown to be taken seriously by brief interpretive remarks to the patient, the developmental process taking place in the patient can be stimulated and sustained.

The following twelve dreams occurred in the course of one month:

1st Dream

"I am sitting on the beach by the sea. In the sky an illuminated fish is fighting with a round thing (circle, disc, sun); outcome uncertain."

Here we see, first of all, the conflict that emerged in the clash between the patient and her "superior." A "sun" could very well represent the superior. But then the dreamer herself is the fish, and the fish in the dream is not right at all. A fish does not belong in the sky, and it is not illuminated. A fish belongs down below in the water where unconsciousness rules. The conflict is too much for the patient; she finds herself in a situation which demands conscious (illuminated) height and in which she is as helpless as a fish in the air (in the sky). The round thing also raises the question of wholeness (circle); whether, in her unconsciousness (fish), she is strong enough to deal with that problem is unclear (outcome uncertain). The dreamer herself is not identified with the fight; she watches it. Accordingly, she ought to be in a position to state her attitude towards her outer and inner problems.

2nd Dream

"Fish dead, water coming out of it. Someone is carrying the fish; it's terrible."

For the moment, the fight has been decided; the unconsciousness (fish) proves to be superseded (dead). It is clearly the dreamer who is carrying the fish; it is she who has the unconsciousness. This is terrible, just as the present clinical condition is terrible. It struck me that the patient was looking at me like a half-dead fish, with a swimming gaze.

3rd Dream

"Dream of a piano."

The problem is in part a problem of feeling (music). The emotional relationship to the therapist is probably also constellated.

4th Dream

"Dream of a tiny baby."

The first appearance of the new life that could develop.

5th Dream

"Dream of half a rose."

The round thing, once a destructive object in the sky, has come to earth and come to life. But it is only half. Half a rose is not a rose. The dreamer had the feeling while she was dreaming that she had to turn onto her other side to make the rose whole. A positive effort is needed to acquire the other half of the whole.

6th Dream

> "Three brothers, all good people, respect their mother; I have to get engaged to a young man I don't know."

The patient received from her upbringing the attitude that you have to be good. This attitude came from her mother, but is represented by three men related by blood (the family animus). Through the number three this attitude is dominant. The dreamer has to achieve a new affective attitude (individual animus), which is still unknown to her (the young man she does not know).

7th Dream

> "Saw a special, mild sun."

Here the round thing is more clearly identified as a sun than in the first dream, and has a shining character (the character of knowledge). The special, mild sun, however, is an image of the Self; compare in this connection the *Memoirs* of Benvenuto Cellini in Goethe's translation (book 2, chapter 13), where Cellini perceives the "pure and bright disc" as a liberating vision in his long imprisonment. The "mildness" of the sun indicates that its light has something of the quality of moonlight. Thus the illumination (manner and form of perception) becomes milder and more appropriate to the femininity (moon) of the patient.

8th Dream

> "Doctor as opera singer, Siegfried, dentist."

The milder character of the dangerous insight is probably attributable to the beginnings of the emotional relationship with the doctor. He can provide the necessary feeling (opera singer), banish danger (Siegfried), and recognize difficulties (the dentist who probes the teeth). As an opera singer and particularly as Siegfried, the doctor is given a larger-than-life character; in that way the animus image reveals something of a more general nature.

9th Dream

"I have to pick berries up off the floor; they are mulberries."

Here there is a hint of the silkworm motif, of the cocoon spun so that the butterfly may emerge. The patient's illness is thus shown in a positive light.

10th Dream

"Have to buy strawberry-colored sunshade in a shop."

The berry motif is taken up again, but this time in the form of strawberries. It provides protection against the dangerous sun. The German word for "strawberry," *Erdbeere,* contains the word for "earth": *Erde.* Thus it is a question of the earth, of natural reality. The relationship to the doctor, for example, is not just exalted romanticism; it may also be physical desire. This question ought not be avoided, for only then can one be sure one is safe. The doctor faces the same problem, since the atmosphere in a long course of therapy is not always completely objective, for example, when the doctor is seen as a Siegfried. Often male vanity is flattered, and inflation or therapeutic error can be the result.

11th Dream

"Have to get into the coffin. Brother has hanged himself."

It becomes apparent that the old life has to die before the new life can be born. The inherited affective attitude (family animus, brother) has been overcome; it is also no longer dominant (only one brother).

With this dream the clinical picture took a significant turn for the worse. The patient was actually lying there as if she were in her coffin, could hardly move, and showed clear catatoniform acrocyanosis. The doctor who occasionally deputized for me with the patient visited her at that time, and declared without hesitation that he considered it a matter of urgency that she be admitted to a nursing home. I had to agree with him insofar as something had to be done, though I chose a different course. With considerable physical effort, I forced the patient to get out of bed and to get dressed. I took her out of the building and drove her in my car to a good restaurant, where I ordered a pleasant meal with some Burgundy and mineral water. We had a pleasant and civilized conversation, and the patient was absolutely delighted to be in an ordinary human situation again for once. Hardly had she gotten back home again, though, when she returned to her earlier catatonic state. But she was able to tell me that the reason was that she had not drunk all her mineral water at the restaurant. That night she dreamt the final dream:

12th Dream

"The mineral water has to be mixed with the wine."

Again it would seem that the earth (mineral) had been forgotten and only the wine (spirit) had been drunk. The patient had greatly enjoyed the meal with its educated and civilized conversation, but had visibly repressed the pleasure it gave her to think how she had seduced a relatively young man (at that time!), as it were, to rape her. This also shows how far the patient can get the therapist to go in the transference situation! The suppression of the dark aspects of the shared meal explained the patient's immobility (catatonia); as long as only the good side is there, it is impossible to move.

All the same, the catatonic symptoms receded sufficiently in the next few days to avoid the need for hospitalization. But then new compulsive symptoms appeared. Whenever the patient heard a clock strike (there was a church tower nearby), she had to stand completely still for five minutes. And she felt a compulsion to spit, although at the same time spitting was a guilty sin.

The clock symptom shows the tendency to escape from time into eternity. Only a person who lives in eternity is freed from the earth with its darkness and its dirt, and the striking of the hours is a painful reminder that, as human beings, we live in time. It was as if the patient wanted to escape from time by standing stock still. On the other hand, spitting, as a sign of aggressive disgust (reaction against the "superior"), belongs to the dark side of the personality, which is precisely what wanted to make itself felt; the patient felt herself driven to commit "sins" of that nature. Plato gives a famous metaphorical description of this human problem in the picture of the charioteer in *Phaedrus* (246ab, 247b, 253a-e):

> To describe the nature of the soul as it is would require a long exposition of which only a god is capable; but it is within the power of man to say in shorter compass what it resembles. Let us adopt this method, and compare the soul to a winged charioteer and his team acting together. Now all the horses and charioteers of the gods are good and come of good stock, but in other beings there is a mixture of good and bad. First of all we must make it plain that the ruling power in us men drives a pair of horses, and next that one of these horses is fine and good and of noble stock, and the other the opposite in every way. So in our case the task of the charioteer is necessarily a difficult and unpleasant business. [...] The teams of the gods, which are well-matched and tractable, go easily, but the rest with difficulty; for the horse with the vicious nature, if he has not been well broken in, drags his driver down by throwing all his weight in the direction of the earth. [...] One of the horses, we say, is good and one not. The good horse is upright and clean-limbed, with a high neck and a hooked nose; he is white with black eyes; his thirst for honor is tempered by restraint and modesty; he is a friend to genuine renown and needs no whip, but is driven simply by the word of command. The other horse is crooked, lumbering, ill-made; stiff-necked, short-throated, snub-nosed; his coat is black and his eyes, a bloodshot grey; wantonness and boastfulness are his companions, and he is hairy-eared and deaf, hardly controllable even with whip and goad.

If a stimulus approaches this pair, the good horse responds obediently, but the dark one kicks, *spits,* and runs wild, until perhaps it is possible to bring it to a halt with a jerk on the reins. So mortals do not travel a steady path like the gods, but in bursts pushing forward, then halting and stumbling, like humans. Plato gives the light character of the reasonable side of man and the dark character of his shadowy side a vivid reality in his description of the two horses. If a person tries to escape from this contradictoriness, this erratic human progress, he withdraws from time and is unable to move; in our patient's case, such withdrawal produced the rigid, catatonic clinical picture.

In order at least to avoid a rigid routine in what was clinically still a critical situation, I had the patient transferred from the sanatorium to a hotel where she was looked after by a private nurse. This marked a new stage in the treatment. Up until that point the nurses had changed according to the rota in the sanatorium, and the only constant relationship the patient had had was with the doctor. Now she had a second permanent partner, a woman. The patient was extremely difficult for the nurse. Whereas she made some effort to accommodate herself to the doctor, she was obstinate towards the nurse in her compulsions like a stubborn horse (cf. Plato's image!). Also, the position of the nurse was somehow closer to that of the patient on a human level and less objective than that of the doctor, so that the nurse was far more inclined than the doctor to see certain compulsions not as symptoms, but as malice and nastiness. The nurse's complaints grew more insistent; she was particularly upset that the patient hardly spoke to her, whereas with the doctor she spoke haltingly but clearly and logically. The nurse felt this as contempt. For her part the patient saw the nurse as being hateful to her.

Thus there was a repetition of the original situation to which the patient was fixated. Once again there was a conflict between two women, and once again it was "the other one" who was the evil one in the patient's eyes. However, her own dark side, the "dark horse," was now also visible. So when the patient came with fresh complaints, I was able to point out to her the facts of her own behavior, emphasizing how the nurse was upset by the way she hardly ever spoke to her. Indignant and also stunned, the patient spontaneously exclaimed: "Now I won't say another word!" She meant that what I had said was the most incredible accusation anyone could possibly make against her. But the effect of her exclamation was quite the opposite. What I heard was the literal sense of the words. That the patient should respond to the accusation that she spoke too little with the nurse by saying that she would not say anything at all now seemed to me so grotesque that I burst out laughing.

That moment was a turning point. Only a few days before the patient had told me it was too late, there was no hope left; and she had seemed even more swollen and rundown. Now the doctor's laughter enabled her to accept her own dark side. Humor is absolutely essential in coming to accept one's own shadow; this acceptance can never work with deadly earnest. Also the affective side, the patient's emotionality, had loosened up and become more responsive after the months of psychotherapy including her emotional relationship with the doctor. As a result, she was able to see her other side (the other "half of the rose").

This turning point took place after eleven and a half months of psychotherapy. The patient began to speak freely, and the compulsions, both the compulsive eating and the washing, disappeared within three days. She then had two dreams which speak for themselves:

13th Dream

"I have given birth to a child."

14th Dream

"I am carrying a small child in my arms."

The new development, which had already been announced in the fourth dream, now arrived and became a reality for the patient. Now she did not just dream "about a child," but had given birth to it and carried it in her arms.

The actual meaning of the psychological problem only emerged, however, in the following, final state of treatment.

The patient found a dentist and had her teeth put back in shape. With almost incredible speed, her weight went from 211 pounds back down to 128 pounds; she was reborn and rejuvenated. Meanwhile, her husband had come over from America. Despite his wife's good condition, he was strangely out of spirits and decided to return home with her immediately.

So after twelve months, the treatment was successfully concluded – or, as we were to discover, almost concluded. The reason for the husband's strange mood was still to emerge.

To be on the safe side, the husband decided to have the familiar nurse accompany his wife on the journey home. They left on board a ship. But I soon received two letters from America. In one of them the patient renewed her complaints about the impossible behavior of the nurse. In the other letter, the nurse reported that she had been aggravated and annoyed by the patient in every way imaginable during the crossing, so that the ship had become a hell for her. Moreover, in America the patient's condition had rapidly deteriorated again.

I instructed the nurse to return to Europe immediately. And to the patient, I wrote a strongly worded letter; I asked her to consider her unacceptable behavior and the injustice of her complaints against the selfless nurse.

This time the lesson worked. Often it is necessary to re-emphasize what has been acquired through psychotherapy in order to fix it in consciousness. Consciousness demands that insights be retained; otherwise, even the best insights are ephemeral and are dissipated like smoke.

The patient recovered immediately after receiving my letter and has remained healthy in the years since then; I was able to follow her progress through correspondence with one of the daughters. Now the patient began to act from the perspective of the newly acquired dark side. She did what she ought perhaps to have done at the beginning of her illness. She put pressure on her husband – no wonder he was less than delighted when he came to collect his wife, because she asked a lot of him. She demanded that he quit the company of which he was an employee and start his own company in competition. For better and also for worse (!) she had her way. And so at last she was able to meet the wife of the president of the board on an equal footing and no longer had any "superiors" to anger her with spiteful remarks. She had reached the point where she could get annoyed, even properly angry, and then react appropriately. I had no influence on the final confrontation with her husband; I only heard about it later. Anyway, genuine action has to come from within the individual; it was not the place for medical advice. The firm the husband started up developed very successfully, and his income also rose significantly. He died a few years ago.

The problem of the shadow is discussed by Pascal:[5]

> What does man do? He would like to be great, and he realizes that he is small. He wants to be perfect, but finds nothing but faults in himself. He would like to be loved and respected by other people, but his faults can only earn him dislike and disapproval. He makes every effort to ensure that neither he nor others are aware of his own faults, and he cannot endure it when he is forced to see his own faults or when they are seen by others. There is no doubt that it is a terrible thing to be full of faults, but it is a worse thing to be full of faults and not to acknowledge it.

What is particularly important here is the observation that people cannot bear to have to see their own faults. It is in such situations that the deviation into mental disorder occurs. It often takes a long time before you see your own shadow. And when you see it, what you feel is a sense of annihilation. This sense of annihilation can be lifted through serious contact with other people.

In the case we have been discussing, the patient was at first not ready for the experience of the shadow, probably owing to her conventional "good" upbringing. In the conflict situation, therefore, everything unpleasant was projected onto the opponent. In the first stage of psychotherapy, the personal resources of the

patient were developed. A primary factor was the affective relationship to the doctor, and the doctor was sometimes experienced
as a mythological figure (animus figure, e.g., as Siegfried).
Thought and poetry were not neglected either, e.g., the reading of
Gottfried Keller. In this sense, the psychotherapy was also a sort
of lesson. The literature quoted here (Jung, Freud, Plato, Pascal)
should be seen in the same light by the doctor: The words of a
master do not serve merely to throw light on the facts of a
situation; they are set in the right context only when they are seen
in relation to a real person. That is where one sees the difference
between book learning and knowledge from experience. And that
is how the doctor learns, too.

In the second stage of therapy, the original fixation situation
was repeated in the encounter with a woman. The patient could
be made to see her own shadow, since this time there was a
genuine conflict. The spontaneous reaction of the doctor, a burst
of laughter, led to acceptance of the shadow and so to a turning
point, which immediately brought about a clinical cure. Laughter
– humor – made possible the painful and difficult step which
Jung called the step towards accepting "the ugliest man" (Nietzsche, *Thus Spake Zarathustra*), the real man.[6] Jung says of this
step: "Our resistance to taking this step, and our fear of it, show
how great is the attraction and seductive power of our own
depths. To cut oneself off from them is no solution; it is a mere
sham, an essential misunderstanding of their meaning and value.
For where is a height without depth, and how can there be light
that throws no shadow? There is no good that is not opposed by
evil.... What is down below is not just an excuse for more
pleasure, but something we fear because it demands to play its
part in the life of the more conscious and more complete man."
Thus the patient's fear was first of the "superior" and then of the
nurse, until finally she realized that she too had an unpleasantly
dark side which she feared in herself.

The final stage of treatment brought the stability of a cure. The
question of the patient's own shadow had to be restated and taken
in again. Then the patient was ready to act. She was able to

confront her husband and his employers. She was also able to express anger and annoyance, so that her actions produced results and achieved a new independence for the family.

It goes without saying that the course the treatment took was not planned. Nor can one claim that every neurosis is already a step towards a meaningful development. That development can only happen when a path is found through the chaos of neurosis. Although planning may not be so useful, it cannot be disputed that the guidance of the doctor is important. The case we have been studying also makes it clear, however, that the decisive moves of the patient in real life cannot be prompted or even guided by the doctor. The decisive act has to be the result of the patient's personally taking a position.

We noted at the start of this discussion that the observation carried out during a course of psychotherapy can be likened to a refined form of psychiatric exploration. What are the conclusions to be drawn from the case in psychiatric terms? It becomes apparent that psychotherapy blurs the clear pictures usually given by psychiatrists. This is understandable since, in psychiatry, we make a diagnosis on the basis of the actual symptoms and course of an illness, whereas the latter are themselves influenced by psychotherapy. In our case depressive signs, compulsive neurotic symptoms, and schizophrenic (catatonic) symptoms appeared in various forms. With hindsight, the case can be seen to have been neurotic. But it is not improbable that the diagnosis would have had to be psychosis if no psychotherapy had taken place. Often it seems as if, when psychotherapy is successful in cases of psychosis, the cure is proof that it was not psychosis after all, but neurosis. Psychosis, one could then say, is not cured by successful psychotherapy but is, so to speak, disproved. Where that proof is not forthcoming and the course remains unfavorable, the diagnosis of psychosis has to stand.

The psychological diagnosis in our case is more straightforward. There are clear signs of a clinical disorder caused by the problem of the shadow. In psychotherapy, therefore, we move on from psychiatric diagnosis to psychological diagnosis. And then we are no longer describing objective clinical pictures, but rather a problem that can often become for the person concerned a painful and dangerous experience.

XX

THE USE OF SCULPTURE
IN THE TREATMENT OF PSYCHOSES

In psychotherapy it is often crucially important that the psychic content is recorded. Otherwise it often disappears like a fleeting shadow. Moreover, Jung has shown that an active relationship to emerging fantasies can assist the healing process in a person and stabilize the psychic situation. He called this active relationship "active imagination."

Artistic expression is one form of active imagination. It permits physical activity, and the concrete result gives positive support to the stability of the psychic situation. For psychotics and borderline psychotics whose activity is paralyzed or distracted and whose inner stability is undermined, artistic expression is therefore of great therapeutic importance.

Artistic expression through the medium of sculpture would seem to be particularly suitable in this connection. The psychic content is expressed in a solid, three-dimensional object, the making of which allows physical work with the hands. The teaching of sculptural expression in psychotherapy is considerably more difficult, however, than the teaching of drawing or painting.

Almost every person can draw and paint spontaneously. Almost everyone has had a minimum of preparation in primary school, which can be a start. In our clinical work when, for example, we have set up a studio, the leader of the creative therapy will observe extreme restraint with regard to technical guidance so as not to disturb spontaneous production. There can be problems if one or another of the patients who has perhaps been in the clinic for a longer period wants help as an artist, which cannot in itself be the purpose of therapy. The therapy leader needs a lot of psychological tact in dealing with such situations. The problem is even more evident with sculptural work. On the one hand, it is very rare to find any sort of prior training in patients. On the other hand, most people do not want simply to knead a lump of clay; they also want to produce something worth looking at and lasting. It is an advantage if the leader of creative therapy is himself active as a sculptor. Without having to give instructions, he can provide a stimulus simply through his own activity. That way, there are always examples available for anyone who would like to create sculpture. Clay seems to be the best material, which can then be fired and painted.

Another problem emerges even more clearly with sculpture than with drawing and painting, and that is the problem of interpretation. Even with pictures, we have to be careful not to undermine the language of creative, active imagination with the interpretive language of concepts and so rob the picture of its *direct therapeutic effect*. This holds far more with sculptures. As a rule, sculpture has to be understood as direct expression, and the only important thing is the patient's commentary. Sculpture shows an inner situation translated into a solid object. *This solid object gives the patient a hold*. It can also provide *orientation* for the therapist in his attempt to understand. Talking about it a lot usually means talking it to death. The essential thing is to *appreciate* the "work"; and often it is not even the result that is decisive, but the process of making it.

I will now give four examples to illustrate the place of sculpture in psychotherapy. These examples relate to sculpture as self-diagnosis, sculpture as representation of the transference, work with sculpture as an instrument of therapy, and the sculptural object as the expression of a turning point in psychotherapy. The examples are drawn from my personal practice; thus the therapist in each case is the author.

Self-diagnosis

A forty-year-old woman in an unhappy marriage became an alcoholic. The marriage ended with divorce; the two children were put in the care of the father, and the woman's relationship to her own family was undermined by this development. Attempts at psychotherapy both inside and outside the clinic always ended with serious relapses into drinking. The woman was a likable and gifted person when she was sober. After very lengthy treatment, which had had its ups and downs, she gave me a sculpture that she had made without my knowledge; it was her first sculpture. The sculpture represents the head of a bacchante. Viewed from the right-hand side, it has the features of an aged woman who may once have been beautiful (fig. 1). The left-hand side of the face, however, is seriously damaged, and where the eye used to be there is blood dripping from an empty socket (fig. 2). Thus the head bears the gruesome features of a one-eyed, badly wounded maenad (fig. 3). With this sculpture the woman made her own diagnosis: "Though I am well-preserved on the conscious [right] side, I am badly injured and instinct-blind on the unconscious [left] side."

The sculpture shows that the patient is traumatized and how badly traumatized she is. Psychic traumatizations can indeed be that serious. Situations like this are not simply an invention of Freud's, and they cannot be dealt with in a couple of sessions of analysis with a look at a couple of dreams. The findings represented here by the patient herself need long and difficult work before they heal. The left eye that sees into the unconscious is lost. It can no longer look outward. A positive development, healing, is only possible if a way of relating to the unconscious is sought in introspection.

This woman's self-diagnosis needed no commentary. It showed the therapist, and the patient, where things stood. That way, it became possible to look for a solution. In clinical terms, the sculpture brought *an end to the absence of insight* with regard to the patient's alcoholism.

Transference

A forty-eight-year-old unmarried woman was suffering from paranoid schizophrenia with delusions of saving the world. The relationship to the therapist seemed to her to promise deliverance, but it was disturbed by a tendency to familiarize the relationship. Then she gave me a ceramic sculpture, a relief, which she said represented "King Henry and his wife" (fig. 4). The sculpture shows the transference situation; my name is in fact Heinrich. In the sculpture the transference relationship is raised out of its realistic familiarity onto a higher, general level, which brings out its general, intellectual content. What is meant is not an ordinary marriage, but a special one; not intimacy or sexuality, but an elevated marriage, a royal marriage. It is true that in transference psychotherapy a marriage, a *coniunctio*, is supposed to take place. To look for it on an earthly, familiar level is a tragic misunderstanding. And if the therapist simply rejects this misunderstanding, the situation becomes really unproductive, or even dangerous. Therapeutically, on the contrary, the tension has to be endured until what has been understood as "planned marriage" is recognized as something *symbolic and spiritual*. In this case the tension led to the patient's employing active imagination: spontaneously, without the therapist's advice, she created a sculpture which expressed the right attitude in the transference situation.

Sculptural Work as an Instrument of Therapy

An unusual fifty-seven-year-old man visited the clinic, which he had seen mentioned in a newspaper. Outwardly he seemed all right. He said he had practically never worked; evidently his means were such as to allow that. In private studies he had devoted himself to art history. Now he was in a crisis because he needed a wife. Above all, though, he was suffering from wind (flatus), which was quite uncontrollable and which lately had forced him to withdraw completely from the world, although it was obvious that in this world people need each other and that one should not cut oneself off. His most scurrilous story, which was also recorded in writing, aroused the suspicion that there were also paranoid symptoms. Radio and television were repeatedly mentioned as disturbing factors. The patient stayed nine days in the clinic. He busied himself in the studio where, of his own accord, he began to produce sculptures, all of which he broke again, however. On leaving, he assured us that he would stay in touch. The subsequent development was as curious as the findings. Back home he wrote a description of a journey to see the statues of Greece, which he had imagined, and which he undertook in the company of a Zurich psychotherapist. The description went into great detail and was astonishingly accurate; the patient had obviously taken precise bearings. Then he sent a large parcel containing three sculptures that he had produced at home. The sculptures were badly broken since he had not been able to bake them at home. The patient had portrayed a billy goat (fig. 5), a human head (fig. 6), a winged goddess (one wing is broken off) (fig. 7).

In other words, he had modelled the animal, the human, and the spiritual. And he had portrayed the male, caught between sexuality (billy goat) and anima (goddess). The production of the sculptures had two immediate consequences. For one thing, the patient at last had a profession! He had new visiting cards printed, on which – beneath his name (where other people might put "Chartered Accountant," for example) – he described himself as "Plasticus"; this was no doubt intended to mean someone who produces sculptures. Furthermore, he undertook the imagined journey to Greece in reality. He also sent us a detailed account of the journey, proving that he was really there by sending postcards from the main stops along the way.

Both the sculptures and the real journey were probably connected psychologically with the "uncontrollable wind" the patient complained of on admission to the clinic. Such flatulence is common in cases where nothing real is being done (after all, it is via the colon that one "does" things).

The possibility of going back out into the world from the encroaching schizophrenic isolation was constellated by the imaginary journey in the company of the psychotherapist. But the journey became a reality only after the patient had produced his three sculptures. The sculptures themselves are very small; they are only 5 cm to 15 cm high. But for the patient they were a very big thing, big enough to make him a "Plasticus."

One may smile at this. But one would not smile if, as a psychiatrist, one knew what it means for a person to break through the barrier of psychotic stultification. In this case, the liberation occurred through the simplest modeling activity, in which at last something personal and creative was done. It was only a small thing, a very small thing, but *very little is simply infinitely more than nothing at all.*

The ensuing, lengthy correspondence was very important in the treatment of this man, who had spent only a few days in the clinic. This case shows how important it is to accept even the strangest individual, the most curious case, with the greatest care and to wait attentively to see what develops. The patient saw direct psychotherapeutic influence as a phenomenon in the clinic, without any contents becoming conscious to him. He wrote: "I was very impressed by the doctors, who did not prescribe any medicines for me but who, after a first, very thorough interview, then just had long conversations with me that were very soothing. The conversations concerned my past life, starting with my grandparents. At first I did not really understand why they were so soothing." Did the doctor establish psychic contact with the patient, or did his aura produce an effect on the patient? All that happened in the clinic, it would seem, was that a certain constellation took place. The further development only became apparent later.

To complete the story of this little thing that was created, I would like to mention another example, which shows what spontaneous creativity can achieve in a person when it is set in motion on a large scale. In a park in Hauterives, France, is a bizarre building twenty-six meters long, fourteen meters wide

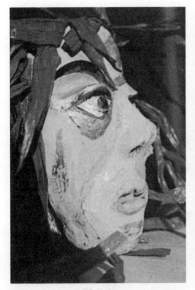

Fig. 1

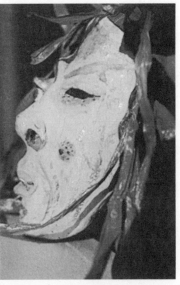

Fig. 2

Fig. 3

Fig. 4

Fig. 5

Fig. 6

Fig. 7

373

Fig. 8

Fig. 9

Fig. 10

Fig. 11

and twelve meters high. It is the *palais idéal* of the postman Cheval (fig. 8). Ferdinand Cheval lived from 1836 to 1924, and died at the age of eighty-eight. When he was twenty-eight, he dreamed that he had to build a palace. Fifteen years later, at the age of forty-three, in the middle of life, he suddenly realized that he had to make the dream a reality. For thirty-three years, from 1879 to 1912, he worked on the construction of his monument, the "ideal palace," using stones he collected on his postman's rounds. The building is covered with primitive but intriguing figures. It is a wonderfully skillful piece of work (figs. 9, 10). Cheval himself thought he was insane when he started work on the building, but gradually he realized that there was a healing force at work in him which was his sole happiness. "A farmer's son, I will live and die a farmer – yet having proved that, even among people of my kind, there are some who have genius and energy," he wrote in his autobiography (1905; ed. André Jean, 1937). Here we see the creative divinity at work in a person. Cheval himself realized that he was not mad after all, and precisely because he was building this crazy, or at least bizarre, monument. Even creating something eccentric is permitted; it is not psychotic. On the contrary, *creative work can be a release from psychosis,* as well as a protection against it.

Sculpture as an Expression of a Turning Point in Psychotherapy

A thirty-six-year-old man in an intellectual job was admitted for emergency treatment at his own request. He was severely depressed and very agitated, though not actually psychotic. The condition had been triggered by a considerable affective tension with his wife. The patient declared himself scarcely capable of working or of doing anything. When psychotherapy got under way, an attitude of violent opposition became apparent. The findings then improved quickly so that the patient could again pursue his work. Apart from that, however, nothing changed for months; the situation in the marriage remained blocked, and the patient's mood remained one of despair. Eventually, however, there was a reversal, when the patient handed me a sculpture as a present. From that moment on, he had recovered *his inner equilibrium*. The sculpture, in the manner of Henry Moore, shows two figures joined at the base, whose upper parts communicate with one another by means of black and white threads (fig. 11). The right-hand figure (on the left for the viewer) is male; the left-hand figure (on the right for the viewer) is female. The male figure is tied to the female figure in two places. The top of the man's head, his skull, his consciousness, is tied to something behind the woman's head, the unconscious. That link is white, in other words, healthy and conscious. The man's mouth is tied to the surrealistically represented breasts of the woman and so receives maternal nourishment. That link is black, in other words, dark, instinctive, and unconscious. But both figures form a single whole, since they are joined at the base.

In this sculpture the patient rediscovered contact with his emotionality (anima). This contact was both spiritual (from consciousness to the unconscious) and instinctive (maternal-nourishing function of the anima). In creating the sculpture he must have revived the contact. It also came to light that there was an objective side matching the subjective side, namely the patient's need to clarify his relationship with his wife (reconciliation? divorce?). Unfortunately, my social circles and those of the patient did not permit me to investigate that question further.

The decisive therapeutic effect of producing this sculpture cannot have come simply from the fact that the patient was actively creative. It was probably equally important that he was doing something for someone else in giving the sculpture to the therapist as a present and a document. This had the effect of a liberation from the autism, the isolation in opposition, that was closing in on him dangerously.

The latter consideration also played a part in the three other cases that have been mentioned. In each case the sculpture was produced "for the therapist." With sculptures that are so solid and "real" it is often important not only that they were produced but also that they were intended for a particular person. So not only is "something done," but "something creative is done for someone else." A modest deed for another person also protects against excess, inflation, which threatens when the creative god comes alive in a person. Man is not divine; only creative power is divine.

In conclusion, we can say the following:

In order to work with sculpture in psychotherapy, there is no need for instruction (lessons), but there is a need for a certain stimulus. For example, it is an advantage if the leader of a clinical, therapeutic studio is an active sculptor. Examples were cited to illustrate the following aspects of the subject: The patient can express his problem in the form of a sculpture (diagnosis). He can represent the meaning of the relationship to the therapist in the sculpture (transference). He can find a new attitude to himself and the world through the act of producing the sculpture (therapy). And he can embody, or even achieve, a successful outcome of therapy in the sculpture (lysis). The creation of a sculpture has a direct effect. Of course, the sculpture also has to be understood. It has to be appreciated; but as a rule in therapy, in conversation with the patient, it needs no interpretation. On the other hand, it is essential that the therapist recognize the importance and significance of the sculpture in the therapeutic process. That knowledge can guide his reactions and foster his relationship to the patient.

XXI

ANALYTICAL PSYCHOLOGY AND SOCIETY: THE LOST SYMBOL, OR AN INQUIRY INTO THE NATURE OF MASS PSYCHOSIS

The loss of a symbol can shake humanity to the core and be like an earthquake in world history. The history of our culture, Mediterranean culture and European culture, provides some striking examples.

The first example is the decline of the ancient Egyptian empire, which lasted from 4500 to 2500 B.C. and disintegrated over a period of 350 years. This was the empire of the pyramids, those sixty stone "hills" on the west bank of the Nile opposite Cairo, extending as far as Fajum. In the new empire Memphis was the center. The Egyptian state had a fully developed bureaucracy, with the king at its head. The king (pharaoh = great house) towered far above his subjects and was an incarnation of the gods, above all of Amon-Ra and Horus.

The head of this state-pyramid, then, was a god-king. In him the world above was symbolically embodied. The "above," as a symbol of something relatively unknown[1] was best represented by the God-King. As a living symbol he, the Pharaoh, gave order to the people.

This world, which knows an above, also has a "below." Below are the dead and the other world, whose empire is described in the *Egyptian Book of the Dead* (the text handed down to us, however, is one thousand years more recent). The essential and longest part of the *Book of the Dead* is chapter 125, which has come down to us in thirty-four copies and deals with the weighing of the soul after death in the Hall of Double Justice.[2] In the Hall of Double

Justice the dead soul confesses in front of forty-two witnesses the sins of which it is free and then its heart is weighed. The two justices are those of the East and the West. Thus the clash of opposites, for and against, conflict and sin, are placed in the below and in the tension of East and West, whereas above the god-king symbolizes the unity and permanence of the pyramid-state.

The collapse of the pyramid-state in the years 2500 B.C. to 2160 B.C. meant for its subjects the loss of their organizing symbol. The above, the god-king, lost his power, and so his symbolic significance was lost, too. What this meant for people is clearly expressed in the "Conversation of a Man Tired of Life with His Ba [soul]," composed around 2200 B.C. H. Jacobsohn, who has written a new commentary on the document, says:

> The contemporaries of the man tired of life discovered – probably for the first time in Egyptian history – the terrors and the dread of separation from God and loss of God. The omnipotence of the god on earth and divine son, of Pharaoh, was broken. For the first time people faced one another and saw themselves as individuals. That must have been impossible for the Egyptian to bear, having been used to the collective religious community; and the frequency of suicide in those days is no doubt attributable to that inner shock.[3]

The loss of the above, of the divine, royal head, led to external and internal chaos in Egyptian society. In the course of history, various attempts were made to find a new order following the collapse of the old, archaic order. One of the most notable attempts was that of Pharaoh Amenhotep IV, who ruled from 1375 B.C. to 1358 B.C. and called himself Akhnaton. With a fanatical singleness of purpose that ran far ahead of his time, he tried to separate the divine and human spheres. In place of the old gods, who were really nothing more than deified mortals, he put Aten, the sun. At the same time, he directed his followers' attention to a far more comprehensive and distant force than the blinding disc of the sun in front of which they bowed.[4] In an age when people still believed that a god was simply a more powerful earthly creature, with a form conceived along natural lines, Akhnaton proclaimed that God was a formless being, the seed of reason, and the power of love that penetrated all space and time.

Akhnaton was unable to win acceptance for his abstract monotheism. After his death he was publicly portrayed as an apostate and a heretic.[5] It was not until 1350 years later that Mediterranean mankind once again faced the question of a clear distinction between God and man.

This question arose when the monotheistic Jewish people encountered the Roman Empire. That moment is rightly taken as the turning point in our calendar. It was an encounter not only between two peoples, but also between two figures who were to dominate history for years to come: Christ, whose kingdom is not of this world, and Caesar, the ruler of the empire.

Ideas about these two figures were at first unclear. Messianic hopes were often directed outwards, and even on the cross Christ is called *Rex,* King. On the other hand, Antony and his friends dedicated a veritable Passion to the murdered Caesar, the *divus Julius.* In it we read:[6]

> His divine ancestry was so genuine that he only had one purpose in life: to save wherever there was someone to be saved. They received forgiveness even before they asked for it, they were saved even before they realized they were in danger, and he himself never asked to whom he had shown mercy. And he, the father of the Fatherland, the invulnerable one, the demigod, suffered death, slaughter in the Senate, unarmed the victorious commander, defenseless the emperor of peace, cut down by his own companions, he who always had pity on them.

And Caesar's successor, Augustus, is elevated to the rank of messiah and savior by Virgil in his fourth eclogue:[7]

> Justice returns to earth, the Golden Age
> Returns, and its first-born comes down from heaven above.
> Look kindly, chaste Lucina, upon this infant's birth,
> For with him shall hearts of iron cease, and hearts of gold
> Inherit the whole earth – yes, Apollo reigns now.

> You at our head, mankind shall be freed from its age-long fear,
> All stains of our past wickedness being cleansed away ...

We see, then, that the longing for a god-king, a savior-prince, was very much alive at that time, and that there were clear signs of a wish still to see the above as one, and Christ as king or Caesar as a messiah.

The historical development then led to a split, which meant that the church and God stood on one side, with the state and Caesar on the other. The world now had a new above, but not a unified above as in the Egyptian pyramid-state ruled by the god-king. The above was a pair, God and Caesar.

There was often extreme tension between these two powers. The battle between church and secular rulers was a moving force in the Middle Ages; Canossa was considered a victory for the church, and the exile of the popes in Avignon, a victory for the princes. Internal upheaval at the top – the Reformation in the church, and in the state the Wars of Succession and the revolutions, for example, in England and France – rocked the foundations of Europe, but on the whole the structure remained astonishingly stable right up until recent times. People on the European continent felt secure in the knowledge that an emperor, king, or government had the affairs of state in hand, while on a metaphysical plane God was guiding their destiny. Where there were upheavals, they were a misfortune that was bound to pass and did not fundamentally challenge the symbolic reality of the supreme pair, "God and emperor."

Here and there, however, the reality of the "supreme pair" was seriously under threat. The shock waves of the French Revolution were significant, if short-lived, when the Sun King with his Catholic clergy, who had dared to revoke the Edict of Nantes, was replaced by a revolutionary tribunal and a cult of reason. But soon a new emperor was crowning himself in the presence of the pope, and people could go on living, quarreling, and even fighting wars, knowing for whom and under whose protection they fought. Nor was there any doubt about what constituted a sin.

The tremor of the French Revolution, however, was a warning sign, and it was not long before the "double apex of social life," God and emperor, came under a far more serious threat. This time it took place in Germany – in Germany, of all places, the ruler of which had for a thousand years been called "Roman Emperor," and which had given the world the last great prophet of the religion of the Son of God, Martin Luther. In the nineteenth century both the Protestant and the Catholic faiths were still flourishing, with churches in every parish. The Holy Roman Emperor still had his residence at the Hofburg in Vienna and, in Berlin, Germany had seen a new birth of empire.

In the course of the nineteenth century, however, signs began to appear that the double apex of God and emperor was being undermined. Religious worship began to seem questionable. As early as 1811, August Wilhelm Schlegel, at that time living in Bern, wrote to the Duke of Montmorency: "Protestant worship leaves me cold; all I see in the priest is a man who makes what are often mediocre observations on the most exalted truths, or even takes it upon himself to interpret Revelation according to his own opinions. The service leaves me devoid of the blessings that Holy Communion affords the faithful." Schlegel then thought of turning to Catholicism, but was deeply disillusioned by its association with political reaction, so that in 1819, disgruntled and full of gloom, he wrote from Bonn to Berlin: "For twenty-eight years now I have been sailing the turbulent seas of Europe and believe I have acquired some knowledge of the weather. Since my return last year the horizon in Germany has darkened considerably and unexpectedly quickly; and I can see other, unfavorable changes in the weather in the offing."[8]

What Schlegel felt about the Protestant service was felt by ever-wider circles, and no one was surprised that Germany's visionary philosopher, Friedrich Nietzsche, could declare in 1882: "God is dead! God will stay dead!"[9] *The Gay Science* is the title of the work in which this announcement is made. But there is little cause for gaiety in the announcement of this death!

While the power of the religious authority was fading, that of the state and the symbolic emperor was not in much better condition. Here is how a loyal royalist, Prince Philipp of Eulenburg-Hertefeld, spoke of the heroic Emperor Wilhelm I, the first emperor of the new German empire, in 1885:[10] "The emperor's old doctor, Lauer, has been completely fossilized for years. He has found himself a fat captain with ugly legs as an assistant, and the two of them never take their eagle eyes off the emperor. Lauer says that the old gentleman's need for rest is increasing. General Hartmann calls him 'a walking corpse.' " Indeed, why should an emperor not be senile? It is not the senility, but rather the private and detached point of view of the observer, which shows how for the faithful servant – whether he realizes it or not – the figure of the emperor no longer carries any symbolic weight and has become a corpse to be ridiculed.

The grandson of the hero, Wilhelm II, was self-consciously brash and modern. He was a failure, because one cannot be the carrier of a symbol that way.

Both emperor and empire, lacking a true spiritual orientation, sought compensation for this sharply felt lack in the external world, in sterile materialism. They felt constantly disadvantaged, constrained and, with astonishing hubris, defrauded of a future. Yet they were rich and could have had a good life. Stefan George accurately characterized the attitude:[11]

> *Alles habend, alles wissend seufzen sie:*
> *"Karges Leben! Drang und Hunger überall!*
> *Fülle fehlt!"*
> *Speicher weiß ich über jedem Haus*
> *Voll von Korn, das fliegt und neu sich häuft –*
> *Keiner nimmt ...*
> *Keller unter jedem Hof, wo siegt*
> *Und im Sand verströmt der Edelwein*
> *Keiner trinkt ...*
> *Tonnen puren Golds verstreut im Staub:*
> *Volk in Lumpen streift es mit dem Saum –*
> *Keiner sieht.*

[Possessing everything, knowing everything, they sigh: "Meager existence! Stress and hunger all around! There is no abundance!" But I know there are storerooms over every house full of corn that is blown around and lies in heaps – no one takes and uses it... Cellars under every farm where the wine seeps out of barrels and disappears in the sand – no one drinks... Tons of pure gold scattered in the dust: People in rags brush it with their hems – no one sees it.]

In fact, they thought that they should take it, that they should drink it and that they could see it. But unfortunately, disoriented as they were, they saw it in world politics, where the devil of power had led them to believe it was to be found.

So Germany stumbled into the carnage of the First World War as a community whose symbolic above was already undermined. Religious faith was in doubt, God had been declared dead, and it was impossible to take the emperor seriously. The war ended in defeat. The reputation of God, with whose blessing the war had ostensibly been started, suffered still further, and the emperor, with all his subsidiary princes, lost power and rulership.

What was left behind was an impoverished country whose heroic dream was over. But still that was not the worst of it. The worst was that there was no longer a collective symbol. The more sensitive individuals had already felt this lack before the war, and found themselves in the same situation as the man tired of life in Egypt four thousand years before. Hermann Hesse described their reaction in *Walter Kaempff* (1908), where Kaempff says: "The Good Lord. He is nowhere, there is no such thing." And, "It was not he that weighed me in the balance, but I that weighed him, and I found that he was a fairy tale." Walter Kaempff never got beyond this topic, Hesse wrote. His God was to him an idol, whom he provoked and cursed in order to make it speak. Thus the meaning of his existence was lost. His light burned out suddenly and sadly. "One night the maid heard him talking and walking to and fro in his room until late, before everything was quiet. In the morning he did not answer her knock. And when the maid finally pushed the door gently open and crept into his room, she sudden-

ly gave a scream and ran off in a fright, for she had seen her
master hanging by a leather strap from the ceiling."[12]

The poets dealt with this topic even before the First World
War. But after the war there were few in Germany as sensitive as
Kaempff or the ancient Egyptian, and there was not, as then, a
suicide epidemic. Apparently the great suicide epidemic was still
to come.

In the meanwhile people went on living, working, running
factories, serving in the state bureaucracy, sitting in schools,
going to cafés, and attending concerts, as if nothing had happened.
Hardly anyone saw how dangerous it was that there was no
longer a symbol above, neither God nor emperor. There were a
few incidents that should have served as warnings, but no one
took much notice. Germany's most gifted statesman, Walter
Rathenau, was treacherously murdered in broad daylight on the
streets of the capital. And yet there was very little appreciation of
just how bad the situation must have become for such a godless
and politically damaging act to be perpetrated without the whole
country rising in revolt. But that is just it: Without God murder is
not a sin, and without a state the murder of a statesman is no loss.
Above was a vacuum. Maybe there was a brief uproar. But then
the same thing happened as happens in Spitteler's *Prometheus
and Epimetheus* after the abduction of a divine child:[13]

> Then a voice was heard speaking with superior knowledge: "Dear
> brothers! What is it you want? And why are you getting so heated
> and worked up? Can't you see that the houses are still standing? And
> look how merrily the little streams are racing along!" And they
> looked around in amazement; and when they saw that the houses
> were all still standing and the streams were all racing merrily along,
> they turned with a smile and went peacefully back to their homes.

It was soon to become apparent whose voice it was that was
talking so shamelessly and appeasingly: the voice of Behemoth,
the devil. But then Spitteler wrote his epic in 1880!

Above, there was no longer any symbol, and wherever it still survived it was demolished. The physics of Einstein and Planck and the depth psychology of Freud and Jung had already opened up whole new perspectives, which could have confronted a conscious mankind with unexpected problems and insights. But that sort of thing was not liked. Opportunities for new insights received the same treatment as the jewel in Spitteler's story,[14] of which people said: " 'And so the sooner we rid ourselves of this curse the better; we'll leave it for the others so that, God willing, all the evil will befall them.' And so they hurled the jewel down onto the street, so that it cried out and groaned and wailed bitterly. And to them, it seemed, this was a great comfort, as was the groaning."

The vacuum created by the loss of the symbols of God and king seemed terrible at first. But then cultivated Europe experienced something unexpected: consolation. It came when a degenerate painter and hysterical loudmouth had the nerve to insert himself into the vacuum. Unfortunately, the man himself was a nobody, which was to have serious consequences.

The vacuum that had been hanging over people was so intolerable that at first everyone was relieved when the emptiness was once again filled. Of course, people soon noticed that the way it had been filled was not ideal. But it became apparent that even in this sphere the law that nature abhors a vacuum holds true, and so the person who had occupied the vacuum was not removed.

The situation would not have been so bad if the person filling the vacuum had not been a nonentity. In the places once occupied by God and emperor there now sat a new God-pharaoh who was nothing of the sort. This was a grave catastrophe. When the symbol is invested, but invested in a figure of inadequacy and nullity, then its archetypal opposite comes alive. The consequences prove that the activation of the archetypal opposite is no theory, but a deadly serious fact. A nobody was sitting on the throne of the God-king, but under his rule the opposites of God and king assumed new vitality and power as the *devil* and the *criminal*. The devil is the Anti-God. The criminal breaks the law that the king protects. In an essay written in 1936, Jung recognized the vacuum, but his apprehension that the vacuum might be filled by the old Germanic god Wotan proved too optimistic.[15] It was not Wotan; no, it was the devil and the criminal. It is moving to see how clearly this was foreseen by the Swiss writer Gottfried Keller whose poem "The Public Slanderers" was frequently admired by members of the German Resistance Movement in Germany's darkest hour.[16] It runs as follows:[17]

> *Ein Ungeziefer ruht*
> *In Staub und trocknem Schlamme*
> *Verborgen, wie die Flamme*
> *In leichter Asche tut.*
> *Ein Regen, Windeshauch*
> *Erweckt das schlimme Leben,*
> *Und aus dem Nichts erheben*
> *Sich Seuchen, Glut und Rauch.*
>
> *Aus dunkler Höhle fährt*
> *Ein Schächer, um zu schweifen;*
> *Nach Beuteln möcht' er greifen*
> *Und findet bessern Wert:*
> *Er findet einen Streit*
> *Um nichts, ein irres Wissen,*
> *Ein Banner, das zerrissen,*
> *Ein Volk in Blödigkeit.*
>
> *Er findet, wo er geht,*
> *Die Leere dürft' ger Zeiten,*
> *Da kann er schamlos schreiten,*
> *Nun wird er ein Prophet;*
> *Auf einen Kehricht stellt*
> *Er seine Schelmenfüsse*
> *Und zischelt seine Grüsse*
> *In die verblüffte Welt.*
>
> *Gehüllt in Niedertracht*
> *Gleichwie in einer Wolke,*
> *Ein Lügner vor dem Volke,*

Ragt bald er gross an Macht
Mit seiner Helfer Zahl,
Die hoch und niedrig stehend,
Gelegenheit erspähend,
Sich bieten seiner Wahl.

Sie teilen aus sein Wort,
Wie einst die Gottesboten
Getan mit den fünf Broten,
Das kleckert fort und fort!
Erst log allein der Hund,
Nun lügen ihrer tausend;
Und wie ein Sturm erbrausend,
So wuchert jetzt sein Pfund.

Hoch schiesst empor die Saat,
Verwandelt sind die Lande,
Die Menge lebt in Schande
Und lacht der Schofeltat!
Jetzt hat sich auch erwahrt,
Was erstlich war erfunden:
Die Guten sind verschwunden,
Die Schlechten stehn geschart!
Wenn einstmals diese Not
Lang wie ein Eis gebrochen,
Dann wird davon gesprochen,
Wie von dem schwarzen Tod;
Und einen Strohmann bau'n
Die Kinder auf der Haide
Zu brennen Lust aus Leide,
Und Licht aus altem Grau'n.

[A pest lies dormant in dust and dry mud, like a flame in the ashes. A shower, a breath of wind, wakens it to life, and from the void there emerge plagues and fire and smoke. / From out of the dark den a thief creeps forth to roam abroad; purses are what he is after, but he finds more valuable booty: He finds a quarrel over nothing, false learning, a torn banner, and an abject people. / Wherever he goes, he finds the emptiness of meager times, so he can be unashamed, and he becomes a prophet; a rubbish heap is his platform, and he hisses his greetings to a baffled world. / Cloaked in malice as in a cloud, a liar to the people, soon he towers in strength with the number of his supporters who, ranking both high and low, spying their opportunity, offer him their services. / They spread his word the way the messengers of God once distributed the five loaves, it grows and grows! At first there was only the one dog telling lies in their thousands; and like a roaring storm, his standing grows. / The seed is sown, the country is transformed, the masses live in shame and laugh at mischief! Now what used to be an invention has become a reality: the good have disappeared, and the bad have rallied together! / One day, when this time is past, it will be spoken of as the Black Death was; and the children will build a straw man in the field to burn happiness out of sorrow and light out of old terrors.]

The catastrophe gathered speed like an avalanche, although people were still jubilant for a while because at last the vacuum had been filled. The fact that it was occupied by lower archetypes, devils and criminals, was not recognized until it was too late. In other words, the typical pattern of behavior associated with the archetype imposes itself, where it has free passage, with enormous power and speed. So people soon realized that any form of resistance was difficult and dangerous, and perhaps also useless.

Other poets, too, had sensed the catastrophe long before. As early as 1846, Heinrich Heine wrote in the final poem of *Atta Troll*:[18]

> *Wahnsinn, der sich klug gebärdet!*
> *Weisheit, welche überschnappt!*
> *Sterbeseufzer, welche plötzlich*
> *Sich verwandeln in Gelächter!*
>
> *Welch ein Sumsen, welterschütternd!*
> *Das sind ja des Völkerfrühlings*
> *Kolossale Maienkäfer,*
> *Von Berserkerwut ergriffen!*

[Madness in the guise of cleverness! Wisdom gone crazy! A dying breath that suddenly turns to laughter! / What is that droning sound, world-shaking? It is the colossal cockchafers of the springtime of nations, gone berserk!]

The humming of the bombers that went berserk in destroying Europe come to mind.

The consequences of the archetype of the criminal need hardly be described in further detail. The criminal corruption of justice, the broken treaties, the ruthless assassination of an imperial chancellor in his home, and much else besides are all well known. And let me recall a truly devilish plot, exceeding the imagination of a Hieronymus Bosch, with this single testimony. Dr. Ella Lingens stated in court in Frankfurt on 2 March 1964 that she once had to watch as a child was thrown alive into the flames of the camp crematorium at Auschwitz. At first she could not believe her eyes and thought the child was a dog, until her fellow prisoners told her that the camp commander had authorized this additional method of killing to ease the pressure on the crematorium.[19]

The negative influence of the devil-criminal archetype also produced typical results for the individual. The reproduction of the nation was brought down to an animal level; as with dogs and cattle, the sole consideration was that of race. The spiritual side of man was fundamentally negated.

Christoph Steding, speaking in 1938 under the patronage of the president of the Imperial Institute for the History of the "new" Germany, said: "An empire is better than all psychotherapy and psychoanalysis because it lifts people above themselves if they voluntarily submit themselves to it, which effectively eliminates the cause of all psychopathic behavior, namely, a feeling of self-importance." For that reason there could be no "split people" in the Third Reich. This claim was an obvious lie. But it lent the German people, which was now supposed to consist solely of "whole people," the prestige of a "chosen people." The insecure and false nature of this claim meant that people had to affirm it through confrontation with others. In a devilish and criminal way, they therefore turned on the one other people that in a quite different and genuine sense had the right to call itself the chosen people: the Jews. The Jews were all the more suited to the role of scapegoat, since waging war against this deeply religious, non-Christian people enabled the new chosen people to forget just how far they had betrayed their own religion, Christianity. Jakob Schaffner, an inglorious Swiss National Socialist, contemptuously referred to the Bible as a "foreign collection of texts."[21] The most sinister, tragic thing was that, owing to the absence of the higher, divine-royal archetype, the devilish and criminal aspect could rampage all the more indiscriminately. The victims were neither guilty nor innocent; they were random. And regarding the butchers, it was often difficult to say whether they saw the wrongness of what they were doing. The devil spoke with flattery, or threats, of duty and honor, until nobody knew any more what was above and what was below.

In one respect, though, the criminal-devil was right: in the prophecy of the thousand-year empire. Except that that prophecy, like everything else he said, has turned into its opposite. Through his efforts, Germany did shift a thousand years, only not forward, but backward. Germany's borders, the borders of the Federal Republic of today, are as they were in 919, when Heinrich I of Saxony became the first German king. He then began to extend German territory eastward by building castles and towns in the East; that is why he was known as the founder of cities. Everything that was gained in the one thousand years since then was lost in the brief period of criminal rule.

The invasion of the archetype of the devil-criminal is over *for the moment*. The whole nightmare ended in fire, smoke, and death. And yet the danger lurks everywhere, and a new screaming fool could unleash a new catastrophe at any time, a catastrophe that would be worse than anything known previously. So we have to beware of relaxing simply because "the houses are still standing and the streams are still merrily flowing." We have to ask whether there are any lessons to be drawn from what happened.

One thing is certain: The danger arising from the loss of the "higher symbol" is in no way a purely German problem. The circumstances – the lost first war, the coming together of religious crisis and political crisis, and the fall of the monarchy – all contributed to the fact that Behemoth was able to seize power in Germany rather than elsewhere. At bottom, however, all the countries and peoples of the Western world face the same question: The above as God-king is archaic. The above as God and church on the one hand and as state and emperor on the other, such as we have inherited it from antiquity, has become problematic today. And the fact that the below was able to take over in the form of devil and criminal and become so powerful deserves serious consideration.

The conclusions we draw from this situation are meaningful only if they are simple and practical. Today a person who asks serious questions detests generalities.

First of all, one has to ask whether the symbolic summit of society that was once called God-pharaoh and later manifested itself in Christ and Caesar, should still be left in its position at the top in the traditional sense, since "up there" it is always possible that something evil and uncontrollable will happen. This would mean that religion cannot remain a simple matter of going to church. It has to be lived out as an individual responsibility, regardless of any theology or catechism. Christ, one might say, is not "above you; he is with you and in you." The challenge is to responsible individuation. Luther said: "Here I stand, I can do no other." He had understood.

But the Caesar cannot stay above either. From this there follows the democratic responsibility of the individual for the community. Subservience to authority, party bondage and a weakness for slogans are incompatible with the demands of the age. This seems self-evident today. But still most people talk more foolishly on this subject than they ought to.

Furthermore, we have to see that twice so far this century there has been a regression, brought about by the forces of evil in two world wars, which constitutes a slap in the face for our age with its faith in progress. Under these circumstances, we will have to look carefully at our faith in progress. Where, exactly, do we want to end up if the world is to continue to get better and more perfect all the time? Better, that is, in the sense intended by those who believe in progress. We have to balance faith in progress with our duty to the past. People do not just live for the future but also from the past. The false *Blut und Boden* romanticism of the criminal period should not fool us into thinking that there is not a genuine link to one's homeland and ancestors which is more than nostalgia for the "good old days." Thus, for example, we must stop the destruction of the European countryside through speculative development, and youth must be taught the tradition of history. A progress paid for with losses would indeed amount to a step backward.

Finally, we face the most difficult question. God-king and devil-criminal are an antimony, a genuine contradiction. If the below, the devil and the criminal, can emerge so suddenly and literally, would it not be best to go to work on the below before it once again gains control? If we remember, in the Egyptian chamber of the dead there was no good and evil; instead there were "two types of justice," which were simply distinguished as a neutral pair of opposites, East and West. When the above does not suppress the below, but the below encounters the above, then the below has a different meaning and effect. For then the devil is also Lucifer, the fallen angel, who with his contrasting light illuminates the above; and the criminal is also Prometheus, who breaks the supposedly eternal laws as a creative act.

In practice this means that the contradictions in all actions and judgments have to be appreciated. It is true that, as in Goethe's *Faust*, the devil can be the force that "always intends evil and yet always does good." But in order for that to be the case, one needs consciousness, since unconsciousness conjures up archaic brutality.

So in place of the antimony God-king and devil-criminal, we need a living quaternity which would provide order and mediate tensions. In practice this means that one must take the ambiguity of right and wrong upon oneself. And one must accept the dubious nature of good and evil.

An attitude based on those principles is more difficult to maintain than one might think. It would be a lot easier to rely on the king to be a good fellow and God to be a good father. Then, one would only have to obey naively, or at most rebel childishly. But in order to prevent the sort of catastrophe that arises when a contrary archetype assumes control, everyone will have to accept the dual justice of right-wrong and good-evil, of king-criminal and God-devil, as a personal responsibility.

This requires constant self-examination and a constant readiness to change. No one who has recognized the dubiousness of judgments can simply choose the right thing and always do good. He can only continue to examine himself and make fresh decisions. Right and wrong, good and evil, are truly opposites comparable to the cross, of which Christ says, "Let him deny himself, and take up his cross daily, and follow me!" (Luke 9, 23).

Where, then, can we find again that symbol the loss of which would expose whole populations to chaos? Not in its regressive restoration. The regression to the God-Caesar was hollow, and the Antichrist raised his head. The age when the symbol that carries the community was to be sought as a figure and a power outside and above seems to have reached an end. Therefore, people must discover the symbol within and guard it in their hearts. In political terms, that means the responsibility of the individual as a citizen of the community. In metaphysical terms, it requires us to realize that our intentions and mistakes are forever leading elsewhere than we had planned to go. And still the result is what we are. We have to grasp that consciously and responsibly.

Since the original symbol of the God-king is a collective symbol, its revival in the soul of the individual entails our acknowledgment of the other, even if he thinks and acts differently from us. We should face him, neither destroying him nor allowing ourselves to be subjected to him, but constantly seeking dialogue. It goes without saying that the dark and dangerous side of emotionality will come alive in the process, both in ourselves and in the other person. But if the light is not extinguished, there is no cause to fear a disaster. The resulting tension should not be evaded, because it is part of life. Mankind is not ready for this solution today. It is the task of future generations to move further in that direction. But the catastrophe in Germany has given a sign that bids extreme caution.

To conclude, the archaic symbol of the God-pharaoh is to be found today in the soul of the individual in the form of an ethical-political and an intellectual-religious responsibility. This way of putting it likewise remains a symbol, a formula for a relatively unknown and yet existing fact.[22] The fact itself, which is formulated symbolically, is not located in people's souls. It extends far beyond them and remains, as God-king, a timeless archetype: the lord of human history.

XXII

PSYCHIATRY, PSYCHOTHERAPY
AND ANALYSIS TODAY (1982)

Fifty years have passed since my first session of analysis with C. G. Jung (the expression "training analysis" was unknown in those days). Forty-four years have passed since I began my clinical psychiatric work as a doctor (which I still carry on today) after the medical training Jung advised me to get. Let me review briefly what I have seen.

1) In 1938 *classical psychiatry* was fully developed. Cullen (1710-90; *Neurosis*) and Pinel (1745-1826) had established the basis of psychopathology; Charcot and P. Janet had demonstrated the dynamics of the psyche; and Kraepelin, E. Bleuler, and K. Bonhoeffer – following Esquirol (1772-1840) – had founded the psychiatric institution in which the psychiatric patient was examined, observed, looked after, diagnosed and treated with simple activities as well as with a few simple drugs.

2) I will pick out a few aspects of the *development* over the four decades since 1938.

a) In 1938 almost all psychiatric *hospitals* were much too big, either barrack-like and outside town, or converted monasteries and convents. They were called "institutions," which discriminated against the inmates, though they often had poetic names, such as Burghölzli, Waldau, Friedmatt, or Bel-air. The patients were locked up, and even the doctors were confined to the institution. Many psychic disorders were the direct result of the confinement of the patients. These enormous institutions were often in poor physical repair. Today there is a lot of renovating and improvement, and the institutions are called "clinics." But the problem of clinics that are too large has not been solved; renovation tends rather to perpetuate the situation. Small psychiatric units in general hospitals are not the solution either, since they cannot accept severe cases. Liberalization is the thing today. But there are new dangers that arise as a consequence. Unfortunately we have more suicides. Drugs are smuggled into the clinic; they are even sold there. Dangerous patients are sometimes discharged far too soon. One thing in particular is missing: Politicians show an interest in universities and railroads (and much else besides), but they have little interest in psychiatry, whose buildings are among the largest in society today. And if they do show an interest, they talk in ideological terms without therapeutic knowledge.

b) *Diagnosis*. Since Kraepelin and E. Bleuler, we have at our disposal a clear system of diagnosis. For forty years diagnostic concepts have been becoming less and less clear. People look for new words; they believe society produces mental disorder artificially; they get confused. One of the favorite expressions is "borderline case," which means that the case is difficult but unclear. People get confused for two striking reasons: First, they reify psychiatric concepts. I mentioned this tendency and the danger of "labeling" patients in the introduction. This reification (hypostatization), of which psychiatrists are mostly unaware and the opponents of psychiatry always so, rightly makes people uneasy and leads to a fight against concepts. A second reason for the lack of clarity lies in the fact that the clinical tests are often carried out by test psychologists and the physical examination by the "team medical specialist," so that the doctor, left on his own, is unable to make a diagnosis any more, which makes a unified view and thus clarity more difficult to achieve. But maybe the lack of clarity is a positive thing. For one thing it prevents schematic thinking and encourages psychological seeing and experiencing in therapy, as described in chapters 14 and 15 of this book. In addition, it can lead to a new psychological formal diagnosis (e.g., when the Jungian typology is taken as a starting point).

For example, you might then ask, How are problems distributed in youth, in mature middle age, in old age, and also among the possible psychological types (from introverted to extraverted; then, e.g., with feeling as the main function, intuition as the first subsidiary function, or thought, or sensation; and in all sixteen variations of typology)? And all this, factored not only into three age groups, but also into the two sexes, and with regard to progression (conscious structure) or regression (the unconscious counterposition) in the actual circumstances. This would already yield 192 combinations. There is a lot to be done here in the way of research.

c) *Medication.* Over the past forty years there have been great advances in this field. Although after Wagner-Jauregg overcame syphilitic progressive paralysis with the malaria cure in Vienna in 1917, there was a long wait. Electroshock treatment was the first step twenty years later. Modern neuroleptics were a breakthrough. Manic-depressive illness can usually be brought under control with Tofranil (or equivalent) or Haloperidol, and then stabilized with lithium. The management of schizophrenia can at least be made more humane with the help of Largactil (or an equivalent), which has changed the atmosphere in psychiatric clinics. The neuroleptics can also make psychotherapy viable for many more patients. Furthermore, we now have medicines to treat epilepsy or delirium tremens. However, the neuroleptics raise two questions. For one thing, the sheer number of new drugs often means that one has too many choices; to keep to what is tried and tested and at the same time to take advantage of what is new, one has to be practically clairvoyant! And one must remember that even the best drugs are no substitute for personal contact with the patient. Without that contact, as we saw in chapter 17, the patients often feel as if they are in the hands of veterinarians and not of doctors. Also, we find the same thing here as P. Rube found with electroshock treatment in 1948: that the success of the treatment is dependent on whether the therapist relates emotionally to the treatment and to the patient, for example, whether there is a feeling of suspense as to the outcome. Of course, the choice of medicine is important, but the actual effect of therapy is – according to analytical psychology – a synchronistic phenomenon.

d) *Doctors*. In 1938 in the University of Zurich psychiatric hospital there were fifteen of us – one professor, three consultants and eleven assistants – to look after the wards, the outpatients, the family clinic, and the pediatric clinic. Today we have four professors, eight registrars, sixteen consultants, one deputy consultant and fifty-eight assistants – in other words, sixty-seven doctors (possibly more). The hospital is getting bigger, and one also needs more time to coordinate one's activities, which again means more staff; it is what is known as Parkinson's Law. For example, admissions (in the area of one thousand a year) have risen some 20 to 40 percent; the number of doctors has risen 200 percent. And since the doctors no longer write reports themselves and, as previously mentioned, no longer carry out tests themselves, the other staff has increased enormously. Forty years ago we learned psychotherapy in private, almost secretly. Today seminars and case conferences are obligatory. Furthermore, even in private, outpatient psychotherapy the rate of turnover has increased enormously. Yet there is still a shortage of doctors. Institutes are founded at which one group trains another group with numerous, compulsory sessions of analysis; the teachers earn their living from the students, the students then become teachers, and the patients have to look out for themselves. A particular disadvantage of this system is the fact that psychotherapists almost all practice in the larger towns with their institutes. The rural areas in every country are poorly served; occasionally psychologists help out, but social security will not pay for them.

e) *Psychotherapy*. Everything is changing so fast in this field. You are a layman if you do not know speech therapy (Rogers); there is an institute for sociometry based on Moreno's psychodrama; even Szondi's "fate analysis" has become institutionalized. Ordinary group therapy is outdated; nowadays you lie on the floor for days and shout at one another or touch one another ("workshop," "marathon"); or bodywork (?), acupuncture, and consciousness raising are linked in a postural integration as propounded by Painter. There is also a European Forum for Sex Education that has been around since 1972 (at first in Tel Aviv, which happens to be in Asia). Gestalt therapy, which aims to give us back our sensuality (?), is now a classic. A young psychiatrist can spend time learning about family therapy with an expert in the United States, only to desert his wife and children later. There is one advantage to all this. Measured against what goes on nowadays, a normal Jungian and a Freudian psychoanalyst are, so to speak, in agreement: For us, analysis is still the personal encounter between analysand and analyst. And one basic factor of therapy does not change: Psychotherapy means that a psychic disorder is not a scandal, but a summons to personal growth. And there is one other factor, too: In the hands of a serious and gifted therapist even an eccentric, perhaps theoretically unfounded form of therapy can be helpful.

f) Psychiatry and *the law*. The tendency to make involuntary admission to psychiatric care an issue for the law to decide rather than doctors is understandable, but nonetheless problematic for the patient, who becomes a "case" rather than a patient. Medicine is discreet and the law is public; and no section of an Act can have the human seriousness of an action. In any case, when an order for involuntary admission is given, it must be clearly necessary, meaning, "It *has to* be; the wayward ego *has to* abdicate; in that way the doors to individuation can be opened." The fact that the courts like to shift the responsibility for the decision onto the psychiatrists, only to castigate their presumption afterwards, is an old problem. It is also increasingly important for psychiatrists to realize that they are called upon to bring about a meaningful reform of the penal system.

g) Psychiatry and *politics*. It is a well-known fact that psychiatry is politically misused in certain states as a means of oppression. In this connection, however, protests are not entirely innocuous, since the oppressor can never accept a loss of face; often a discreet word among colleagues is more effective. The fact that psychiatry is a political issue nowadays is probably more a fashion than anything else, since the layman cannot see that a

madman is in fact unfortunately mad. No one asks the psychiatrists, because they are the heroes or villains of the piece.

h) Psychiatry and *art*. Psychopathological art is modern.
Woelfli/Bern or Schroeder-Sonnenstern are "in." The book *Mars*
by Zorn (Kindler), which contains among other things an account
of severe neurosis, and *March* (Kipphardt, Bertelsmann) are
sensational. I see in them a positive goal. The "mental patient" is
admittedly a problem, but he is visibly authentic, himself, and in
touch with the depths of the soul. This is a warning to everyone.
The days of concerts, museums, and the stage are obsolete.
Today it is the individual who is creative. We are entering the
astrological age of Aquarius, where man with the vessel in his
hand draws water from the well, not as an artist, but as a man
among men. So-called modern art does nothing to prove the
contrary in my opinion! It is largely "bluff."

i) The tasks facing us today: As always, we are interested in
research, in the origin of psychic disorder, and in its treatment.
Then there are numerous problems of *training* to be dealt with,
not only of doctors but of psychologists, nursing staff, and other
specialist staff too. We also need to look at the use of psychiatry
in *schools,* and generally as a prophylactic.

Another very considerable problem that remains unsolved is
that of *drug addiction*. Nowadays, addiction is much more than
simply a psychiatric illness. It raises medical, psychological,
sociological, legal, political, and even theological questions, none
of which has been clearly answered. There is no satisfactory
method of treating addiction. On the whole, society is at a loss for
a way of dealing with addiction. At the same time, drug addiction
is threatening more and more lives. It is a situation we often
encounter in education: When you do not know what to do
anymore, when anything the teacher does is basically wrong,
then you find that the teacher himself is subject to a process of
education. This means that you have to accept the risk of making
a decision, that you have to accept and cope with the responsibility
for the consequences of a wrong decision, that you then must
correct yourself, take responsibility for fresh mistakes, and so

step by step work towards a solution. In the case of drug addiction, however, there is not a single teacher, but a whole group of people responsible. I have counted them; every adult should take his share of the responsibility. Groups of people in positions of responsibility, as well as individuals, must constantly try to make some contribution towards finding a solution, and if possible always in collaboration with other social groups. Mistakes must be openly admitted and accepted, but must not prevent us from continuing to wrestle with the issue. Only then will we be able to find a solution. An analyst cannot provide a general remedy; he is only one among many. He can only try to show from his own experience how best to tackle such "insoluble" problems. It goes without saying that a solution will change the views of society in one way or another.

3) *Where are psychiatry and psychotherapy going today?*

I see three possibilities here:

a) There are an *official* psychiatry, psychotherapy, and analysis, which have become increasingly institutionalized. Laws, or the regulations of respected private training institutes, will determine what sort of training is given and what tests have to be passed to gain a diploma. In that way a decent general standard will be guaranteed. But the enthusiasm of psychiatrists such as Bleuler and Esquirol and of analysts such as Freud and Jung will be gone; the spirit of those pioneers will be a thing of the past.

b) Various forms of psychotherapy and of research that were originally connected with psychiatry are branching out in new directions of their own, following *paths of salvation*. Groups and institutes are formed, among them psychosophical, parapsychological, or even "meditative" societies with a Zen or Tibetan line (some with their own newspapers). It then becomes clear that *du sublime au ridicule il n'y a qu'un pas,* since much of what you hear is wisdom and much is folly; often you are fascinated, and then you just have to laugh. But one thing is obvious: People are being offered a faith situated on the borderline between faith and superstition, a borderline which is a genuine concern to many.

We should not be overhasty in condemning superstition. The theological notion that our lives are governed by a good God is discredited in many circles. The fact that in such times of transition many new promises of "salvation" seem (and often are) absurd should not delude us as to the importance of the basic issue.

c) The third possibility is *esoteric*. Properly understood, a psychiatrist or psychotherapist is a person who serves the ideals of his profession for the sake of the soul. This service is an archetype (a typical form of attitude and behavior) which – with varying force – is present in each of us. A knowledge of how to handle the unconscious is today more vital than ever. A person who has acquired that knowledge himself through his work can help others. A diploma cannot prove that a person possesses that knowledge, nor can membership in a psychotherapeutic association. Anyone who does have such knowledge and experience, and who on the basis of that experience can assist a fellow person, is an analyst. The term "guru" is probably too farfetched, but it conveys the idea. Analysis is the best offspring of nineteenth and twentieth century psychiatry. And so we can hope that, in the future, there will still be people who are analysts in this sense.

It is very much to be desired that some analysts should belong to the "official" school of psychotherapy, whereby they provide a link between analysis and the collective and can sometimes impart to "standard" care something of the élan of the pioneers.

Analysis itself, as C. G. Jung taught us in his day, should be private, since it contains something of what the alchemist Lambspring advised us to hide: what is most personal. I quoted Goethe's words "Tell it only to a wise man" *(Selige Sehnsucht)* with reference to Lambspring (Chapter XV). His words apply equally to analysis.

REFERENCES

Chapter I: The Practical Application of Analytical Psychology

1 I. Betschart, *Theophrastus Paracelsus* (Einsiedeln and Cologne: 1941), 17.
2 C. G. Jung, *CW* 8 par. 198.
3 *Ibid.*
4 C. G. Jung, *CW* 8 par. 561.
5 *Ibid.* par. 546.
6 *Ibid.* par. 555.
7 H. E. Fierz-David, *Die Entwicklunesgeschichte der Chemie* (Basel: Birkhäuser, 1945), 241.
8 C. G. Jung, *ibid.,* par. 545.
9 C. G. Jung, *CW* 6 par. 812-813.
10 *Ibid.* par. 779.
11 C. G. Jung, *CW* 8 par. 554.
12 C. G. Jung, *CW* 5.
13 C. G. Jung, *CW* 12 pars. 44 ff.
14 C. G. Jung, *CW* 16 par. 431.
15 *Ibid.* par. 419.
16 *Ibid.* par. 365.
17 Werner Braunbeck, "Auswirkungen der modernen Physik auf unser Weltbild," *Cosmos* 50 (1954): 53.
18 Quoted from Markus Fierz, "Über den Ursprung und die Bedeutung der Lehre Isaac Newtons vom absoluten Raum," *Gesnerus* 11 (1954): 67.
19 C. G. Jung, *CW* 8 par. 280.
20 Ludwig Binswanger, "Symptom und Zeit," *Schweizerische medizinische Wochenschrift* 81 (1951): 510.
21 G. Benedetti, "Die Welt des Schizophrenen und deren psychologische Zugänglichkeit," *Schweizerische medizinische Wochenschrift* 84 (1954): 1029.
22 J. N. Rosen, "The Treatment of Schizophrenic Psychosis by Direct Analysis," *Psychiatric Quarterly* 21 (1947): 3.

23 Heinrich Pestalozzi, "Ansichten und Erfahrungen, die Elementar-bildung betreffend," in *Heinrich Pestalozzis lebendiges Werk* (Basel: Birkhäuser, 1946) 3: 266.

Chapter II: The Father Archetype

1 Paul Daniel Schreber, *Memoirs of My Nervous Illness,* trans. Macalpine and Hunter (London: Dawson, 1955) 162, 165, 238.

2 E. A. Wallis Budge, *The Gods of the Egyptians* (London: Methuen, 1904) 1: 372.

3 C. G. Jung, *CW* 7 par. 245.

4 Pierre Janet, *Névrosés* (Paris: Flammarion, 1909) 358.

5 Marcel Jouhandeau, quoted in Marcel Arland, *Les Cahiers de la Pléiade*, 49.

6 C. G. Jung, *CW* 4 pars. 707-715.

7 *Ibid.* pars. 703-706.

8 C. G. Jung, *CW* 5 par. 617.

9 Frau Dr. Med. Luisa Hösli kindly passed on the details of this case.

10 C. G. Jung, *CW* 17 par. 35.

11 C. G. Jung, *CW* 5 par. 354.

12 C. A. Meier, *Healing Dream and Ritual: Ancient Incubation and Modern Psychotherapy* (Einsiedeln: Daimon, 1989) 20.

13 *Iliad* XIV. 346-351., see also Jung, *CW* 5 par. 363.

14 C. G. Jung, *CW* 4.

Chapter III: The Mother Archetype

1 M. Boss, *Der Traum und seine Auslegung* (Bern/Stuttgart: Huber, 1953) 125.

2 C. G. Jung, *CW* 6 par. 783.

3 L. Binswanger, *Ausgewählte Vorträge und Aufsätze* (Bern: Francke, 1947) 125.

4 C. G. Jung, *CW* 8 par. 53.

5 C. G. Jung, *CW* 8 par. 960.

6 C. G. Jung, *CW* 9 par. 384.

7 M. Fierz, *Verhandlungen der Schweizerischen Naturforschenden Gesellschaft,* 130.

8 G. Bally, *Schweizerisches Archiv für Neurologie und Psychiatrie* LXX.2 (1952) 234.

9 Pascal, *Pensées* (Paris: Garnier, 1930) 65.

10 C. G. Jung, *CW* 8 par. 273.

11 *Ibid.* par. 280.

12 S. Freud, *Three Essays on the Theory of Sexuality,* trans. J. Strachey (London: Hogarth, 1962) 3rd ed., xiv-xvi.

13 C. G. Jung, *CW* 6 par. 61.

14 Pascal, *ibid.,* 67.

15 C. G. Jung, *CW* 16 par. 462.

16 H. Biaesch, *Verhandlungen der Schweizerischen Naturforschenden Gesellschaft* 130, 101.

17 Von Tscharner, quoted in Biaesch, *ibid.*

18 Pascal, *ibid.,* 65.

19 L. Wittgenstein, *Das innere Bild* (Stuttgart: Hippocrates, 1952) 12, 14.

20 *Ibid.* 13.

Chapter IV: The Importance of the Family

1 R. A. Spitz, "La genèse des premiers relations objectales," *Revue française psychoanalytique* 18 (1954) 479-575.

2 G. Keller, "Frau Regel Amrain und ihr Jüngster," in *Die Leute von Seldwyla.*

3 H. Pestalozzi, "Wie Gertrud ihre Kinder lehrt," *Heinrich Pestalozzis lebendiges Werk* (Basel: Birkhäuser, 1946) 3: 174, 181.

Chapter V: Rapport in Clinical Psychiatric Therapy

1 M. Bleuler, *Zürich Spital-Geschichte,* n.d., 396.

2 C. G. Jung, *CW* 16 pars. 353ff.

3 L. Szondi, *Schicksanalyse* (Basel, 1944).

4 L. Binswanger, *Schweizerische medizinische Wochenschrift* 75 (1945) 49.

5 P. Janet, *Les Névrosés* (Paris: Flammarion, 1909).

6 J. G. Frazer, *Taboo and the Perils of the Soul* (London, 1911).

7 R. L. Denkins, *Archives of Neurology* 64 (1950) 2.

8 L. Lévy-Bruhl, *Les fonctions mentals dans les sociétés inférieurs* (Paris, 1912).

9 J. Layard, "The Incest Taboo and the Virgin Archetype," *Eranos Jahrbuch* 12 (1945) 253.

10 P. Rube, *Journal of Nervous and Mental Disease* 108 (1948) 304.

11 Bleuler, *Fortschritte der Neurologie und Psychiatrie* 19 (1951) 429.

Chapter VI: Psychological-Psychiatric Findings and Therapy

1 E. Bleuler, *Dementia Praecox or the Group of Schizophrenias,* trans. Zinkin (New York: International Universities Press, 1950).

2 C. G. Jung, *CW* 3.

3 C. G. Jung, *CW* 16 par. 198.

4 C. G. Jung, *CW* 8 par. 198.

5 *Ibid.* par. 200.

6 C. G. Jung, *CW* 9.ii pars. 193-212.

7 G. Schwab, *Sagen des klassischen Altertums* (Gütersloh: Bertelsmann, 1921) 32.

8 C. G. Jung, *CW* 3.

9 C. G. Jung, *CW* 9.ii pars. 193-212.

10 C. G. Jung, *CW* 5 par. 253.

11 La Rochefoucauld, *Maximes* (Porrentruy: Portes de France, 1947) 142.

12 Montaigne, *Essais* 50.2.12.

13 E. Bleuler, *Psychoide als Prinzip der organischen Entwicklung* (Berlin: Springer, 1925).

14 H. Driesch, *Philosophie des Organischen* (1909).

15 C. G. Jung, *CW* 9.ii par. 212.

16 S. Freud, *Civilization and its Discontents,* in *The Standard Edition*, ed. J. Strachey with A. Freud (London: Hogarth, 1961) 21: 69-71.

17 L. Binswanger, *Der Mensch in der Psychatrie* (Pfullingen: Neske, 1957) 15.

18 C. G. Jung, *CW* 3 par. 570.

19 *Ibid.* par. 575.

20 H. Zimmer, *Kunstform und Yoga* (Berlin: Frankfurter Verlagsanstalt, 1926) table 27.

21 R. Wilhelm and C. G. Jung, *The Secret of the Golden Flower,* trans. C. Baynes (London: Routledge, 1962), Jung's commentary also in *CW* 13.

22 *Sacred Books of the East* XLIL.ii, 161ff. Cf. Jung, *CW* 11 par. 923.

23 C. G. Jung, *CW* 8 par. 396.

Chapter VII: The Assimilation of the Incompatible Complex

1 C. G. Jung, *CW* 13 par. 65.
2 *Vita di Benvenuto Cellini,* II.3, trans. Goethe.
3 *Ibid.* III.1.
4 C. G. Jung, *CW* 11 par. 431.

Chapter VIII: Meaning in Madness

1 E. Ionesco, quoted in Anni Carlsson, "Der Steppenwolf und die Nashörner," *Neue Zürcher Zeitung* 299 (n.d.) 162.
2 See H. Schmidt, *Philosophisches Wörterbuch* (Leipzig: Körner, 1934) 9th ed., 700.
3 E. Kraepelin, *Psychiatrie* (Leipzig: Abel, 1889) 3rd ed., 109.
4 E. Bleuler, *Lehrbuch der Psychatrie* (Berlin: Springer, 1937) 6th ed., 50.
5 G. Ewald, *Neurologie und Psychatrie* (Munich/Berlin: Urban und Schwarzenberg, 1959) 4th ed., 268.
6 Julien Green, *Journal 1946-1950* (Paris: Plon, 1951) 45.
7 C. G. Jung, *CW* 9.i par. 275.
8 C. G. Jung, *CW* 5 par. 1.
9 Bertolt Brecht, *Gespräch auf der Probe* (Zurich: Sanssouci, 1961) 93.
10 C. G. Jung, *CW* 11 par. 758.
11 *Ibid.*
12 E. Bleuler, *ibid.*

Chapter XII: Fear, Truth and Confidence

1 C. G. Jung, *CW* 14, par. 125.
2 H. Schmidt, *Philosophisches Wörterbuch* (Leipzig: Körner, 1934) 9th ed., 713.
3 A. Jores, "Rektoratsrede über den Sinn der Krankheit," quoted in Jaspers, *Studium Generale* (Berlin: Springer, 1953) 6: 436.
4 A. Jores, *Klinische Medizin* 48 (1953) 924.
5 R. Leriche, *Souvenirs de ma vie morte* (Paris: Seuil, 1956) 118.
6 Quoted in H. Schmidt, *ibid.,* 714.
7 O. H. Bowen, Questionnaire on Truth in the State of Indiana, *Medical Times* (Oct. 1955).
8 F. Singeisen, *Psychologische Probleme in Allgemeinspitälern* (Veska, 1959) 805.

9 C. G. Jung, *CW* 2 pars. 560-638; see also L. Binswanger, *Journal für Psychologie und Neurologie* 10 (1908) 149.

10 E. Bleuler, *Psychoide als Prinzip der organischen Entwicklung* (Berlin: Springer, 1925).

11 C. G. Jung, *CW* 8 par. 368.

Chapter XIII: Medicine and Spiritual Welfare

1 H. Pestalozzi, "Wie Gertrud ihre Kinder lehrt," *ibid.* (ch. 4) 177.

2 J. W. von Goethe, *Die natürliche Tochter,* IV.2051.

Chapter XIV: Dreams, Resistance and Wholeness

1 C. G. Jung, ed. "Preface," *Psychologische Abhandlungen* (Leipzig: Deutike, 1914).

2 C. G. Jung, *CW* 16 par. 198.

3 C. G. Jung, *CW* 6.

4 H. Bergson, *Einführung in die Metaphysik* (Jena: Diederichs, 1912) Pts. 2 & 3, 15.

5 C. G. Carus, *Psyche: On the Development of the Soul. Part One: The Unconscious* [1846] (New York: Spring, 1970) [distinction not maintained in trans.].

6 C. A. Meier, *Healing Dream and Ritual: Ancient Incubation and Modern Psychotherapy* (Einsiedeln: Daimon, 1989); and *The Meaning and Significance of Dreams* (Boston: Sigo, 1987) 69ff.

7 C. G. Jung, *CW* 7 par. 263.

4 H. Bergson, *Introduction to Metaphysics,* parts 2-3, opening section.

8 *The Diary of Samuel Pepys* (London: Bell, 1926) 58.

9 C. G. Jung, *CW* 6 par. 779.

10 *Ibid.* pars. 812-813.

11 G. T. Fechner, *Elemente der Psychophysik* (1899), 2nd ed., pt. ii.

12 C. G. Jung, *CW* 8.

13 A. Portmann, broadcast on Swiss Radio 2, 3 Nov. 1974.

14 J. W. von Goethe, *Faust,* V.11954.

15 A. Schopenhauer, *Parerga und Paralipomena* (Leipzig: Brockhaus, 1908) I.

16 C. G. Jung, *CW* 8.

17 La Rochefoucauld, *Maximes* (Porrentruy: Portes de France, 1947) 142; see also Montaigne, *Essais* 52.12.

18 C. G. Jung, *CW* 9.ii par. 218.

19 *Ibid.* par. 219.

Chapter XV: The Lambspring Figures

1 *The Hermetic Museum,* ed. A. E. Waite (London: Watkins, repr. 1953).

2 A. Jaffé, in *Du* (1955).

3 See Waite, ed., *The Hermetic Museum.*

4 *Musaeum Hermeticum* (Frankfurt am Main, 1678) 579.

5 J. W. von Goethe, "Selige Sehnsucht," *West-östlicher Diwan.*

6 A. Muschg, "Über Goethes Umgangsformen mit der Natur," *Der Brückenbauer* 11 (Spreitenbach) 19 March 1982.

Chapter XVI: The Treatment of Depression

1 C. G. Jung, *CW* 8 par. 19.

2 C. G. Jung, *CW* 9.ii pars. 217-218.

3 Th. Paracelsus, *Labyrinthus Medicorum – vom Irrgang der Ärzte* (Frankfurt am Main: Insel, n.d., Inselbücherei n. 366) 45.

4 H. Lewrenz, in *Der Nervenarzt* 23 (June 1951).

Chapter XIX: Psychotherapy and the Shadow

1 C. G. Jung, *CW* 8.

2 S. Freud, *Introductory Lectures on Psychoanalysis,* trans. J. Strachey, Standard Edition (London: Hogarth) 16: lec. 18 par. 5.

3 *Ibid.* par. 6

4 *Ibid.*

5 Pascal, *Pensées,* n. 100.

6 C. G. Jung, *CW* 10 par. 271.

Chapter XXI: The Lost Symbol

1 C. G. Jung, *CW* 6 par. 815.

2 E. Naville, ed., *Das Aegyptische Totenbuch* (Berlin: Ascher, 1886) 159.

3 H. Jacobsohn, "The Dialogue of a World-Weary Man with His Ba," in *Timeless Documents of the Soul,* by H. Jacobsohn, M.-L. von Franz, and S. Hurwitz (Evanston: Northwestern Univ. Press, 1968) 50.

4 A. Weigall, *Echnaton* (Basel: Schwabe, 1923) 66.

5 *Ibid.* 25.

6 E. Stauffer, *Jerusalem und Rom im Zeitalter Jesu Christi* (Bern: Francke, 1957) 23.

7 *Ibid.* 25.

8 B. von Brentano, *August Wilhelm Schlegel* (Stuttgart: Cotta, 1943) 195, 197.

9 F. Nietzsche, *Werke* (Leipzig: Kröner, 1930) 256.

10 Ph. Eulenberg-Hertefeld, *Aus 50 Jahren* (Berlin: Patel, 1925) 128.

11 S. George, "Stern des Bundes."

12 H. Hesse, *Kleine Welt* (Berlin: Fischer, 1933) 96.

13 C. Spitteler, *Prometheus und Epimetheus* (Jena: Diederichs, 1923) 255.

14 *Ibid.* 149.

15 C. G. Jung, *CW* 10 par. 385.

16 I. Scholl, *Die Weisse Rose* (Frankfurt am Main: Fischer, 1955) 50.

17 G. Keller, *Gedichte* (Berlin: Cotta, 1902) 1: 283.

18 H. Heine, *Atta Troll* (Hamburg: Giese, 1847) 156.

19 *Neue Zürcher Zeitung* N.898, 1964.

20 K. Schmid, *Unbehagen im Kleinstaat,* (Zurich: Artemis, 1963) 155.

21 *Ibid.* 166.

22 C. G. Jung, *CW* 6 par. 18.

Index of Names

Subject Index

PARIS 1989
Personal and Archetypal
Dynamics in the Analytical
Relationship
*edited by Mary Ann
Mattoon*
ca. 510 pages
ISBN 3-85630-524-6 (paper)
ISBN 3-85630-529-7 (cloth)

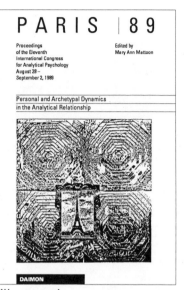

PARIS │89

Proceedings
of the Eleventh
International Congress
for Analytical Psychology
August 28 –
September 2, 1989

Edited by
Mary Ann Mattoon

Personal and Archetypal Dynamics
in the Analytical Relationship

DAIMON

The official Proceedings of
the 11th International Congress for Analytical Psychology are now available. The
Paris Congress was contro-
versial, provocative and
stimulating as always, and
this volume contains all the
papers presented, many richly illustrated.

From the contents: "Countertransference Dynamics in Analysis ,"
"Destructive and Creative Forces in Analysis," "Analytical Psychol-
ogy and Women," "Child Analysis: Transference/Countertransfer-
ence," "Psychodynamics in Training," "Analytical Psychology and
Art," "Analysis and Culture," "Analytical Psychology and Inter-
Cultural Experience," "Jung and Anti-Semitism."

Susan Bach
LIFE PAINTS ITS OWN SPAN
On the Significance of Spontaneous Paintings
by Severely Ill Children
with over 200 color illustrations
Part I (Text): 208 pgs., part II (Pictures): 56 pgs., 240 x 200 mm
ISBN 3-85630-516-5

Life Paints its own Span with over 200 color reproductions is
a comprehensive exposition of Susan Bach's original approach to the physical and psychospiritual evaluation of
spontaneous paintings and drawings by severely ill patients.
At the same time, this work is a moving record of Susan
Bach's own journey of discovery.

E.A. Bennet
MEETINGS WITH JUNG
Conversations recorded during the years 1946-1961
125 pages, paper
ISBN 3-85630-501-7

In this collection of diary entries made by British psychiatrist E.A. Bennet during his visits with the Swiss analyst C.G. Jung over a 15-year period, Bennet's colorfully spontaneous accounts reveal Jung's down-to-earth personality and his extraordinary mind, at ease in his daily surroundings. We are provided an intimate introduction to the impromptu Jung, his circle of friends and colleagues, and the places he loved. In relaxed conversation with Bennet, Jung's ideas were often formulated more clearly and directly than in other presentations. Thus, *Meetings with Jung* serves as an ideal introduction to Jungian psychology while providing a rare, intimate perspective into Jung's life and work for those already familiar with the more scholarly literature.

Rafael López-Pedraza
HERMES AND HIS CHILDREN
220 pages, paper, illus.
ISBN 3-85630-518-1

Hermes and his Children has become something of a classic among therapists, poets, artists and readers of every ilk around the world. Rafael López-Pedraza approaches the soul through myth, pathology, image and the very living of them all. The love and passion of a man fully in his element radiates throughout this unique work, now updated and expanded for this edition.

Rivkah Schärf-Kluger

The Gilgamesh Epic

DAIMON
VERLAG

R. Schärf-Kluger
THE GILGAMESH EPIC
A Psychological Study of
a Modern Ancient Hero
Edited by H. Yehezkel Kluger
Foreword by C.A. Meier
ca. 200 pages, paper,
illustrations
ISBN 3-85630-523-8

The long-awaited life-long opus of Jung's brilliant disciple, Rivkah Kluger, this book consists of a detailed psychological commentary on the ancient Sumero-Babylonian epic myth of Gilgamesh. The great beauty and depth of the Gilgamesh epic, one of the world's most ancient myths, render it a unique instrument for learning about the human soul. Rivkah Kluger ably applies it to illustrate the significance of myths for an understanding of the development of consciousness and of religion: we are shown how an ancient myth is highly relevant to the state of our world today.

Available from your bookstore or from our distributors:

In the United States:
The Great Tradition
11270 Clayton Creek Road
Lower Lake, CA 95457
Tel. (707) 995-3906
Fax: (707) 995-1814

Chiron Publications
400 Linden Avenue
Wilmette, IL 60091
Tel. (708) 256-7551
Fax: (708) 256-2202

In Great Britain:
Element Books Ltd.
Longmead, Shaftesbury
Dorset SP7 8PL, England
Tel. (747) 51339
Fax: (747) 51394

Worldwide:
Daimon Verlag
Hauptstrasse 85,
CH-8840 Einsiedeln Switzerland
Tel. (41)(55) 532266
Fax (41)(55) 532231

ENGLISH PUBLICATIONS BY **DAIMON**

Susan Bach – *Life Paints its Own Span*

E.A. Bennet – *Meetings with Jung*

George Czuczka – *Imprints of the Future*

Heinrich Karl Fierz – *Jungian Psychiatry*

von Franz / Frey-Rohn / Jaffé – *What is Death?*

Liliane Frey-Rohn – *Friedrich Nietzsche*

Aniela Jaffé – *The Myth of Meaning*
 – *Was C.G. Jung a Mystic?*
 – *From the Life und Work of C.G. Jung*
 – *Death Dreams and Ghosts*

Siegmund Hurwitz – *Lilith – the first Eve*

Verena Kast – *A Time to Mourn*
 – *Sisyphus*

James Kirsch – *The Reluctant Prophet*

Rivkah Schärf Kluger – *The Gilgamesh Epic*

Rafael López-Pedraza – *Hermes and his Children*
 – *Cultural Anxiety*

Alan McGlashan – *The Savage and Beautiful Country*

Gitta Mallasz (Transcription) – *Talking with Angels*

C.A. Meier – *Healing Dream and Ritual*
 – *A Testament to the Wilderness*

Laurens van der Post – *A «Festschrift»*

Jungian Congress Papers:

Jerusalem 1983 – *Symbolic and Clinical Approaches*

Berlin 1986 – *Archetype of Shadow in a Split World*

Paris 1989 – *Dynamics in Relationship*